Jens Nielson, Bishop of Bluff

David S. Carpenter

Master's Thesis
Brigham Young University
Department of History
2003

Dissertations in Latter-day Saint History

Produced by BYU Studies

Volumes in the series:

A Study of the Origins of The Church of Jesus Christ of Latter-day Saints in the States of New York and Pennsylvania, by Larry C. Porter

A Call to Arms: The 1838 Mormon Defense of Northern Missouri, by Alexander L. Baugh

Alexander Schreiner: Mormon Tabernacle Organist, by Daniel Frederick Berghout

The Mormon Reformation, by Paul H. Peterson

The Mormon Ideology of Place: Cosmic Symbolism of the City of Zion, 1830–1846, by Steven L. Olsen

Sister Wives and Suffragists: Polygamy and the Politics of Woman Suffrage 1870–1896, by Lola Van Wagenen

Early Mormon Pamphleteering, by David J. Whittaker

The Emergence of Brigham Young and the Twelve to Mormon Leadership, 1830–1841 by Ronald K. Esplin

"Give It All Up and Follow Your Lord": Mormon Female Religiosity, 1831–1843 by Janiece Lyn Johnson

The Joseph Sr. and Lucy Mack Smith Family: A Family Process Analysis of a Nineteenth-Centry Household by Kyle R. Walker

Cover image *Ledge of Sunland* (oil on canvas) by Maynard Dixon, Brigham Young University Museum of Art, gift of Kelly Ullmann.

Cover design by Robert E. M. Spencer.

ISBN 978-0-8425-2771-2

Printed in the United States of America

10 9 8 7 6 5 4 3 2 1

Dissertations in Latter-day Saint History

Over the years, graduate students have written many important dissertations on LDS topics. Unfortunately, they have typically been unavailable or unknown to lay readers. All too often, good copies of dissertations reside only at the institution at which they were written or on a few researchers' book shelves. BYU Studies hopes to fill this gap by producing and distributing selected dissertations and theses of interest to Latter-day Saints, making them available to a larger audience.

The works in this series have been reformatted from the originals and a subject index has been added. Nevertheless, these dissertations have undergone only minimal editing. For example, some typographical errors have been corrected and the footnotes and bibliography have been made to conform to the *Chicago Manual of Style*. Original page numbers are referenced by superscripted italicized numerals in brackets (e.g., [3]). Occasionally, the author has included additional information in the endnotes to update old material. Those additions have been placed in brackets and italicized to distinguish them from the original text.

Contents

Acknowledgments

I am grateful to those who took time after plowing, between sandstorms, and even during roundups to preserve parts of Bluff's past, whether they were clerks, letter writers, census takers, or simply those who recalled stories, and whether or not they were conscious of their contributions. Francis A. Hammond and Albert R. Lyman were extremely conscientious diarists, almost always backtracking when they missed a day. They have preserved better than anyone the past life of Bluff and its settlers, from heroic to petty, triumphant to discouraged. President Hammond's journals illuminate the administrative side of the town, from the top down, and we would know little about its workings or Bishop Jens Nielson's life during certain years without these records. Albert Lyman started his journals as a thirteen-year-old boy, and nothing in my research gave me as much pleasure as figuratively growing up in Bluff with this guileless, enterprising lad. His diaries discuss many of the same events as Francis Hammond's, but from the much different view of youth looking up at life.

Much has changed between the late 1800s and now, and without the developments of our modern world I could not have written this history. Donna Jensen and Mike Halliday's work to collect documents and photographs related to Jens Nielson on CD-ROM has been enormously helpful; many of these items would have escaped me without it. The Internet has only begun to live up to its potential for historical research, but it was helpful in many ways. Footnoting is not nearly as arduous as digging ditches or maintaining a frontier household, but without this computer and its software (which crashed only at noncrucial times and in nonfatal ways), I could not have done it. I am glad our society thinks enough of its past to invest in the libraries and archives, as well as their able staffs, that were invaluable to this project. The Department of History at Brigham Young University sponsored me through scholarships and assistantships, and the Alpine School District allowed me to take a sabbatical year, all of which helped keep food on our table while I contributed nothing immediately useful to society. I am not sure I would be comfortable finding out the impact air conditioning had on the interpretations found in this history, but I am glad it exists.

The members of my graduate committee have contributed not only their knowledge and professionalism but also their understanding, patience, and sympathy throughout the process of writing this thesis. They are responsible for many of the improvements; I retain ownership of all the mistakes. I am especially grateful to my dear wife, Jolene, for her encouragement and long-suffering. She and the five children we have welcomed since I started writing about Bluff could have had a lot more fun, especially in the summers, if I did not do it. I dedicate the finished product to her and to my idiocratic grandma Ila Nielson Sundwall, who was, until a few weeks before I finished my thesis, my living link to Bluff.

Introduction

Jens Nielson's last task was to stay where he was. This was made harder by the fact that he was used to moving. As a young man he was driven by ambition into Denmark's landholding class. Just as he arrived at that status he converted to Mormonism and was driven by faith across the Atlantic and most of America. Along the way he lost his former friends and reputation, his homeland, much of his money, his firstborn son, and almost his life. After he arrived in Utah, the Zion of his new religion, Church leaders assigned him to settle in five different towns over the next two decades. As he approached sixty, Jens volunteered to start a remote outpost somewhere in the southeastern corner of the territory. The trek there was almost impossible, and it was only the beginning of labors for the pioneers who traveled through the Hole in the Rock to found the town of Bluff. Jens soon became the bishop in Bluff, a position he held for twenty-five years. He determined he would not leave this place that was so unlike where he was born.

Bluff was the back eddy of empires, settled on one of "the last blank spot[s] on the United States map."[1] It was planted in 1880 near the end of Mormon colonization [1] and in one of the few unsettled corners left in the country.[2] Bluff's citizens confronted many of the problems most westerners faced. Water was their first and enduring concern. Relations

---

1. Aton and McPherson, *River Flowing from the Sunrise*, 1.
2. Mormon colonization in the West is analyzed in Arrington, *Great Basin Kingdom*; Meinig, "Mormon Culture Region," 191–209; Wahlquist, "Settlement Processes in the Mormon Core Area"; and Sherlock, "Mormon Migration and Settlement."

with their native and new neighbors were often unpredictable and could turn violent. The federal government was an important force in this region, at times helping and at times hindering their development. It was hard for tenderfoot lawmen to administer justice. The colonizers were isolated and intimidated by the scale and the ruggedness of the land. But much of Bluff ran counter to the trends. Its pioneers traveled east, to worse land than they previously had, to help, they believed, the Indians of the region. Rather than grant the settlers homesteads, Congress almost gave their homes back to the Native American tribes. Bluff's residents often felt more threatened by the cowboys around them than by the Indians, and they were very hesitant to call in the cavalry. Finally, this town's sturdy settlers endeavored not to be rugged individualists but rather to form an orthodox cooperative community based on inherited patterns and directed by religious authorities from afar.[3] [2]

In many ways, Bluff was different from typical western towns for the same reasons most Mormon settlements were different. They were usually settled by the direction of Church leadership, and they pursued principles of cooperation and unity. These towns followed a basic settlement template in laying out the land and establishing institutions. Many had some sort of economic or political mission to fulfill, making the whole town, not just a segment of specialized churchmen, into missionaries. But even among Mormon settlements, Bluff was unusual in some ways. The "second exodus" through the Hole in the Rock to Bluff, a six-month ordeal, caused its pioneers to develop a unique sense of identity that grew with time in those who endured in the settlement. They were cut off by the Colorado River and austere canyon country from the main core of Mormons. Geography aimed their town more toward the fledgling non-Mormon outposts and economies in Colorado, which made the Mormons feel like strangers in their home territory. The sense of separateness, not just from the non-Mormon world but from most of Mormonism, was strengthened as they endured prolonged crude living conditions and an atrociously high level of

---

3. Mormon town planning was more a pattern than a prescription. For its basic premises, characteristics, adaptations, and exceptions, see Nelson, *Mormon Village*; Ricks, *Forms and Methods of Early Mormon Settlement*; Peterson, "Imprint of Agricultural Systems"; Jackson and Layton, "Mormon Village"; Jackson, "Mormon Village: Genesis and Antecedents." See also May, *Three Frontiers*, for how a Mormon town differed in its principles and practices from two other western towns.

labor to stay where they were. In our time, when opportunities for physical work have to be rented in health clubs and microwaves are too slow, all pioneer life looks difficult. But the toil and discomfort exacted from those who lived in Bluff daunted even experienced colonizers.

Bluff's missionaries expected to be a civilizing force amid opposition, a "fort on the firing line," as one of the town's children put it.[4] They believed strongly in their [3] religious errand and quickly assumed the legitimacy and authority of the new government of San Juan County to help them organize the area in their image. But the cattlemen, outlaws, miners, and small-scale settlers who arrived around them, as well as the Navajos, Utes, and Paiutes who had been there for some time, usually had other ideas. Bluff's advantages helped the Mormons control the county, but not always in the ways and to the degree they hoped. Bluff's frontier turned out to be more of a restless borderland, in which each of the groups converging on the county pursued its own goals, at times in sympathy and at others in antagonism toward each other.[5] Some had

---

4. Lyman, "Fort on the Firing Line."

5. San Juan County in the late 1800s is a particularly good spot to see interaction in the West. Each of the three major schools of historical thought toward the West add meaning to what happened there. Bluff's settlers certainly would have been sympathetic to the perspective of Frederick Jackson Turner, most directly stated in "The Significance of the Frontier in American History." They felt they were "the outer edge of the wave," albeit an eastbound wave of settlement, and if they didn't quite feel they were at "the meeting point between savagery and civilization," it was because of the sympathy they had toward the Native Americans generated by the Book of Mormon, a history of ancient inhabitants of America. Turner would have been disappointed in Bluff, since it did not meet, except for maybe its unruly children, his predictions for democratization and institutional improvisation. Ray Allen Billington has updated this approach in his studies of the West. Herbert E. Bolton's multilateral borderlands framework is a helpful way to look at the various groups in San Juan County, especially considering that the Mormons, surrounding states, and the federal government, while not exactly rival empires, all had their own interests, particularly in dealing with Native Americans. Bolton's ideas were written in his cornerstone work, *The Spanish Borderlands: A Chronicle of Old Florida and the Southwest* and updated by John Francis Bannon, *The Spanish Borderland Frontier, 1513–1821.* The continued priority to pay attention to everyone and a regional focus on competition for limited resources are important contributions made by the "New Western Historians." Who controlled the range and the water were highly important in how things turned out in San Juan County during this time. The seminal

more success than others, but few left empty-handed. This was also true of those who lived in Bluff. They brought and held a strong Mormon presence in the county, but only by spawning new settlements. Bluff [4] itself was a sieve for settlers; no more than a fifth of those who came before 1906 stayed for any significant length of time. The San Juan missionaries established more peaceful relations with the Indians than most non-Mormon bands but made little headway in assimilating or converting Navajos, Utes, or Paiutes. As time passed, the Bluff Saints emphasized the effects their mission had on themselves at least as much as what it did for those around them.

To stay where they were, Bishop Jens Nielson and the others in Bluff had to adapt. They originally hoped to embody the pioneer principles of cooperation and unity by building an independent agricultural village. But the San Juan River denied their crops dependable water, and most of the colonists left. Those who stayed, though increasingly dogmatic about holding Bluff, were practical enough to recognize that the ideal of the agricultural village would not permit them to survive. So they switched much of their energy to raising livestock as a new means to sustain their mission, and they tried to do it cooperatively.[6] Those who stayed also generated the towns of Monticello, Verdure, and Blanding. This diversification helped the communities prosper and keep more people, but the cowboy lifestyle and the wealth it brought threatened their spiritual and social principles to an unacceptable degree.[7] The older citizens were especially alarmed when they saw what [5] was happening to their

---

works of this group are Limerick, *Legacy of Conquest*, and White, *"It's Your Misfortune and None of My Own."* The three schools may, as some have suggested, function as an overall process, as frontier yields to borderlands, which becomes region. See Cronon, Miles, and Gitlin, "Becoming West: Toward a New Meaning for Western History," in *Under an Open Sky*, 7.

6. This argument is similar to that used by Leone in "Evolution of Mormon Culture in Eastern Arizona" to describe why some of the settlements on the Little Colorado River survived. The Church of Jesus Christ of Latter-day Saints produced "individuals capable of adapting themselves to changing economic realities while preserving their ideological independence within American culture."

7. Abruzzi, "Ecology, Resource Redistribution," argues against Leone that instead of cooperative adaptation, what saved the colonies on the Little Colorado was the effective redistribution of resources that multihabitat settlements and the tithing network allowed. San Juan County was different from the Arizona settle-

children. The shift to livestock also made the town more dependent on outside markets and susceptible to the national economy, which both helped and hurt their mission. Mormons seized control of more of the county's rangeland, which helped them secure the area politically, but this undermined their efforts with the Indians by creating more direct competition for the region's limited resources. Bluff's leaders saw these disorienting influences and fought against them to maintain the settlement's precarious balance. Economic failure could force them to abandon their mission, but success could ruin them as well. Church leaders' rearguard actions against individualism, partisanship, and unbounded capitalism, though ultimately unsuccessful, were in force throughout Utah at this time. Although Bishop Nielson and the other leaders of his generation belonged almost entirely to the pioneer age and its principles, modernizing forces had made Bluff less peculiar to Mormons, and to westerners in general, by the time he died.[8]

Bluff was never far from failure during Jens Nielson's life. Many Mormon towns in harsh environments were abandoned, and Bluff's physical and cultural environments were especially harsh.[9] On the periphery of Mormon settlement, Bluff's residents sometimes [6] felt misunderstood and neglected in their struggles. Pragmatic adaptation and diversification helped the town continue, but it could not have survived on these alone. By most rational measures, Bluff should have been abandoned, and a farmer as hardheaded as Jens Nielson should have led the exodus. But Bishop Nielson was not an entirely reasonable man. He had bound himself to obey Church authorities, and this stubborn faith required him to stay in Bluff, no matter how impractical. This was not a question of orthodoxy versus apostasy. Those who left Bluff generally did not leave Mormonism. Other equally faithful men viewed the town differently from Jens: the General Authorities of the Church were usually divided

---

ments. Economic and regional diversification helped to make life more tolerable and further the goals of the mission.

8. For the general tension between communal and individual endeavors in Utah settlements, see Arrington, Fox, and May, *Building the City of God*, xi–xii. The mainstreaming of Mormon politics, economy, and culture is described in Larson, *"Americanization" of Utah*; Lyman, *Political Deliverance*; and Alexander, *Mormonism in Transition.*

9. See Rosenvall, "Defunct Mormon Settlements."

on preserving it, and Jens's immediate leaders were appalled at what it cost to maintain the place. Regardless of others' arguments, until the Church's leaders released him from Bluff, Jens Nielson would not go. This impractical steadfastness in the bishop and some others preserved Bluff on many occasions when no amount of adaptation alone could have saved it.

Much has already been written about Bluff. The first group of histories (and still the great majority) consists of recollections by the original settlers and their numerous descendants. These are indispensable sources of information, but largely episodic and uncritical. They are fully sympathetic to the Mormon settlers, paying little attention to their neighbors except as friends or foils to the heroic quest. Typical of these recollections are the many works of Albert R. Lyman (the "Old Settler," who was born just before Bluff began and lived into the Kennedy administration) and the *Saga of San* [7] *Juan*, by the Daughters of Utah Pioneers.[10]

Broader studies began emerging in the 1950s and 1960s. University of Utah historian David E. Miller wrote the classic account of the Hole-in-the-Rock Expedition but stopped when the settlers arrived at Bluff. Bryant Jensen continued the story from there in his master's thesis. He unearthed much valuable information, but his coverage was sketchy, and many important sources were not yet available. Franklin Day devoted his thesis to the cattle industry in the county, which led to further investigations of this aspect by Don D. Walker.[11]

In the next decades, some of Utah's top historians turned their attention to this corner of the state. Charles S. Peterson came the closest to a revisionist view of Bluff in the first section of *Look to the Mountains*,

---

10. Among the most important of this generation are Jones, "Writings," and Perkins, Nielson, and Jones, *Saga of San Juan*. Albert R. Lyman was an inveterate writer, whose vigorously lyric pen has written recollections of many of the first settlers, including Jens Nielson, as well as a number of loose histories of the area. See especially "History of San Juan County," for many important pieces of information and *Indians and Outlaws* for rollicking tales of "the fight for San Juan."

11. Miller, *Hole-in-the-Rock*; Jensen, "Historical Study of Bluff City"; Day, "Cattle Industry of San Juan County"; Walker, "Cattle Industry of Utah"; Walker, "Carlisles: Cattle Barons."

published in 1975.[12] He agreed with the majority of the early settlers of Bluff, who suspected the mission extracted too much work to justify the results. Leonard Arrington surveyed Bluff's history as a backdrop for the [8] Redd family in his biography on Charlie Redd.[13] Today's leading scholar on the history of San Juan County is Robert S. McPherson of the College of Eastern Utah's Blanding campus. His many well-crafted works have done an admirable job of evening accounts by bringing neglected aspects of San Juan County, such as Native Americans and the environment, back into the picture. He has also written articles on episodes in Bluff's story (the Indian removal question, the cattle industry, law enforcement, the gold rush) in the *Utah Historical Quarterly* and the regional journal *Blue Mountain Shadows*.[14] In short, while recent scholars have brought enormous talent to the study of Bluff, the town itself has usually been collateral to their main interests. No one has attempted to write the early history of the town using the documentary and statistical sources that are now available.

Jens Nielson was a large man in stature, enthusiasm, and personality. This combination seemed to attract attention, and he quickly became a leader wherever he went. One of Jens's associates indicated the range in his character by describing him as having "indomitable courage" as well as being the "old comic boy."[15] Joseph F. Smith [9] called him "one of the grandest men the church ever had."[16] Albert Lyman has composed brief, moving sketches of Bishop Nielson's life, but aside from these and family reminiscences little has been written about him. As the bishop of Bluff, Jens Nielson was the community's mainspring, "connected directly or indirectly with all its life-giving activities."[17]

---

12. Peterson, *Look to the Mountains.*

13. Arrington, *Utah's Audacious Stockman.*

14. See McPherson, *Northern Navajo Frontier;* McPherson, *History of San Juan County;* and Aton and McPherson, *River Flowing from the Sunrise;* as well as the other works listed in the bibliography.

15. Lemuel H. Redd Sr., letter to family, January 22, 1889; Lemuel H. Redd Sr., Autobiographical Sketch, 1902.

16. Nielson, "Jens Nielson," 58. The occasion for the comment was when Floyd, Jens's grandson, returned from his mission to England in the 1920s and reported his activities to President Smith.

17. Lyman, "Bishop Jens Nielson: The Old Wagon," 72.

This book is a detailed history of late-pioneer-era Mormonism in one of its harshest environments. It will describe the life of Bishop Nielson and the history of Bluff from 1880 to 1906, explaining how and why the settlers persisted where they did during these years, and what difference it made that they did. [10]

Arrival, 1820–1880

April 6, 1880

Most of them could not go on. Even if the people found strength to make themselves move, the animals were through. Their expedition to a new settlement on the San Juan River was supposed to take six weeks. Now, six *months* later, the last few miles were too far to go. It took almost all they had to reach this strip of bottomland, and the planting season was moving on without them. As more settlers straggled into the valley and surveyed the red bluffs that rose starkly around it, they began to understand that this might *have* to be the place for them. It was April 6, 1880, the fiftieth anniversary of the church that sent them on this grinding migration across the Colorado River into one of the remotest corners remaining in the West.

This was not the first difficult trek for many of them. And it was certainly not the first for one of the oldest among them. Jens Nielson's sixty years had carried his sturdy frame from a sea-sprayed island of southern Denmark to this arid outpost in Utah. His convictions had traveled at least as far. [11]

Jens Nielson's Journey

Conversion

As a young Dane, Jens Nielson's greatest hope was to move up into respectable society. He was born April 26, 1820, on the island of Lolland, separated from Germany by a finger of the Baltic Sea. He did not know his father and expected no inheritance. So Jens hired out his labor until he could become an independent farmer.[1] At the age of thirty his physical and emotional efforts were rewarded. He married Elsie Rasmussen, who had labored through similar struggles herself, and Jens Nielson bought five acres of land later in the year. A son arrived shortly after. "I was looked on as a respectable neighbor," Jens assessed later, "and many times invited to the higher class of society."[2]

Two men preaching a disreputable foreign religion found the Nielsons' neighborhood in the fall of 1852. Out of curiosity, Jens attended a nearby meeting, and his pastoral life was transformed. "As soon as I saw those men's faces, I knew they were not the men as represented to be, and I told my friends so before I heard them speak. Before the meeting was out, I knew the testimony they bore was of God. We bought some few of their tracts and studied them for a few weeks and were perfectly satisfied the [12] work was of God." Both Jens and Elsie began to believe the doctrines of Mormonism.

Still, they did not join The Church of Jesus Christ of Latter-day Saints immediately. If they had, it would have required tremendous spiritual and material sacrifices of them, and Jens had labored too long to cast away his good fortune so quickly. "Now the struggle commenced to give up all my possessions," he wrote later.[3] He wrestled with himself for over a year

---

1. The most complete account of Jens Nielson's early life is Lyman, "Bishop Jens Nielson." Lyman's account incorporates an autobiographical letter Jens wrote to his son Uriah in 1901 into additional facts Lyman heard the bishop tell in their time together in Bluff. Regarding Nielson's parentage, Lyman mentions that "it was a delicate secret that Jens did not know his father." See Lyman, "Bishop Jens Nielson: The Old Wagon," 71. Lyman also commented in "Bishop Jens Nielson" that "we know that he was denied the care of his real father, that he had a step-father and half-brothers and sisters. One of his half-brothers, Francis, sailed away to the west and is supposed to have been lost at sea, for they never heard of him again."

2. All direct quotes in this chapter, unless otherwise noted, are from Jens Nielson, letter to his son Uriah Nielson, March 20, 1901.

3. Jens Nielson, "Short History of Jens Nielson." This seems to be a copy or revision of the letter Jens Nielson wrote to his son Uriah in 1901. Most of the differences between this document and that letter (as well as the sections of it quoted in Albert Lyman's "Bishop Jens Nielson") are changes in wording. But it also has a few significant additional ideas not found in the other two versions.

before he and his wife were baptized into their new faith on March 29, 1854, by Johan Sandberg.[4]

Emigration

Almost immediately the Nielsons were displaced by their conversion. Their social standing evaporated once they were baptized. "From that time on," recalled Jens, "all of my former friends turned against me and spoke all kind of evil against me, and that falsely." On one occasion he was even assaulted by an anti-Mormon pack that left him injured and outraged. "He presented his tattered clothes to the local magistrate in an appeal for justice, but was told there was 'no law in Denmark to protect the Mormons.'"[5] Converts throughout Denmark faced such treatment, in spite of the supposed religious liberty granted by the more liberal constitution of 1849. "That awful delusion, [13] Mormonism," had converted over two thousand souls since its first missionary, Erastus Snow, had arrived in 1850, and the backlash was severe.[6] Opposition was notably fierce on Lolland, where "it had become a common saying that all who joined the 'Mormons' should have their windows broken."[7] In the long term, these insults would not matter, since Latter-day Saints (the more official name for Mormons) were expected to gather to the body of the Church in "Zion," the territory of Utah in the United States. "All my possessions had no power over me then," Jens wrote. "My only desire was to sell out and come to Zion." He found a buyer for his home and was about to remove with his family when again his plans were abruptly changed.

A regional Church leader, perhaps Lolland Conference President Johan Svenson, admonished Jens that he was not doing his duty. Before he left his homeland, he should warn others, just as he had been warned. This meant Jens should become a missionary. "That counsel came right

---

4. Andrew Jenson, *Latter-day Saint Biographical Encyclopedia: A Compilation of Biographical Sketches of Prominent Men and Women in The Church of Jesus Christ of Latter-day Saints*, 4 vols. (Salt Lake City: Andrew Jenson History, 1901–36), 2:203.

5. Lyman, "Bishop Jens Nielson," 1.

6. The epithet comes from a petition presented by one Chamberlain Esquire Wickfeldt of Lolland to the King of Denmark in 1856. See Mulder, *Homeward to Zion*, 42.

7. Jenson, *History of the Scandinavian Mission*, 77.

in contact with my natural feelings, but the Spirit whispered to me I
must obey, for obedience is better than sacrifice." For more than a year
he labored to save the souls of his countrymen, leaving Elsie to manage
the challenging circumstances at home. He served well, presiding over a
"branch," a small congregation of the Church in the area of his labors. He
baptized about fifteen people and considered his labors a success.[8] [14]

In the spring of 1856, Jens was honorably released from his mission.
At once he liquidated his property, paid his debts and his tithing, and bid
farewell to his homeland. Jens and Elsie, along with their five-year-old
son Jens, whom they called Niels, and Bodil Mortensen, a nine-year-
old girl another convert entrusted to their care, boarded the steamship
Rhoda in Copenhagen and started west.[9] They were part of a larger
stream of Danish pilgrims who comprised 163 of the 764 Latter-day
Saint passengers aboard the triple-masted U.S. vessel *Thornton* that left
Liverpool, England, on May 4, 1856. Now the Nielsons found themselves part of a flood of Saints and could associate with hundreds in
the same circumstances. Like most Mormon emigrant companies, the
throng aboard the *Thornton* made the best of what was usually a trans-
atlantic ordeal. Organized under returning European missionary James
G. Willie, they were a model community, extremely well-regimented and
behaved.[10] When they arrived in New York on June 14, after forty-one
days at sea, ship's captain Charles Collins called them "the finest body of
emigrants I have ever had the pleasure to convey across the Atlantic."[11]

---

8. Jens Nielson to Uriah Nielson, 27.

9. Jens Nielson to Uriah Nielson, 28. Jens was so proud of paying his first sixty
dollars in tithing in Copenhagen before he left that he kept the receipt for the
rest of his life. See Jenson, *History of the Scandinavian Mission*, 112, for travel from
Copenhagen to Liverpool. A list of passengers on the *Rhoda* can be found at http://
www.ldsep.org/scand/em/56rh.htm, accessed January 3, 2002.

10. May, "Rites of Passage," 40, felt these regimented ocean crossings were something like a "crash course" or "boot camp" for the relatively new converts in communal skills and "practical Mormonism."

11. The complimentary letter from Captain Collins to James Willie as well as the
passenger list of the *Thornton* are from National Archives and Records Administration, film M237, reel 163, as quoted on the web site of the Immigrant Ships Tran-
scribers Guild, http://istg.rootsweb.com/1800/thornton18560615.html (accessed
July 10, 2001). See also Samuel Rowley, "Autobiography," and Thomas Rowley, "Life
of Thomas Rowley," for more details of this voyage.

The immigrants were welcomed in New York by Mormon Apostle John Taylor. [15] Three days later, they continued their *en masse* odyssey by locomotive and steamboat.[12] Aside from an unpleasant exchange with surly railroad men in Toledo, the journey went well. The Nielsons and their fellow Saints moved through a country agitated by escalating violence in Kansas and electrified by the beating of Senator Charles Sumner on the floor of the U.S. Senate just weeks before. While the migrants made their way west, the infant Republican Party met in Philadelphia to nominate John C. Frémont as their first presidential candidate, on a platform which called on Congress "to prohibit in the territories those twin relics of barbarism—polygamy and slavery."[13] The Nielsons may not have grasped much of this with their embryonic understanding of English, but what they did comprehend confirmed to them why they were fleeing to Zion. The company reached the end of the Rock Island Line at Iowa City, Iowa, on June 26.[14] Their lurching, steam-powered introduction to the eastern United States had lasted twelve days.

In Iowa City the Nielsons met another obstacle. Even though they had the money [16] to travel with a full wagon and team, they had been counseled in Denmark to contribute as much as they could to the less fortunate. This meant they would have to forego a full outfit and travel by handcart, according to Brigham Young's optimistic plan to gather more souls for less money. But poor communication between European

---

12. Jenson, *History of the Scandinavian Mission,* 112, gives the itinerary of the *Thornton* group as arriving by rail in Dunkirk, Ohio, on June 19, reaching Toledo by steamship on June 21, and arriving in Chicago on June 22, probably by rail. But *Thornton* passenger George Cunningham took a steamship up the Hudson to Albany, crossed New York by rail, traversed the Great Lakes to Chicago by ship, then took one more railroad to the Mississippi. See Carter, *Treasures of Pioneer History,* 5:252–56; and Madsen, *Journey to Zion,* 635–39.

13. "Republican Party Platform of 1856," in Johnson, *National Party Platforms,* 27–28.

14. The information for the ill-fated Willie Company, unless otherwise noted, comes from Stegner, *Gathering of Zion,* chap. 8; and Christy, "Weather, Disaster, and Responsibility." The migrants probably had to ferry across the Mississippi even though the first bridge built over that river was completed right on their route on April 22 of that same year. Two weeks after the first train ran across this marvel of engineering, though, the steamboat *Effie Afton* ran into one of the piles and destroyed a section of the bridge. It most likely was not repaired by the time this immigrant train came through. Incidentally, Abraham Lincoln defended the railroad interests in the *Effie Afton* case, one of the most important of his career.

mission leaders and Church immigration agents in Iowa left the agents
surprised by the number of Saints arriving so late in the season. They had
already outfitted three handcart companies that year, and there were not
enough vehicles left for the *Thornton* group. So the pioneers had to wait
three more precious weeks as carts were thrown together out of whatever
wood became available, properly seasoned or not. About five hundred
eager emigrants, 120 handcarts, and a few supply wagons finally set out
on July 15, once again under the leadership of James G. Willie. As on the
Thornton, long-established principles of organization pervaded the camp.
The band was organized into hundreds, with a leader over each. Jens Nielson was assigned to be in charge of his tent, which housed twenty people.
Each handcart held from four hundred to five hundred pounds, most of
it provisions for the trip. Every adult was authorized to bring seventeen
pounds of personal property, each child ten. But while the passage of the
Willie Company across the Atlantic had been exemplary, no one would
ever hope to emulate the Willie Company's crossing of the plains.

At least seventy-five members of the company dropped out in Iowa.[15]
The rest arrived at the final outfitting post of Florence, Nebraska (at the
eastern end of the territory, near today's Omaha), on August 11. They
refitted for a week, but also held a mass meeting to decide if they should
try to cross the mountains so late in the year. Most [17] of the immigration agents and expedition leaders favored making the attempt. Those
who thought the risks too great, particularly Levi Savage, were derided
for a lack of faith. Jens knew little about the country ahead; it was utterly
unlike Denmark. Therefore he had to rely on the judgment of those who
did. The great majority of the assembly voted to leave.

The company pulled out of Florence on August 18. From there, misfortunes multiplied on the hapless travelers. Their slapdash carts broke down
regularly. Many of their draft and beef cattle were driven off in a buffalo
stampede. Fort Laramie had few supplies left for them when they arrived.
Other way stations expected no more immigrants and were abandoned.
Cold and snow came extraordinarily early. And all the delays translated into
increasingly cruel arithmetic when applied to their dwindling rations: by
the time they passed Devil's Gate, the men were allotted ten and one half
ounces of flour per day, down from a pound, and the women and children

---

15. Lyman, "Bishop Jens Nielson," 3.

still less. Some began to beg the leaders to please pack down the flour into the cups to fit a bit more in. All along the Sweetwater River, the lives of consumed Saints flickered out when they sat down during the day or while they rested at night, "as smoothly as a lamp ceases to burn when the oil is gone."[16] The last flour was eaten on October 19, and the company would have been completely extinguished if not assisted somehow.

On the same afternoon the flour disappeared, hope arrived with messengers from Salt Lake City heralding more substantial relief soon. The first rescue wagons came two days after, with just enough food and warm clothing and promise to get the group moving again. But the worst lurked ahead. In spite of the meager relief, more of the travelers [18] gave out and were placed in the carts to be pulled by the rest. On October 23, the company tried the unforgiving ascent up Rocky Ridge. A keen wind sliced through them as they trudged through knee-deep snow up steep and broken slopes. Some were absolutely unable to budge their carts, weighed down by those who could no longer even try, and they, like oxen, were doubled up to move one cart forward a few yards, and then the other. When they staggered into camp, few pitched their tents but rather "sat shivering with cold around their small fires."[17] The pitiful stragglers were brought into the camp at Rock Creek by teams and wagons just before dawn.

When the burial detail surveyed the company in the morning, they found there were thirteen who had frozen during the night. Among the dead was Bodil Mortensen, clutching brush she would never throw into the fire. Also among the dead was little Niels Nielson; his numb parents could not protect their only child from exhaustion and unending cold. All the bodies, large and small, were stacked in the same square hole chiseled into the frozen ground. After a bit of a funeral the corpses were covered with willow boughs, then dirt, then shale to keep the wolves from them. Two of the gravediggers died that night and were buried nearby the next day, making fifteen total who never left the frigid camp at Rock Creek, still three hundred miles from Salt Lake City.

The company moved on, and its members continued to die daily. Jens was the only survivor of the five men who started the trip in his tent, and

---

16. John Chislett, member of the Willie Company, quoted in Stegner, *Gathering of Zion*, 245.

17. From Levi Savage, Journal, Thursday, October 23, 1856, quoted in Riverton Wyoming Stake, *Remember*, 10.

he had to enlist some of [19] the "largest and strongest women" to help set
up the shelter at night.[18] Then Jens faltered. Frostbite had deformed his
feet, and now it was his turn to sit down in the snow and die. He urged
Elsie to go on without him and save herself. She would not. Instead,
she persuaded her husband to get into the cart. Somehow she got her
small body, less than five feet tall, to pull her large husband far enough
to recover his strength and will.[19]

Relief wagons kept arriving to feed the starving and carry the disabled,
and after the emigrants crossed over South Pass the weather improved.
But the danger was not past, as old and young continued to expire
almost every day. Of the 404 members of the Willie Company who
left Florence, 68 died, and many who survived suffered lingering effects
from frostbite or other afflictions.[20] Jens kept his feet, but they had been
frozen at odd angles, giving him a permanent limp. From at least Fort
Bridger the Nielsons were able to abandon their cart and ride in a relief
wagon.[21] Finally, on November 9, the Willie Company emerged into Salt
Lake City to the welcome of hundreds of people who had turned out
to greet them. The bishops of the various wards in the valley made sure
each of the families was comfortably accommodated, and the survivors
began to recover and consider their new lives in Zion.

But somewhere back in those unmerciful mountains, Jens reaffirmed
the choice he [20] had made before being baptized. "I remember my prayers
as distinctly today as I did then," he told his son Uriah forty-five years
later. If God "would let me live to come to Salt Lake City," then "all my days
should be spent in usefulness under the direction of his Holy Priesthood."
So far priesthood direction had delayed his departure from Denmark until
this disastrous season and cost him most of his money, his only son, and
almost his life. Yet emerging from the ordeal he was still faithful. His feelings matched the "Reformation" in Utah that year, as the Saints sought to
purge their souls of any remaining impurities. Most pioneers were rebaptized when they reached the Salt Lake Valley as a way of rededicating

---

18. Lyman, "Bishop Jens Nielson," 4.

19. Lyman, "Bishop Jens Nielson," 6. "Short History of Elsie Rasmussen Nielson," 79, says that Elsie pulled the cart "all one day until he again took courage and
determined to see the journey through."

20. Christy, "Handcart Companies," 2:572.

21. Perkins, "Address Made in Evening Services," 41.

themselves to the faith in their new home. Whether Jens Nielson was physically baptized again or not, he emerged from his travails reborn.

Colonization

Once Latter-day Saints gathered to Zion, they were expected to build it up under the direction of Church authorities. Sometime in the next two years, the Nielsons were assigned to settle in Parowan. Established six years before, in the wake of Parley P. Pratt's explorations, it was the oldest Mormon community in southern Utah. It was originally part of the "Iron Mission" to manufacture that metal out of the ore in the mountains nearby. It also became the center from which other southern settlements radiated, as the Nielsons later found out firsthand when they were sent to settle new land. But for the time being, Jens and Elsie occupied themselves in rebuilding their lives. They were alarmed, as the whole territory was, at the reports of a United States army advancing toward Utah in the summer of 1857. From August on, Jens probably drilled with the [21] territorial militia, unless his twisted feet excused him from this service.[22]

Through all this, the Nielsons hoped to have more children but were disappointed again during their first year in Utah. Still, they believed they would be blessed this way if they lived the whole gospel, all of the commandments of their faith, as well as they could. But part of that "whole gospel" might disrupt the family before it helped: by late 1857, Jens felt he should marry a second wife. Plural marriage, more often called polygamy, had been openly avowed by the Church since 1852. While not everyone had the spiritual or economic means to live up to the principle, it increasingly became an ideal. In the fervent Reformation spirit of 1856–57, leaders exhorted eligible members to do their duty in this area as in others. Declarations such as this one from Heber C. Kimball seemed aimed directly at the Nielsons' difficulties: "I have noticed that a man who has but one wife, and is inclined to that doctrine, soon begins to wither and dry up, while a man who goes into plurality looks fresh, young, and sprightly. Why is this? Because God loves that man, and because he honours His work and word."[23]

---

22. If the Nielsons were in Parowan in the summer of 1857, they might have seen the Fancher Train as it passed through Parowan, traveling toward Mountain Meadow.

23. Heber C. Kimball quoted in Alexander, *Utah, the Right Place*, 188. The incidence of plural marriages was never higher than in these supercharged years, 1856–57. See Stanley Ivins, "Notes on Mormon Polygamy."

For most Mormons polygamy was not a salacious concept but a spiritual one, and the Nielsons had as much difficulty embracing it as most members did. Jens may have heard about the doctrine in Denmark, or he may have been counseled to take a second [22] wife by Church leaders in Utah who felt he met the standards to do it.[24] Even if he was not individually invited, every major decision Jens had made since he was baptized three years before, no matter how cataclysmic to himself or his family, had been based on trying to live up to the requirements of his faith. There could be no exceptions. Whatever problems he and Elsie encountered could be resolved only by obedience.[25]

Before a man asked a second wife to marry him, he often had to ask his first. Almost everything had changed for Elsie since 1850, the year she married Jens. They had sold their farm, lost their son, and now he was asking to alter their union. But Jens would not continue without her consent. He prophesied that if she accepted this principle, she would be blessed with children once again.[26] Elsie agreed, and on October 4, 1857, Jens married Kirsten Jensen in the Endowment House in Salt Lake City. Jens was thirty-seven years old, Elsie twenty-seven, and Kirsten twenty-three.[27] [23]

---

24. Most men who entered plural marriage were asked by Church authorities to do it. See Arrington and Bitton, *Mormon Experience*, 199–200. If such an invitation were given to Jens Nielson, he could hardly refuse if he hoped to live up to the desperate covenant he made in the snow a few months before. It could also indicate that the Nielsons made a strong start for themselves economically in their first year in Utah. The 1860 Manuscript Census for Iron County, Utah, 183, shows Jens Nielson as a farmer in Parowan with $300 in real estate and $375 in personal property. These amounts are about average for the community, but a good start for someone who had been there no more than three years. See also Bachman and Esplin, "Plural Marriage"; Embry, *Mormon Polygamous Families*; and Foster, *Religion and Sexuality*, for more on the religious imperatives and social practices of plural marriage.

25. Jens and Elsie were not unusual in their motive. Embry, *Mormon Polygamous Families*, 52, asserts that the desire to live up to one's faith was the leading reason a Mormon entered into plural marriage.

26. Lyman, "Bishop Jens Nielson," 7.

27. Exactly when the Nielsons first settled in Parowan is troublesome. It seems logical they would have gone in early 1857 so they could get out of crowded Salt Lake City (an unusually high number of immigrants came in 1856, and there had been poor harvests in 1855 and 1856) and arrive in time to plant that year. Arrington,

Kirsten and what was left of her family had arrived in Utah not long before. But she already knew Jens Nielson: he had baptized her while he was a missionary in Denmark. Kirsten's parents and two brothers crossed the Atlantic with the Nielsons on the *Thornton* in 1856 but left Kirsten, a brother, and a sister in Denmark since the family did not have enough cash to travel together. Kirsten's parents and brothers stayed in the Midwest to earn money for the remnants' passage rather than go to Utah immediately. But the joyful reunion the family expected in the United States never happened. Instead, after Kirsten and the others crossed to America and trekked to Council Bluffs, Iowa, in 1857, they were informed that their mother and one of their brothers had died from cholera in St. Louis. Another brother died as they crossed the plains with their father as members of the Christiansen handcart company that summer.[28] Less than a month after her afflicted family pulled into Salt Lake City, Kirsten, after quiet struggles of her own, became the second wife of Jens Nielson.[29] [24]

From Quaker to Latter-day Saint, 343, mentions regarding the handcart companies of 1856, "As each company came in, ten or more immigrant families were assigned to each ward to be housed and sheltered, until they could be sent to southern settlements to locate the following spring." But the small interval between the arrival of Kirsten Jensen, Jens's second wife, to Salt Lake City (September 13, 1857) and her marriage to Jens in Salt Lake City (October 4, 1857) make it difficult to believe the Nielsons were in Parowan already. In his letter to Uriah, Jens wrote only that "From here [Salt Lake City] we went to Iron County, Utah and settled in Parowan." They were definitely in Parowan by the time their daughter Mary was born in October 1858. It is also possible that the Nielsons' wrestling with polygamy began earlier than the family stories indicate, and they arranged something with the Jensens on the *Thornton* in 1856.

28. See Gabbart and Redd, "Kirsten Jensen Nielson," in Nielson, "Bishop Jens Nielson: History and Genealogy," for a sketch of her life. She is on the Christiansen Handcart Company list in Carter, *Our Pioneer Heritage*, 14:321–23.

29. Most likely the Jensens stayed in Salt Lake City during this month, as indicated in Lenora Jones, "Pioneer Story." Kirsten's brother John Lolland was very upset that she married into polygamy. He offered to build her a house and take care of her for the rest of her days if she refused to marry into such an arrangement. But Kirsten, according to her youngest daughter who heard her tell the story many times, felt, as Jens and Elsie did, that she had to obey every principle of the gospel and could not afford to discriminate against the principle of polygamy. See Kimmerle, "Little Visit," 233.

Jens's promise to Elsie came true. In October of the next year, she gave
birth to a daughter, Mary. Kirsten had a boy named Jens, but he died the day
he was born. The next six years in Parowan, however, brought many more
children. Elsie had another daughter, Julia, and Kirsten had two boys, Hans
Joseph and Jens Peter, as well as a girl, Margaret. Now Jens had achieved
something he had never dreamed of in Denmark: he was a respected member of the community and the head of not one, but two, households.[30]

Once more his faith did not let him stay still. Due to scarce water and
a declining wheat crop, Church authorities in Parowan sent out explorers
to find new land.[31] Jens was called to start a new settlement.[32] In March
1864, fifty-four families from Parowan and Beaver cut a winding road up
frosty canyons to a place they eventually called Panguitch, about twenty-
five air miles east of Parowan on the upper Sevier River. Jens Nielson
was [25] appointed the presiding elder, then bishop, responsible for the
venture.[33] When the settlers arrived, they quickly set to work digging
irrigation ditches, planting crops, and constructing their homes from the
plentiful timber in the area. But with only one team of animals for every
three families and the short growing season that exists at an altitude of
6,666 feet, not much crop was raised. The following winter was severe, and
when their flour gave out, the families were reduced to grinding wheat
in a little coffee mill or gnawing on boiled kernels to survive. Seven men

---

30. That Jens became a respected member of the community is implicit in his
call as presiding elder over the Panguitch settlement in 1864, a position that carried
considerable responsibility.

31. See Newell and Talbot, *History of Garfield County*, 57.

32. A "call" is an official request issued by Church leaders for a member to do a certain job. Many settlers of new Mormon communities were called to do it. They were
under obligation to remain in this "mission" until they were released by a Church
authority. Sometime between 1856 and 1864 Jens lived in Paragonah, a town near
Parowan. He lived there for only a short period of time, since none of his children
were born there, and they came regularly. Jens Nielson did not mention Paragonah in
his 1901 letter to his son Uriah, but he did say he had been called to make six homes
in Utah, and a home in Paragonah would round out that number. It is possible that
Jens moved one of his families to Paragonah and kept the other in Parowan.

33. The basic unit of the Church is a "ward," the equivalent of a congregation or
parish. A ward is usually led by a bishop. But a "branch" is a less-developed ward,
headed by a branch president or presiding elder. In the Panguitch Branch, Jens
Nielson was the leading religious authority.

were sent to Parowan for supplies and were able to proceed over the deep
snows in some places only by arranging a relay of quilts to walk on. But
the colony survived to celebrate its anniversary the next March. As one girl
recalled the feast, "We had pies made of bulberries and service berries and
the bishop made forty gallons of beer."³⁴ The settlers soon completed the
small log structure that was a schoolhouse, church, dance hall, or assembly
room, depending on the occasion. Sunday meetings found the Nielsons in
the front row, with Elsie's two little girls in matching dresses.³⁵

Elsie bore a third daughter, Agnes, in the spring of 1865, but the
infant died the [26] following December. During her short life, new trouble came to the settlement. Relations between Indians and Mormons
boiled over in Sanpete Valley to the north, and various Indian bands
began to loosely organize under the Ute Black Hawk to raid Mormon
settlements. They hit perimeter outposts such as Panguitch particularly
hard, and the settlers fought a number of skirmishes against the Indians. Those embattled residents stayed close to their fort and organized
a strict militia to guard themselves and their livestock. When George A.
Smith reviewed the troops in March 1866 he found forty men, twenty-
two guns, and a few revolvers, with about half the guns "scarcely fit for
service."³⁶ Even under these precautions, Panguitch was too vulnerable,
and it became one of the many exposed settlements Church leaders
decided to abandon during the conflict. Late in the spring of 1866, the
colonists cleared out, leaving their third crop in the fields.

With Kirsten ready to give birth at any moment, the Nielsons moved
twenty-six miles down the Sevier to Circleville, another settlement started

---

34. Julia Robinson, quoted in Newell and Talbot, *History of Garfield County*, 61.
The beer was most likely "Danish beer," a low or non-alcoholic brew. The "Word of
Wisdom," the Church's health code, did not usually carry as much formal force in
the nineteenth century as it would later in the twentieth. Some high Church leaders,
such as John Henry Smith and Brigham Young Jr., felt as late as 1901 that Danish
beer was permissible. See Alexander, *Mormonism in Transition*, 258–60, for views
of the Word of Wisdom in the late nineteenth century.

35. Gwen H. Jones, "History of Kumen Jones," 104. If Kirsten settled in Panguitch, it was not until after the town was settled. She had three children under
five years old, and the third was born April 1, 1864, in Parowan, weeks after the
Panguitch expedition left.

36. Winkler, "Circleville Massacre," 12.

in 1864. There she delivered another son, John, shortly after they arrived. But the Indian pressure on Circleville was at least as heavy as it had been in Panguitch, and it, too, was abandoned later in the year. Before that happened, though, a brutal act occurred. Circleville, like Panguitch, had been raided by Indians late in 1865. But unlike Panguitch, settlers were killed in these attacks. When difficulties and rumors continued the next spring, the residents of Circleville decided to take preemptive action. They confined all the members of the nearby Piede group of Paiute Indians in their meetinghouse while they awaited [27] instructions from authorities in Parowan. When some of the Indian men slipped out of their ropes and attacked their captors, the alarmed settlers killed all sixteen of them. Then they proceeded to execute at least ten captive women and children to keep them from telling about the murders. Only four small children were allowed to survive.[37] The Nielsons, recently arrived, had little influence. Jens protested strongly against confining the Indians to the church and pleaded against the massacre, but in the end he retreated declaring, "I wash my hands clean of this."[38] When Circleville was abandoned, the Nielsons returned to Parowan.

Within two years, the young family moved to Cedar City, about eighteen miles south. Compared to where the Nielsons had lived recently, Cedar was a mature community, having been established a few months after Parowan in 1851. Originally it was the center for the county's attempts to produce iron, but those efforts had been abandoned by the time the Nielsons arrived in 1866 or 1867. Jens most likely knew a number of Cedar residents already through church and commercial connections. He quickly became a prominent figure in his new community. In 1869 he was called to the high council of the Parowan Stake.[39] By then Jens had also been elected to the city council, and he would serve as a councilman for ten years. In 1873 he appeared before the Utah Second District Court judge and became a citizen of the United States. [28]

---

37. Winkler, "Circleville Massacre," 18; and Newell and Talbot, *History of Garfield County*, 82–85.

38. Lyman, "Bishop Jens Nielson," 5; and Kimmerle, "Little Visit," 234–35, tell of Nielson's reactions to these events as he told them years after they happened.

39. Dalton, *History of Iron County Mission*, 300. A "stake" is a larger unit in the Church that usually includes from five to twelve wards. The high council is a group of twelve men that helps the stake president operate the stake.

Jens prospered enough in Cedar that by 1874, either by invitation, inclination, or inspiration, he married again.[40] Ane Katrine Jorgensen was also born on the island of Lolland in Denmark.[41] Her mother died before the baby turned two, and her father died by the time she was ten. She was placed with a foster family named Beabaum, probably the same family that raised Elsie. While Elsie was a farm worker, "Trena" found work as a domestic servant in Copenhagen. She was employed in the homes of some of the city's wealthier citizens and became an excellent cook. Mr. Beabaum migrated to Parowan and later paid for Katrine to come to Utah, possibly to look for her brother. She visited Elsie in Cedar City and stayed on for six months as a boarder before Jens asked her to be his third wife. After taking the long trip to Salt Lake City accompanied by Kirsten's oldest daughter, Jens, now fifty-four, and Katrine, who was twenty-nine, were married on February 23, 1874, in the Endowment House. By this time the Nielsons lived in a large, rectangular home in Cedar City. Elsie and her two daughters resided on one end, while Kirsten and her children lived in the other. When Jens married Katrine, he added two more rooms for her, making the house into an "L" shape, with Elsie and her children occupying the junction and the households of Kirsten and Katrine on the ends. Jens [29] rotated through the sections, living a week at a time with each family.[42]

The Nielsons needed all the space they could get. Although Kirsten's baby from Circleville, Johnny, died not long after his first birthday, she had three more healthy children in Cedar City: Francis, a boy, and two girls, Lucinda and Caroline. One last boy, Hyrum, was stillborn in 1876.[43]

---

40. Whatever the reason for this third marriage, it placed Jens among the minority of those in plural marriage with three or more wives. Ivins, "Notes on Mormon Polygamy," found that in a sample of 1,784 polygamous husbands, 66.3 percent had two wives, 21.2 percent "were three-wife men," 6.7 percent had four wives, leaving 5.8 percent with more than four wives. Smith and Kunz, "Polygny and Fertility," found similar percentages. In their sample of 1,687 polygamous husbands, 70.2 percent had two wives, 20.7 percent had three wives, and 9.3 percent had four or more wives.

41. See Butt, "Ane Katrine Jorgensen Nielson," in Nielson, "Bishop Jens Nielson: History and Genealogy," for details about Katrine's life.

42. Reeve, "Lucinda Diantha Nielson Hyde," 205–6.

43. Kirsten had been out chopping wood a few days before the delivery, when some of the wood flew up and struck her in the abdomen. At that moment, she said

Katrine had three children, Annetta, Uriah, and Freeman from 1875 to
1879, making for a total of eleven children, six daughters and five sons, in
Jens's large family. The father's other responsibilities continued to grow
as well. In 1877 he was called as the first counselor to Bishop Christopher Arthur in the Cedar Ward, and on November 27, he dedicated the
cornerstone for the new meetinghouse.[44] The Nielsons, just like their
neighbors, contributed to the construction of the St. George Temple
and rejoiced at its completion in 1877.[45]

Their life, however, was not entirely idyllic. Cedar City's "United Order
of Enoch," an attempt organized by Brigham Young to bring the Saints'
economic affairs into close cooperation, fell apart within three years
of its organization in 1874, leaving [30] fractured feelings and finances
behind.[46] Then there was a great division in the stake when some supported Jesse N. Smith and others William Dame as their stake president.[47] This controversy hit Parowan the hardest, but still sent ripples

---

she felt the baby "just drop," and when it was born dead a few days later, she was
convinced that was the cause. See Kimmerle, "Little Visit," 234.

44. See Dalton, *History of Iron County Mission*, 301; also Jones, *Henry Lunt*, 304.

45. According to a family story, while the temple was being built, a man came
to Kirsten at home to ask for donations. Regretting she had nothing to give at the
moment, she promised to donate the next money she gained and prayed intently
about it. Soon after, Margaret came running in to show her the shiny button she
found in the dirt. The "button" turned out to be a five-dollar gold piece, which
Kirsten gladly gave to the cause. See Reeve, "Lucinda Diantha Nielson Hyde," 207;
and Gabbert and Redd, "Kirsten Jensen Nielson," 2–3, which splits this story out
to two separate occurrences.

46. See Arrington, Fox, and May, *Building the City of God*, for the various types
of united orders that were attempted in various Utah settlements as well as their
failures and effects.

47. Seegmiller, *History of Iron County*, 80; Peterson, *Take Up Your Mission*,
48–49. This strange confrontation quite possibly had something to do with the
original impetus for the San Juan Mission. William Dame, who had held the position since the 1850s, won this contest for the stake presidency. Soon after, the First
Presidency was informed that Silas S. Smith, brother of the failed candidate, Jesse
N. Smith, wanted to "remove from Paragonah and form a new settlement with some
of his friends." The First Presidency and the Quorum of the Twelve, the highest
governing bodies of the Church, therefore issued him a call to lead a colony to the
San Juan "if it be in accordance with his feelings." Later, however, they found out
that Silas Smith had never expressed any such desire, but he apparently decided, in

through Cedar's society. The Cedar Saints did manage to preserve some cooperation, continuing to operate a store and beginning to herd their sheep and cattle in cooperative companies. The older Nielson boys often found themselves alone on the range watching stock.

Overall, by 1879, Jens Nielson could be content. He had followed the high standards and forded the difficult challenges of his faith. He had been carried to a strange new land and had sacrificed much, but like Joseph of the Old Testament, whose story he loved dearly, he had been recompensed many times over.[48] He had a large family whose eleven children spanned an entire generation. The oldest, the very energetic Mary, had wed [31] one Kumen Jones, a wiry cattleman from Cedar, just before Christmas in 1878.[49] The youngest, Freeman, was born a few months after Mary's wedding, in August 1879. By his family, church, and community, Jens Nielson was recognized as a "strong character, strengthened or developed more or less by his association with the Mormon Church."[50] Once again, Jens could say, as he had regarding his early years in Denmark, "The Lord blessed me on my right hand and on my left." He could be excused if, at the age of fifty-nine, after establishing one home in Denmark and five in Utah, he anticipated a tranquil retirement, disrupted only by his growing children and an increasing gaggle of grandchildren. But he may also have suspected from his previous experience that other fates awaited.

---

spite of poor health, to lead the mission anyway. See Larson, *Erastus Snow*, 637; John Taylor, letters to Erastus Snow, January 9, 1879; February 15, 1879.

48. Lyman, "To the Family of My Dear Bishop," 46.

49. Jens approved of this union even though young Mr. Jones had gotten his daughter in a wreck a short while before. A large group went up Bear Canyon in a lumber wagon, and while they all launched into the chorus of "Sweet Belle Mahone," the vehicle tipped over, trapping everyone but Mary and Kumen underneath. Miraculously, they lifted the wagon and freed the others, and no one was seriously hurt. This was probably not the first time Jens was concerned about Mary's social activities. Kumen wrote, "They called her Wild Bill in the bunch she ran with. There never was a girl could dance as hard and as long as Aunt Mary." But she was "without a trace of an unvirtuous, impure thought." See Kumen Jones, "Writings," 163; also Kumen Jones, "Aunt Mary Jones," 90.

50. Kumen Jones, "Bishop Jens Nielson."

To the San Juan

The Call

The Mormon Church was the greatest colonizing institution in the American West.[51] From the arrival of the first pioneers in the Salt Lake Valley in 1847, the Church [32] created more than five hundred communities in successive waves of colonization. Most of this was done under the imperatives of gathering and supporting over a hundred thousand immigrants and their posterity with the scarce and scattered resources of the region. But this physical necessity was coupled with "their own particular version of Manifest Destiny": the extension of Mormon control throughout the Rocky Mountain region, eventually overspilling U.S. borders into Canada and Mexico.[52] Even after the establishment of the Cotton Mission around St. George in southern Utah during the 1860s, population pressures continued, becoming especially acute toward the end of Brigham Young's life in the late 1870s. Settlement continued within Utah Territory in marginal areas. One hundred new settlements jumped over the boundaries of Utah from 1876 to 1879, located in places such as the San Luis Valley in Colorado, the Upper Snake and Goose Creek valleys in Idaho, and the Little Colorado and Salt River valleys in Arizona. In some of these areas, agricultural lands and pastures were reclaimed from the desert through laborious irrigation projects. It was important not only to cultivate new colonies for the present, but also to secure land for future growth, particularly in places that might be settled by non-Mormon "Gentiles."[53] One of these areas was the four corners region. In the late 1870s it was still largely unsettled, but immigrants were approaching swiftly, and [33] better they be Mormon than not, "that the Saints may have room to dwell."[54]

---

51. See Arrington, *Great Basin Kingdom*, for the ideals and experiences in this massive settlement process.

52. Peterson, *Take Up Your Mission*, 7–9. See Sherlock, "Mormon Migration and Settlement," for the particular features of this last wave of Mormon colonization.

53. Mormons, in their theology, are part of the House of Israel and inheritors of the covenants the Lord made with Abraham. Therefore, non–Latter-day Saints, being outside of these covenants, are sometimes referred to as "Gentiles."

54. Silas S. Smith in Parowan Stake, General Minutes, March 23, 1879, see also March 22, 1879. "President Snow expressed himself ... spoke of the importance of

As usual, more colonization meant increased constriction of Native Americans. In spite of Mormons' good intentions toward them and Brigham Young's policy of feeding rather than fighting them, more for the Mormons meant less for the Indians.[55] The livestock of the new settlers was difficult to resist for cultures accustomed to raiding their neighbors. Even with the end of the Black Hawk War in the late 1860s, and the continued best efforts of Indian missionaries such as Jacob Hamblin and Thales Haskell in the 1870s, difficulties persisted between Mormons and Native Americans on the southern frontier.[56]

Given these factors, Brigham Young almost certainly considered sending a mission into southeastern Utah or the nearby corners of Arizona or New Mexico, and perhaps discussed it at a conference in St. George in 1877.[57] But the great colonizer died in August of that year. While this may have delayed the endeavor, Young's successor, [34] John Taylor, along with Erastus Snow, the Apostle who oversaw southern settlements, did not let the matter rest long. Specific preparations to occupy the area began during a stake conference in Parowan days after Christmas in 1878. One name read just before the close of the conference altered Jens Nielson's golden years immensely.[58]

The name was that of his oldest son, Hans Joseph Nielson. Joe was nineteen years old and unmarried. Like his father, he was tall, sturdy, broad-faced, square-jawed, and incurably outgoing. And like the others on the long list of names read by Elder Snow at the conference, this

---

setting upon and occupying the Territory of Arizona, New Mexico, & parts of the State of Colorado, and parts of the Territory of Utah that is not now occupied."

55. See Arrington, *Brigham Young*, chap. 13 for President Young's views and policies toward the Indians.

56. The twin goals of settling land for strategic political purposes as well as for pacifying and proselyting Indians were not new for the Mormons. See Meinig, "Mormon Culture Region," 191–209, for the waves of settlement that radiated out from the Mormon core area in the late 1800s. The Elk Mountain Mission (where Moab is today) tried unsuccessfully to achieve these ends in the late 1850s.

57. See Miller, *Hole-in-the-Rock*, chap. 1, for details on the call to the San Juan. See also Albert R. Lyman, Journal, November 25, 1897, for a speech given by Brigham Young Jr. in which he recalls that his father wanted a colony "between the Navajo and Ute nations to make friends with them and prepare them for the gospel when the time came."

58. See Parowan Stake, General Minutes, December 29, 1878.

public announcement was the first he knew about his call to relocate
to the Four Corners region. Furthermore, Joe was also chosen to be a
member of the exploring party that would reconnoiter that area early
the next year. Jens was particularly attached to this son who was his firstborn after he had to bury Niels in the frozen ground near Rock Creek.[59]

The mission call caused turmoil in the stake as soon as the names
were read. A week after the conference, a special meeting was held in
the social hall in Cedar City. Bishop Christopher Arthur and the stake
president, now Henry Lunt, assured those assembled that there had
been "no prejudice" in the selection of names. Their colonizing mission
was just as important as a foreign mission and would require the same
amount of guidance from the Holy Spirit. Bishop Arthur assured them
there was no compulsion, but advised all who were going to do so "with
a cheerful heart." He invited those who were called and their parents
to express themselves on the matter. Jens, among others, arose and [35]
announced "his willingness to assist all that laid in his power for his son
to go and fill the mission." Joe also expressed his willingness "to go and
do the best he could."[60]

But something else was working in Jens aside from his desire to help
his son. During the meeting, Bishop Arthur also invited volunteers to
submit their names for this mission. Over the next weeks, Jens contemplated doing just that. Of course he was concerned about Joe, but
there may have been other factors that influenced him during these early
months of 1879. He probably agreed with the major purposes of the proposed outpost. He had lived near the southeastern border of Mormon
settlement for more than twenty years and could see the need for better
relations with the Indians. Furthermore, if gentile cattle ranchers, or
even worse, outlaws, dominated the southeastern corner of the territory,
as it looked as if they were starting to do, then they would not only use
up resources that Mormons needed for the future, but also antagonize
the Indians there.[61] Despite their run-ins, Mormons felt a spiritual obligation toward Native Americans, possible descendants of the Book of

---

59. Lyman, "To the Family of My Dear Bishop," 46.

60. Cedar Ward, General Minutes, January 2, 1879.

61. For reasons why the San Juan Mission was started, see Miller, *Hole-in-the-
Rock*, 4–9; Jensen, "Historical Study of Bluff City," 3–6; Crabtree, *Incredible Mission*,
1–6.

Mormon's "Lamanites." Better relations had to be established with them before the Mormons could convert them. In other words, the proposed settlement would be started for both offensive and defensive reasons: to pacify Indians in the hope of eventually converting them and to defend Zion by preempting this large section of land from outsiders.

Jens might also have worried about something else. Federal officials began to [36] step up their prosecution of polygamists after the passage of the Poland Act in 1874. Brigham Young was embroiled in legal difficulties surrounding the divorce suit of his last wife, Ann Eliza Webb, for several years before his death. Then, scarcely a week after the Parowan Conference issued the first calls to settle the San Juan region, the Supreme Court of the United States upheld the conviction of the late Brigham Young's private secretary, George Reynolds, for polygamy. And Congress seemed to be brewing up more trouble for those who lived in "L"-shaped houses with more than one wife.

Sometime in the next month or two, Jens approached a Church leader, perhaps Erastus Snow himself, and asked to be called to this mission. He was volunteering to go but also hoped for the validation of an official priesthood call.[62] It came in the next conference of the Parowan Stake, held in Cedar City on March 23, 1879.[63]

---

62. This explanation of Jens Nielson's call to the San Juan Mission takes into account both his own conviction that he was called by Erastus Snow (see Jens Nielson letter to Uriah Nielson) and Albert R. Lyman's uneven insistence that he was not called but went to accompany Joe. According to "Bishop Jens Nielson," 6, written in 1936, he was called to the mission, but in Lyman's biography of Lemuel Redd published in Redd, *Lemuel Hardison Redd, Jr.*, 19, he was not. In "To the Family of My Dear Bishop," written in 1965, he wrote, "However, because it was a new, hard country and because of his love and concern for his son, he decided to go with them." He developed this idea more in "Bishop Jens Nielson: The Old Wagon," n.d. While many others accompanied the colonizing expedition without a formal call, it is my opinion, given his convictions and past experiences, that Jens came to feel he was supposed to go, and he wanted this formalized into a priesthood calling so that this became a duty not just an impulse. As Kirsten's oldest daughter Margaret put it in 1944, "Jens Nielson's oldest son, Joe, was called to go so his father, Jens Nielson, volunteered to go also." Margaret was fifteen when all of this was happening in 1879. See Mary Kisten Adams, "Life of Margaret Adams," in "Jens Nielson History," 187.

63. Parowan Stake, General Minutes, March 23, 1879.

Some of the Nielsons began to prepare for their removal. Not all of them would go. Katrine, who may have had some troubles with her health already, was expecting Freeman to be delivered just before the expedition would leave. It was better for her to stay in the house at Cedar and manage the fields and flocks. For the time being, Elsie and [37] Julia would stay as well to help. Elsie's oldest daughter, Mary, would accompany her husband, Kumen Jones, who had also been called. Kirsten and her six children would go, and they began to accumulate supplies and expectations for the journey to their new home.

On April 14, 1879, Joe Nielson and Kumen Jones left Paragonah with the twenty-four other men, two women, and eight children who made up the scouting party. Church authorities had not designated a specific spot for the colony, so this party's goal was to explore the region and find a suitable place to settle. Its members might have contemplated what they were leaving. Many besides themselves had worked very hard to make their towns what they were. Cedar City had almost 750 settlers now, with almost 2,000 acres of fields enclosed against the nearly 12,000 sheep and 3,000 cattle. It had built up its industries, with gristmills and sawmills, a tannery, a furniture shop, and two mercantile stores. In all it had become comfortable: "a beautiful little village with its orchards and shade trees, the envy of many passers-by."[64] Plunging into the wilderness forfeited all of that.

All of those who were called to settle in that wilderness wrestled with their feelings. Kumen Jones had a dream shortly after he and Mary were wed in St. George, days before the December 1878 Parowan conference. In it, "he was helping erect buildings from rock. There were Indians watching and nearby was a muddy stream. The next morning he asked his mother to interpret the dream, whereupon, she [having already heard rumors] began to cry, 'Oh Kumen, you will be called to pioneer into the San Juan [38] River country.'"[65] James Davis was distressed by his call, but tried to rally his spirits: "Feel very low and sad about it. So did Mary and the children, but by the help of God I am determined to obey counsel. We are still feeling gloomy over the mission."[66] He sold his farm in Cedar

---

64. "Cedar Ward Manuscript History."

65. See Gwen H. Jones, "History of Kumen Jones."

66. Davis, Journal, January 1, 1879. Two weeks later he was still trying to talk himself into it in his January 13, 1879, entry: "I cannot help but feel bad when any

and took his whole family out with the scouting party. Twenty-two-year-old Lemuel H. Redd Jr. in New Harmony had been married for less than a year and was determined to succeed in business when his call came. His father-in-law, who was his partner in the business, was also supposed to go, but decided he would not. "Lem," as the young man with intense eyes was known, told his own father he could not afford to accept the mission call. But his father directly replied that he could not afford *not* to go, and young Brother Redd found the motivation to accept.[67] The Woods, who lived across the street from the Nielsons in Cedar City, were called in 1882 to strengthen the mission. "We spent the evening talking about our call to San Juan," Jody Wood recalled. "Some thought they would just as soon stay in Cedar. But when a call comes from the President of our Church, we go."[68] But as was usually the case, not everyone did. Some pleaded difficult circumstances and were released from their call. Some just stayed put.[69]

The scouting party returned in September, having traversed a circle of almost a [39] thousand miles. The explorers curved south, then turned up through the Navajo Reservation at Moenkopi in Arizona, and left the Davis and Harriman families in a promising spot near where Montezuma Creek flowed into the San Juan River, in southeastern Utah. They came home by the northern arc, across the Colorado and Green rivers, then up the Sevier. They reported two or three sites that could sustain settlements, but also had mixed experiences with the Indians and the water in the area.[70]

The scouting party's report was acceptable, but not encouraging. And the roundabout routes they took to the proposed settlement were too long for the main body to return on if the settlers hoped to reach their new home before winter. There had to be, they believed, a more direct way

---

one comes to buy me out after toiling so hard to get what I have got but I am determined to fill my mission."

67. Arrington, *Utah's Audacious Stockman*, 12.

68. Noall, "Mormon Midwives," 130.

69. This range of reactions was not unusual. See Peterson, *Take Up Your Mission*, 54–58, to see the same sorts of reactions to calls to settle on the Little Colorado in Arizona.

70. See Miller, *Hole-in-the-Rock*, chap. 2, for a more detailed description of the entire scouting expedition.

that would bisect the circle of the scouting party's path and take the settlers straight to the San Juan. Just in time, scouts from Escalante, a town
eighty-five miles east of Cedar City, reported such a "back door," a probable passage across the Colorado River that would open a shortcut to the
San Juan. All the while preparations continued, and people decided if
they were going. The Nielsons had an easier time of it since they did not
have to sell their house and fields. Still, they had to take what they would
need for their migration and what they wanted for their new home. But
Jens had no doubts. During his last sacrament meeting in the Cedar City
Ward, he once again emphasized that he "felt it the voice of the Lord to
him to go, and he was going by the help of the Almighty."[71] [40]

The Epic

In late October, wagons creaked out of many of the southern Utah settlements, rolling toward Escalante. The Lymans moved south from Oak
City with six wagons and 180 head of cattle. The Paces and Goddards
and Redds pulled out of New Harmony, and the Hutchingses and Lil-
lywhites from Beaver. But the largest contingent came from the Parowan
Stake. On Wednesday, October 22, 1879, the Nielsons' three wagons,
with about twenty others, left Cedar City. The expedition picked up
more families in Paragonah, though not Silas S. Smith, a cousin of the
martyred prophet Joseph Smith, who was called to lead the expedition
but was not ready to leave. The company then turned up Little Creek
Canyon and followed the same road Jens blazed fifteen years earlier
when he led the way to Panguitch. At the head of Little Creek Canyon,
the Nielson party caught up with the large group from Parowan, which
had many clans of Deckers, the Butt brothers, the Rowleys (whose
father, Samuel, also survived the *Thornton* and Willie handcart experiences when he was a lad), and the Nielsons' half nephew-in-law, Hanson Bayles.[72] There the mass moved over to the Upper Bear Valley and
camped for three nights, where "Jens Nielson, Danishman, recognized as
leading elder, proceeded to organize his flock and lay down some simple
regulations for the conduct of his charges, the people of the San Juan

---

71. Cedar Ward, General Minutes, October 19, 1879.

72. Hanson's father, Herman Daggett Bayles, married Kirsten Jensen Nielson's
younger sister, Dorthea, as his fifth and final wife.

mission."[73] Jens made rules similar to those of most Mormon migrations: "The Sabbath was observed at all times, and under all [41] conditions. Every evening, hymns were sung and prayers were said. Occasionally dances were held," as Kumen Jones remembered.[74]

The group pushed down the Bear River Valley, then up the Sevier to Panguitch, which had been resettled in 1871. In fact, the leader of this second settlement, George Washington Sevy, later joined the expedition. By early November the host arrived in Escalante, then pushed ahead through the Potato Valley to the end of anything resembling a road at Forty-mile Spring. Here, about a month after they left the older settlements, they made camp to wait for the groups behind and to scout the terrain ahead.

The Nielsons were well outfitted for this trip. They had three wagons for their eight family members and supplies. Like most pioneers, they had furnished at least some of their wagons as rolling apartments as well as freight haulers. Three beds and a stove were set up in them, so none of the family had to sleep on the ground. As for food, in addition to wheat, corn, bacon, potatoes, and molasses, they had some extras. Elsie sent along five gallons of honey from the hives she faithfully kept, and Kirsten made at least that much ground cherry preserves to take with them.[75]

Beyond the usual rigors of wagon travel, Kirsten had to feed the family along the way. Baking bread on the coals of a campfire was routine. For supper each night, she filled her big, black pot with corn cereal sweetened with molasses. Her job was sometimes made more difficult by her own family. One day, Margaret and Caroline were riding in the back of a wagon, with Kirsten riding up front with Joe. The girls smelled [42] freshly baked bread, which was supposed to last all day. Abetted by their father, they ate one piece, then another, until they found they had devoured everything. Their mother's crestfallen face and the extra work they had to do to replace the lost loaves discouraged them from repeating the performance.[76]

---

73. Miller, *Hole-in-the-Rock*, 50–51, quoting Margaret Nielson's account based on George Decker's journal.

74. Gwen H. Jones, "History of Kumen Jones," 106.

75. These details come from Reeve, "Lucinda Diantha Nielson Hyde," 208; and Kimmerle, "Little Visit," 235.

76. Leland Redd, "Bishop Jens Nielson," 35.

Yet on the whole the children were assets. Most of the families on the trip were younger, with two or three small children. But the Nielsons had six, most of them adults by frontier labor standards. Joe, close to twenty, was skilled with animals and could also help gather and herd stock, as well as build the road ahead. Jens Peter, at seventeen, had similar skills and was already a giant, nearing the six and a half feet in stature he would have as a man. Francis, or "France," as he was called, was notably shy for a generally affable family, but at eleven he was old enough to drive one of the wagons, and he could also go out to gather firewood and scout pasture for the animals. The three girls, Margaret, 15, Lucinda, or "Cindy," 7, and Caroline, 5, sometimes scouted with France, and helped their mother with her many tasks.[77]

The Nielsons' livestock were indispensable. There were two oxen to pull one wagon, two mules to pull another, and four head of cattle to pull the third. The family also had some dairy cows and an unspecified number of beef cattle among the thousand or so loose head that were strung ahead or behind the company as the feed warranted. Fueling these beasts became difficult: finding enough grass and water was one of the major challenges of the expedition, and it only got worse as they moved farther [43] from Escalante and deeper into winter.

At Forty-mile Spring the strung-out companies gathered. Jens sent Kumen Jones and three others to find a route to the Colorado River and beyond. These scouts were not encouraged by prospectors they encountered who informed them that "if every rag, or other property owned by the people of the territory was sold for cash, it would not pay for the making of a burro trail across the river."[78] Silas S. Smith, the president of the expedition, arrived amid these dim prospects on November 24. He sent out a larger exploring party to find a passable route. "After about one week's tramping," almost everyone in this group also felt it was impossible to pass through what Platte Lyman called "the worst country I ever saw."[79] On their way back to camp, the disappointed explorers informed the men who were pushing the road out from Forty-mile Spring that

---

77. See Reeve, "Lucinda Diantha Nielson Hyde," 208; Kimmerle, "Little Visit," 235; Adams, "Margaret Nielson Adams," 187; Redd and Gabbert, "Life of Kirsten Jensen Nielson," 144.

78. Kumen Jones, "Writings," 10.

79. Quoted in Miller, *Hole-in-the-Rock*, 62.

their work was in vain; a bird could not cross that country, let alone teams and wagons.[80]

By the time the exploring party returned, the full camp of almost 250 settlers in more than 80 wagons had finally assembled at Forty-mile Spring. The group had many mouths and muzzles to feed. Heavy snow was falling on the Escalante Mountains behind them, making a retreat more perilous. As the scouts filed into President Smith's tent to give their reports, they had more than themselves to consider: most had brought families. Caroline was the youngest Nielson at five and a half years old, but more than a fifth of the group was younger than she was. The trail forward seemed too treacherous and the road [44] back too desolate.

After the scouts gave mostly negative reports to the assembled leaders of the expedition, Jens Nielson made a motion that was both spiritual and strategic. First, he prophesied that if they decided to go on, a road could be made to their new home and crops raised there the next season.[81] Then he proposed that the party "unanimously … sustain Brother Smith in whatever course he thought best for us to pursue." Silas Smith, a quiet but steady man and an experienced pioneer, determined to proceed, even if it took over three months to build the road, since he considered it impossible to withdraw through the heavy snow behind them.[82] The next day, a general meeting was held, and many members spoke their support for President Smith's resolution. Jens Nielson declared that they should "go on whether we can or not." Then, in a fervent attempt to produce a fairly new and intricate English word through a Danish-trained throat, he affirmed that if they had enough "stickety tootie" they would succeed.[83]

With new resolve, the expedition advanced over the rugged country to the Fifty-mile Spring. Some camped there, but the Nielsons most likely

---

80. Walton, Diary, 32.

81. Walton, Diary, 32.

82. Platte D. Lyman, "Diary," December 3, 1879.

83. Miller, Hole-in-the-Rock, 67. According to Webster's Ninth New Collegiate Dictionary, the word "stick-to-itiveness" was first manufactured in 1867. The definition, "dogged tenacity," is appropriate. Mulder, in Homeward to Zion, believed the phrase was "sticket to trude," an attempt to say "stick to the truth," also an appropriate resolution.

accompanied the Cedar City contingent to the camp near the Hole in the Rock, a narrow slit in the sandstone overlooking the Colorado River. The site had a breathtaking view: the river was three-quarters of a mile away, two thousand feet down. Little Caroline peeked through the [45] crevice one day and eagerly summoned her mother to look at the small white kittens she saw in the distance. Kirsten had to tell her they were not kittens, but her father's white mules far down the gorge.[84]

The party's food supplies dwindled, despite what they imported from Escalante. Flour ran out, and they had to parch their wheat or grind it in small coffee mills. George Hobbs reported that his "first meal of chopped wheat would shame a dose of salts in its purging propensities."[85] Despite these hardships, the travelers continued to enjoy themselves when possible by singing and dancing. While the area around the Hole in the Rock had no natural amphitheater such as Dance Hall Rock back near the Forty-mile camp, a number of nights found the Saints doing the best they could with the fiddle and harmonica under the stars.

They also used the time in camp to follow Mormon pioneer precedent and organize more formally for the trip ahead. Silas Smith was sustained as the head of the company and Platte D. Lyman as his assistant. The camp was split into groups of ten families with captains over each. Jens Nielson was made captain of the first ten, as well as chaplain for the entire group. President Smith, a former member of the Utah legislature, hurried to the capital town of Fillmore to lobby for money and road-building supplies from the territorial congress.

The work on the road to the river began. Benjamin and Hyrum Perkins, stout coal miners from Wales, drilled and blasted a wagon road down the first part of the Hole, a [46] sheer stone drop of forty-five feet. To do this, men were often suspended by ropes to drill holes and set powder. Once this first section was hewn from the rock, they proceeded to construct "Uncle Ben's Dugway" down a fifty-foot drop lower in the canyon. To get down this "slantindicular" surface, the men drilled holes in the stone face and inserted oak staves.[86] These were covered with perpendicular poles, brush, rocks, dirt, and gravel to widen the path enough

---

84. L. Wayne Redd, "Jens Nielson Family," in "Jens Nielson History," 63.

85. Miller, *Hole-in-the-Rock*, 90.

86. This original adjective came from Nathaniel Alvin Decker, as remembered by Albert R. Lyman in *Indians and Outlaws*, 31.

for a wagon. While the "Cedar boys" toiled on these upper parts of the road, other groups labored in the lower canyon and across the river. Debris blasted loose from the top was used to make fills farther down. Cornelius Decker remained impressed by these efforts many years later. "I don't think I ever saw a lot of men work with more zeal and will to do something than that crowd. We were all young men and the way we did make the dirt and rock fly was a marvel."[87]

By late January, the tired migrants were ready for the great adventure: to take the wagons down to the river. The upper part of the road averaged a steep eight feet of drop for every rod (sixteen and a half feet) of distance. But some places, particularly the first stretch of road, plunged down at a precipitous forty-five degree angle. The back wheels of each wagon were rough-locked with chains and moored by as many as twenty men anchoring ropes behind it. The first wagons skidded down on January 26. Many animals were unwilling, and there were a number of narrow escapes and nasty scrapes, but no wagons tipped over, and no creature was killed. After the breathless descent, the [47] exhilarated and exhausted drivers pulled onto Charles Hall's large ferryboat and crossed the river. Road crews had already cut a dugway up the opposite bank. This ascent was easy only in comparison to what they had already endured. Seven teams had to pull each wagon up Cottonwood Hill, and the only two tipovers of the trek happened on this treacherous road.[88]

Beyond the Hole in the Rock

From the top of Cottonwood Hill, the expedition was still two months away from its destination, longer by itself than the six weeks originally planned for the entire trek. Supplies from Escalante and Parowan kept the party from starvation. But for those two months they picked, blasted, and dug their way up and across mesas, down chutes and canyons, and somehow past every obstacle that presented itself. Not all the travails were against the landscape: two healthy babies were born on the way. The pioneers developed stronger ties as they endured and celebrated together. "All the hurt feelings and disgruntled tempers were washing

---

87. Decker, "Pioneering in Utah, Arizona, and Colorado," 11.
88. Kumen Jones, "Writings," 18.

away in fun under the stars," Eliza Redd remembered.[89] And Joe Nielson started paying particular attention to Ida Lyman, one of the three single women on the trip.

As their wagon wheels sifted through the deep sand down Comb Wash, Jens Peter asked his mother how this trip compared to her handcart journey back in 1857. "I don't remember everything about the handcart company, but we could get along," Kirsten [48] replied. "We can't even get along in this sand."[90] In the end, the members of the Hole-in-the-Rock expedition worked a collective total of 3,200 days on the road from Escalante to the San Juan, an average of forty-one days of labor for every male over fifteen years old.[91] No pioneers died, but many animals did. Hanson Bayles started the trip with twenty-one head of cattle and arrived at the San Juan River with six. The Nielsons' milk cows dried up, and the family lost one ox and two of its cattle. This left Jens with no choice but to yoke an ox and a mule together to power one of their wagons. All of the emigrants would have agreed with the speculation of Platte Lyman's brother, Marion, in a letter that might have reached them about this time: "This is a very trying winter in all parts of the territory. I presume none are having a more serious time than you and your company."[92]

The final pull up San Juan Hill was almost infernal. The teams had to be multiplied once again to drag the wagons up the road. The beasts had given what they had over the past weeks, but to clear this last, large obstacle they had to be beaten into giving more. Even with seven teams to a wagon many of the animals faltered and fell, smearing hair and blood from their forelegs onto the rocks. At the top of the hill, Jens Nielson's second ox sank to the ground and died. Those creatures who survived that final drag were beyond exhaustion. Some wagons took days to cover the few miles between that awful hill and the spot next to

---

89. Arrington, *Charlie Redd*, 16.

90. Jens P. Nielson, "Settlement of Bluff," 186.

91. Kumen Jones, "Writings," 212, relates that the road cost $4,800 at $1.50 per day. The legislature eventually appropriated $5,000 for the project, and the Church gave $500, mostly in tithing supplies from Parowan. According to these figures, if one man were going to do all this work, he would go at it seven days a week for eight full years and into August of the ninth.

92. Francis Marion Lyman, letter to Platte D. Lyman, February 27, 1880.

the river where they all huddled together and decided [49] their journey was over.

So there they were. As exuberant celebrations took place among Mormons throughout the territory, and many in debt were released from bondage on April 6, the Day of Jubilee, this group began to recover its strength and go about the business of colonizing. Not all of them liked their prospects. Upon seeing the place, Margaret Nielson looked up at her father and asked dubiously, "Is this where we are going to stay?" "Why yes," Jens replied. "Where did you want to go?"[93] [50]

---

93. Adams, "Margaret Nielson Adams," 187.

Survival, 1880–1881

1880: Initiation

First Days

When they held a meeting that first evening, the settlers did not debate what to do; after starting so many communities, Mormons knew that. Jens Nielson had followed the standard plan in Panguitch, as had many of the others in settlements across the territory.[1] This meeting was held so they could get to work. Under the direction of acting leader Platte Lyman, five men were chosen to survey the land, and the rest were set to dig the irrigation ditches. The next morning, Wednesday, April 7, they started the chains and shovels moving.

By Saturday they had a problem. The surveyors found less land than they had anticipated, so they called another meeting. Rather than live on such small lots, the [51] colonizers decided to hold a lottery for the available land. A slip of paper was prepared for every family and unattached individual. Forty of the slips had the number of a lot on them; twenty-two were blank. Those who drew a number would stay on that parcel, those with blanks would move on. In the tense drawing, Jens Nielson

---

1. For the pattern and modifications of Mormon settlement, see Nelson, *Mormon Village*; Arrington, *Great Basin Kingdom*, 354; Ricks, *Forms and Methods of Early Mormon Settlement*; Peterson, "Imprint of Agricultural Systems"; Jackson and Layton, "Mormon Village"; Jackson, "Mormon Village"; and Arrington and Bitton, *Mormon Experience*, 120.

most likely drew a number. Platte Lyman drew a blank. And then this group of settlers they were overseeing began to unravel.

The divisive issue intruded on their church meetings the next day. James Pace, who held a number, proposed sharing equally with those who did not but was voted down. Many others who held lots did not want to share them and made that blaringly clear with "illiberal feelings" toward those who were supposed to get out. On Monday they held another meeting and things got worse. Some who were supposed to move on had started settling on parcels of land anyway. At the end of the contentious gathering, those holding numbers again voted out those with blanks. But on Tuesday, the dispute almost miraculously dissipated. Some of the men again proposed throwing out the lottery results, seeing as how "it is out of the question for us to move any further at present." This time, after much discussion and negotiation, the idea passed. Fifty-nine smaller lots would be distributed. Self-interest had almost destroyed in days the union they had forged through six months of shared hardship. Work on the ditch, which had been almost entirely suspended during the dispute, resumed that afternoon.[2]

Each individual or family of settlers received a town lot that measured just under [52] an acre plus a field lot of anywhere from eight to twenty acres based on its location and quality. These were small even to Mormons, who had smaller fields than other western settlers. For the most part, Mormons looked to their land more to sustain their families than to raise a large crop for market.[3] If things continued as they were, most of the boys who were helping Jens clear, water, and plant their acres would have to look elsewhere for their own farms when they grew up.

---

2. The most useful contemporary source on the early days of the settlement is Platte D. Lyman, "Diary." The particulars on the land dispute can be found in the entries from April 10–13, 1880. Jens Nielson probably drew a number since Platte Lyman's diary listed some of the noted settlers who did not.

3. See May, *Three Frontiers*, 146–84, for a discussion of land use in the Mormon settlement of Alpine, Utah, compared with non-Mormon communities in Idaho and Oregon. The average farm size in Alpine was 15 acres, while in Middleton, Idaho, it was 151 acres, and in Sublimity, Oregon, it was 292 acres. Figures are from 1857 to 1860. Peterson, *Take Up Your Mission*, 161–62, found that the average family in the Little Colorado settlements in Arizona had twenty acres.

With the land controversy dispatched, the colonizers set up their homes. For the Nielsons, like most of the families, this meant modifying the same domiciles they had used for the past six months: their wagon boxes were removed from the wheels and parked on their town lot. Others threw together crude brush wickiups. But there was no time yet for real homebuilding. All available labor had to go toward getting life into the town, which meant getting water into the ditch.

As the men threw themselves and their animals into scraping and digging a channel, it did not take long for the regular rhythms of life to reassert themselves. Alvin Morris Decker was born that first Monday night. And Roswell Stevens, at seventy-two easily the oldest member of the group, died on May 4. He had come out with three of his nephew's sons, and long before, in 1847, had marched across the Southwest as a private in Company E of the Mormon Battalion. But the Hole-in-the-Rock trek finished him. [53] The others could not saw straight lumber for his coffin out of the twisted cottonwoods nearby, so they pried the planks from a wagon box.[4]

Their neighbors up the river at Montezuma, the Davis and Harriman families as well as a few other individuals who were deposited there by the scouting expedition in 1879, greeted the newcomers with mixed emotions. On the one hand, they were thrilled the expedition had arrived, since they desperately needed supplies. On the other, they were disappointed most were not coming to settle with them. A few of the pioneers had gone directly to Montezuma, and three more families headed there during the land squabble. But the best news that came down to Bluff from Montezuma was that Thales Haskell, the veteran Indian missionary, was there. During the spring he had come by to see if any of those left on the San Juan were still alive. When he found they were, he moved his own family in, and his experienced and stoic presence was immensely reassuring to the settlers.

On Sunday, April 25, amid wind, rain, and even some snow, the settlers gathered together again and gave their infant town a name. William Hutchings seized on the most obvious feature surrounding the place and proposed "Bluff City."[5] The name was unanimously approved.

---

4. Albert R. Lyman, ed., "History of San Juan Stake," 93.
5. Platte D. Lyman, "Diary," April 25, 1880, 258.

Whether the reddish bluffs suggested protective ramparts against outside dangers or looming walls imprisoning them was a matter of personal interpretation.[6] [54]

The next day was Jens Nielson's sixtieth birthday, and he had a new job. The Utah Legislature had just created San Juan County with Silas Smith as county judge, Charles Walton as clerk, and a board of selectmen, or county commissioners, consisting of Platte D. Lyman, Zachariah B. Decker, and Jens Nielson. The officials in Bluff held the first meeting of the county court, "by appointment of the judge" (probably meaning that Smith sent word to go ahead without him), on Jens's birthday. There they added another hallmark of civil society by appointing Lemuel H. Redd Jr. as the tax assessor and collector. The acting county court then adjourned for the time being.[7]

Later in the day, Jens was also left in charge of Bluff, or what was left of it. Silas Smith was still back in the settlements, now recovering from illness. After the meeting of the county court, Platte Lyman followed those who had headed back up the road toward the Hole in the Rock to fetch family and supplies from the older settlements.[8] But other settlers had already left for good. A few families never planned on staying, but had linked up with the San Juan expedition to get them to Colorado or Arizona more quickly, they thought, than the usual routes. Other individuals had come to help their relatives relocate, and with that job done they returned to their homes. Still others, called to the mission or not, took a look at the country and kept right on going.[9] In all, 61 people, almost one-quarter of the 234 who came, left the San Juan permanently before [55] June. Hopefully a successful first year's crop would stop the hemorrhaging of population. Jens's leadership did not last long on this occasion. Silas Smith arrived in May, and when Platte Lyman returned to Bluff on June 2, he marked the progress the residents had made: "The

---

6. Albert R. Lyman, "History of San Juan Stake," 61. George Hobbs is quoted here, saying there was much disappointment, "for they expected to find a large open valley; instead they found a narrow canyon with small patches of land on each side of the river." Hobbs also identified Hutchings as the man responsible for the name of the town.

7. Platte D. Lyman, "Diary," April 26, 1880; San Juan County Minute Book, April 26, 1880.

8. Kumen Jones, "Writings," 21; Platte D. Lyman, "Diary," April 26–June 2, 1880.

9. See Appendix B, "After the Hole in the Rock," to see who left, when, and why.

water is in the ditch and some seed has been sown which has come up and is looking well, but taken all together, I do not think the prospect very encouraging."[10]

Who They Were

Bluff was planted just in time to be counted. The census taker came through town on June 19 and was on to Montezuma by June 21.[11] His numbers confirmed what the settlers already knew: they were astonishingly young. The enumerator found 193 people living in these two towns, all of them Mormons, and their average age was seventeen years and six months old.[12] Children swarmed all over the settlement, with exactly half of the population under sixteen, and more than two out of five under the age of ten. Among the thirty-six married couples, there were twenty-five infants less than two years old, and forty-nine less than five. Jens and Kirsten Nielson, at sixty and forty-six years old, were [56] the oldest couple still there. In fact, aside from Jens, only one other soul was over sixty, and overall fewer than one in seven were over thirty. There was one man in his fifties, nine settlers in their forties, and sixteen in their thirties. But most of the adults barely fit the age requirement: fifty-three of them were in their twenties, and three wives were younger than that.[13]

---

10. Platte D. Lyman, "Diary," June 2, 1880.

11. The manuscript census was signed by "Brigham T. Young," Brigham Young's grandson through his son Brigham Young Jr.

12. See the appendix for more specific statistics on the 1880 residents of Bluff and Montezuma. There were some Mormons, the Harrises, near Bluff when the pioneers arrived, but they sold their homestead to Platte Lyman and left around the time of the land lottery. The census taker did not seem to take great pains in seeking inhabitants of areas outside Bluff and Montezuma. He listed only nine cowboys and miners living outside these towns, though these migratory occupants might have been hard to locate. Also, the claim sometimes made that Bluff had a larger population at its founding than it has enjoyed ever since is untrue. The original population on April 6 was perhaps 250 people in Bluff and Montezuma with the Harrises added, and was 202 for San Juan County in the June 1880 census. The 2000 census found 320 people living in Bluff. Incidentally, the census shows 194 residents for Bluff and Montezuma in 1880, but Peter Mickelsen was listed twice.

13. Wahlquist, "Population Growth," profiled twelve Wasatch Front towns in 1880 and found 44 percent of the population under age 15 (down from 46 percent and 52 percent in the previous two decades), and an average age of 23 (up from 20 in 1860).

Most of them had been born in Utah. Naturally, almost all the settlers over thirty had been part of the exodus to Utah from other states
or foreign countries in the 1840s and 1850s. But among those in their
twenties, fewer than one in four had been born elsewhere, and hardly any
of the youth and children. Overall, just over three-quarters of the settlers
were Utah-born and had known no other way of living than the Mormon communities in which they were raised. One in six came from foreign lands, and more than three-quarters of these were from the British
Isles.[14] But the Nielsons could converse in Danish with Lars Christensen,
Samuel Mackelprang, or J. P. Jensen. In fact, Samuel Mackelprang and
the parents of Peter Mickelsen and his sister, Anna Mickelsen Decker,
came from the same region of Denmark as the Nielsons.

Almost everyone was attached to a family somehow. The typical household in Bluff and Montezuma had four people in it with a
fifth on the way. The average husband [57] was thirty-one, his wife was
twenty-eight, and the couple was about to celebrate its eighth wedding
anniversary.[15] As was true in most Mormon towns, the typical husband had just one spouse. James Harvey Dunton set up the only multi-
spouse household in the towns for his two wives and ten children. Jens
Nielson and Platte Lyman had plural wives living elsewhere.[16] Unlike

14. Wahlquist, "Population Growth," found 30 percent foreign born in his
twelve Wasatch front towns in 1880, 57 percent of those over age 20 and 68 percent
over age 30. These towns had 73.6 percent of their foreign-born residents from
the British Isles, 14.1 percent from Scandinavia, and 5.2 percent from other countries in Europe in 1870. May, *Three Frontiers*, 294–95, found that the 667 towns in
the western United States in 1870 had an average of 31 percent foreign born. The
170 Mormon settlements from that same year contained, on average, 36 percent of
the population born in foreign countries.

15. But few of the actual settlers met this average profile: half of the husbands
were under twenty-nine and half of the wives were under twenty-six, since the ages
of the few older couples brought the overall average up. See also Bean, Mineau,
and Smith, "Effect of Pioneer Life on the Longevity," who compiled data for
marriage ages in Utah. There were 41,218 in the sample, and they showed that the
average ages were, from 1860 to 1874: men 25.28, women 20.40; and from 1875 to
1889: men 24.54, women 20.23. The couples in Bluff in 1880 married at these average ages: men 23.4, women 19.8.

16. Ivins, "Notes on Mormon Polygamy," estimates that 15 to 20 percent of Mormon families were polygamous at the peak of the practice. Logue, *Sermon in the*

most western towns, there were a few more females than males in Bluff
and Montezuma, though this was due to the children, since there were
slightly more adult men than women.[17] The three single women who
came without their parents stayed with brothers or sisters, as propriety
demanded. Only three single men lived completely unattached; of the
six other bachelors, four lived with relatives and two were brothers to
other settlers, but lived alone.

As remote, fledgling outposts, Bluff and Montezuma were less than
half the size of [58] the average community in either Utah or the West.[18]
They had significantly fewer foreign-born residents and polygamous
households than the average Mormon community, and a few more
females. But it was not unheard of for half of the population in a developing Mormon community to be under sixteen. What was missing was
the middle: more mature families whose parents were in their thirties,
forties, or fifties. The Nielsons were not typical settlers in Bluff and
Montezuma. These colonies were dominated by young couples and their
toddling children, so the average age was more than five years less than
that of most Utah towns. With so many young families, these were vulnerable settlements; either their environments or their neighbors could
overwhelm them. The earnestness of the settlers in setting up their new

---

Desert, found that 33 percent of all St. George households, and 38.4 percent of "eligible" households were polygamous. Bennion, in "Incidence of Mormon Polygamy,"
found 30.4 percent of LDS resident in the Kanab Stake in a polygamous family in
1880, and from 19 percent to 32 percent in the wards of the Davis Stake.

17. May, *Three Frontiers,* 294–95, composed a mythical "Allton," representing the
averages of the 667 towns existing in the Western United States in 1870, and found
there were 180 males for every 100 females. He also assembled the average for the
174 Utah towns in 1870 and saw a much narrower gap: 105 males to 100 females.
This is close to the figure of Wahlquist, "Population Growth," in his twelve Wasatch
Front towns in 1880: 49 percent of the population was female.

18. According to the census, there were 107 in Bluff and 86 in Montezuma,
though according to residences suggested in Platte Lyman's diary, the placement of
families in the census is not entirely accurate. A few more probably lived in Bluff
and a few less in Montezuma than the census suggests. May, *Three Frontiers,* 294–95,
found 383 in the typical western town in 1870 and 499 in the average Mormon town
in that same year. The average population of Wahlquist's twelve Wasatch Front
settlements in "Population Growth" was 279 with 31 percent foreign born. The average number in a household was 4.5 people.

homes was often not far from anxiousness, or even desperation, since they knew they could not withstand many mistakes.

Where They Were

San Juan County was still "the *terra incognita* of the country," as a member of the Hayden survey had dubbed it a few years earlier.[19] Some of its settlers were astonished by their first glance: "This is the most God-forsaken and wild country I have ever seen, [59] read or heard about," recorded one.[20] Other newcomers were a little more restrained: "It is the wildest, oldest looking country on earth, I think."[21] Parley Butt felt that "when God finished makin' the world he had a lot of rocks left over an' he threw them down here in a pile in Utah."[22] The untamed terrain entranced some and haunted others.

The bottomland around Bluff extended two miles east and west along the San Juan River, and it was one mile across from the cliffs on the north to those on the south. These rock slabs were adorned with "numerous fantastic and strange formations." The most distinctive of these, the Navajo Twins, stood to the northeast as sandstone sentinels. Rocks also immediately hemmed in the east. The western boundary of the settlement was Cottonwood Wash. Miles beyond that, the sun set over the fantastic petrified writhing of Comb Ridge, named after the shape atop a rooster, but on a scale more suited for some mythic vermillion serpent.

On top of the sandstone wall across the river to the south, Navajos occupied lands stretching into Arizona. The northern wall and northeastern rocks submerged themselves under the shale of Tank Mesa and

---

19. *New York Times*, September 9, 1875, quoted in Peterson, *Look to the Mountains*, 39.

20. Josephine Catherine Chatterley Wood, Journal, October 30, 1882, quoted in Noall, "Mormon Midwives," 130–31. Wallace Stegner later agreed with her assessment, writing that "San Juan was then [1880], and is now, the most barren frontier in the United States." See *Mormon Country*, 229. Both of these descriptions were about as kind as that of a Utah newspaper in 1861, when it printed that southeastern Utah was "one vast continuity of waste and measurably valueless, excepting for nomadic purposes, hunting grounds for Indians, and to hold the world together." See Perkins, Nielson, and Jones, *Saga of San Juan*, 9.

21. Hammond, Journal, March 7, 1889. Hammond's faithful and extensive journals are split between the Church History Library and Perry Special Collections.

22. Riis, *Ranger Trails*, 51.

Bluff Bench, on top of which grew sage, grass, cedar, and pinyon pine that stretched forty miles to the Abajo, or Blue, Mountains and Elk Ridge. By there the elevation climbed from 4,320 feet at Bluff to 7,000 feet before the Blues [60] quickly rose to over 11,000 feet in altitude. The ponderosa pine forests on the flanks of these mountains were the closest source for good lumber. The mountains also pushed up the dry desert air, cooling and condensing it into precipitation, which was sent down to the south in a series of shallow, intermittent streams. Comb and Butler washes surrounded Comb Ridge; Cottonwood Wash ran just west of Bluff, while Recapture and Montezuma creeks came down to the east. All flowed, when they did, through their cottonwood-covered banks into the San Juan. This river came from the San Juan Mountains in Colorado, wound south into New Mexico and northwest into Utah Territory. It swept gently by Montezuma and Bluff before plunging through contorted canyons, the "Goosenecks," into the Colorado. The creeks and rivers had gradually deposited the blessing of "deep, rich alluvial soil" that caused the settlers to stop here.[23] How long they remained depended on how ingenious and industrious they were and how generous the rivers would be in irrigating that soil.[24] It also depended on how well their neighbors welcomed them.

Neighbors

The San Juan missionaries were quite conscious of where they were *not*. Within a few weeks of their arrival, they found a tree stump inscribed a couple of years before by Ferdinand Dickert, a government surveyor, that told them they were 328 miles [61] south and 128 miles east of Salt Lake City.[25] They knew from painful experience that they were 117 miles as the crow flies from Escalante, and that was certainly not how they traveled. They considered themselves in a hinter or nether region, largely

---

23. Erastus Snow and Brigham Young, "The San Juan Country," *Deseret News*, September 22, 1880, 540.

24. The area was tempting for farmers. It has a long growing season. Although the rainfall is only about eight inches a year, the San Juan brings water all year, if only it can be brought up onto the land. See Aton and McPherson, *River Flowing from the Sunrise*, 84.

25. Platte D. Lyman, "Diary," April 26, 1880. See Peterson, *Look to the Mountains*, 26, for clarification on this surveyor and others who came through the region before the pioneers.

isolated from people like themselves. And so, when they journeyed west, they traveled back to "Utah," as if they were in some separate territory.[26]

In a way they were. They were far from any other white town, and geography aimed them more toward the developing settlements of frontier Colorado than toward their homeland. Colorado had just become a state in 1876, and its southwestern corner was bustling with the activities of ranchers, miners, and some other Mormon colonizers. Durango, in fact, was being assembled at the same time Bluff was, but almost a hundred miles away. By 1880, various settlers were also returning to Moab, almost ninety miles to the north in Utah. To the southeast, Farmington, New Mexico, had been founded four years before the Bluff settlers arrived, but was still 150 miles away. All of these settlements were easier to access than Bluff's parent communities, or at least would be as soon as anything resembling roads were made. The San Juan settlers were nowhere near the interstate of that age—the railroad. The closest railhead was in Alamosa, Colorado, 180 air miles away.[27] Bluff was an isolated outpost of white settlers, but the community still had plenty of neighbors. [62]

To the south were the Navajos.[28] According to archaeologists, the Navajos' Athabascan ancestors wandered south from northwestern Canada around AD 1000 They arrived in New Mexico about the time the Anasazi left in AD 1300. But the "Dine" ("the people," as the Navajos call themselves) assert their ancestors emerged from the last of a series of underworlds to this Fourth or "Glittering World" at a place in the La Plata Mountains of Colorado or somewhere near Navajo Dam in New Mexico. They inhabited an area bounded and protected by four mountains and four rivers, the San Juan being the northernmost riparian border.

The Navajos earned the enmity of their neighbors by perpetually raiding them. As they learned the uses of horses and herd animals from the Pueblo Indians and the Spanish, livestock became an important target. The Navajos also borrowed agriculture from those around them and began planting corn, beans, and squash in addition to pursuing the hunting and gathering lifestyle that they brought with them. But in the late 1800s, they felt the same pressures of encroaching white settlers as other western

---

26. See Albert R. Lyman, Journal, January 1, 1897, for an example of this usage as late as 1897.

27. Jensen, "Historical Study of Bluff City," 109–10.

28. For the history of the Navajos, see McPherson, *History of San Juan County*, 53–66.

tribes. The American military leaders urged the Utes to attack, enslave, and reduce the Navajo Nation. Then the army took direct action.

In 1864, the same year William Tecumseh Sherman was burning through Georgia, Colonel Kit Carson waged a similar brand of demoralizing warfare on the Navajos, igniting their homes and fields, hatcheting their orchards, and driving off their flocks. As winter and starvation closed in, over eight thousand Navajos immediately or eventually marched three hundred miles, beyond their defensive borders, to the Bosque Redondo [63] Reservation in New Mexico. Even holdouts such as Manuelito and Ganado Mucho gave in when they saw the suffering of their followers. On the reservation, they found physical and spiritual half-lives, scarcely subsisting on short rations and enduring attempts to convert them to a different way of life. By 1868, after an inspection of the reservation by General Sherman, the government gave up the attempt. Not only were the captives allowed to return home, but the thousands of fugitives, including leaders such as Hashkeneini and Kaayelii in Utah, emerged from their places of refuge. But they did not forget the "Fearing Time" inflicted by the soldiers. Some refused to plant fruit trees when they returned, certain that invaders would raze them.

The Navajos' reservation in 1868 was only a quarter of what their traditional lands had been, but by 1880 they were expanding their fields and flocks beyond the official boundary of the reservation north to the San Juan.[29] "The people" had returned to their promised land and were enlarging their borders at a time when most Indian lands were being constricted.[30] Some Navajos, such as Kaayelii, often lived north of the San Juan. Others crossed tentatively to trade with the Utes and Paiutes, put in some crops, or graze their sheep. The colonists in Bluff were aware of the recent aggressiveness of the Navajos, which was partially responsible for their mission. But that knowledge also led the settlers to wonder about how they would be welcomed as they glanced anxiously toward the southern cliffs from time to time. The Navajos, given their recent history, were also in [64] suspense as they peered over the rim into the busy new towns.

---

29. President Chester A. Arthur issued an executive order on May 17, 1884, officially adding the land south of the San Juan River to the Navajo Reservation.

30. For more comparisons between Navajo and Mormon beliefs, see chapter 3 in McPherson, *Northern Navajo Frontier.*

Utes and Paiutes roamed the lands on the north of the San Juan River. Some of them probably heard the explosions as the pioneers blasted their road to Bluff. These Indians' Numic-speaking progenitors had migrated from southern California and arrived in the Great Basin perhaps as early as AD 1150. As the migrants spread across the Colorado Plateau, they subdivided into numerous groups with related languages. The Utes, ranging farther to the east, split from the Paiutes by about AD 1600, as they were occupying the Four Corners region.

The Utes in San Juan County were the westernmost of the three Southern Ute bands, and according to the United States government, they were not supposed to be there. These Weeminuche Utes had a complex relationship with their neighbors, and some helped the government terrorize the Navajos in the 1860s. Nevertheless, their turn for confinement came immediately after. In 1868 a large Southern Ute reservation was created, comprising almost the western third of Colorado, but by 1880 it was reduced to a 15-mile-wide by 110-mile-long strip of land in the southwestern corner of the state. Reservation agents tried to persuade the Utes to embrace agriculture, but many of their charges, seeing no need to change their ways, continued to roam over their traditional homelands. They pursued game and gathered food as the seasons dictated into the Blue and La Sal mountains and visited the Northern Utes on the Uinta Reservation once in a while. Sometimes they fished, and sometimes they planted corn, beans, squash, and melons in small plots. They traveled in flexible bands, usually of twenty to one hundred people, following whoever in their number commanded their respect at the time. And so [65] Utes who rode with leaders such as Red Jacket, Mariano, and Narraguinip were renegades from the reservation according to the United States, but in their own reckoning they were simply living as they always had. As long as the game held out and the U.S. government did not take too much of an interest in them, they could continue to do so. Although the Utes knew the government tended to take more interest in an area occupied by white settlers, the new town might offer compensating advantages.[31]

---

31. Aton and McPherson, *River Flowing from the Sunrise*, 29–33. See these pages for more details of the seasonal living patterns of the Utes and Paiutes in the Four Corners region.

The San Juan Paiutes were the only branch of their people to extend east of the Colorado River. The government had not yet created a reservation for any Paiutes, so they were under no obligation to leave San Juan County, though they were often considered renegades by the few whites in the area. Adopting less of the horse and plains culture than the Utes, the Paiutes roamed in small, fluid family groups hunting, gathering, and occasionally farming for their existence. Both the Utes and Navajos looked down on the Paiutes but also found them useful. The Utes sometimes intermarried with the San Juan Paiutes to the point that in some bands they were almost indistinguishable and were referred to solely by one name or the other. Navajos also married Paiutes, hired them for certain tasks, and used them as a screen against the Utes during times of intense raiding. Some young Navajos had teamed with Paiutes to launch raids of their own into southern Mormon settlements in recent years. The new towns on the San Juan were, to some extent, the settlements' counterstrike, a sort of peace offensive.

So Bluff and Montezuma were founded on the seam of these three tribes that had variously killed and cooperated with each other. The easternmost Paiutes met the [66] westernmost Utes and the most northern Navajos in San Juan County.[32] Animosity between the Navajos and Utes lingered, though it was sometimes softened by trade and marriage. The Paiutes were often in the middle geographically and politically, mediating between the other tribes. Now the Mormons hoped to do some of the same, and the fact that they were potential trading partners made them more welcome to these earlier residents of the county.[33] But there were no guarantees any of them would get along. The Bluff settlers had heard that the two miners they had met while traveling to the San Juan were killed soon after by upset Indians in Monument Valley. Although each tribe blamed the others, the murders did little to reassure the young families moving in that their new neighborhood was entirely safe. The colonizers were occupying an area that all of their neighbors found desirable at times, and all of the groups, Mormon and Native American alike, felt some degree of entitlement to the land or the resources along the San Juan.

---

32. Salmon and McPherson, "Cowboys, Indians, and Conflict," describes the region well from the perspective of the Indians at this time.

33. McPherson, *History of San Juan County*, 87.

Other newcomers made this mix more volatile. Cowboys began riding into southeastern Utah just as the Mormons took interest in it. Individual cattlemen such as Tom Ray, "Spud" Hudson, and Preston Nutter crowded cows into the northern part of the county when they found they could corral fifteen to twenty dollars per head if they bought cattle in Utah and sold it in Colorado. And since San Juan County, the area in between, was unorganized before 1880, they could graze their cattle tax-free. Such profits soon [67] began to glint in the eyes of more substantial investors.[34] The San Juan region also attracted those attempting to avoid another kind of government attention. Outlaws found easy refuge in the area, whether working for one of the cattle outfits or holing up in one of the countless crannies of such a broken country.

A small but steady parade of miners also marched across the county, hoping to recreate the bonanzas of Colorado on this side of the border. A few others came west from Colorado hoping to homestead. None of these newcomers had any obligations toward the Indians, and the actions of any one of them could easily inflame the whole area. By 1881, United States Army troops stood ready at Fort Lewis, Colorado, southwest of Durango, to protect white settlers. Soldiers were the last people the Indians wanted in the area, and the Mormons, while grateful for the protection if necessary, were not in favor of any increased federal presence either.

The Bluff colonizers had injected themselves into a remote corner of the West, but one that was quickly getting crowded, at least by the standards of that isolated place. They had to live peacefully with their Native American neighbors for their mission and themselves to survive. But they also settled in a strategic spot from which they could command that corner of the territory against the Gentiles who were starting to come in. Vested with full religious and political authority, they continued to build the towns they hoped would fulfill both parts of their mission. [68]

Pillars of the Community

In early June, Silas Smith came downstream from his camp at Montezuma to further organize the settlement. On June 6, a Sunday, acting as president of the San Juan Mission, he organized the Church in Bluff. The next day, as provisional judge of the county, he presided over the

---

34. Peterson, *Look to the Mountains,* 80–85.

second session of the county court. Church and state were never far from each other in Mormon towns because their purposes reinforced each other. Communities were constructed not just to make a living, but also to "make saints." Building up "the waste places of Zion" occurred as much on an individual's moral landscape as on the town's lots and fields. Conversely, "'making the desert bloom' ... was a form of religious worship."[35] And so religion, politics, and the economy were always intertwined, though nominally separate. The settlers had already distributed land, set up irrigation, and resolved their early disputes under Church authority. As they strengthened the pillars of their community, their ecclesiastical leader, Jens Nielson, would also come to embody the strong relationship between spiritual and material government.

At the Sunday meeting, Jens was once again called to watch over the souls of the settlement. As chaplain of the Hole-in-the-Rock expedition, he already had responsibilities of this nature, but now they were made more formal. Jens was appointed as the presiding priest in the Bluff Branch, and James Bean Decker became the Sunday School superintendent.[36] The Sunday School got off to a rousing start that same day. Since they had no building, class was held under a massive cottonwood, eventually dubbed "The Swing Tree," in Samuel Rowley's field south of town near the river. During the meeting, young Sarah Williams recalled, "a bunch of Indians came riding up [69] and I wondered what would become of us, but Bishop Nielson and Bro. Jones were so calm I found there was no reason to be afraid."[37] On that same eventful Sunday, Cindy Nielson was baptized by Charles Walton in the San Juan River, thus becoming the first person to receive this ordinance in the new community.[38]

The next day at the county court, Jens continued to act as a county commissioner. Under Judge Smith, they set a tax of six mills (.6 cents) on every dollar of assessed property value.[39] Lemuel H. Redd, the assessor and collector, swiftly went out as the first governmental ambassador

---

35. Arrington, *Great Basin Kingdom*, 25–26.

36. Platte D. Lyman, "Diary," June 6, 1880.

37. Albert R. Lyman, "Notes on the Life of Sarah Williams Perkins," 6.

38. Reeve, "Lucinda Diantha Nielson Hyde," 209; for location of the tree, see Rowley, Autobiography, 21.

39. San Juan County Minute Book, June 7, 1880.

to the previously unmolested cattlemen in the county and, despite some resistance, started to assess and collect. Most of the money he brought in went to two causes: roads and schools. George Sevy was appointed supervisor of roads. The settlers needed to improve the road back to Utah and build better roads to Colorado and Moab. But there was so much to do that summer that they mostly just improved routes as they traveled them. Kumen Jones was appointed school superintendent, and classes started late that fall. France and Cindy Nielson were two of the pupils instructed in Bluff by Ida Lyman, who was paid an old cow named "Blue" for her efforts.[40] Additional offices, such as pound keeper and coroner, were added when necessary. While the county court eventually permitted alcohol to be sold, they set the fee [70] prohibitively high: one-year liquor licenses were $200 each, "paid in advance."[41] Better no organized drinking at all in their county, but if it did happen, at least it would pay for some roads and schools.

The government continued to develop over the summer. The county held its first regular elections in early August, and Jens was chosen as a commissioner again, as he would be in the next two elections as well.[42] The new county court set up some law enforcement, with Sunday School superintendent Decker as constable and Platte D. Lyman as prosecuting attorney.[43] Charles E. Walton was appointed postmaster before the year was out, but the appointment was discontinued in the absence of any predictable post. Mail, for the time being, came by surprise, with any traveler who happened to pick it up in Utah or Colorado. Nor was it encouraging that James Lewis, the man elected as county judge, saw "nothing that pleased him" in the area and headed home to Kanab right after the election, never to return.[44]

For any of this organization to do any good, the colonizers in Bluff had to make a living, and they had to do it together. The ideal of the

---

40. Kumen Jones, "Writings," 213, Perkins, Nielson, and Jones, *Saga of San Juan,* 321.

41. San Juan County Minute Book, December 11, 1882; McPherson, "Navajos, Mormons, and Henry L. Mitchell," 58.

42. San Juan County Minute Book, August 4, 1880, September 5, 1881, September 4, 1882.

43. Austin and McPherson, "Murder, Mayhem, and Mormons," 39–40.

44. Silas S. Smith, letter to Platte D. Lyman, August 5, 1880.

standard Mormon settlement was to become a cooperatively independent agricultural village. Jens and his flock not only had to raise crops,
but to get along with each other and work together to make their town
[71] independent of outside influences. Part of the motivation for this was
practical: past experience and persecution showed it was better to enrich
each other than outsiders with their trade. Part was philosophical: in the
old Jeffersonian tradition, agrarian habits made more virtuous citizens.
But part was spiritual: a city of God could not be polluted with outside
influences, and its citizens must be united. The scriptural warning, "If
ye are not one, ye are not mine" applied to their economic enterprises as
much as to their religious relations.[45]

The Nielsons and the other settlers of Bluff had all tried to practice unity in their previous settlements. All of them had been part of
cooperative industries, herds, or stores. Almost all had participated in
united orders in the mid-1870s, such as the one the Nielsons lived under
in Cedar City, in which private property was subordinated to Church
authority in varying degrees.[46] The settlers had seen the theoretical
advantages and practical flaws of such attempts. These ventures allowed
industries to form in capital-starved lands and also aimed to bind the
Saints more tightly together. But it seemed almost impossible to hold
these concerns together against centrifugal self-interest. Unlike the colonizers sent to the Little Colorado in Arizona in 1876, those going to Bluff
were not supposed to set up a united order at the settlement's inception.[47]
The impulse toward organizing [72] new united orders dwindled with the
passing of the general depression of the 1870s and the death of Brigham
Young in 1877. So Jens and the others were not going to cooperate to that

45. Doctrine and Covenants 38:27. This is a book of revelations received mostly
by Joseph Smith.

46. The charts in Arrington, Fox, and May, *Building the City of God*, appendi-
ces IV and IX, show that all of the major sources of Bluff colonists, Cedar City,
Parowan, Panguitch, Paragonah, New Harmony, and Oak City had some type of
united order organized in 1874. Since so many of the details were left up to local
leaders, united orders during these years differed from one another in their organization and requirements. If these united orders were like most, they had disbanded,
like Cedar City's, by Brigham Young's death in 1877. All of these settlements except
Parowan had some type of cooperative mercantile association as well.

47. See Peterson, *Take Up Your Mission*, 93–95.

extent. But all of them had lived in Utah long enough to be permeated with the communal ideals of independence, home manufactures, and cooperation. Although some of the particular communal experiments, such as the united orders, had waxed and waned, the principles themselves still reigned.[48] The practical and spiritual advantages of economic cooperation were, in the words of John Taylor, "obvious to all those who desire to serve the Lord."[49] But that last qualification was an important one: nature, neighbors, or circumstance might destroy them from without, but they were as likely to destroy themselves from within.

Nature began to say something in June. Soon after the first water came into the ditch it went right out. There was so little fall from the head of the ditch to the town that it was hard to keep the stream flowing. Jens marshaled his workforce again, and the men flung themselves into the task of building a dam at the head to raise the water level in the ditch. Suddenly high waters washed the dam downstream, and the same fate awaited the two other dams they tried to build soon after. So they extended the ditch another half-mile upstream to increase its overall decline, and the same troubles bedeviled them there. But late June surges brought enough water to their fields to allow the tired diggers and those working on the dam to spend their labors elsewhere for the moment.[50] [73]

These problems caused many to suspect that they would not be able to raise enough crops to feed themselves, and there were many products they could not yet produce themselves. Like it or not, they would have to trade for these things somewhere else. And so once their seed was in the ground, many men exported the only commodities they had: their labor, wagons, and teams, to the nearest source of employment in Colorado. This was a compromise with the ideal of independence, but without the compromise there would be no community, ideal or not. And it was not an unusual one: Cedar City had regularly sold its surpluses to mining camps in Nevada and western Utah.[51] So the older Nielson boys, Joe and Jens Jr., took teams and went with the others. For many of the younger men like them, it was the first time they would live outside

---

48. John Taylor reaffirmed this soon after becoming President of the Church. See Arrington, Fox, and May, *Building the City of God*, 315.

49. Quoted in May, "Making of Saints," 77.

50. Decker, "Pioneering in Utah, Arizona, and Colorado," 16–17.

51. Seegmiller, *History of Iron County*, 75.

of a mostly Mormon place for very long, and there was concern among themselves and their parents about how they would behave.

Those who went to Colorado soon reported that they did well for themselves. Many traveled all the way to Alamosa to work on an extension of the railroad. Platte Lyman made from five to thirteen dollars per day, a windfall wage, cutting and hauling railroad ties. He also did some scouting along with Silas Smith for more promising settlement sites in Colorado and New Mexico.[52] President Smith, the man who was largely responsible for the fact that settlers were trying to survive on the San Juan, became convinced that Manassa, Colorado, was a more desirable place to live.

Events in Bluff, meanwhile, did little to recommend that anyone should stay there. [74] Jens Nielson was once again responsible for the town as the presiding religious and civil authority. With the luxury of two older sons to send to Colorado, he was one of a handful of men who could stay all summer to look out for the welfare of the families there. The intentions of Bluff's neighbors were still unclear. Each day saw "fervent prayers morning and evening, that the Indians would be peaceably disposed towards the defenseless town."[53] But Jens also had more immediate problems to address. As the heat rose late in July the level of the San Juan fell, and the water abandoned the irrigation ditch. Since there were only about ten men left to try to lower the ditch or raise the water, most crops dried up, and more discouraged settlers gave up and left.[54] The leader of the Bluff Branch was rapidly losing any members over whom to preside.

Jens also had plenty to concern him in his own home, or the wagon boxes in which his family still lived. Kirsten had been stricken with an illness that left her in bed most of the time, unable on most days to raise her arms to her head.[55] The family still had no dairy cows and had to get along without milk.[56] With his two oldest sons gone, Jens had to rely

---

52. See Platte D. Lyman, "Diary," June 14 to September 24, 1880, for details of this trip.

53. Albert R. Lyman, "History of San Juan County," 17.

54. Platte D. Lyman, "Diary," August 3, 1880. See appendix B, "After the Hole in the Rock."

55. Gabbart and Redd, "Brief History of Kirsten Jensen Nielson," 3.

56. Kimmerle, "Little Visit," 226.

on the help of sixteen-year-old Margaret and eleven-year-old Francis to care for Kirsten and the two younger children, as well as look after the family's stock, gardens, and fields. Despite his crooked feet, Jens liked to work hard. "He limped heavily wherever he went, yet he went nonetheless on that account; he went early and late. He [75] liked to rise in the gray dawn and get impressions from crossing the fields before the sun came out."[57] Because he stayed at it all summer, and perhaps due to his experience and the location of his fields, the canny old Dane was the only Bluff farmer to bring in a crop of wheat that fall.[58]

The rest of the farms did not fare as well. The town's products included some vegetables, corn, and sorghum cane, but due to the difficulties with the ditch and the long absence of most men, Bluff was not able to raise a general crop.[59] Those who suspected that the place might not support them were confirmed in that belief. If more men had stayed in Bluff, they might have been able to save the crops, but that was too risky. Their labor in Colorado undoubtedly bought the supplies that would allow the colony to survive. When Jens Peter and Joe returned from Colorado, they brought important provisions for the family. Flour was very expensive, at nine dollars per hundred pounds, but they were able to bring enough. Their wagons were also loaded with clothes, hay for the horses, and even some dried fruit and sugar. These, with what their family had grown, would hopefully see them through the winter.

Fortunately, some help came as the summer waned. Silas Smith was able to disburse some of the five thousand dollars the legislature appropriated for building the road into the San [76] Juan, but not as much of it as the settlers would have liked.[60] By early September, William Hyde, a forty-eight-year-old merchant, arrived from Salt Lake City. He had been

---

57. Albert R. Lyman, "Bishop Jens Nielson," 10.

58. This is the tradition found in Albert R. Lyman, "History of San Juan Stake," 76, and it could refer to the fact that he was the only one to bring in a full crop. Rowley, Autobiography, 21, reports that the Rowley fields brought in "a little wheat." Silas S. Smith, letter to Platte D. Lyman, August 5, 1880, tells that as late as August, just the Bartons and others who had fields in the bottoms near Cottonwood Wash had the only sure crop. Smith did not specify what they were growing, however.

59. Erastus Snow and Brigham Young Jr., letter to John Taylor, September 6, 1880, in Deseret News, September 22, 1880, 540.

60. Silas S. Smith, letter to Platte D. Lyman, August 5, 1880.

asked to come by President John Taylor, and he set up a trading post in Montezuma. When he looked the land over, though, he was not too eager about it: despite "a rich sandy soil that will grow almost anything," the problem was "it will take a good deal of labor to get the water out of the river." Altogether, Hyde judged, " I do not think I want any of it; it is too hard a country and too hard to get at." But the trader in him was enticed by some items shown to him by a Navajo, "some of the finest blankets I ever saw."[61]

Two Apostles, Erastus Snow and Brigham Young Jr., along with Marion Lyman, also arrived in early September to survey the settlement. They held a number of meetings, still in the open air, and gave advice and encouragement to the settlers. They were very impressed with the soil and the climate, which were "all that could be desired." They congratulated the Saints on their road- and community-building efforts so far. Even though the Indians appeared to be friendly during the first summer, the Apostles advised the settlers to stay with the tradition of building their homes around a hollow square to form a fort. "Let no man think of scattering or locating families upon farms or claims isolated from their brethren, or of abandoning the posts to which they have been appointed, or to go at the beck and call of unauthorized individuals in search of other locations not yet appointed or consecrated for the gathering of saints." Working in Colorado was allowed, as long as it was done under the direction of the presiding [77] authorities of the mission. They also cautioned against land speculation. Everyone who improved their lot was entitled to compensation for that, but land itself should be apportioned by Church authorities, with ownership given to those actually present. This counsel highlighted the change in the town since spring. At the start, settlers had argued over the privilege of occupying the land; now the future of their vacant lots had to be determined.

The Apostles confirmed what the colonists had learned the previous summer: "Your chief difficulty will be how to arrange your water sects, flood gates, wing dams or other contrivances for controlling the waters of this fluctuating stream, but experience gained by a few failures will enable you to accomplish it. Let none be discouraged or abandon the enterprise." They called back all the absent members of the mission and

---

61. William Hyde, letter to *Salt Lake Herald*, September 5, 1880, in Journal History, October 3, 1880, 4.

urged them to direct their primary efforts toward the water problem the upcoming winter. The Apostles envisioned "flourishing towns and villages" along the San Juan and believed that after some initial success, there would be five hundred Saints there instead of fifty. If the settlers followed their instructions, the Apostles blessed them with "peace and prosperity, fellowship and love."[62] If any of the settlers hoped the Apostles would release them from such a difficult mission they were disappointed. Still, their efforts of the first summer received marginally passing marks from the Church authorities, and the vision and blessing of the Apostles were inspiring to the isolated Saints.

Bishop of the Bluff Ward

Neither man might have realized it at the time, but Erastus Snow was doubly [78] responsible for Jens Nielson being in Bluff. He was the one who had pioneered the Danish Mission thirty years earlier that had brought the Nielsons out from among their neighbors. And as the "Apostle of the South," Snow spearheaded the settlement on the San Juan and called many of the people to populate it. Now he was about to make sure Jens Nielson would stay here for a long time.

The Apostles finished the religious organization of the settlement. Silas Smith and his sons were set to move to Manassa, Colorado, which was still considered part of the San Juan Mission, soon after the conference. Platte Lyman, as first counselor, would be in charge of Bluff and Montezuma in the absence of President Smith. The Bluff Branch was made into a ward, and to nobody's surprise, Jens Nielson was ordained bishop. George Sevy was appointed first counselor, and Bishop Nielson's son-in-law, Kumen Jones, was made his second counselor.[63] Zachariah Decker Jr. was to preside over the Montezuma Branch.

As shepherd of the Bluff Ward, Bishop Nielson would have a lot to do. The duties of a bishop in the late 1800s were both spiritual and temporal. Presiding Bishop of the Church Edward Hunter had pointed out in 1861 that there were even more difficulties in being a country bishop than a city bishop. In the country, a bishop became the authority in many

---

62. Erastus Snow and Brigham Young Jr., "Instructions to San Juan Saints," September 5, 1880, in *Deseret News*, September 22, 1880, 540–41.

63. Platte D. Lyman, "Diary," September 19, 1880.

areas. In addition to being theologian and statesman, he was a "pastor, constable, judge, arbitrator, foreman, and mayor."[64] While Bishop Nielson's ward was smaller than average, its mission and situation made its concerns larger, as the [79] land, ditch, and Indian questions had already made manifest.[65]

A good illustration of the required mix of spirituality and practical sense was the principle of tithing. As a spiritual requirement, Saints were commanded to give the Church 10 percent of their increase. This was received and managed by the bishop. But in cash-poor Utah, cash tithing amounted to only about 20 percent of the total in 1880.[66] A small amount of the rest came in labor, but the great majority was in kind. This meant that loads of hay, corn, and potatoes, as well as cows, horses, and pigs were regularly being dropped off to the bishop. He had to have a storehouse and yard in which to keep them, but he also had to be able to manage them well so they did not rot, deteriorate, die, or get stolen. Furthermore, he had to meet with each member for an end end-of-year tithing settlement where the bishop and the Church member computed how much that member had raised or earned and how much he had tithed. Finally, the bishop was responsible for allocating tithing resources to local purposes, the poor, or Indians, or converting the items to cash to be forwarded to Church headquarters. This required a wide range of abilities. Bishop Nielson seemed to possess the range required. His age and experience helped. As Albert Lyman appraised him later, "It is the fine balance of the temporal and spiritual that makes the well-balanced man. For quality of balance, Jens Nielson was one among thousands. He was old enough to be the father of these other [80] men, and they accepted him as such."[67]

Bishop Nielson was also responsible for carrying into effect "the program of the church." In 1880 this meant an array of meetings and organizations. Every Sunday the Saints continued to assemble for Sunday

---

64. Quoted in Arrington and Bitton, *Mormon Experience*, 209.

65. The average ward in 1877 had 81 families and 437 members. This average was pulled up by the Wasatch Front wards. Salt Lake wards averaged 566 members, while those in Utah County averaged 808. See Hartley, "Common People," 250.

66. This estimate, as well as other information about bishops and tithing that follow, come from Arrington, "Mormon Tithing House."

67. Albert R. Lyman, *Lemuel Hardison Redd, Jr.*, 39.

School in the morning, and Superintendent Decker led them in songs such as "Children Haste to Sunday School, Nor Tarry on the Way."[68] Although they could not get the *Juvenile Instructor* magazine regularly in Bluff, classes were still conducted, complete with recitations, catechisms, and examinations.[69] They also held a sacrament service in the afternoon, with Bishop Nielson announcing in his musical intonation, "Men you vill come to order; ve vill commence our meeting." The bishop also closed the meeting in his Danish-laced English, endorsing what the speakers said and adding his own comments, sometimes forgetting himself in his eagerness and slipping entirely into the mother tongue. During his thirty years in the Church, he had built up great enthusiasm for it, and this vigor was the defining characteristic of his talks, "the fervor of his words more winning than his fluency."[70] On the first Thursday of each month, Saints were expected to fast and contribute to the poor the equivalent of what they would have eaten. In the early afternoon a fast meeting was held, in which farmers and their wives were expected to come in from their fields and give testimony of the truth of the gospel as they had witnessed it in their lives. From the start, these essential [81] Church meetings went well. The first Sunday after Platte Lyman returned from Colorado, he felt that "there is a good spirit in this ward." Later, he remarked that the Sunday meetings "are generally well attended and always interesting."[71]

But there were other elements in the program of the Church, most of recent invention, which also needed to be carried out. Back in the 1850s and 1860s, the Church gave parents little institutional support in raising their children aside from Sunday School, which was not always held, and sacrament and fast meetings, which children rarely attended. As complaints came to Salt Lake City in the 1860s and 1870s of the bad

---

68. Albert R. Lyman, "Experiences and Impressions," 1:4.

69. Hartley, "Common People," 263.

70. See Albert R. Lyman, "Bishop Jens Nielson: The Old Wagon," 71, 73 for these quotes on the bishop's speaking style.

71. Platte D. Lyman, "Diary," September 26, 1880; March 3, 1881. Hartley, "Common People," 251–56, warns about reading too much into such appraisals. Meetings always seemed well attended because the meetinghouses were so small relative to the population. Measured by the percentage of members of the ward who attended, the results usually did not look as good.

behavior of "unchurched youth," Church leaders devised new programs to support parents in the difficult job of proper breeding. "Retrenchment" associations to root the youth in basic gospel principles commenced, then faltered in the early 1870s. The youth program was retrenched itself into the Young Women's and Young Men's Mutual Improvement Associations, with weekly meetings in which the youth studied "history, literature, debate, and elocution" as well as doctrine.[72] Often they had readings and recitations and performed musical numbers or dramas. The YWMIA and YMMIA also held one meeting together each month, nicknamed the "conjoint." Bluff started a YMMIA in late 1880, with Charles E. Walton as its president, but did not yet start the young women's [82] organization. By October, however, a branch of the Relief Society, the Church's women's organization, was up and running under President Jane McKechnie Walton.[73] According to Church instructions in the late 1870s, young men were also expected to be ordained deacons in the Aaronic Priesthood, help keep the church clean, and, as mice guarding the cheese, keep order during meetings.[74] Bishops were expected to hold weekly Aaronic Priesthood meetings with the boys, though these often adjourned from April through August. A Primary organization for children had been started by the Church in 1878, and even though the Bluff Ward was not lacking children, the bishop did not yet organize this group.

Still, the organizations that did exist made for an endless round of meetings through the week and a difficult schedule for a struggling farming community to keep up. But led by their bishop, the ward members did their best to meet the institutional expectations the Church had for them. As a result, the ward became the focus of activities in the community. It seems that one organization or another was always holding some sort of party, performance, or dance. YMMIA president Charles Walton distinguished himself as a protean actor in these productions: "comedian, tragedian, whatever else was demanded." He still fiddled at the dances, and his bugle also called the Saints to holidays, meetings, and other special occasions. Samuel "Ginger" Cox (so designated for the

---

72. Arrington and Bitton, *Mormon Experience,* 214.
73. "Bluff Ward Manuscript History," October 28, 1880.
74. Hartley, "Common People," 257–59, 264–67.

color of his beard) could fiddle along with Walton and sing. The Perkins brothers, Hyrum and Ben, crooned old Welsh ballads, sometimes with Kumen Jones, such as "Pull for the Shore," "Nora Darling," and "Will You Love Me When I'm [83] Old?"[75]

In between all these meetings and activities, families added their houses to the fort. Using a pattern in place since at least 1846 when the Saints were stationed in Winter Quarters, they arranged their homes close together in the shape of a square, with about twenty-four rods, or almost four hundred feet, per side. A picket wall filled the spaces between the homes. Since their arrival, they had lived out of their wagon boxes "for about another six months before our first log cabins were ready to occupy," as Kumen Jones remembered.[76] To build these cabins, they used the only wood they had, ram's horn cottonwood logs, saddle-notched at the corners. The plentiful gaps were chinked and daubed with wood chips and mud, but the result was less than perfect. "My home is made of cotton wood logs crooked as can possibly be used," a fourteen-year-old Bluff boy candidly observed.[77] The Bluff women and children, who spent far more time in these homes than the men, must have had mixed feelings. On the one hand, many felt like Kumen Jones, who exclaimed, "But oh, what a luxury to get out of the blazing sun under a cool dirt roof, even if the floor was dirt, too."[78] But many of the homes had doorways without doors, and windows without glass that first year. Women sprinkled the floors to persuade the dust to settle, and when it rained the permissive roofs did it for them. Residents quickly learned that most San Juan storms came swiftly and furiously. Whatever combination of willow boughs, dirt, sand, and weeds they tried, these roofs [84] "never turned away the rain, which dropped dismally long after the sky cleared."[79] And when the wind blew, nothing could keep the sand out, either. It found its way into everyone's clothing, bedding, and food. For Kirsten Nielson, especially as she was recuperating from her illness, it was a great relief to move out of her wagon. But the rude log cabin she moved herself and her children into was not much compared with

75. Albert R. Lyman, "History of San Juan County," 33, 37.

76. Kumen Jones, "Writings," 187.

77. Albert R. Lyman, Journal, January 4, 1894.

78. Kumen Jones, "Writings," 187–88.

79. Corinne Roring, *Beautiful Bluff*, 8.

the brick home she had occupied in Cedar. Still, she and everyone else
kept house as well as they could in such homes, all easily within view of
each other in the fort block.

Finally in the fall, they put together the largest building in the fort:
the schoolhouse. The rectangular building was assembled out of the
same sort of cottonwood logs they used on their homes, with coal-oil
lamps mounted on the wall and most likely a fireplace on one end. It was
not only a schoolhouse but, like the one Jens helped build in Panguitch,
also held church meetings, dramas, programs, dances, and every other
type of public gathering that happened in Bluff.[80]

As they put the finishing touches on the meeting hall and gathered
there, the survivors in Bluff were pleased, if not entirely satisfied, with
their efforts so far. In six months they had turned a thread of river bottom
into their home, complete with government, church, and school. They
had established a village similar in form, though smaller and cruder in
many ways, to those they had left. They had sacrificed the world not just
in the general way all Mormons were supposed to do, but also in the form
of the [85] very specific comforts in the older settlements. They labored
together on their ditch and celebrated together during holidays and public
events. They set themselves up as an example to the Indians and Gentiles
in a previously unorganized county. And while they were still on shaky
economic ground, they had the consolation of knowing they were being
true to their faith, that they were different not only from the Indians and
the Gentiles, but from those Saints who had pulled out of the mission.[81]

---

80. It is possible that women sat on one side and men on the other, as the Nielsons and others used to do in the Parowan Tabernacle. See Hartley, "Common
People," 256–257. The building was constructed sometime between September 27,
1880, and January 2, 1881, according to entries in Platte Lyman's diary.

81. See Holzapfel and Allred, "Peculiar People." This article builds on the work of
sociologist Rosabeth Moss Kanter in *Commitment and Community: Communes and
Utopias in Sociological Perspective*, (Cambridge: Harvard University Press, 1972). She
proposed that a utopian society must retain members, achieve group cohesiveness,
and establish social control through sacrifice, investment, renunciation, communion,
mortification, and transcendence to achieve enough strength and solidarity to survive. This article applies these six measures to Mormon pioneer society in general.
While the Bluff community was not completely utopian, their mission required
the same level of commitment, making these factors useful measuring sticks in
examining Bluff's success.

Yet all was not well. In spite of the advice of the Apostles, some continued to become discouraged and abandon the enterprise. William Hutchings, the man who gave the town its name, packed up his family and left in late September, "disgusted with this country."[82]

Winter

Platte Lyman accompanied the Hutchingses out in September on his way to Oak City to retrieve his family, and Bishop Nielson left in November to visit the portion of his family residing in Cedar City. The trip was a difficult one for Jens, for more reasons than the rough ride back. He left his children in Bluff with an ailing mother, a rude house, and probably enough food to survive the winter, though not comfortably. The Indians had started raiding Bluff's livestock as the weather got colder, and the bishop could not [86] be certain they would allow the settlement to survive, nor could he be certain that his little ward in Bluff would not get smaller before he got back. Plus he had responsibilities as a county selectman. But two of his wives and four of his children were still in Cedar City, and he had not seen them in almost a year. As Katrine wrote to her husband, the children "would like to know why their father doesn't stay with us all the time."[83] And so he went. The trip back over the Hole-in-the-Rock road, while by no means easy, was at least faster than the first time he had traveled it.[84] Jens covered the distance between Bluff and Escalante in about two weeks on this trip, as opposed to five months the first time.[85]

---

82. Platte D. Lyman, "Diary," September 29, 1880.

83. Katrine Nielson, letter to Jens Nielson, 233.

84. Albert R. Lyman, in Carter, *Our Pioneer Heritage*, 19:287, described the trip this way: "A trip back to Cedar at that time took longer and cost more in money and anguish than a journey halfway around the world today.... It meant the slow and laborious dragging of cumbersome, iron-tired wagons over more than three hundred miles of unsoftened rocks and unhardened sand, with pony teams to tug and puff, to rock with sweat and develop raw sores on their shoulders."

85. Jens probably traveled to Cedar with Kumen Jones and may also have been accompanied by Joseph A. Lyman, George Westwood, and Joshua Stevens since Platte Lyman crossed the path of all four. See Platte D. Lyman, "Diary," November 18, 1880. Travel times on the Hole-in-the-Rock road come from Platte Lyman's trip to Escalante, which took from September 27 to October 9. Also see Kumen Jones, "Writings," 22–23.

When Jens arrived at the familiar home in Cedar perhaps a week later, he was greeted by Elsie and Julia, who was now eighteen years old, as well as Katrine and her three young children: Annetta, five; Uriah, three; and Freeman, a couple of months past his first birthday. Katrine, a notably good cook, most likely pulled out all the stops. On his first Sunday back, Jens occupied the entire sacrament meeting giving a "very encouraging" report about the settlement on the San Juan and urging all those who had been called "to respond cheerfully."[86] Jens renewed old acquaintances in Cedar and looked after his [87] household there in relative comfort until the next spring.

Whatever mail got through brought mixed news from Bluff. Kirsten's health continued to improve through the winter, and the family had enough provisions. But a skunk got into the honey, meaning they had to eat their regular doses of corn mush unsweetened. Christmas was more bitter. No one in town had very much, but they had dances to celebrate the season, and on Christmas Eve the hopeful children hung up their stockings. Kirsten tried to explain to Caroline and Cindy, who were six and eight, that Santa Claus would not be able to find them clear out in Bluff. But the girls kept their faith, and after the others turned in they tacked their stockings to their bedposts. When they woke up eagerly in the morning, they found those stockings as forlorn as they had left them the night before. Kirsten was just as heartbroken as the girls, and she promised Santa would always find them in the future.[87] In the meantime, Indian raiders found the town's livestock regularly during the new year. There was also quite a bit of excitement in January, when Mr. Critchlow, a construction engineer, passed through Bluff with a team of six men. They were scouting a railroad route from Colorado to St. George. The dream lasted until the first day of spring, when Critchlow and crew returned, "having satisfied themselves that there is no chance for a railroad from here west."[88]

As Jens was preparing to return in early April, he read a report about Bluff, courtesy of the *Deseret News*. Platte Lyman had written Erastus Snow at the end of February, and the Apostle forwarded the report to the newspaper. Bishop Nielson had to be encouraged by [88] what he

---

86. Cedar Ward, General Minutes, November 1880.

87. Leland Redd, "Bishop Jens Nielson," 36; and Alice Redd, "Sketch of the Life of Caroline Nielson Redd," 217.

88. Platte D. Lyman, "Diary," January 24 and March 21, 1881.

read. More families had come in and more homes were built, which were filling the perimeter of the fort. The weather had been fine. Work went forward on the ditch, and prospects looked good for a crop. But most importantly, "all is peace with the Indians on both sides of the river, although we have seen very little of them of late." But Jens might have been alarmed when he read the next line: "We are herding our horses all the time, however, as a precautionary measure."[89]

In the early spring Jens prepared to return to Bluff. In his last sacrament meeting in the Cedar Ward, he urged those who hesitated to depart for the San Juan to be true to their calling. Then he asked for the faith and prayers of all the Saints in Cedar "in behalf of himself and his little flock."[90] On April 12, he said goodbye to Trena and their three young children. Elsie and Julia came with him to relocate in Bluff. Elsie brought mulberry shoots to plant so she could continue to feed the silkworms the Relief Society encouraged Mormon women to raise in the 1860s.[91] She may have also brought some of her beehives so they could produce their own honey for the people—and skunks—in Bluff.[92]

Erastus Snow did his own advertising in the *Deseret News*. "Ho! for San Juan," read a headline on April 13, the day after Jens left Cedar City. Any Saints "with means and muscle" should meet Bishop Nielson in Escalante by April 16 so he could accompany [89] them to their settlement. The resources of the region "will abundantly reward persevering industry and labor."[93] Nephi and Annie Bailey and their family went with Bishop Nielson from Cedar, and three more families joined them on the way.[94] Someone among them, possibly the bishop, brought a wagonload of grape cuttings and young apple trees.

89. *Deseret News*, March 30, 1881, 136.

90. Cedar Ward, General Minutes, April 10, 1881.

91. See Arrington, *Great Basin Kingdom*, 227–28.

92. No source that I have found tells exactly when Elsie and Julia came to Bluff the first time, but if Jens brought them, this was most likely the trip. He did not visit Cedar City in the winter of 1881–1882, and there is no evidence that he visited in the winter of 1882–1883, though he could have gone at the end of the year. In a letter written to Jens on April 15, 1883, Katrine suggested that Elsie was not in Cedar City, so she should have been in Bluff by then.

93. *Deseret News*, April 13, 1881, 161.

94. Albert R. Lyman, "History of San Juan County," 23.

On his way back, Jens found that the Hole-in-the-Rock road, carved with so much toil the year before, was already obsolete. An easier route had been scouted and built by George Sevy and men from Escalante, and Charles Hall had moved his ferry upstream. The bishop's party rejoined the old road on the other side of the river, four or five miles beyond Lake Pagharit. The Hole in the Rock, Cottonwood Hill, and Grey Mesa were no longer obstacles travelers needed to worry about, but most of the road on the east side of the Colorado was still in use. According to the railroad man Critchlow, the new road was a little longer and "very little if any better" than the old.[95]

1881: Failure

Back to Bluff

On Monday, May 9, well before Jens got to Bluff, he was surprised to see Joe coming up the road to meet him. His son had things to tell him: to start with, he was shot at a few days before. As they headed home, Joe had plenty of time to fill his father in on the details, though these may have unsettled the new recruits traveling with them. It [90] seems Platte Lyman's letter in the *Deseret News* was overly optimistic about the Indians. They raided Bluff's livestock regularly during the winter, finding in Bluff, it seems, a new source of subsistence during the lean cold season.[96] That was why the settlers herded and guarded the horses all the time. Joe was on watch at the Bluff Bench northeast of town on May 5 when a band of Indians cutting out horses shot at him. Joe rode quickly back to the settlement and burst into the fast meeting then in progress. The meeting swiftly adjourned as eight or nine of the men got on their horses and headed out to cut off the thieves, and a few more followed soon after. Joe was one of them, and they caught up with about ninety Indians, thirty of them men, near Boiling Springs in Butler Wash. Among the 150 or so horses the Indians had, the Bluff posse found eleven that belonged to

---

95. *Deseret News*, April 6, 1881, 157; Platte D. Lyman, "Diary," March 21, 1881. See also the map in Miller, *Hole-in-the-Rock*, showing the new "Hall's Crossing" route.

96. See Platte D. Lyman, "Diary," January 11, February 26, and March 23, 1881, entries for incidents. The last incident happened soon before Lyman wrote his cheerful letter to the *Deseret News*.

their herd, two of them stolen last year. When the men expressed the
intent to take their horses back, some of the Indians pulled their guns,
and so did the Bluff gang; they were a trigger pull away from war. But
then one of the Indians mentioned something about "Mormons," and the
others quieted down and put away their guns. The Mormons led away
their horses and returned to town, their mission barely intact. They put a
heavy guard on their horse herd that night, and the next morning a group
returned early to the Indian camp. The Indians were generally friendly,
but some were quickly upset when two more horses were reclaimed. As
the Bluff men looked over the herd, they noticed close to forty branded
horses. The Indians also had a lot of cash, "to which they assigned very
little value." They must have raided a ranch somewhere, but despite seeing this, the villagers went home, and the [91] Indians rode on.[97]

After the headlines, Joe may have also reported to Jens the other news.
William Hyde, who still had not reconciled himself to the idea of digging
a ditch, had found a solution for their water problems. He put in a water
wheel at Montezuma. It cost him four hundred dollars, but it was sixteen
feet in diameter and could hoist more than twenty-three thousand gallons

<hr />

97. My telling of this story is a composite of a number of sources. Platte D. Lyman,
"Diary," May 5–6, 1881, is the only contemporary account of Bluff's dealings with
these Indians, but Lyman's journal is consistently laconic. Lyman suspected they were
"renegade Utes and Navajos" who usually camped on the Navajo Reservation. Lyman's
description of the events is characteristically restrained and makes no mention of
any Indian referring to Mormons. Kumen Jones was also at these events, but wrote
his account years later in "Writings," 212, noting that "one of the Indians mentioned
the name Mormons." But he also pushed the tense confrontation until the morning of May 6. Albert R. Lyman, "History of San Juan County," 21–22, followed the
rough account of his father's diary, but added some details. Albert R. Lyman, *Indians
and Outlaws*, 39–43, gives the full dramatic story, but this time his account follows
Kumen Jones's version more closely and embellishes a number of points for dramatic
effect. The Indians involved were "Piutes." Lyman dramatizes further on this version
for *Lemuel Hardison Redd, Jr*, published in 1967. Austin and McPherson, "Murder,
Mayhem, and Mormons," 40–42, claims Jens Nielson chose the posse, which was
"a church vigilante committee." While there is some truth to the charge that Bishop
Nielson often had a lot to do with civic affairs and sometimes chose posses, that
was not the case in this situation. Constable Decker rode with the posse, and Jens
Nielson was still on the road home rather than deputizing Church brethren. Like
most western tales, this one took on a life of its own.

an hour out of the river, giving brothers Hyde and Haskell more water than they could use. Brothers Davis, Cox, and Harriman installed wheels there also.[98] But all was not well in Montezuma, despite the miraculous water wheels. There was a lot of contention among the few families there, and they were no longer holding regular church meetings. To make matters worse, the Harrimans lost their two-year-old daughter to illness, despite the best efforts of Sister Haskell, the most skillful nurse in the settlement.[99]

Unfortunately, Bluff did not have the same solid rock banks as Montezuma, so the [92] wonder of water wheels was not an option for them. Instead, they formed a ditch committee in mid-January and all the available men dug, scraped, and hacked away at it through February and March. On April 2 the river rose seventeen inches, filling the ditch with water and the town with joy. But this quickly fled as swells of water broke through the banks in several places. By April 11, the river fell, taking all of the water back out again, and by April 23, they had played so much of this cat and mouse with the ditch that a crew had had to be kept on the job ever since, to make perpetual repairs to it.[100]

Aside from the unenviable labor on the ditch, Jens also missed the most festive occasion of the past few months. On April 6, the townspeople celebrated the first anniversary of their arrival. They held an all-day celebration just like they used to have on big occasions in Cedar City and other previous homes. A marshal and chaplain for the day were chosen. There was a meeting with speeches and songs in the morning, then a children's party in the afternoon, followed by a dance for adults in the evening.[101] Although he missed the party, Bishop Nielson returned with reinforcements for the second campaign.

More Disappointment

Prospects for the second year, though tempered by the hard experience of the first, looked promising. In addition to the four new families

---

98. Platte D. Lyman, "Diary," March 29, 1881; Journal History, April 1, 1881, 3; Albert R. Lyman, "History of San Juan County," 23.

99. Platte Lyman, Diary, March 28, 1881.

100. Platte Lyman's diary gives a day-by-day account of the struggles with the ditch for this period.

101. Platte Lyman, Diary, April 6, 1881. See also Walker, "Golden Memories," 61–67, for typical celebration schedules in pioneer Utah.

that came in with the bishop, five more had already arrived. And June brought still another family: John Allan settled in [93] Montezuma. Allan was a Scot with a "magnificent beard," and, at age 57, he was nearly the contemporary of Bishop Nielson. He brought both of his wives, Agnes and Jane, and five of his children. Bishop Nielson decided soon after his return that the ward could not get along anymore without a Primary organization to teach its children. At least a dozen had been born since the previous summer, and about the same number came in with the new families. Sister Paulina Pace was put in charge of making the program work with this rambunctious swarm.[102]

By the end of the month, Jens found out how narrowly his own son and the whole town had avoided disaster. The Indians who shot at Joe and almost opened fire on the town's posse had killed three cowboys at Paiute Springs before they arrived at Bluff and ten more men a few weeks later in a battle at Pinhook Draw, on the northwestern slopes of the La Sals.[103] If violence had erupted near Bluff, it would have cost not only lives, but the livelihood of the mission.

That summer repeated the pattern of the year before. After planting crops in June, Joe and Jens Peter, along with many other men from Bluff, freighted for the railroad in Colorado. Once again they made good money with their teams and wagons and reminded themselves why they were not Gentiles. Amargo, New Mexico, was "the wickedest and most lawless town" there ever was, according to Platte Lyman. The [94] freighters stayed in Colorado into the fall, and some remained until December before buying supplies and heading home.[104] With President Lyman among them, Jens Nielson was again the leading authority in Bluff all summer.

---

102. Platte D. Lyman, "Diary," February 3, 1881. Most likely there were more, since the Baileys brought three children with them in May. Families who probably came in 1881 aside from the Baileys and Allans were those of James and Elizabeth Craig, Orren and Emeretta Kelsey, Lars and Mattie Jensen, Henry and Sarah Moody, and Joseph and Mary Woolsey (Joseph was one of the original settlers, but had left by the 1880 census). Hans Bayles also returned with his new wife, Mary Ann Durham.

103. Albert R. Lyman, "History of San Juan County," 21–22; Salmon and McPherson, "Pinhook Draw Fight."

104. Platte D. Lyman, "Diary," June 2, October 8, 1881, tells about this year's freighting.

As such, Bishop Nielson supervised the season's struggle with the ditch. The remaining men installed a headgate to try to tame the heavy floods that washed out the top of the ditch. But the river won, washing out the gate and sending it "on a voyage to the Gulf of California." Hans Bayles and others tried desperately to lasso it, but their ropes caught nothing but water. This year's failure was more discouraging than the last. This time they had organized, started early, and devoted months of labor to the effort, but the river defeated them and their crops again. They were still a "dry camp" without a reliable source of irrigation and dependent on wages and supplies from the Gentiles in Colorado.[105]

In early fall, two cowboys came into town looking to trade horses. A short time after, some of the town's horses were missing. Bishop Nielson determined that three men should trail the cowboys toward the Utah settlements, where the thieves' trail pointed. Lem Redd, Hyrum Perkins, and Joseph Lyman were chosen. Days later, Perkins came back with a desperate report. They had recovered their property, but "Jody" Lyman had been shot while ferrying the animals back over the Colorado, and a bone in his leg was shattered. Lemuel Redd was bringing him in as best he could, but Jody was in agony, and they could not move very fast. The bishop, Jody's elderly mother, and some others [95] quickly left Bluff to bring him in. By the time they arrived, Jody had improved, thanks to a prickly-pear poultice made by Baililii, a passing Navajo. They brought the wounded man home, and his brother Platte probed his wound daily to remove bone fragments. The men who shot him were never captured, though one of them was reported down the Colorado at Lee's Ferry with the provisions of the other. Bluff's settlers found they were not immune to the depredations of others in this wild country. And the decisions of the bishop, even in nonreligious matters, could carry grave consequences. Jody Lyman spent the next two months in bed, and then his brothers carted him back to Oak City.[106]

Joe Nielson also had his life changed in the fall. Somehow between the freighting and digging, he and the schoolteacher, Ida Evelyn Lyman, got to know each other well enough to decide to get married. They set

---

105. See Albert R. Lyman, "History of San Juan County," 19, 23, for the failures of the ditch and the crop.

106. Platte D. Lyman, "Diary," October 11–December 6, 1881; Albert R. Lyman, *Indians and Outlaws*, 45–51.

out on the long trip to the nearest temple, in St. George, where they were married on November 30, 1881. The newlyweds stayed the rest of the winter back in the older settlements, probably spending some of the time with Katrine in Cedar City.

But Jens did not go back that winter.[107] There was too much to do in Bluff after the second year of failed crops, and his concerns were shared in the top levels of Church leadership. By November, Church President John Taylor was worried about the mission. Hearing that it could continue only if the men worked among the Gentiles, President [96] Taylor remarked that the mission was not so urgent that the people should be required to stay if it were not a good place to live.[108] To acquire more information and evaluate the situation, he sent a representative to the colony. Many of Bluff's residents had known Edward Dalton in Parowan; Jens had served with him for at least eight years on the Parowan Stake High Council. The sixty-four-year-old Dalton arrived in early December and found the Saints in Bluff once again in disharmony.

Another Ditch

It was the ditch again. The four-mile-long channel they had labored to excavate for two years was useless. There was too little fall to it, too much sand in it, and the headgate was still traveling south somewhere. There was only one solution, no matter how unappealing: they needed to make a new ditch, with its head a couple of miles higher up the river. This alone was daunting to those who had exhausted themselves so often on the first ditch. But there were two additional problems.

The first was technical. In making the first ditch, the Saints had used all the bottomland dirt along a hundred-rod stretch, more than a quarter mile of riverside. Over that length, they were right up against the smooth

---

107. Kumen Jones, "Writings," 22–23, says he traveled with Kumen Jones back to Escalante in 1881, then came back by the new road in the spring of 1882. He must have been referring to the winter of 1880–81, since that was when the new road he described was built, and also because three other contemporary sources put Jens in Bluff in January of 1882. Nor is there any record of Jens speaking in the Cedar Ward that winter. See Platte D. Lyman, Diary, January 16, 1882; Davis, Journal, January 21–22, 1882; and San Juan County Minute Book, December 28, 1881; March 6, 1882.

108. Quoted in Peterson, *Look to the Mountains*, 38.

rock swept by the river. How could they dig if there was no dirt? Unwilling to give up the mission, Bishop Nielson and others determined to manufacture an artificial bank. They would construct log cubes, similar to the walls of a cabin, with one end open. One of these "cribs" would be placed in the river and filled with rocks and brush to anchor it against the current. Then another would be splashed next to it and so on, crib by crib creating a jetty that would hold the water close to [97] the bank. But with less than twenty men in town when the idea was conceived, it required a disheartening amount of work; they would require roughly one hundred cribs. Nevertheless, those available set to it in late November, and Orren Kelsey, who had arrived earlier in the year with his large family, distinguished himself in constructing cribs.[109]

The second problem was financial, and by arousing settlers' feelings against each other it threatened the community as much as the failure to bring water. Residents had earned ownership in the first ditch based on how much labor and money they contributed to it. Over two years, many had toiled their way to considerable equity in the project. But now that it was abandoned was their stock worthless as well? Some of those who had worked the most understandably felt it was not; they should be given credits in the new ditch to match their labor on the old. Others were vehemently opposed. The old ditch was a useless item, and any credit carried over to the new ditch would only diminish the amount of work the shareholders would desire to do. Edward Dalton arrived in the middle of this controversy.

The first impression the would-be mediator made was not a good one. Brother Dalton presented a letter from President Taylor, advising the Saints in Bluff to fort up and take small pieces of land, "all of which we had done more than a year ago."[110] It seemed that the leadership of the Church, while not unsympathetic, was underinformed. Dalton toured the old ditch and was immediately impressed by the amount of work it would take to construct the new one. He heard arguments on both sides of the credit question. And [98] then he proceeded to solve the dispute in the regular Mormon way—with a meeting.

---

109. Albert R. Lyman, "History of San Juan County," 27–28, describes in detail this cribbing process.

110. Platte D. Lyman, "Diary," December 3, 1880.

On Saturday morning, December 10, ward members gathered in the schoolhouse. There was much animated discussion, as both sides aired themselves. Then the visiting authority, present on behalf of the President of the Church, spoke in favor of throwing out all the old credits. After this they held a vote, unanimously affirming the resolution: they would get credit only for work done on the new ditch since November. His job done, Brother Dalton departed. To recommit to each other and the crushing burden before them, some were rebaptized in the afternoon.[111] They continued their work on the ditch, starting three months earlier than the year before. The division and hard feelings had, for the time being, been defeated by the more important priorities of unity and obedience to Church authority.[112]

The great problem was solved just in time to allow the Nielsons and their neighbors to enjoy the festive Christmas season in Bluff. Work on the ditch was suspended for the last week of the year to haul wood, look after the stock, kill some beef, and do plenty of dancing. Santa Claus did find the Nielsons this time, at least in the form of older brother Jens Peter, who made sure he brought some dolls back from Colorado for the girls. [99]

---

111. Platte D. Lyman, "Diary," December 10, 1881.

112. See May, "Making of Saints," for similar conflict-solving processes in Kanab, as well as how they relate to studies of social cohesion in early New England Puritan towns.

Heights and Depths, 1882–1884

1882: Hope

Union

When James Davis decided to visit Bluff for a few days in January, he was surprised by what he found. Unlike the cool feelings the residents in Montezuma often held toward each other, the people in Bluff welcomed him warmly. He ate with the Coxes, the Baileys, and the Mackelprangs, and with the Nielsons twice. He went to a dance, and a Brother Roper even rounded up his horses for him. At the end of his six days in Bluff, he recorded that he had been "overwhelmed with invitations [on] every hand. I can safely say I never spent a better time in all my life."[1]

Those who remained of Bishop Nielson's flock were being knit together through their common ordeals and festivities. They interacted often in surviving together. What one person could not produce, he borrowed from his neighbor; what one family could not consume it shared with its friends.[2] Common courtesy required residents to help each other with their stray animals and children. The possibility of danger from Indians or [101] outlaws kept them closer.

---

1. Davis, Journal, January 20–24, 1882.

2. See Walker, "Golden Memories," 50–53. No source directly says why there was more contention in Montezuma. It might have been that many of its settlers lacked the bonding migration through the Hole in the Rock. It might also have something to do with the leadership or personalities in each town.

Bluff's settlers also did a lot together. Aside from the public holidays and entertainments put on by Church organizations, each household sponsored dinner parties, receptions, and celebrations of its own. Even those who feuded about the ditch in December entertained each other by January. And the women had their own circles as well, visiting and caring for each other's families frequently. Jens and Elsie's oldest daughter, Mary Nielson Jones, often visited those in need and was well suited for the job with her "sympathetic, understanding heart."[3] She also assisted Margaret Haskell as a midwife.

Some of the camaraderie in Bluff was the inevitable result of everyone living in the one-block area of the fort, with scores of children raising dust, and all the doors and windows pointing toward each other all day and all night. The settlers could either get along or be miserable in their small square together. But these constricted logistics also contributed to the reasons why some people decided to leave. Contentions existed, sometimes with surprising force, but few of them were permanent among those who remained. In such a condensed society, it was easier to leave than endure a dispute that would not go away. While the settlers' attempts to put roots into the San Juan ground were often thwarted, they were certainly developing stronger ties with each other.[4] [102]

Frontier Diplomats

The Mormon settlers now had more frequent contact with the Indians. Navajos, Utes, and Paiutes visited the settlements often, not only to trade at Hyde's store, but also to visit the other inhabitants. The settlers' safety and mission depended on making these interactions positive, but they found their visitors difficult to predict. Sometimes Native Americans dropped by Bluff's homes to talk, sometimes to work for food or other supplies, and sometimes to beg or demand items. Generally the settlers preferred the Navajos to the Utes and Paiutes, since the former did more trading and less begging. One settler felt the Navajos were a "more manly" race.[5] Their farming, herding, and home industries were

---

3. Kumen Jones, "Writings," 201.

4. See May, *Three Frontiers*, ch. 6, on how a similarly "dizzying round of church-sponsored voluntary activities" in Alpine, Utah, caused not only more frequent contact and closer ties with each other, but also strengthened attachments to the town.

5. Hammond, Journal, May 22, 1885.

more identifiable to the Bluff settlers than the migratory existence of the
tribes to the north. The Navajos' industries also gave them much more to
trade, originally wool and goatskins but increasingly blankets and other
home manufactures. Bluff's residents were attracted to other recognizable characteristics. Kumen Jones became friends with a twenty-year-
old Navajo named Jim Joe (or Hurteen Joe) in the first summer of the
settlement. Jones found him the paragon of what he admired in sturdy
pioneers: "industrious, thrifty ... always frank, open, straightforward."[6]

But problems persisted. Utes and Paiutes protested the incursion of
cattle onto their lands by stealing them or sometimes just killing cows
and leaving them to rot.[7] The [103] settlers kept two men out guarding
the horses now, but they still were not enough. So the bishop regularly
appointed men to recover stolen horses. The settlers could not afford to
let these animals go; next to the river, the beasts were the most important
resource in sustaining their lives. Without horses they could not manage
their small herds, haul freight for themselves or for hire, or even plow their
fields. Bishop Nielson did have one small advantage over other settlers in
this respect. One of his teams consisted of a yellow mule with ringbones
and a white mule with spavins on three legs. Such sad-looking creatures
were never stolen.[8]

The man Bishop Nielson turned to most often in negotiating with the
Indians was Thales Haskell. Brother Haskell had been a noted Indian
missionary before he was called to come to Bluff, and he spoke Navajo
and Paiute. As with many successful negotiators, he spoke more in
demeanor than he did in words. Usually he and one or two others would
go out for a few days and return with horses, sometimes those stolen the
previous year rather than the last week. To keep up cordial relations, at
times the searchers would even pay the Indians a reward for "finding" the
stolen horses.[9] At other times, settlers enlisted Indians such as Jim Joe to

---

6. Kumen Jones, "Writings," 167.

7. Platte D. Lyman, "Diary," October 26, 1882, May 5, 1883; Albert R. Lyman,
"History of San Juan County"; McPherson and Hurst, "Fight at Soldier Crossing,"
258–59.

8. Albert R. Lyman, "History of San Juan County," 15.

9. Platte D. Lyman, "Diary," January 11, 1881; Rowley, Autobiography, 21, reported
having to pay $25.00 to recover one of his horses.

help track down and recover items stolen by Indians and whites alike.[10] The bishop called on Haskell so often to undertake these errands that he apologized for their frequency. "Don't feel bad about that," Brother Haskell replied, [104] "You know that is what I am here for."[11]

Bluff had become an immediate buffer for the "Utah" settlements. If thefts by Indians were fewer in the Mormon towns across the Colorado River, it was because the herds of Bluff were a closer target. Sometime within the first two years of the settlement, the beleaguered residents of Bluff asked leaders of the Church what they should do about these thefts. Erastus Snow wrote them that "inasmuch as the Latter-day Saints of the San Juan Mission would live their religion and obey counsel, the Indians who would not be friendly, but would steal and persist in their hatred and meanness towards us, the hand of the Lord would be made manifest in their destruction."[12] Some Indians became notorious for their thieving, the worst at this time being a burly man known as Navajo Frank. He was often friendly when he visited the settlements, but "he has stolen our horses before, and has also insulted the women on several occasions."[13] In late February and early March of 1882, Navajo Frank went on a spree. Bishop Nielson asked Thales Haskell to take some men and recover the animals. When he found Navajo Frank this time, Haskell looked at him for a while and then "quietly but seriously told him that if he continued to [105] steal from the Mormons he would take sick and die." Frank laughed, then he returned one of the missing horses. After another theft, Frank

---

10. Kumen Jones, "Writings," 167.

11. Albert E. Smith, *Thales Hastings Haskell*, 50.

12. Kumen Jones, "Writings," 42 is the only mention of this warning I know by someone who was there. Albert Lyman wrote various accounts of it in *Indians and Outlaws, Lemuel Hardison Redd, Jr.*, and "Bishop Jens Nielson: The Old Wagon." They vary in a number of details, including whether it was Erastus Snow or Francis Marion Lyman who issued the warning, if the Saints wrote a letter about Indian depredations to Salt Lake, and if General Authorities made a special visit in response. My best guess is that Erastus Snow wrote this in a letter sometime in 1881. The residents of Bluff wrote a letter in 1883 on whether or not to stay, but it was more about the ditch and their general situation than about the Indians. Marion Lyman was with Erastus Snow and Brigham Young Jr. when they came in September 1880, though he was not yet an Apostle, and he also came for a conference in Bluff in September 1883, possibly leading to his inclusion in some versions of this story.

13. Platte D. Lyman, "Diary," March 23, 1881.

disappeared for months. He finally resurfaced in Montezuma, "thin and haggard," his chest sunken in. He asked Thales Haskell to "write a letter" to the Lord for him saying he would not steal from the Mormons again. Haskell guaranteed nothing but told Frank that if he stopped stealing and tried to get others to stop he might recover. The settlements had no more trouble from Frank, and he lived into his nineties, though never the picture of health again.[14]

Sometimes the crime was not as large and the consequences not as serious. Hyrum Perkins recruited Kumen Jones to help recover a pair of shoes stolen by a Navajo woman. When the men found the suspect seated in her hogan, she earnestly proclaimed her innocence and invited them to search for the shoes. Their efforts uncovered nothing, until they asked the woman to stand. When she delayed, the two men, one to an arm, hoisted her into the air, "revealing the stolen shoes amid her screams and jabbering. She was a big, fat husky lass and it was no child's play," remembered Kumen Jones. The men returned to Bluff, and for a long time after the woman erupted in laughter whenever she saw either of them.[15]

Despite such diplomacy, the problem of theft by the Indians did not go away. [106] Later in 1882, William Hyde sardonically informed the readers of the *Salt Lake Herald* of their lack of progress: "We have made the effort to prevent them from stealing our stock, etc., and have been attended with that same success that has blessed nearly all white settlers on frontiers for the last 300 years. We have managed to stand it, however, and hope to report that they have quit it entirely when the millennium shall have begun." But Hyde was proud that "despite scheming bad men"

---

14. The essential story and quote are from Kumen Jones, "Writings," 40–43. Jones, who reported accompanying Haskell when the ominous prophecy was made, added, "This instance may seem strange to some, but there were so many who knew of it at the time, that it could have been substantiated in any court of justice." He also recalled, with the help of his wife Mary and some neighbors, fourteen "of the worst of the Utes and Paiutes that had died off within a few years, all of them healthy-looking men." Both Kumen Jones and Albert Lyman testified of seeing sunken-chested Navajo Frank in his old age. See Albert R. Lyman, *Indians and Outlaws*, 38. Platte D. Lyman, "Diary," February 25 and March 9, 1882, corroborates Frank's activities and the groups sent out to get him. Lyman mentioned nothing about the stern warning to the Navajos, though he was not on the scene when it was given.

15. Kumen Jones, "Writings," 215–16.

the settlers had largely turned the Indians into "our friends, and not one bloody combat have we to record."[16]

By Mormon accounts, one of the "scheming bad men" was Henry Mitchell up the river. From his base near McElmo Creek, Mitchell tried to play both sides of the Indian question. He invited the Navajos to cross the river and trade in his store, and he even wrote "passes" for them to graze their sheep off the reservation on the north side of the river.[17] But Mitchell also refused to sidestep any provocation and instead called for troops from Fort Lewis in Colorado to deal with the "murderous savages." He felt the Mormons were conniving with the Indians to drive out others. The Mormons were not setting Indians against Gentiles, nor did they have enough influence to do such a thing. But Mitchell pointed out something else that rankled him—all the Indian tribes in the area were friendlier with the Mormons than they were with him.[18]

This charge was closer to the truth, and it showed the fundamental success of [107] Mormon diplomacy to this point. Cursing thieves and hoisting squaws was not the full Indian policy of Bluff. The Mormons came into the area with no spiritual or practical choice but to cultivate peace with the Indians, and the natives knew it. The settlers brought their families and left them largely undefended. Bluff's citizens never organized a militia, and they patiently negotiated their differences rather than summon federal troops from Fort Lewis. The settlers wanted to teach the Indians without being taught in turn, but they were not too pushy about it. And while the Mormons consumed important resources, their purpose was not to drive the Indians out but rather to draw them in through trade and goodwill.[19] As Kumen Jones expressed it, "From the time of our first landing in this part of the country to the present we aimed to not let a chance go by for convincing them of our friendship for, and our interest in their welfare or behalf."[20] In this, the colonists were simply extending

---

16. Quoted in Journal History, December 16, 1882. The letter was written December 1, 1882.

17. Platte D. Lyman, "Diary," October 26, 1882; McPherson, "Navajos, Mormons, and Henry L. Mitchell," 59; Peterson, *Look to the Mountains*, 57.

18. McPherson, "Navajos, Mormons, and Henry L. Mitchell," 54–57.

19. Peterson, *Look to the Mountains*, 58–59.

20. Kumen Jones, "Writings," 190. Kumen Jones recalled learning these rules from Thales Haskell and Silas Smith about how to negotiate with Indians: "Always

what had been the Church's policy since the early 1850s. Mormons hoped
to win the sympathies of the "Lamanites" through patience, train them in
a more agrarian lifestyle, and then hopefully convert them to Mormonism.[21] While they had not done much of the latter yet in Bluff, relations
were stable enough by early 1883 that Church leaders were ready to call
specific missionaries to the Indians to make [108] the attempt.

Cooperative Success

With the spring showers came another stream of new settlers. William
Adams, an Irishman from Parowan, arrived with his German wife, Mary,
and their four children, aged eight to sixteen. Adams had helped save the
Parowan United Manufacturing Company a few years before and was
called to Bluff "for his excellent judgment which would assist the young
men laboring there."[22] Other families came with him and so did the newlyweds Joe and Ida Nielson. Jody Lyman came back on crutches, his shot
leg two or three inches shorter than the other.[23] He was immediately
made postmaster, even though there was still no regular mail service. As
usual, some left as well, though this time not voluntarily. Hyrum Perkins
started out for Cedar in early spring "with John Gower, who is nearly
dead with consumption."[24]

   By this time it had become obvious that George Sevy, though he
was admired by everyone, was not coming back to serve as first counselor in the ward. Bishop Nielson chose Sevy's erstwhile neighbor in

---

be plain, frank, and straight in talking with them. Treat with them as you would
with children. Don't accuse or charge them with wrong doing without being *sure*
of your grounds. Never attempt to run a 'bluff.' As a rule you will be safer *without* a
gun or weapon of any kind, if your aim is to be a peacemaker. Be unselfish, patient,
let them do most of the talking, get their viewpoint and deal with them from what
they think is right." Jones also admired natives for keeping their word once a peace-
able agreement was made, saying the Indians "have *never* broken these agreements."
Kumen Jones, "Writings," 135.

   21. See Arrington, *Brigham Young,* ch. 13, for Brigham Young's evolving policies
toward the Indians in Utah Territory.

   22. William Adams, "History of William Adams," 1894, on "Jens Nielson History," CD-ROM, eds. Mike Halliday and Donna Jensen, 303; Cedar Ward, General
Minutes, September 23, 1882.

   23. Platte D. Lyman, "Diary," February 12, 1882.

   24. Platte D. Lyman, "Diary," March 19, 1882.

New Harmony, Lemuel Redd Jr., to fill the vacancy as second counselor, moving Kumen Jones to the office of first counselor. The two were an effective contrast: Redd was direct, even blunt in his manner but could hold his emotions, while Kumen Jones, though more moody, could also be more soft-spoken and [109] endearing when the occasion warranted. Each had enough courage to carry out difficult assignments.[25] For the first time the Bluff Ward had a full bishopric with the sixty-one-year-old Dane supported by the two men each less than half his age.

That spring, the bishop and others also decided it was time to set up another customary Mormon institution—a cooperative store. Since the founding of Zion's Cooperative Mercantile Institution (ZCMI) in Salt Lake City in 1868, most wards and settlements had opened a local cooperative store, which often became a retail outlet not just for ZCMI wholesale goods, but also for local home industry products. The store was usually directed by Church authorities, and members bought low-priced shares in the enterprise. Latter-day Saints were expected to patronize only the cooperative store, thus strengthening not only their shares of stock, but also their unity and collective economy.[26]

Bluff's co-op was a relatively late arrival. By 1882, many of the other cooperative stores were declining or passing into private ownership. In fact, just two weeks before Bluff residents pooled their resources, President John Taylor officially authorized Mormons to patronize private retailers once again. Nevertheless, on April 24, 1882, the Bluff Cooperative Store was organized. Predictably, Platte Lyman was elected president, with Jens Nielson as vice president, Charles E. Walton, Kumen Jones, and Hyrum Perkins as directors, Lemuel H. Redd Jr. as secretary, and Benjamin Perkins as treasurer. Jody Lyman was appointed as the first salesman, to help the crippled father provide for his increasing [110] family, at least until the mail started coming in.[27] Before the store opened for business a month and a half later, members subscribed to its stock,

25. See Albert R. Lyman, *Lemuel Hardison Redd, Jr.*, 55–59, 62–63, for his assessment of Lemuel Redd's character later in life.

26. See Arrington, *Great Basin Kingdom*, 306–14; Arrington, Fox, and May, *Building the City of God*, ch. 5 and ch. 14, for descriptions of and reasons for the rise and decline of local cooperative stores.

27. Kumen Jones, "Writings," 213; Platte D. Lyman, "Diary," June 11, 1882. William Adams's extensive experience with cooperative ventures in Parowan might help

and the store may have bought out Ben Perkins's store and perhaps some of Hyde's for its original inventory.

Bluff's leaders felt the town needed a co-op for many reasons. First, the store moved the town closer to the ideal of the agricultural village. As usual, the Church provided the broad principles, and Bluff's leaders filled in the practical details as they organized the cooperative.[28] The Bluff store also eased acute economic ills. It provided more variety in products than an individual's store could, while also passing the profits around the community instead of funneling them into one pocket. It channeled trade with the Indians into that one store instead of dispersing it around the community and creating friction between Mormons and Indians alike in competing for business. It gave the residents an official outlet for locally produced articles; residents could bring in corn and take out eggs, for instance. Bishop Nielson could also handle his tithing accounts through the store, issuing co-op credits to the needy or to Church officers for their expenses and transferring tithing cash, stock, or produce to the store in compensation. Most importantly, it provided the men of the community with employment. The stockholders took turns freighting local products and produce to towns in Colorado and hauling back [111] flour, cloth, shoes, and various other products for the co-op. In effect, men could work for the co-op instead of depending on the jobs of Gentiles. The freighters were usually paid in store credit, a convenient way to balance their account in a cash-strapped economy.[29] Co-op freighting did not replace working for the Coloradans entirely, but it gave the citizens of Bluff a measure more of independence and

---

explain his call to the San Juan at this point. See William Adams, "Autobiography," 35–36.

28. Arrington, Fox, and May, *Building the City of God*, 11. The purposes for Bluff's Co-op were remarkably similar to the purposes outlined by Moses Thatcher for stake boards of trade that were being organized in 1879: find markets for products, organize and sustain home industries, prevent hurtful competition, match supply and demand, prevent self-interested middlemen, set "living prices" for laborers, promote organization and union. There is no evidence that the San Juan Stake had a board of trade during Jens Nielson's lifetime, but its co-op attempted to put into practice the same principles. See Arrington, Fox, and May, *Building the City of God*, 324–25.

29. Albert R. Lyman, "Biography," in *Lemuel Hardison Redd, Jr.*, 34.

unity. But public spirit was required: once the cooperative store opened, the residents of Bluff were expected to patronize it and no longer trade with Indians on their own account.[30]

The small co-op building in the northeast corner of the fort quickly became a gathering place. Townsfolk leaned on the L-shaped counter to "chew the fat," and children peeked in at the striped candy on the counter, the colored beads and pictures, and especially the Indians, as they "jostled each other, smoking and laughing" in the "festive, drawn-out affair" of bartering with the clerk.[31]

The colonizers needed all this help because the first object of their hopes, the ditch, was still spurning their best efforts. Every available man had been working on it since the previous November. Once again they elected ditch officers, who organized crews with foremen to accomplish the tasks they needed to do. On average, each man [112] worked ninety days building and anchoring cribs, scraping and digging the ditch itself.[32] So many men were working on it that only two showed up for February's fast meeting.[33] Despite their labors, the wary laborers knew better than to trust too much in their efforts. Long gone were the days when they quarreled with each other for every arable acre. This year they were preparing to plant only 200 out of the 690 available acres, and they would give land to anyone who came.[34]

The ditch was entirely too chancy for some. Platte Lyman took Joseph Barton and Orren Kelsey to the Blue Mountains, hoping to find a less labor-intensive site to fulfill their mission in the "little valleys" east of the range. They crossed Elk Mountain into Dark Canyon but concluded later that year the water there was too low for irrigation.[35]

---

30. Bluff's co-op was unusual in that it was not called the B.C.M.I., or Bluff Cooperative Mercantile Association, according to the pattern of most of the local stores, but simply "the co-op." It was also different since it did not distribute Z.C.M.I. merchandise, but due to its remote location it worked with Colorado wholesalers.

31. Albert R. Lyman, Summaries of Each Year, book 1, p. 22; Albert R. Lyman, "History of San Juan County," 36.

32. Albert R. Lyman, *Indians and Outlaws*, 54; Kumen Jones, "Writings," 40.

33. Platte D. Lyman, "Diary," February 2, 1882.

34. William Hyde, "The San Juan Country," *Deseret News*, August 16, 1882, 475. This is a letter from Hyde to President T. J. Jones in Parowan written in June 1882.

35. Albert R. Lyman, "History of San Juan County," 30–31.

In April the cribs were completed. The labor crews watched with suspense as the water flowed into their artificial bank for the first time. To their
alarm, the stream seeped out through the porous bottoms of the cribs. But
these holes soon filled with sediment, and the town rejoiced when the water
trickled in by the end of the month. They rushed to prepare their ground
for planting, earlier than ever before in the year. The river, as it turned out,
had other plans. Its spring surges overwhelmed the head of the ditch, carried
off the headgate again, and eroded away the first thirty rods of the channel.
After the settlers' most superhuman effort, the river foiled them. With a
collective deep breath, [113] they determined to lay off 214 rods of new ditch
to extend it more than half a mile upstream, and they flew into the project.
Mere digging seemed less of a challenge by now, and by the end of May, they
were done. The water dropped out of the ditch again in July, so they had to
muck out the sediment and deepen the bottoms. August was very hot, but
the water stayed in. Then in the middle of September, rains caused Cottonwood Wash to flood over some of the best crops, but when it drained away
the next morning, the farmers found the damage was minimal.[36]

At the end of it all Bluff produced a crop. Even the usually reticent
Platte Lyman pronounced that "the corn crop here is beyond all comparison the best I ever saw anywhere." And for the first time Bluff had
something like a harvest festival. They had produced potatoes and even
some small grains. They reaped their corn and imported a cane mill to
turn their sorghum into molasses. The "sweet odor" of boiling molasses
filled the air, and soon after the children held their first candy pulling
into the late hours of the night.[37] The men hauled their bounty to the
railhead in Durango in regular shipments. The water wheels in Montezuma worked just as well, leading presiding elder William Hyde to
exclaim "the perseverance, industry and indomitable will of the people
here, who have had the moral personal courage and tenacity, combined
with that particular abiding faith, have demonstrated the fact beyond
a peradventure, that it can [114] be taken out and made a success."[38] He

---

36. See Platte D. Lyman, "Diary," April 29–November 9, 1882, for a blow-by-blow
account of that year's adventure with the ditch. See also Albert R. Lyman, "History
of San Juan County," 31.

37. Albert R. Lyman, "History of San Juan County," 31.

38. Letter from "W. H." of Montezuma to Salt Lake Herald, written December 1,
1882, in Journal History, December 16, 1882.

was even more sure in the fall than he had been in June that "this river will afford homes for hundreds of families, and with less labor than any settlement in Southern Utah," and that the Saints were "united with Bishop Nielson in building up Zion and developing this country."[39]

For the first time in three attempts, Bluff looked ahead to winter on a solid economic foundation. They had raised a crop and improved their independence on orthodox cooperative principles through their store. Even better, the co-op paid a 10 percent dividend to its shareholders only five months after opening its doors.[40] The county also received a thousand dollars from the Utah Legislature to improve the road to Escalante. Bishop Nielson administered the money and endeavored to guarantee that "for ever dollar spent one dollar and a half of actual improvements have been made."[41] William Hyde was planning to open another trading post at Rincon, ten miles below Bluff, and many others also planned economic ventures. Their stock was fat, they were in good health, and they even had a "ripple of excitement and a slight rush of miners" in early December when gold, silver, copper, iron, and coal were discovered fifty miles downstream. The Church did not sponsor cooperative ventures in speculative mining, but some amateur [115] Bluff prospectors investigated promising claims for themselves.[42]

Adding to their satisfaction was the fact that on October 26, a landmark day to all who were there, regular mail service started in Bluff. Gone were the days when they might wait two months for some freight wagon or random rider to bring their letters through from Colorado. Now they could have predictable correspondence with family, friends, and Church headquarters. They could get regular updates on Utah and the world through the *Deseret News* (at four dollars per year, delivered) and whatever other newspapers or magazines they chose to patronize. This dependable connection was another sign that they were taming the wilderness, and it greatly reduced their feelings of isolation.

---

39. Hyde, "San Juan Country," 475.

40. Platte D. Lyman, "Diary," November 6, 1882.

41. Letter from "W. H." of Montezuma.

42. See Platte D. Lyman, "Diary," December 3, 8, 1881; Platte Lyman, letter written February 19, 1883, to *Deseret News*, March 28, 1883, 147. Orren Kelsey along with Platte and Joseph Lyman found promising gold and silver claims for themselves on a ledge two miles up Cottonwood Wash.

Overall the settlers felt good about their mission. It looked as if they would be able to successfully hold on to this corner of the territory, and their relations with the Indians were "very friendly, and as a rule [they] conduct themselves as well at least as the average white citizen."[43] At the ward fast meeting in December, two men were confirmed by Platte Lyman, who had baptized them that morning. Eberhardt Meskin was the mission's first convert to Mormonism. He had come from Colorado a few months before and had studied the doctrines of the Church while in Bluff. George Ipson was already a Mormon, but was re-baptized, symbolizing a rededication to the mission that most felt that season.[44] [116]

The number of settlers again increased. Reinforcements, including the Nielsons' neighbors from Cedar City, Samuel and Josephine Wood, had been called by the Church and arrived in Bluff in two companies. The labor pool of the town increased to fifty men by the end of the year, with nearly that number of families.[45] Bluff mothers had an abundant harvest as well, giving birth to a dozen babies in the last six months of the year.

One Bluff mother who did not have a child that fall, or in any of the four years of her marriage so far, was Mary Jones, Jens and Elsie's oldest daughter. She probably helped deliver many of the infants who came in late 1882 and may also have been present when the Decker and Kelsey babies were lost soon after they arrived. But her own lack of children troubled her and her husband more as time passed. As her husband Kumen put it later, "It seemed like being lost in a desert to have a home without children." Jens spoke with Mary about it. His solution was that she needed to permit Kumen to take another wife, "and not put it off,"

---

43. Platte Lyman, letter to *Deseret News*, 147.

44. Platte D. Lyman, "Diary," December 7, 1882.

45. Those with families who definitely came with these expeditions were Samuel and Josephine Catherine Chatterley Wood, as well as Frederick Isaac and Mary Mackelprang Jones. Those who possibly came in 1882 were David and Eliza Ann Barton Edwards, Brigham and Johanna Maria Haskell Harrison, Henry and Sarah Barney Moody, and Thomas and Margaret Rowley. Charles and Emma Smith Willden also came with the Woods in 1882, but seem to have gone through in short order to Mancos. Emma was the sister of Joseph Stanford Smith, who had gone on to Mancos earlier. Josephine Wood also mentioned Alma Smith, David Adams, "Peter," and "Aunt Mamie" in her journal as accompanying the expedition. See Noall, "Mormon Midwives."

since they had heard Congress was considering stronger anti-polygamy legislation. Furthermore, he promised that if she did, she would have children of her own. After all, he may have reminded Mary, she was the result of such a promise a quarter century before. Mary consented, and on October 4, she and Kumen left Bluff with Kumen's choice for a second wife, seventeen-year-old Lydia May Lyman. Mary [117] stayed with her mother and sister, now back in Cedar City, while Kumen and Lydia went to St. George and were married. If anyone could have helped Mary through these days, it was Elsie.[46]

The holidays in Bluff were chilled by freakishly cold weather, the thermometer hitting an unthinkable twenty-three degrees below zero. Aside from that spell, the weather was "remarkably pleasant," good for laboring on the ditch and looking forward to the year ahead.[47]

1883: Indecision

Another Victory

For once the ditch was improved rather than rebuilt during the winter. The Bluff labor gangs widened the bottom of it to ten feet across and doubled its capacity. The whole thing was five miles long now, with only six feet of fall over the entire distance.[48] All the men pitched in, despite the continuing stream of miners passing through town with reports of "new discoveries of fabulous richness."[49] Some of the miners attended Sunday meetings and listened with respect. At the end of January, Apostles Brigham Young Jr. and Marion Lyman held five meetings with the Bluff Saints. The community had grown large, stable, and prosperous enough that it was time to intensify their efforts [118] toward the Indians. Thales Haskell, Kumen Jones, and other men were called to learn the Navajo language, explain to them the purposes of the settlement at Bluff, and teach them agricultural methods.[50]

---

46. The particulars of this whole episode come from Kumen Jones, "Writings," 150; Gwen H. Jones, "History of Kumen Jones."

47. Platte Lyman, letter written February 19, 1883, to *Deseret News*.

48. F. W. Young, letter to *Deseret News*, in Journal History, September 4, 1883, 3; "Bluff City," *Deseret News*, May 23, 1883, 273. This article was based on a letter from William Adams written in April.

49. Platte D. Lyman, "Diary," January 15, 1883.

50. Platte Lyman, letter written February 19, 1883, to *Deseret News*; "Bluff City," 273.

On April 26, the settlers found enough time to celebrate a new holiday, the bishop's birthday, three weeks after their founder's day commemoration. Soon after the festivities, however, high waters came, and the banks of the ditch started breaking again. With "almost the entire attention of all hands," the water was kept flowing to the fort, but once more planting was delayed until early June. Heavy sands blocked the head on the Fourth of July and took ten days to clear out. Breaks continued into August. Some showers helped the crops, but also brought more flooding down Cottonwood Wash.[51] Throughout the summer, guards patrolled the banks of the ditch to fix problems immediately. On some occasions, they had to blast out boulders "as big as a wagon bed to a two-story house" that fell into the ditch from the cliffs above. John Morgan, a visiting Church authority, was of two minds when he saw the ongoing project in September. To the *Deseret News* he boasted that it was "one of the most stupendous undertakings that has been accomplished by the same number of people, in the history of the settlement of the Saints."[52] More privately, when he saw the sheer amount of hard labor the ditch required, he confided to Jody Lyman, who was still bothered by his injured leg, "I believe I'd prefer having both legs shot than have the job the boys [119] have on that canal."[53]

By the middle of August, the crops looked good and the Indians were largely peaceful. In fact lately they even allowed their women to come to Bluff alone, which was an encouraging sign of trust.[54] Under such favorable circumstances, settlers began to abandon the fort. With the blessing of their leaders, many people moved their houses out to their city lots and ended the collegial but confined experience of all living on the same block, hearing every clang from Amasa Barton's anvil and the wail of every baby. Children no longer "played in a flock" in the middle of the fort.[55]

The houses had been improved as well. Many more colonists had imported doors, curtains, furniture, and glass windows from Colorado or ordered them from the fairly new catalog of Montgomery Ward and Co.

51. Platte D. Lyman, "Diary," May 5 to August 1, 1883.

52. John Morgan, "Correspondence," *Deseret News*, October 17, 1883, 611.

53. Kumen Jones, "Writings," 216–17.

54. Morgan, "Correspondence," 611.

55. Albert R. Lyman, "History of San Juan County," 36.

Most had hung their homes with "factory," a thick, unbleached muslin that lined the walls and covered up the ugly underside of the roof. It also allowed those at home to funnel rainwater into a few convenient holes, rather than endure a general downpour. The factory had to be washed clean of the mud that oozed down, but it was an improvement. And each family added whatever additions it could to beautify their surroundings. The Nielson girls put paper flowers on their curtains.[56] Some families even hauled lumber from Colorado to put in a plank floor to give their families something worth sweeping. [120]

Jens left Bluff, with two other men, two women, and three children, on August 9, taking still another new road to Cedar City.[57] This one went from Hall's Crossing over to the Fremont Valley and through Loa before linking up with existing roads to Iron County. Jens proudly told the locals in Loa about the Bluff ditch and that the residents of Bluff "think their water sure now."[58] When he arrived in Cedar City, he saw his wife and children for the first time, possibly, in two and a half years. Annetta was eight already and doing well in school. Uriah was six, and Freeman, the baby, was now four. The farm in Cedar was prospering, aside from the unavoidable inconveniences of frontier agriculture. He reported to his old friends in the Cedar Ward that although "some of the brethren called to the San Juan country had backed out and returned to Iron County," that "those who remained at Bluff City were a good, industrious, hard-working people."[59]

Questions

While he was gone, Jens missed the capstone of Bluff's religious organization. The San Juan Mission was converted into the Church's twenty-seventh stake. The first quarterly conference of the new San Juan Stake was held in Bluff on September 22 and 23, with Apostle Marion Lyman and Elder John Morgan visiting from Church headquarters. Bluff had been a full-fledged ward for over three years, but the San Juan Mission

---

56. Reeve, "Lucinda Diantha Nielson Hyde," 209.

57. This may have been a family trip. The two women could have been Kirsten (whose sister lived in Parowan), Elsie, Julia, or Margaret; the two men Jens Peter and Joe; the three children Francis, Cindy, and Caroline.

58. Young, letter to *Deseret News*.

59. "Parowan Stake Manuscript History," September 23, 1883.

now gained full legitimacy as a stake, which included Bluff and Montezuma, [121] as well as Mormon settlements in Mancos, Colorado, and
Burnham, New Mexico. Platte Lyman, just turned thirty-five, became
the stake president, since Manassa, Colorado, where mission president
Silas Smith still resided, now belonged to a separate unit. For most of
the Saints, the move meant little in their day-to-day lives. But it did
mean they would hold, as all stakes were supposed to, quarterly conferences, which would eventually rotate among the units in the stake. Saints
who were able, and especially ward and stake leaders, would travel to the
location of that quarter's conference. And at least once a year that meant
visitors would crowd into the homes of Bluff for meetings and celebrations. Organization as a stake also justified the Saints in that region: it
was at least as strong a sign to them as regular mail service that they were
remaking the county in their image.

With the stake now established, its president wanted to know how
long the Saints in Bluff would be required to continue their extraordinary
efforts to subsist there. The first ditch cost ten thousand dollars in wasted
man hours without producing a general crop, and the second, in its two
years, had consumed close to forty thousand dollars. This meant they
had expended almost $80 per acre per year in labor for every one of the
five hundred combined acres they cultivated in the last two years.[60] And
this was just the work required to bring water to the fields. Beyond that
they still had to plow, plant, tend, and harvest. In other words, while the
situation was about as good as it ever had been in the history of the mission, Lyman was worried about the question that loomed larger than the
prospects for the next [122] season. He suspected the mission might not be
worth what its members were pouring into it. The two visiting authorities
in September had no definite answer about how long the mission should
be held. Lyman immediately after went to Durango, where he caught

---

60. Morgan, "Correspondence," 611, put the cost of the ditch so far at almost
forty thousand dollars. They cultivated two hundred acres in 1882 and perhaps
three hundred in 1883 (see Kumen Jones, "Writings," 213). Platte D. Lyman, "Diary,"
December 3, 1883, said the ditch tax for the approaching season was set at $29 per
acre, meaning the three-year total for the ditch would be $48,300. But the taxes
were assessed for all seven hundred acres of farmable land, resulting in his lower
total of $69 per acre total for the years 1882 to 1884. My $80 figure is per acre actually
cropped in the two years 1882 and 1883.

the new railroad to Salt Lake City. There, on October 1, as the Church's authorities were gathering for their general conference, President Lyman "reported the San Juan Mission to President Taylor and the Apostles who were somewhat divided with regard to the wisdom of continuing that mission under the unfavorable circumstances which so far have attended it." Lyman did not get the answer he was looking for by the time he left.

He returned to Bluff by the railroad, which now made Salt Lake more accessible to his stake than Escalante. As he drove back from Durango, he passed a number of cheerful Bluffites freighting their sizeable harvest and co-op items to Colorado. But when he arrived in Bluff, he found the people "considerably exercised over a report of the probability of the abandonment of this mission, which however strikes many of the people quite favorably."[61] By November they had received no answer.

Bishop Nielson heard about some of this through Erastus Snow, who gave him a letter to take back to Bluff. Whether he planned to return so soon or not, the bishop headed back and presented the long-awaited reply to Platte Lyman on December 1. "After due consideration," the verdict read, "the First Presidency and apostles generally deem it unwise to encourage the abandonment of your homes and your efforts to establish your settlements on that stream and its vicinity, notwithstanding we all deeply sympathize [123] with you in your difficulties in controlling the stream."[62] But the Saints needed to retrench: if they would try to stay closer to home and be more self-sustaining, the crisis would pass and prosperity would dawn. It was questionable where the combined opinion of the General Authorities of the Church ended and those of Apostle Snow personally began, since he was the sole signatory to the letter. He continued that President Lyman and anyone else who wanted to leave the mission could go, but the release was not phrased in flattering terms. When he read it, Platte Lyman felt "the only inference to be drawn is that those who leave are destitute of faith and a contented spirit." To him such a release seemed a dishonorable escape and, "in consideration of all [his] labors [t]here," he felt it unjust that he was singled

---

61. See Platte D. Lyman, "Diary," September 23–October 25, 1883, for this entire episode.

62. Erastus Snow, letter to Platte D. Lyman and Jens Nielson and to the Saints on the San Juan, October 26, 1883.

out "in a letter written to the people generally, and to be read and re-read by them."[63]

The word spread quickly upriver, so that most of the men from Montezuma came down and "freely discussed" the issue during Sunday meetings the next day. A majority emerged for staying for at least one more season. The ditch was a tremendous challenge, but they had brought in a crop the last two years with it, and maybe the worst was behind them. According to President Lyman, a majority of those in favor of staying acted out of "a rational view of the matter," but he contrasted these with others who were possibly the swing voters: a few "whose sentiments may … be materially changed by circumstances [124] aside from the general welfare of the place." They "spoke in a very bigoted and inconsistent way in favor of remaining here."[64]

There was no question that Bishop Nielson favored staying and little question that he was one of those who held the "rational" view of a Mormon who had repeatedly shown that obeying priesthood authority was more important to him than personal ease or profit. But President Lyman and Bishop Nielson were drifting toward different conclusions on the overarching question of whether Bluff was worth holding. Neither man disputed the worthiness of the goals of their efforts, but they differed on whether the cost required to maintain this particular place was worth it. Ironically, it was only due to the vagueness in the geography of the mission call that allowed them to settle at Bluff in the first place. Montezuma was where the original scouting party expected them to locate. But since they had settled on the San Juan, Apostles of the Church had assured them

---

63. Platte D. Lyman, "Diary," December 1, 1883. The text in question from the Erastus Snow letter read, "Meantime if Bro. Lyman or others desire to withdraw from that mission we have no disposition to require them to stay and will continue to pray for prosperity elsewhere among the saints of other places, for we recognize their longsuffering and patient labors, but if a spirit of faith and contentment shall revive in them so they can be happy in their labors, we believe they will get see satisfactory fruits of their labors."

64. Platte D. Lyman, "Diary," December 3, 1883. The meeting was held the day before this entry. Platte Lyman never specified whom or what he meant here. He could have been referring to some who were dazzled by the dividends of the cooperative store and wanted to stay only to reap more of the same, or to some who saw other lucrative, uncooperative activities in the county.

that their particular spot, and not just the county in general, was vital, located as it was where the friction was the greatest. Therefore, Bishop Nielson, as he had conditioned himself to do since he emerged from the waters of baptism and the snows of 1856, would wait on that same priesthood authority, the general leadership of the Church, to direct differently. President Lyman, born on the banks of the Platte River in Wyoming to distinguished pioneer parents, had come to believe that there had to be a better base for the mission than Bluff. And he felt he had the responsibility to present the circumstances of [125] his stake to the authorities so that they could clearly direct him. He most likely felt that he had accurately described the conditions of the area when he gave his report in Salt Lake City. At least some of the authorities, it seems, interpreted his realism regarding Bluff as pessimism toward the mission.

The two men also had different personalities. Platte Lyman was, by all accounts, an excellent and faithful man. He worked as hard and endured as much, if not more, than anyone. But his talents and personality made him somewhat different from many around him and inclined him away from a frontier life. He was "kind, quiet, thoughtful, ... [and] studious."[65] It may have been this more refined nature that caused some of the Church leaders to feel his presentation showed a lack of faith. Erastus Snow certainly thought so, especially when contrasted with Jens Nielson's unrefined exuberance. There was no recorded rivalry or feud between the sixty-three-year-old bishop and the thirty-five-year-old stake president. They were both deeply faithful men who thought highly of each other. But their faith had led them to different conclusions about what was right in these circumstances. Both men agreed, however, that the next year would be crucial to the survival of Bluff. At the end of the meeting in the schoolhouse on December 2, Lyman felt that most of the settlers "will no doubt be governed very much by the success of the next season."

The decision made, they all got to work right away. That same evening the Irrigation Company met again to choose new trustees and levy twenty-nine dollars more per acre in ditch [126] taxes. And they still had

---

65. Kumen Jones, "Writings," 194–95. Jones wrote that Lyman was "an inspiration and an education," and that he was "loved and honored by all who had come within the scope of his acquaintance."

other duties to do. Bishop Nielson accompanied President Lyman to Montezuma. The Saints there were still scattered physically and spiritually. William Hyde had resigned as presiding elder earlier in the year. John Allan Jr. was appointed in his place, but there was still wide dissatisfaction with their isolated situation. In the previous stake conference, the bickering Montezuma branch had been folded into the Bluff Ward, under Bishop Nielson's responsibility, though Brother Allan would continue to preside when the bishop was not there.

The ward members prepared for their second stake conference in Bluff by expanding the schoolhouse. They put a fourteen-foot extension on the north side, part of which was occupied by a platform to serve as a stand for meetings and a stage for theatrics.[66] The weather for the conference was poor, but "the Spirit of the Lord was poured out abundantly upon the people" as they discussed unity, cooperation, and building up the waste places of Zion in their meetings on December 22 and 23.[67] The Nielsons ate Christmas dinner at Kumen, Mary, and Lydia Joneses' home, along with Platte Lyman's family. Together, they "filled the house to capacity." And the bishop's family soon got bigger: two days after the holiday feast, Joe and Ida gave him the slightly tardy gift of his first grandchild. [127]

1884: Catastrophe

Promises

The settlements on the San Juan were rejuvenated as the year turned. Bluff and Montezuma had 245 people living in them, about as many as they had when the Hole-in-the-Rock expedition arrived. Even though almost four years had passed since then, these towns were still very young. The colonists themselves had aged, of course, and older settlers like the Hydes, Allans, and Adamses had added experience, but the children kept coming. More than half of the 245 were under fifteen years old now, and the average age of the settlers was still a little short of eighteen. More than three of four residents were Utah-born, and most of those

---

66. Platte D. Lyman, "Diary," December 22, 1883.

67. Charles E. Walton, "San Juan Stake Conference," *Deseret News*, January 9, 1884, 813.

who weren't still came from the British Isles. But there were also seven other Danish-born settlers with whom Jens, Elsie, and Kirsten could converse in their native tongue.

Some things had changed. Plural marriage had a much larger presence than it did when these towns were settled. While James Harvey Dunton had left, since 1880 Peter Mickelsen, Benjamin Perkins, and Lemuel Redd had all joined Kumen Jones in marrying second wives. Like Brother Jones, they may have been encouraged to do so by their bishop, particularly as rumors of the Edmunds Act of 1882 approached and the act itself materialized. Bishop Nielson, John Allan, William Hyde, and possibly Platte Lyman also had two wives living in Bluff by this time.[68] Now one out of four settlers lived in polygamous families, more than doubling the number from four years before. Those who [128] practiced plural marriage were again expressing their faith in obeying the whole program of the Church, just as Jens and Elsie had chosen to do back in their early years in Parowan. Such faith could only help the fortunes of the settlements in the upcoming year. But the best demographic news was that there were now fifty-seven men over the age of sixteen to work on the ditch, more than ever before.

Right after the New Year, the ward enlarged its organizations just as it had enlarged its meetinghouse. The bishop instituted the Young Ladies' Mutual Improvement Organization under President Irene U. Haskell on January 3. It was the only major institution in the Church that Bluff had neglected, and now the ward, though it was still only half the size of the average ward, had every program in place.[69] They wanted to leave no cause, physical or spiritual, for failure in this pivotal year. It seemed to be working. Rain and snow descended in greater quantity than the colonists had seen before in the early months of the year. While this blocked their mail for a few weeks, it made "the ground ... sufficiently wet to bring up any kind of a crop."[70] The ditch looked good as well.

But then they had to use their new cemetery again. The previous spring the Rowleys lost their three-year-old boy, John Taylor Rowley, to a measles outbreak. Because of the wet weather then and the floods the

---

68. Platte Lyman had two wives, but it is uncertain if both lived in Bluff at this time. So by 1884, eight of Bluff's forty-three families (19 percent) practiced polygamy.

69. "Bluff Manuscript History," January 3, 1884.

70. Platte D. Lyman, "Diary," February 24, 1884.

Cottonwood caused, Samuel Rowley requested that he be permitted to bury his boy on a high hill overlooking the town, rather than in the sandy hills toward the wash where bodies were buried heretofore. The idea [129] made so much sense that the one very old and five very young bodies Bluff had lost so far were reinterred in the new cemetery along with young Brother Rowley.[71] Now in 1884, on January 10, as the cold wind whipped around them, the Nielsons and most of the town buried Joe and Ida's daughter, Jens' first grandchild for all of two weeks, in that hill. At the end of February, Kumen Jones's first child (by Lydia May, not Mary) followed, a few weeks short of surviving five months. Aside from dinners, holidays, and shows, the town also periodically assembled for that last walk up the hill.

In between these sad events, in early February, Jens accompanied Platte Lyman and Lemuel Redd as they slogged through muddy, unfinished roads ninety miles upriver to the Burnham Branch in New Mexico. President Lyman felt better on this trip. About a week before, he had received a letter from his brother Marion, explaining that the Church leadership as a body had taken no action on the mission. This confirmed that Erastus Snow's perceived swipe at Lyman's faith was his opinion only. But Marion also reported that the leadership was still divided: some felt the mission to be very important, but others, including President Taylor, "did not feel like requiring men to remain in any place they were not satisfied with."[72] After setting the branch in order, the three left "in a blinding snow storm" and endured "a bitter cold and disagreeable trip" home.[73] [130]

Deluge

The wet weather continued to portend great things for their crops until it overwhelmed them. By mid-March the San Juan had risen seven feet, washing away some stretches of the ditch while filling others with sand. Cottonwood Wash disgorged floods, which swept over the western side of the town. The torrent, as Platte Lyman described it,

> struck the southwest corner of the Fort, filling a number of houses with water and mud to the depth of 8 or 10 inches, and causing the

---

71. Albert R. Lyman, "History of San Juan County," 34; Rowley, Autobiography, 23.
72. Platte D. Lyman, "Diary," January 30, 1884.
73. Platte D. Lyman, "Diary," February 15, 1884.

inmates to move to higher ground. Cellars, pigpens, and chicken coops were flooded, and corn in the shock buried from 1 to 2 feet deep in mud, doing in this way hundreds of dollars damage, besides burying fences beyond the possibility of redemption, and covering a part of several of the best claims on the river 18 inches deep with worthless white sand.

Surveying such damage, some settlers were "a little discouraged by these misfortunes, but most of them seem as determined as ever to hold on until they conquer all the various obstacles to be met with in reclaiming this forbidding looking country."[74]

When the waters receded, the people plowed some deeper furrows down the wash to the San Juan, to try to keep the stream from spreading out over such a broad delta again.[75] Then they held their stake conference as scheduled on March 22 and 23. Some had started causing contention between those who favored leaving and the majority who still hoped to stay, and this dampened the spirit of the meetings. Again the leaders spoke on the most pressing themes: unity, cooperation, building up Zion. Someone spoke on "reclaiming the desert land" so soon after they were almost washed into the San Juan. [131] One anonymous Saint felt sunny enough to predict soon after the conference that "there has been some talk of this mission breaking up, but that time I think is past. The crisis is over and there will be enough people stay to make it a success with the help of the Lord."[76] But one ominous talk of the conference hit the heart of their situation more closely. Its theme was "preparing for the great events about to transpire."[77]

The weather was very unstable in April, "being warm and cold, wet and dry, windy and pleasant by spells." The Cottonwood continued to flood occasionally. But Bluff farmers were able to plant much earlier than ever before, putting in crops by the middle of the month.[78] Indian

---

74. Platte D. Lyman, "Diary," March 15, 1884.

75. Albert R. Lyman, "History of San Juan County," 38.

76. "Beams from Bluff City," *Deseret News*, April 23, 1884, 221, from a letter written by "a subscriber" on April 2, 1884.

77. For the stake conference see Platte D. Lyman, "Diary," March 22–23, 1884; Charles E. Walton, "San Juan Stake Conference," *Deseret News*, April 16, 1884, 207.

78. Platte D. Lyman, "Diary," April 12, 1884.

relations contorted to match the weather. On April 20, there was a major fracas at Mitchell's, killing at least one Navajo and wounding two more. The Saints in Montezuma, closer to the trouble, were especially concerned. Jane Allan was alone at the time with five children, but a Navajo, "Old Peejo," yelled at her from across the river to stay at home and they would not be harmed. Troops came out from Fort Lewis, and Navajos disappeared from Bluff for two weeks, pulling back at least two-days' ride from the San Juan until early May.[79] [132]

The waters kept coming.[80] The San Juan surpassed the Cottonwood in maliciousness by washing out a third headgate and the whole head of the ditch, even though the Bluff men had extended it another three-quarters of a mile upstream the past winter. By May 20, most of the settlers were nearly vanquished. If this was to be the year of decision, the San Juan country had failed them. But they still could not find it in themselves to pick up and abandon their mission. President Lyman, Bishop Nielson, and almost every other man in town signed a letter to President Taylor spelling out their difficulties, reminding him of their sacrifices, and asking permission to move elsewhere unless he could send them sufficient help. Regarding the river, they concluded, "Our experience has taught us that we cannot reckon with any certainty on what it may do."[81] Finally their will had been eroded away like the banks of the ditch, their troubles, like sediment, heaped too high. No one felt the tragedy more than Bishop Nielson, who had labored so hard on both the ditch and the ward's spirits. Jens and Elsie described in Danish the sad state of their fields, the hope of a harvest completely gone, in a letter to Katrine on May 28.[82] Still, Jens and many others would not leave until released

79. See Platte D. Lyman, "Diary," April 28 and May 4, 1884; Albert R. Lyman, "History of San Juan County," 38; Peterson, *Look to the Mountains*, 68.

80. See Aton, "River, the Ditch," for the theory that these heavy rains in 1883–84 were caused by the eruption of Krakatau in Indonesia and the El Niño effect that followed.

81. See Bluff Ward, letter to President John Taylor, May 19, 1884; Platte D. Lyman, Diary, May 20, 1884.

82. Katrine Jorgensen Nielson, letter to Jens and Elsie Nielson, June 9, 1884, 240. All that is known about the May 28 letter is what Katrine mentions about it in her reply. She mentions "When you get ready to leave there …" that they should write and let her know so she can clear the house. The "you" in the sentence is full

by the [133] same authority that called them: that of the Church's general leadership.[83]

While the ward awaited its answer from Church headquarters, the water kept coming. By June 8, the San Juan conquered William Hyde's vaunted water wheel and another one William Adams tried to set up near Bluff. The ditch was so broken that water could be kept in it only about one third of the time, and very few people aside from the bishop bothered to replant their crops. "Most of the people have their minds made up to move and are only waiting the answer of the Apostles."[84]

The fury of the season was still not spent. Rains in the night of June 14 caused the water to rise "two feet higher than we have ever known it before" and washed over even the eastern fields. This flood also delivered the mortal blow to the ditch, breaking so many banks and bringing in so much sand that "we have no idea of attempting to repair it and consequently will not raise a crop." Things were even worse upstream. Hyde's house and the fort at Montezuma were washed away entirely. The Allans were so swamped that one son, Robert, had to rescue the rest of his family in an iron-bottomed molasses boiler.[85] Only one house in Montezuma was left standing.[86] Mitchell's place, further upstream, was wiped out entirely. [134]

Katrine's reply came to Jens before the Church's did. She expressed sorrow for their devastated condition even though she had yet to find out the worst. "It would have been much better if you had left there

---

of possibilities. It could refer to Elsie and Julia, who came sometime in June or July to take care of her. But it could also mean the family, when they are forced to leave that area. Until more information comes to light, that "you" remains ambiguous.

83. A later example of this sort of thinking happened in 1886, when Erastus Snow visited Bluff and found Thales Haskell there without his family, who had moved to Manassa, Colorado. "Apostle Snow then asked why he was not with them to which Thales answered that until the same authority which had called him into the mission released him, he did not feel at liberty to leave the field." See Albert E. Smith, *Thales Hastings Haskell*, 51.

84. Platte D. Lyman, "Diary," June 8, 1884.

85. Platte D. Lyman, "Diary," June 18, 1884, Albert R. Lyman, "History of San Juan County," 41.

86. Sources disagree on whose house it was. Albert R. Lyman, "History of San Juan County," 41, said it was Harriman's; Adams, "Autobiography," 36, said it was Haskell's.

before you had everything destroyed." But this did not mean she simply wanted her husband back with her. She also thought some men should be called "with time on hand to help you out, so none of the folks there should have to leave. It is after all you folks there that have lost practically everything you own." Things looked good in Cedar City. With so much rain, the apple trees were full. Everyone there enjoyed reasonably good health, and they looked forward to Elsie's arrival in the next couple of months, even though she would probably be disappointed with the condition of her bees when she got there.[87] As promised, Elsie and Julia traveled to Cedar to help care for Katrine and the children sometime during the summer months.

As if to be sure the bag of misfortunes was completely emptied on the settlements, there was trouble with the Utes that summer as well. Reports came in from all over the county about conflicts that drove most whites from the range. These skirmishes climaxed in mid-July at a cleft called Soldier Crossing beyond White Canyon. A cowboy and a government scout riding with U.S. troops were shot in an ambush, and their ultimate pleadings were mockingly mimicked by Mancos Jim as they wasted away in the sun. The troops retreated, and the Indians passed the rest of the year subsisting on cattle that Bluff stockmen had taken up there earlier in the year.[88] [135]

Even in this dangerous atmosphere, Bluff settlers tried to scout for a better location. With few crops in the ground and all hope for the ditch abandoned, they had some time to do it. A committee was appointed to look at the prospects of irrigating a site near Yellow Jacket Springs to the east of the Blue Mountains. When they reported it would cost thirty thousand dollars to bring the water up, the plan was abandoned.[89]

Finally, on July 23, the answer they so desperately waited for arrived. In fact, two letters came, addressed to Bishop Nielson. The first was from the First Presidency of the Church. It urged "all who would to remain here and try and build up a place." The decision the Bluff residents hoped would be made by the Church leaders was put back on their shoulders. But another letter came from Erastus Snow informing

---

87. Katrine Jorgensen Nielson, letter to Jens and Elsie Nielson, June 9, 1884.

88. Platte D. Lyman, "Diary," July 7, 1884; McPherson and Hurst, "Fight at Soldier Crossing"; Peterson, *Look to the Mountains,* 69–70.

89. Albert R. Lyman, "History of San Juan County," 42.

them that he and Joseph F. Smith, second counselor to President Taylor, would arrive in Bluff August 3 to see the situation firsthand.

The letter from the First Presidency, aside from being addressed to Bishop Nielson instead of Platte Lyman, suggested that the bishop would make a good stake president. It almost assumed Lyman would not be there much longer. While President Lyman knew he did not enjoy the confidence of Erastus Snow, now it seemed his support from the First Presidency had drained as well.[90] At the time he did not know that someone or some group from Bluff had written to the First Presidency bringing charges against his handling of the stake. Whatever the specific counts against him, this letter gave the impression that President Lyman had little faith left in the place and was about [136] to leave. Those who received it assumed it was true, and therefore Church headquarters began to do their business through the next highest authority, the bishop, rather than through President Lyman. This sort of slight was mystifying and discouraging to Platte Lyman since he knew nothing about the letter and would not for more than a decade.[91]

Still, when the time came in early August, Lyman took Thales Haskell with him to meet the incoming authorities at Montezuma. But they did not come. A few days later, a letter arrived at Bluff, again addressed to Bishop Nielson, with the disheartening news that the pair could not

---

90. For the important points in the letters, see Platte D. Lyman, "Diary," July 23, 1884.

91. Albert R. Lyman, "Platte DeAlton Lyman," typescript, Utah State Historical Society, 43–44, is the only source for the existence of this letter, based on the little his father told him about it later on. Platte never told Albert who had sent the letter. "How much he concealed to keep me from being embittered against some of the men I loved, is but a guess not to be expressed here. I will say that for the brethren of Bluff, he always inspired me with love and confidence, and for the General Church Authorities, very great respect." It is impossible based on the sources I've found to either rule Jens Nielson in or out of those responsible for the letter. He certainly disagreed with President Lyman about the possibilities of the place, and since Church authorities assumed the facts in the letter were true, it must have come from a trusted source. But an underhanded protest like this seems contrary to the more open and regular way Bishop Nielson handled disputes with other authorities in his life. Albert Lyman wrote that his father did not find out about the letter until he was called as president of the European Mission fourteen years later. It seems strange that his half brother, Marion Lyman, an Apostle in the church, would not have informed him earlier if he knew about it.

come until late September. Again, the suspense was extended as the final verdict was delayed.[92] But the abandonment of Bluff appeared inevitable; its remaining residents grimly awaited only the official word to sever the last strand holding them there.

Depths

Under these circumstances, in the middle of August, the bishop himself started looking to transfer rather than abandon the mission altogether. He headed another [137] exploring expedition to the north. A Ute told them about a promising valley seventy-five miles away, northwest of the Blue Mountains. Bishop Nielson, Thales Haskell, and five others found a fine valley with two streams that could water up to twelve hundred acres, nearly twice what they had in Bluff. But the land was scattered in patches along more than fifteen miles of streambed. In the current climate of unrest with the Indians, settlers would be too isolated and exposed. Despite the valley's promises, the party had to conclude that the place was to them, at this time, unusable.[93] When the bishop returned, he found that twelve more men, "most of them with families," had pulled out of Bluff in his absence. Platte Lyman would not hold them to such a hard place, and he granted releases to those who requested them.[94] Despite the bishop's best efforts, the colony continued to wash out from under him.[95]

Jens may have been warned before the blow came. On August 27, a telegram arrived; Katrine was dead. By the time he knew, she had been gone for four days and buried for three. She had long been ill, but when Elsie and Julia returned from Cedar, probably a week or two before the telegram arrived, they reported Katrine to be in better shape. Her rheumatism continued to remorselessly contort her limbs, but she seemed to be out of immediate danger. With August, however, came pneumonia, and it took the life from her lungs in three weeks, too short a time for her husband to see her again, even if [138] he could have left the crisis in

---

92. Platte D. Lyman, "Diary," August 1–8, 1884.

93. Platte D. Lyman, "Diary," August 19, 1884; see also Albert R. Lyman, "Bishop Jens Nielson: The Old Wagon," 73.

94. Davis, Journal, 1884; Rowley, Autobiography, 23; Allred, "Life Sketch of Samuel William Mackelprang and Adelia Terry," 3.

95. Platte D. Lyman, "Diary," August 16, 1884.

Bluff. The Cedar Saints did what they could to make her comfortable in her last days. A Brother Urie wrote to Jens informing him of Katrine's serious illness, but the letter may not have arrived before the telegram. Two days after the news came, Joe took Elsie and Julia back to Cedar City so they could take care of Katrine's three young children.[96]

Meanwhile, the Bluff Ward continued to dissolve. Those who were still there prepared to go home as soon as the visiting Apostles released them.[97] They rounded up their livestock and sold whatever they could in Colorado. Bluff was about to become one of the many settlements founded on marginal resources that failed.[98] Ironically, it was an abundance of water that hastened its end.

In the middle of September, a band of Bluff refugees hauling pigs, chickens, and furniture to sell in Mancos met Apostles Snow and Smith, as well as Elder John Morgan, on their way to Bluff. When the Church authorities arrived in the sodden town, few were left to greet them. President Lyman and some others, not expecting the visitors until later, were a hundred miles away trying to round up their cattle and save them from the Utes. The visiting authorities held two days of meetings with the Saints who were still there. These gatherings, in the minds of many of the settlers, were to build up to the long-awaited [139] official release from their mission. At the very least, they thought, they would be relocated.[99]

Elders Snow, Smith, and Morgan sympathized with their situation and dispiriting struggles. But by Sunday night the Apostles felt "they did not think it was wisdom to evacuate this place and lose one foothold we had gained. It was contrary to the genius of the gospel to go backwards, so they called on all those that could muster faith enough to remain and try it a little longer." According to the public report, "a majority of the people

---

96. Brother Urie, letter to Jens Nielson, August 21, 1884; Letter to Jens Nielson, August 24, 1884; Platte D. Lyman, "Diary," August 27, 29, 1884; See also history of Butt, "Ane Katrine Jorgensen Nielson," 238; Platte D. Lyman, October 16, 1884.

97. Kumen Jones, "Writings," 161.

98. Rosenvall, "Defunct Mormon Settlements," analyzes the 69 of 497 Mormon settlements before 1900 that failed. Of these 69, 43 failed due to environmental factors. Flooding finished off 16 of these settlements, and 11 of the 69 failed between 1880 and 1889.

99. Kumen Jones, "Writings," 141.

responded, and are willing to labor where they can do the most good in building up the kingdom of God here." The Lord, they said, "inspires His servants and they can see through and beyond all the difficulties. They could see good, comfortable homes and orchards, the hill adorned with cattle, and above all, the gospel spread among the Lamanites, and the lost tribes of Israel redeemed."[100] But after this decision, the vote was not unanimous. They made a survey of who would stay and who would go. Joseph F. Smith blessed those who wanted to leave. Then he said, "I promise those who are willing to remain and face this difficult situation that they will be doubly blessed of the Lord." He turned to Bishop Nielson and told him directly, "For your obedient and steadfast response at this time, you shall be blessed and prospered of the Lord both in spiritual and temporal things."[101]

This was the way out of all his difficulties. It was not to abandon the hardships of [140] the mission. It was to hold to the course and be blessed by the priesthood leadership he had promised to obey. His finances were depleted. His ward was almost gone. He could not be with Katrine when she died. But he had done his best to fulfill his mission, and according to this apostolic utterance, it was enough. Platte Lyman, still out of town and out of the confidence of the Church leaders, was released, and Jens Nielson was set apart by Joseph F. Smith as the presiding bishop of the San Juan Mission.[102] Lyman was informed of the changes when he returned the next day.

---

100. The authorities quotes are from C. E. Walton, "Correspondence: Bluff City Not to Be Abandoned," *Deseret News,* October 4, 1884, in Journal History, September 24, 1884, 3.

101. Kumen Jones, "Writings," 142; Walton, Diary, 33. Erastus Snow, letter to John Taylor, September 19, 1884, put the proportion of those who decided to stay at half, "and the others hesitated."

102. "San Juan Stake Manuscript History," September 12, 1884, p. 1. This history mistakenly identifies September 12 and 13 as the dates of the conference. It was probably written awhile after the fact, unlike clerk Charles Walton's immediate report to the *Deseret News,* which set the dates of the conference at September 20 and 21. Jens Nielson's finances were certainly not thriving. Albert R. Lyman, "History of San Juan County," 43, reports hearsay that at the time the bishop could not have settled his debts if pressed for a quick payment. In Katrine's last letter, she was concerned that Jens not go into too much debt over the flood, since it was hard to get money in Cedar that year. The Cedar property, farm, and stock seemed to be

The visit of the Apostles did not end the exodus from Bluff. Those who wanted to leave had been blessed, and many kept on going. September and October saw the departures of the Woods, Baileys, Rowleys, Mackelprangs, Paces, F. I. Joneses, Ben Perkinses, Bayleses, and even the Harrimans, who had lived in Montezuma since 1879 and left behind the graves of two of their children.[103] Platte Lyman remained disappointed in his position. He knew his release was less honorable than he deserved, but felt his own inclinations about this place and the summary way he was dispensed with left him little choice. So he sold his stock and loaded up his family and belongings.[104] [141] On his last night in Bluff he "attended a party in the evening got up as a farewell to me. Did not enjoy myself."[105] He rolled out the next morning, and on his way back to Oak City, took note of the appearance of prosperity evident in every settlement he passed, "in marked contrast to [the] affair on the San Juan."[106]

Those who left felt they had little choice. They were generally the settlers with the largest, youngest families. The average emigrant was almost five years younger than the typical settler who was staying. The average family that was leaving had almost twice as many children under

---

doing well by her account. But Jens had lost a lot in the form of destroyed fields and crops, as well as equity in the decimated ditch. He may still have been in the black overall, but financially speaking, it was not a comfortable position for a man over sixty to be in.

103. See the appendix for a complete list of the families who left in 1884 and where they went.

104. Platte D. Lyman, "Diary," September 22, 1884.

105. Platte D. Lyman, "Diary," October 8, 1884, 316. Platte Lyman later told his son regarding his decision to leave Bluff that "he blamed himself, said it was the mistake of his life and that he had regretted it ever since it happened." See Albert R. Lyman, "Platte DeAlton Lyman," 44.

106. Platte D. Lyman, "Diary," November 2, 1884. Erastus Snow continued to draw a sharp distinction between what he saw as the pessimism of President Lyman and the energy of Bishop Nielson. In Erastus Snow, letter to John Taylor, September 19, 1884, he blamed Lyman for telling the settlements in 1883 that the San Juan would be evacuated, discouraging them from planting in the fall, and preparing to leave the settlement, seemingly with no regard for what the authorities directed. He praised Bishop Nielson, on the other hand, for putting in crops and continuing to believe the ditch could be repaired. As already explained, Platte Lyman's journal and other sources tell a more complex story.

fifteen as those who were staying, and they were much less likely to be in a polygamous family. Unsurprisingly, they were less prosperous, judging by how much they held in the co-op store: the emigrants owned only three-fifths as much as the others. They had labored on the ditch and left their families vulnerable enough to satisfy the demands of any reasonable mission. Nature had demonstrated to their satisfaction that the future of their families resided elsewhere. They scattered to various places. Some of them pushed on to new settlements in Arizona, New Mexico, and Colorado. Many took the Denver and Rio Grande out of Durango to recent settlements in Castle [142] Valley, Utah. And quite a few returned to the places they once again considered home.[107] By and large they had not lost their faith in the teachings of their Church, but they had lost their faith in the future of Bluff.

The pioneers at Bluff made some terrible mistakes in attempting to impose an independent agricultural community on the San Juan shore, but that is what their collective experience and instructions required them to do. They had more than paid for these geographic errors in toil and anguish. And now some were ready to try it again. Only eighteen families remained as winter arrived, but they were rooted to that spot. In 1884, Bishop Nielson began to remark that he had moved six times since arriving in Utah. "When I move from here," he would say, signaling towards the cemetery, "I expect to move to the hill."[108] [143]

---

107. For all of these characteristics of the emigrants compared with those who stayed, see the appendix. Of the 173 who left, 44 (25 percent) went on to settlements in Colorado, Arizona, and New Mexico; 38 (22 percent) went to Castle Valley, 29 (17 percent) went to other settlements in Utah that were not their previous home, and 62 (35 percent) returned to their previous home towns in Utah (the sum of the percentages is over 100 percent due to rounding).

108. Albert R. Lyman, "History of San Juan County," 44.

Revival, 1885–1886

Resuscitation

Remnants

Few Saints assembled in Bluff's log schoolhouse for their December conference in 1884. Out of the 245 who were in the Montezuma and Bluff settlements when the year started, only 79 remained. The bishop's family, along with those of his counselors, were there. William Adams' and Father John Allan's families stayed, and so did those of the Barton, Butt, and Decker brothers. The families of Thales Haskell, Hyrum Perkins, Joe Nielson, William Hyde's first wife, Angeline, and Charles Walton rounded out the entire list of the survivors. The town was much quieter than before. There were fewer than two dozen children under ten; a house with two children in it held more than most. The typical settler was almost twenty-two, about normal for Utah Territory, but unusually old for Bluff. Almost half now lived in polygamous families. About one in seven of the residents still had been born in foreign countries: the town's remaining children could marvel at William Adams' Irish lilt or the Allans' Scottish brogue. Almost all of the Saints born in England had left, however, and the Nielsons were the lone remaining Danes.[1]

Bishop Nielson was the presiding authority on the stand as these relatively few [145] Saints assembled for their December conference. In the

---

1. See the appendix for a statistical comparison between those who left and those who stayed.

way of good news, Thales Haskell reported that the Indians were causing the settlers less trouble. In fact, they hadn't raided the stock at all that
season.[2] But as the members of the Bluff Ward left the conference, they
saw most of the homes empty, most of the yards and fields untended.

There were two dozen men and older boys to repair the washed-out
ditch, less than half the number they had amid the optimism of the previous winter. But as the bishop and others surveyed the wreckage, they
found the damage was less than they had expected. Repairs to the ditch
would take months of labor, but they could be made by extending the
head two more miles upstream. They also hoped to dig the channel two
or three feet deeper than needed to allow sediment to settle. When the
ditch was nearly full, they could cut open a bank and let the sediment
sluice back into the river. The men set to work, hoping once again for
fresh settlers to reinforce them. They received encouraging letters from
some who had left in the fall that they intended to return once the high
snows in the mountains had melted. But many of the others who had
left spread discouraging words about the prospects on the San Juan.[3]

Most importantly, however, the Church was going to help. The General
Authorities called a new stake president, Francis Asbury Hammond, to
replace Platte Lyman. Those in Bluff hoped President Hammond, from
Huntsville in northern Utah, would bring many new settlers when he
came. He tried to visit Bluff in December, but [146] the high snows did
not let him get much closer than the end of the railroad line in Durango.[4]

Stymied by the season from visiting personally, Hammond began
corresponding with Bishop Nielson. He fired off a series of questions
about prospects and practices in Bluff. He reassured the settlers that
there was no longer ambivalence about the mission among the leaders
of the Church, who were

> determined to strengthen your hands, and hold that mission from
> going into the hands of our enemies, and it is designed to call

---

2. "San Juan Stake Manuscript History," December 21, 1884; Jens Nielson, "The
San Juan Country," *Deseret News*, February 18, 1885, 69.

3. Nielson, "San Juan Country," 69; Hammond, Journal, May 9, 1885.

4. See entries in Hammond, Journal, for late December 1884. His journal entry
for March 24, 1885, recollects that he was called by the First Presidency to be stake
president in October 1884, not long after Platte Lyman was released.

from 40 to 50 families to accompany me to settle in that vicinity....
I am told by the Presidency and Twelve that "that mission cannot
be given up, but must be held and maintained as an important
foothold in relation to our labors with our Lamanite brethren."

President Taylor himself emphasized the importance of the Indians:
"'We cannot afford to desert them for if we do they will lose confidence
in us.'"[5]

The bishop wrote at least two buoyant letters to President Hammond,
full of possibilities wrapped in his usual enthusiasm. "Our prospects for
raising a crop have never been better since we came here." There had
been a lot of rain, the stock was good, and the residents of Bluff expected
to have the ditch done by the end of February. There was an "excellent
spirit" among the people, kept up by entertainments and theaters put on
by the youth associations. Even if reinforcements did not come, Bluff's
citizens felt confident that soon they would have enough by themselves,
"for though our field crops have failed us, 'Utah's Best Crop' never has,
and some of the sisters have produced three [147] full crops in less than
five years, which fact removes all doubts or fears about this not being a
fruitful country."[6]

The settlers knew by now that they could not become a completely
independent agricultural village. The bishop related that they were contemplating a number of "home industries" that would make them more
self-sustaining. They had already shown they could make molasses from
sorghum cane. A dairy would be profitable, and the prospects for one
looked good. The town needed a sawmill and gristmill, since there were
none within a hundred miles. They had about five hundred head of cattle,
but they were thinking of exchanging some of these for sheep. Fruit trees
would do well if transported correctly.[7] But the previous years proved
they could not grow enough grain for themselves, and if they could not
do that, they must depend on trade with Colorado Gentiles to survive.

---

5. Francis A. Hammond, letter to Bishop Jens Nielson, January 27, 1885.

6. Jens Nielson, "San Juan Country," 69.

7. See Journal History, February 28, March 13, and March 26, 1885, which cites
the other letter written from Jens Nielson to Francis A. Hammond, February 28,
1885. Parts of the letter were published in *Ogden Herald*, March 3, 1885, and *Deseret
News*, March 27, 1885.

President Hammond urged them to grow corn, beans, and sweet potatoes for the market in Durango. This permanent reliance on outsiders
was a blow to the town's ideal, but the mission itself was more important
than the methods. By the spring the settlers could look forward to a
vigorous new leader and the promised host of new settlers. The mission,
however modified, would survive.

In the meantime, Bluff's ward members did their best to continue
to carry out the full program of the Church with depleted numbers.
The Nielson women began to fill in the ranks of leadership in the ward.
When the Relief Society held its conference in April, [148] Kirsten was on
the stand as a counselor to President Jane Walton. Mary and Margaret
were working with the Young Women's Association. Elsie and Julia had
stayed in Cedar City with Katrine's three children, but they prepared
to sell the home and reunite the family in Bluff after the next growing
season.

Whirlwind

In early May, just as the spring surges began to burst the banks of the
ditch, Francis Hammond arrived to reconnoiter. Five dismayed men in
his expedition had turned around before they had gotten close to Bluff,
but others, including one of Hammond's sons and two of his sons-in-law,
pushed through with him. The new stake president brought news that
Church leadership had plans to call as many as seventy more families,
from all the stakes of Zion, to strengthen the San Juan Stake.

President Hammond lodged near Bishop Nielson's house, and soon
the two patriarchs exchanged their stories. As they inspected the seven-
mile ditch, the bishop and others recited what it had cost to hold this
place, and while President Hammond was feasted by almost every family in town, he told the experiences he had packed into his sixty-three
years.[8] His adventurous life, like that of the bishop, had started near the
sea. In fact, the ocean drew him away from his father's tannery on Long
Island when he was fourteen, and young Francis circled the globe as a

---

8. Francis A. Hammond, "Colorado River to San Juan," *Deseret News*, June 10,
1885, 335; see also Hammond, Journal, May 11, 1885, when he visited around town
and was, in the preceding days, "fed by Adams, Waldron [Walton], Haskell, Allan,
Perkins, & Bishop." He was impressed enough by the fare to report the dinners were
put on as well as "we could have done it in Huntsville in our palmiest days."

cook, cabin boy, and sailor. But somewhere in the Arctic Ocean, a falling
barrel almost broke his back, and the invalid [149] was later set ashore in
Hawaii. After a surprising recovery, Francis Hammond made his way
to San Francisco just in time to meet Mormons from the ship *Brooklyn*
departing overland for Utah. He was quickly converted to their faith and
joined the thinning stream of pioneers that trickled past the gold fields at
Mormon Island in late 1848. Upon arriving in Utah, he threw himself to
work in the Church with the same enthusiasm he had applied to everything. In the next thirty-five years he served three missions, married
three wives, and served in a continuous chain of callings, most recently
as bishop in Huntsville. During the winter of 1883 and 1884, he and his
oldest son Samuel traversed the southwestern states, looking for a good
place to establish a large cattle ranch. Not long afterward, Hammond
was called, at the age of sixty-two, to relocate his enormous energy and
experience to Bluff.[9]

That energy was apparent as soon as President Hammond arrived. He
immediately announced that he was impressed with the "most excellent
spirit" of the people at Bluff and was "well pleased with the bishop and
people of this stake."[10] Then he launched into perpetual motion. In two
weeks he cleared and planted his lot and also sowed some concerns in his
mind about the ditch.[11] With a half dozen other men, he explored the
land to the north for the next two weeks, looking for resources, including
"stock, dairy, and farming facilities, timber, water, power, etc. etc."[12] He
found just what [150] he was looking for: "saw nothing but a first class
country for stock range for summer, and it [is] connected with a good
winter range; the whole country is well-watered for stock purposes."[13]
Elk Mountain looked especially promising, though the Indians they met
there "did not like to have any white men intrude upon them."[14] Neither
did the ranchers in the area, and President Hammond felt that the residents of Bluff would have to act swiftly to secure this outstanding range.
Establishing a base closer to this pasture would help, and the expedition

---

9. See Adamson, *Francis Asbury Hammond*, for details on President Hammond's life.
10. Hammond, Journal, May 10, 1885; Hammond, "Colorado River to San Juan," 335.
11. Hammond, Journal, May 12–May 24, 1885.
12. Hammond, Journal, May 25, 1885.
13. Hammond, Journal, May 28, 1885.
14. *Ogden Herald*, June 22, 1885, in Journal History, June 4, 1885.

found good spots for settlements. White Mesa was "a fine place for a city and farms" once the water from nearby creeks could be brought onto it.[15]

President Hammond quickly started carrying out his plans. He and a few others almost immediately returned to White Mesa in mid-June to further study raising the water, and they dedicated that site "for the use of the Saints."[16] A week after they returned, it was time for stake conference, which was also an opportunity to begin wooing the Indians for the cattle lands Hammond's party had just explored. About a hundred Navajos, Utes, and Paiutes came to feast and receive presents of "bread, coffee, beef, molasses, etc."[17] Many stayed to hear Bishop Nielson report the progress of the Bluff Ward, then listened to President Hammond expound on his plans for the future. "The Lord had sent us here to do them good and not to steal their land or to take away any of [151] their rights but to teach them to work and be honest and live in peace."[18] Within a few weeks, a Ute chief accepted Bluff's purchase of the rights to the land from Elk Mountain to the Colorado River.[19] Whether the Utes agreed out of genuine friendship or a wary calculation that Mormons were safer than Gentiles, this agreement was a significant diplomatic victory for the new stake president.

The spirituality of the San Juan Stake was reinvigorated at the same time as its temporal prospects were revived. For the first time the stake president had counselors: William Halls, a resident of Mancos, Colorado, and William Adams. All the stake organizations were staffed at this conference, mostly with Bluff residents. Home missionaries, including Joe Nielson, were called to travel around the stake and exhort the Saints to do their duty. During the conference, Bishop Nielson reviewed the history of the mission. Out of the roughly 150 men who had been called to the San Juan, only about 25 had stuck to it, verifying the words, in the bishop's view, "Many are called but few are chosen." But now the future looked bright. Stock raising would be important, but the bishop

---

15. Hammond, Journal, June 3, 1885.

16. Hammond, Journal, June 8–June 12, 1885.

17. Hammond, Journal, June 20, 1885.

18. Hammond, Journal, June 20, 1885.

19. Francis A. Hammond, "More of the San Juan," *Deseret News*, August 26, 1885, in Journal History, August 26, 1885, 3.

reminded the Saints they should not be reckless but rather take care "of that which the Lord had made us stewards over."[20]

Soon after the conference ended, President Hammond rode the three-hundred-mile circuit around the stake, visiting Burnham, New Mexico, and the new branch in Mancos, Colorado, that Elders Snow, Smith, and Morgan had organized on their way to Bluff the [152] previous year. Hammond even finished his initiation in San Juan County by arguing with the Mitchells at McElmo on his way back to Bluff.[21] Within a week he was en route to Huntsville once more so he could pack up his whole household and return to Bluff by Christmas. In the few stationary days before he departed, President Hammond experimented with tanning goatskins by using the extract of local brush and persuaded the board of the Bluff Co-op to finish financing a gristmill on which he had put down money in Mancos. He also encouraged the board to follow up on the negotiations started with the Indians over Elk Mountain. On the whole the Indians felt "first rate towards us," Hammond thought, but "they want some ponies for their good will."[22] When President Hammond left in early July, Bluff men were already working on a road to Elk Mountain and preparing to return to White Mesa to dig irrigation ditches up there.

Even away from Bluff, Francis Hammond continued to zestfully boost the region. To counter the negative reports that disgruntled ex-settlers had circulated, he maintained a letter-writing campaign to the *Deseret News* and other papers that was remarkable for its frequency and optimism. He meticulously kept the public posted on his travels, activities, and the advantages of the San Juan region. One of his reports was so enthusiastic that the editors of the paper tacked on the subtitle, "The San Juan Country Proves to Be a Genuine El Dorado," something that would never have been inferred from the more measured reports of Platte Lyman.[23] According to Hammond, the place needed hundreds [153] more people and had only half the stock it could contain, and Jens Nielson "is a fine old gentleman, a father indeed to his people, and

---

20. Charles E. Walton, "San Juan Stake Conference," *Deseret News*, July 15, 1885, 415.

21. Hammond, Journal, July 8, 1885.

22. Hammond, Journal, July 9, 1885.

23. Francis A. Hammond, "A Fine Country," *Ogden Herald*, June 22, 1885, in Journal History, June 4, 1885.

much beloved by the Saints of his ward." The people themselves were "a first-class lot of Latter-day Saints, fully devoted to their mission."[24] With sufficient reinforcements, they would be "salt to save the country."[25]

But Hammond was not satisfied lobbying the public at large. He also tried to influence authorities. He regularly requested money from the Utah legislature, usually for roads to get people into and products out of San Juan County.[26] It did not hurt that his nephew, W. W. Riter, had become Speaker of the House. Hammond also peppered the First Presidency of the Church with so many requests for settlers that by January 1886 they reminded him, "It is best not to become too eager, and to run faster than our strength will allow."[27] The stake president tried to get a miller called to Mancos and looked into importing blacksmiths from the Southern States Mission.[28] Some of his lobbying was effective. The First Presidency wrote to various stake presidents to recruit settlers and asked Wilford Woodruff, President of the Quorum of the Twelve, to have the Apostles speak with the Saints about the San Juan Mission as they traveled around the stakes of the [154] Church.[29]

President Hammond was everything the people of Bluff could ask for and more. He flung his whole soul into the stake and had the connections and vivacity to move its cause forward. In many ways he was like the bishop, which may have created a problem. Bishop Nielson had previously rallied his ward and accomplished his plans "mostly by the force of his strong personality."[30] And now President Hammond, in his tour de force, was doing the same. The new stake president's presence in the county was at least as large as it was in the typical Church meeting, in which he always spoke once and sometimes twice, his remarks often extending over an hour.

---

24. Hammond, "More of the San Juan," 3.

25. Hammond, Journal, December 13, 1885.

26. Francis A. Hammond, "From Here to San Juan," *Deseret News*, January 6, 1886, 814.

27. John Taylor and George Q. Cannon, letter to Francis A. Hammond, January 14, 1886.

28. John Morgan, letter to Francis A. Hammond, February 13, 1886.

29. John Taylor and George Q. Cannon, letters to Francis A. Hammond, September 7 and December 8, 1885.

30. Kumen Jones, "Bishop Jens Nielson Sketch," 21.

The bishop and the stake president agreed on the large principles of the Church and its settlement program. But Bishop Nielson had his reservations about some of President Hammond's particulars, and he drew the line when it came to buying the Mancos Mill. According to President Hammond's recollections of the meeting in which he proposed the venture, "All seemed to favor the matter except Bishop Nielson."[31] The bishop may have thought the investment too risky since the co-op had such limited capital after the floods. He probably disliked the regional approach that came with running a mill in Mancos instead of constructing one in Bluff. Perhaps he resented someone so new taking such decisive action. Whatever the reason, the bishop was unable to persuade a [155] majority of the co-op to vote against it, and the deal went through.[32]

On the whole, though, as the summer days waned the Saints in Bluff felt blessed. With the short manpower they had it seemed miraculous that they brought in a crop. By the time they assembled for conference in early fall, they celebrated a "bountiful harvest," making "the people feel quite encouraged." Their improved log houses and the tracks they continued to beat through the weeds began to look almost like a small village again, and some orchards began to bear fruit. For the first time, the smell of drying peaches competed with that of ripe watermelons in August and September.[33]

When President Hammond returned in early December, he brought thirty-two people and five hundred head of cattle with him.[34] He had been elected a selectman of the county while he was gone and was soon put on the board of directors for the Mancos grist- and sawmills.[35] Even

---

31. Hammond, Journal, July 8–July 9, 1885.

32. The bishop or some others in Bluff might have previously expressed concerns about some of President Hammond's regional plans. When the Hammond group of explorers was about to return to Bluff on June 3, 1885, they held a small meeting in which Hammond "gave some advice as to how we should report our trip." See Hammond, Journal, June 3, 1885.

33. See "Bluff Ward Manuscript History," 1885, and Charles E. Walton, "Quarterly Conference of the San Juan Stake," *Deseret News*, October 7, 1885, 596. The conference was held September 19 and 20, 1885.

34. Francis A. Hammond, letter to *Deseret News*, December 2, 1885, 723. The letter was written November 8, 1885, as he was making his way through Emery County back toward Huntsville.

35. Hammond, Journal, December 8 and 12, 1885.

though the number of new settlers was not as high as promised, falling far short of the 134 families that Church leaders had assessed to the various stakes, thirty new settlers meant there would be more hands to work on the ditch and help hold Bluff that winter.[36] [156]

Reunion

The Nielsons had particularly strong reasons to rejoice as they approached the end of 1885. A week before Christmas, Jens Peter brought Elsie and Julia, along with Katrine's three children, back from Cedar City to live in Bluff for good.[37] The trip was wet, cold, and rough, but Elsie assured the rest of the company they should be thankful their current struggles were not as difficult as those of "the old handcarters." She had to be carried across the Dirty Devil River on Jens Peter's back when she refused to ride a horse, but in the opinion of a fellow traveler, "Sister Nielson stands the rough and heavy roads better than any of us."[38]

Katrine's children had grown considerably since Jens last saw them: Annetta was ten, Uriah was eight, and Freeman six. "Aunt Elsie" was raising them as her own, and Uriah felt she "was the best woman in the world because she ... let him take a cat to bed with him."[39] Elsie was unpretentious and industrious, soon making herself popular with neighborhood boys by sewing buckskin covers on their baseballs when she was not making gloves or tending her beehives and silkworms.[40] And during the winter, another son joined the family. Julia married Willard Butt in the St. George Temple, doing San [157] Juan County the service of ridding it of its oldest remaining bachelor.[41]

------

36. See note inserted into "San Juan Stake Manuscript History," 1885, after page 33 for the assessment on the stakes.

37. Ellertson and Ellertson, "Julia Ann Nielson and Willard (Dick) Butt," 133. The journal Lyman referred to is most likely that of Jody Wood, who kept a detailed account of her two trips to Bluff.

38. Wood, Journal, November 24, December 4 and 14, 1885, 325, 328, and 330.

39. "Short History of Elsie Rasmussen Nielson," 83.

40. "Short History of Elsie Rasmussen Nielson," 79; Meo, "Uriah and Annie Butt Talk about Elsie Rasmussen," 82.

41. Hammond, Journal, December 18, 1885, and Ellertson and Ellertson, "Julia Ann Nielson and Willard (Dick) Butt," 133. Willard Butt was twenty-seven at the time. Julia, Jens and Elsie's second daughter, was twenty-three.

More old friends came back as well. The Baileys and Bayleses had already returned from Cedar City, while Sam and Josephine Wood, along with Sam's new wife Emma, came in with the Nielsons. Bluff's population had doubled since the year before, when not quite eighty remaining residents hoped they could save the mission. Now, the refreshed ward members spruced up the meetinghouse with a new roof and floor before the December conference and anticipated what was to come.

Cattle Country

Holding Their Own

What came in herds to San Juan County were many more four-legged residents. Before Bluff was founded, the area attracted those who had hoped to make themselves rich off livestock. In 1883, around fifteen thousand head of cattle roamed San Juan County, driven in by cowboys such as Tom Ray, "Spud" Hudson, and Preston Nutter. By 1885, however, bigger money was attracted to such profits, and most of the individual cattlemen had been bought out by larger companies. The Pittsburgh Cattle Company ascended the south slopes of the La Sal Mountains, the Kansas and New Mexico Land and Cattle Company, better known as the Carlisles after the English brothers who financed the operation, occupied the north and east drainages of the Blue Mountains, while the Widow Lacy moved her LC Company cattle onto the range near South Montezuma Creek. The Carlisles alone drove eleven thousand head to market in 1884 and branded fifty-three hundred calves the next [158] year.[42]

The Mormons had recognized the potential of the range around them since they arrived. While traveling from Moab to Bluff in September 1880, Platte Lyman's brother Marion reported, "The road lies through the finest range for cattle that I have seen for many years."[43] Francis Hammond's observations in mid-1885 were at least as enthusiastic.[44] But he also felt they had to act fast to secure this livelihood. Just as the Bluff Saints had been

---

42. See Peterson, *Look to the Mountains*, 80–85; Jensen, "Historical Study of Bluff City," 58–59; and Walker, "Carlisles," 269–72.

43. Francis Marion Lyman, "On the Way: The Trip to San Juan," *Deseret News*, September 29, 1880, 558–59.

44. Hammond, Journal, June 1, 1885.

sent to occupy San Juan County in order to hold it against Gentiles, now
they were impelled to hold its ranges against gentile cattle. Their mission
gave the settlers a strong sense of entitlement. At one point toward the end
of his exploring trip the previous summer, President Hammond and those
accompanying him paused while traversing the pass between Elk Mountain and the Blues to enjoy the "magnificent view." Inspired, the group

> sang a hymn and prayed and dedicated the park, the mountain, the
> vales, the water, the grass, the rocks and all the materials in the
> region round about to the Lord our God, and blessed it in the name
> of the Lord Jesus for the use and benefit of his saints, [that] they
> may secure it and hold it forever. It is a very desirable place for
> stock, and we heard that gentiles have their mind upon it, and [are]
> preparing to stock it.[45]

In a similar manner, the Saints worried about holding "our range" against
Navajo herders, [159] who brought their flocks of sheep and goats across
the San Juan River, as well as cattle companies and cowboys, alternately
called "our enemies," "outsiders," and "strangers."[46]

By the end of 1885 the residents of Bluff had already begun to stock
the range themselves. Soon after President Hammond's five hundred
Durhams arrived with him in early December, Jens Nielson's five hundred cattle came from Cedar City with his transplanted family members.[47] Others, such as Lemuel Redd and Kumen Jones, made plans to
buy more cattle in Utah. President Hammond appealed to his friends
and to the Saints in general to come and help them stock up the range
to secure it "from falling into the hands of cattle king monopolists."[48]

Francis Hammond had met the two largest "cattle kings," Edmund
and Harold Carlisle, a few times already, and on the surface their relations were cordial. One of the brothers called on the Mormons' White

---

45. Hammond, Journal, June 1, 1885.

46. Hammond, Journal, January 27, February 26, March 9, March 21, November
20, December 4, and December 17, 1886; George Q. Cannon, letter to Francis A.
Hammond, January 1, 1887.

47. See Francis A. Hammond, "Arrived," *Ogden Herald*, January 8, 1886, in Journal
History, January 8, 1886, 13; Kimmerle, "Visit with Aunt Caroline Nielson Redd," 235.

48. Hammond, Journal, February 11, 1886; Francis A. Hammond, letter to
Deseret News, October 28, 1885, 649.

Mesa camp in June 1885. Francis Hammond remarked that "He is our friend [and] told me he was making a shelter for one of our brethren who are now hiding up from persecution. May the Lord bless him for his kindness to our people. He seems like a fine, liberal English jolly gentleman."[49] The Carlisles returned the compliments, expressing their preference for Mormons as [160] neighbors, since they always returned strays.[50] The "outside" cattle companies employed some of Bluff's young men, such as Jens Peter Nielson, and provided a closer market than Colorado for Bluff's trade.[51] But both sides also moved to secure as much of the range as they could hold and perhaps more. Bluff's White Mesa expedition was trying to establish an advanced outpost against the Carlisles' expansion, while the "cattle kings" attempted to control "36,000 acres of the best cattle range" by digging small irrigation ditches all along the South Montezuma and claiming 640 acres around each trickle.[52]

The Mormons in Bluff felt they were moving just in time by the winter of 1885–86, because they were under siege from a number of other parties as well. Just as the Hammond and Nielson herds arrived in December, ten thousand "outside" sheep were set to graze on the Recapture Wash, which the Bluff residents hoped to use as a winter range. Early the next year, the LC Cattle Company turned a few hundred head loose, and even talked of stocking Elk Mountain. A cowboy named Wilson, then a pair named Eliot and Matthews stopped by Bluff, also on their way to scout Elk Mountain. This was especially threatening since the Mormons felt they had bought rights to this area from the Indians and were counting on it as their summer range. As with the cattle companies, the leaders in Bluff were hospitable to these interlopers, providing lodging and guides for them, but at the same time they developed plans to compete against them. It appeared providential when the cowboys' plans changed. On April 6, 1886, President Hammond reported that [161] Elliot and Matthews "did not think very much of the country. We are pleased that they did not."[53]

---

49. Hammond, Journal, June 12, 1885.

50. Hammond, "More of the San Juan," 3.

51. See Hammond, Journal, July 14, 1885, for Jens Peter's employment building fences for the Carlisles and Nephi Bailey engaging in trade with the cowboys.

52. Hammond, Journal, June 1, 1885.

53. Hammond, Journal, April 6, 1886.

Varmints

The competition continued throughout 1886. Early in the year, the Mormons maintained two armed guards along the eastern rim of White Mesa to be sure they held their ground, though no violence came of it.[54] The Carlisles, through their half-brother foreman, William E. "Latigo" Gordon, continued to claim and fence large portions of the county themselves. By September the range showed signs of wear from being overstocked. Bluff residents resented further incursions by LC Company cattle and also by tens of thousands of sheep "on what we consider our range" later in the year.[55] When Lemuel Redd brought in a herd of cattle at the end of 1886 he brought the town's total to about two thousand head. That was still only a tenth of what the Carlisles ran, but it was enough to occupy important rangeland in the county just in time.[56]

The spring of 1886 also reminded them what kinds of characters outside cattle outfits brought in with them. A pair of "suspicious-looking cowboys" left Bluff without paying for their lodging on Monday, May 31. Soon after, Bill Ball, foreman at the LC [162] Cattle Company up Montezuma Canyon about forty-five miles away, came through looking for the same men. He told a similar story: the pair had stayed with his camp during the winter months and had abused his hospitality by making off with a few of his best horses. A posse of at least a half dozen Bluff men went out with Ball after the bandits. A week later they returned without the fugitives but with a tragic story. They had found the thieves at Navajo Springs in Comb Wash and hoped to shout at them to surrender, being ready to shoot if they would not. But Ball wanted to have a better chance to reason with his former guests and divided up the posse to head them off. Mr. Ball, a decent man by all accounts, was instead ambushed

---

54. See Hammond, Journal, January 19, 1886.

55. Hammond, Journal, December 4, 1886.

56. See Hammond, Journal, December 10, 1886. The 1880s were remarkable in Utah Territory and San Juan County for the increase in the number of cattle. In 1880, Utah had .92 head of cattle per human; by 1890 the ratio rose to 1.32. In San Juan County, the number skyrocketed from 1.3 head per human to 47 in the same decade (from 267 non-milch and non-working cattle to 17,100). Don Walker concluded that never again would "so few people live with so many cattle." See Walker, "Cattle Industry of Utah," 189–190.

and shot, stripped of his spurs and guns, and left to die in the shade of a cedar. He survived a couple more hours then was buried in a sandy grave by the trail.[57]

The Bluff posse felt bad about the killing of a good man like Ball. But they also felt it was suicide to continue pursuing such bloodthirsty men through the "outlaw's paradise" that surrounded them, especially after James Decker's horse was shot out from under him. As President Hammond wrote, "We feel to acknowledge the hand of the Lord in the preservation of our brethren."[58] Justice in general was an important concept in [163] Bluff, but not as important as the welfare of the town itself. Even though a constable resided in Bluff, after the first foray he was willing to let the killers go.[59] But Ball's friends felt the loss more personally. Three weeks after the shooting, a posse of about twenty cowboys arrived in Bluff and took Kumen Jones and Amasa Barton as guides to pick up the trail of the murderers. As so often happened, the outlaws got away cleanly, their trail dissolving somewhere into the Utah settlements. Ball was reburied in the Bluff cemetery months later. People in Bluff found a number of cowboys, like Ball, whom they could respect. But they also found quite a few of another stripe.[60]

---

57. This story has been told many times. The only contemporary mention of it is in Hammond, Journal, May 31 to June 8, 1886. Kumen Jones retold the stories years later in Kumen Jones, "Writings," 207–10. Jones was a member of the posse, but disagreed in some particulars with Hammond's account, raising the question of whether to trust the person who was geographically or chronologically closer to the event. I have voted mostly for chronological proximity by following Hammond's entries. Albert R. Lyman wrote versions of this story in his "History of San Juan County," 46, and *Indians and Outlaws*, 75–78, which add a few more details inconsistent with the Hammond account. Austin and McPherson's account in "Murder, Mayhem, and Mormons," 43–44, closely followed Lyman's versions. James Decker was later reimbursed fifty dollars by the county court for his deceased mare (though he thought it was worth a hundred dollars). See Hammond, Journal, December 8, 1886, and San Juan County Minute Book, December 8, 1886.

58. Hammond, Journal, June 8, 1886.

59. The constable at the time was F. I. Jones. See San Juan County Minute Book, March 31, 1886.

60. See Kumen Jones, "Writings," 217, for Kumen Jones' positive appraisal of many of the early cowboys.

Town Values

This murder highlighted one of the important advantages the Mormons had in their competition against the Gentiles for the range. Instead of approaching the business as independent capitalists, they entered as a cooperating community. While the cattle companies competed exclusively for profits, the Mormons, while not opposed to financial gain, were primarily hoping to find a way to subsist in the county and fulfill their mission. As Elizabeth Kane put it in her tour through Utah years before, "Their ethics teach them simply to provide each settlement with some industry which shall make it self-supporting."[61] The farming ideal had failed, and now Bluff's residents increasingly hoped that livestock would allow them to stay to accomplish their larger purposes. The [164] importance of their mission along with their permanent residence in the county gave them their strong sense of entitlement to surrounding lands, even though legally the range was open to anyone.[62] Furthermore, the Mormons did not have camps, but rather a town. They had families with them and the entire village and Church structure to support them. The cattle companies, on the other hand, had individuals of various calibers coming and going with the seasons. The deeper roots of Bluff gave its people an important advantage in the competition for this marginal land. If Mormons profited, so much the better, but all they had to do to succeed was subsist. Mere subsistence for the cowboys was failure. In a sense the Mormons in Bluff and their cooperative tradition were competing with the cattle companies and their unbridled capitalism.

The danger in all this was that Mormons might throw off their own bridles and become full capitalists themselves.[63] Such a conversion would be harmful in at least two ways. First, in a purely practical sense, Mormons competing against Mormons would weaken their collective place in the contest for the range. But more importantly, if they practiced pure individualism, the settlers at Bluff would deny their mission and their faith. The leaders of the town had been raised on Brigham Young's

---

61. Kane, *Twelve Mormon Homes*, 122.

62. Levi S. Peterson, "Development of Utah Livestock Law," 201–2.

63. See Peterson, *Look to the Mountains*, 45–46, 51 for a comparison of the Mormons and the cattle camps. See also Charles S. Peterson, "Imprint of Agricultural Systems," 99–100; and May, *Three Frontiers*, 81.

principles of self-sufficiency, home manufactures, and cooperation as touchstones of fidelity as long as they had been in Utah. If they denied these principles for individual pursuits, they would no [165] longer be a united stake securing this corner of Zion. Instead, they would look far too much like the enterprising Gentiles they hoped to displace.

Conflict

It was therefore imperative for Bluff's cattlemen to cooperate among themselves. Many of them had been involved in cooperative cattle enterprises before. Jens Nielson was president of the Cedar City Cooperative Cattle Company when it was organized in 1875, and Kumen Jones worked for it for three years as well. But it was very difficult to reconcile the members' interests with the cooperative ideal, and it broke into its component herds in 1883.[64] This experience led the bishop to move cautiously in putting together a similar undertaking in Bluff. In the last weeks of 1885, various residents formed a cooperative stock company after spirited discussions.[65] But the names of Jens Nielson and Francis Hammond, probably the two largest stockholders in town, were conspicuously absent from the list of officers, and the venture fell apart within a month when its members could not agree on a constitution.[66] In the meantime the whole town almost came apart.

It was the ditch again. By the time the ward started planning for it in mid-January, many of the newer settlers had grown skittish about the place. Their land claims were too far from the established ditches to have hopes of getting enough water to grow crops. So [166] the older residents offered to divide and redistribute the land to encourage as many as possible to stay and help labor on the ditch. This gesture seemed to be well received.[67] But a more divisive problem still loomed: the older settlers, who already had built up stock in the ditch through their past labors, wanted to redeem some of that stock to reduce their share of labor this year. The newer settlers resented the prospect of bearing a disproportionate share of the dispiriting burden in the immediate future.

---

64. See Seegmiller, *History of Iron County*, 356; Carter, *Our Pioneer Heritage*, 18:240; Kumen Jones, "Writings," 157.

65. Hammond, Journal, December 21, 1885.

66. Hammond, Journal, March 23, 1886.

67. Hammond, Journal, January 13, 1887.

President Hammond was disturbed by the "lack of union in [the] temporal affairs" of the town. In the afternoon meeting on Sunday, January 17, he addressed the issue in his frank, energetic style, thereby making the divisions much worse. As Bishop Nielson listened to his priesthood leader speak, his indignation grew. Hammond dwelled on "Bluff being a hard place to maintain because of the difficulty of securing water." This much was obvious to anyone who had been there, and these doubts were no greater than those Platte Lyman used to voice. But the bold, entrepreneurial spirit of President Hammond had already developed a program to wean the San Juan Stake off the settlement at Bluff. Many who had come with Hammond had already relocated to Mancos or other places in Colorado, and he himself had property there. Now the stake president said the purpose was to raise enough money to get water onto White Mesa, apparently to relocate the major settlement there. Bluff itself was not vital to President Hammond; it was the overall region that mattered.[68]

That was not how the bishop felt. He and others had invested years of toil in this [167] town. They had been told by higher authorities that Bluff could not be abandoned, and they had been promised specific blessings for staying here. It was not hard for President Hammond to see that "my remarks gave offense to the Bishop Bro. Nielson and some others."[69] The 7:00 PM meeting became a referendum on the president's remarks. Hammond himself did not feel well enough to attend, but his views were defended by some of those present and criticized by others. Bluff was again divided.

The question festered for a week. The next Sunday a priesthood meeting was held in the evening. After the assembled group sang "Come All Ye Sons of God," President Hammond spoke on the duties of the priesthood. Then he warned against the "division liable to spring up in relation to our sentiments as regards Bluff City Ward, its building up and maintenance." He then emphasized the necessity of unity. All present knew he was right. They had to be united or deny their mission. But united on what? President Hammond felt they should be united in forming a settlement on the White Mesa as a more desirable place to live and a strategic base in securing the range. The bishop and others rose to speak with

---

68. Hammond, Journal, January 17, 1886.

69. Hammond, Journal, January 17, 1886, for all the quotations in this paragraph.

"great liberty" on the importance of being united in maintaining Bluff.[70] The discussion continued until after midnight, with both sides weighing in on more particular issues such as ditch credits.

As the tired residents left the schoolhouse that night, a "good feeling prevailed."[71] Once again, both sides felt better after airing out their grievances and backtracking to [168] principles in which they all believed. But this did not resolve everything, because the next morning Bishop Nielson, his counselor Lemuel Redd, as well as William Adams and James Decker called on President Hammond to discuss the "knotty problem" of resolving ditch credits. After further discussions, the older settlers gave in again. They agreed to tax everyone equally for this year's ditch construction, "without reference to capital stock they have in the ditch." They would tax all land to be used during the upcoming season at twelve dollars per acre. Since most chose to work off their tax rather than pay cash, this required a solid week's work per acre of land, though bringing horses and scrapers counted toward the tax as well. This money would not only repair the old ditch, but also pay for construction of a new ditch from Recapture Wash to connect with the main channel. The farmers hoped they could use the less turbulent waters from the Recapture until its level fell too low in the late summer or fall, then switch to whatever water the San Juan had left. By doing this, they anticipated avoiding many of the bank-breaking surges of the San Juan that had occupied so much of their time in the past.[72]

Even with the immediate finances resolved, the larger issue still remained. President Hammond and Bishop Nielson surveyed the new and old ditches together, but they maintained different opinions on Bluff. At the quarterly stake conference in late March, both men emphasized the importance of cooperation and union, "notwithstanding the efforts of our enemies to the contrary."[73] If Mormons sometimes relieved [169] internal tensions by transferring blame to outsiders, they were also quick to condemn themselves for not fully living up to the principles of the gospel.[74]

---

70. "Great liberty" means they spoke their minds without restraint.

71. See Hammond, Journal, January 24, 1886, for what happened at the meeting.

72. Hammond, Journal, January 25, 29, 1886.

73. Charles E. Walton, "San Juan Conference," *Deseret News*, April 21, 1886, 211. Also see May, "Making of Saints," for a consideration of how internal frustrations in a Mormon town might have been vented on outsiders.

74. See Arrington, Fox, and May, *Building the City of God*, 8.

Their enemies would never triumph if the Saints were pure, and Bishop Nielson as well as President Hammond felt the obligation to keep the commandments as fully as they could. Outwardly, the two men had appeared much more united since the controversy in January. In mid-March, for example, President Hammond had helped Bishop Nielson transport barley at his place, and they often had mixed pleasantly in Bluff's endless social season.[75] But each seemed to grow more convinced of his position in the following weeks. The bishop might have felt reassured by a couple of developments. First, the Mancos Mill project he had opposed the previous year lost money from the beginning, and the Bluff Co-op disassociated itself from the mess.[76] Second, Bluff's men and boys got water into the ditch for eight dollars an acre, significantly less than they had anticipated.[77]

But President Hammond still could not understand why the bishop and others chose to huddle by this fickle river when there were more promising locations so close. He often referred to the trouble and cost of maintaining an existence by fighting "this [170] turgid stream."[78] And so he attempted to trump the convictions that Bishop Nielson and others held that Bluff was essential. The main pillar of these feelings seemed to be what President Joseph F. Smith had told the holdouts after their cathartic meetings following the floods in 1884. It just so happened that Joseph F. Smith was an old friend of Francis Hammond's; they had served together as missionaries in Hawaii in the 1850s. So President Hammond wrote to President Smith soon after the disagreements erupted in January. Since Smith was in Hawaii again, a place less likely to be probed for polygamists by federal marshals, his answer took almost three months to arrive. But it came in early April, and President Hammond read parts of it in church.

---

75. Hammond, Journal, March 13 and April 6, 1886.

76. Hammond, Journal, March 1 and 23, May 30, June 19, 1886. The mill resulted not only in financial loss but very hard feelings among the Saints in Mancos. Charges and countercharges were lobbed back and forth into the early 1890s.

77. Hammond, Journal, June 29, 1886. Other settlements had severe difficulties with their irrigation, but usually not of the same magnitude as those in Bluff. The colonists on the Little Colorado in Arizona were upset about the "enormous" burden at Snowflake and other nearby settlements in 1889 from the three-dollar-per-acre ditch tax. See Peterson, *Take Up Your Mission*, 180, 185–91.

78. Hammond, Journal, April 6, 1886.

President Smith wrote that in 1884 he felt the "Sahara of the San Juan" should be held and the key to holding it was the settlement at Bluff. But he also believed that "in the event of the proper development of the country that Bluff was destined to recede into the shade of better locations, if not eventually abandoned." It would clearly have to be abandoned if the water could not be controlled. Still, he pointed out, "Sometimes a thing may cost more than it is worth, but having been purchased at that excessive price, it is too valuable to throw away." President Smith concluded, "My counsel is to hang on to the San Juan Country and if possible make Bluff a 'stronghold.' But men need not ruin themselves in a hopeless cause. Bluff will doubtless some day be built up."[79] While President Hammond may have hoped the letter would tip the balance of the argument in [171] his favor, it was far from conclusive.[80] The two strong-willed leaders continued to co-exist as well as they could. The bishop would have heartily endorsed the sentiment President Hammond inscribed in his journal the night of Bluff's sixth Founders' Day: "May the Lord assist us to yet redeem and make this land lovely."[81]

The county's water continued to wash out the newest version of their best-laid plans by flooding the Recapture ditch in late March and overwhelming other banks at the end of May, doubling the ditch tax estimate from spring and causing the few men in town to wrestle with it daily through the end of June.[82] "We have had a good deal of trouble to keep the water out of our ditch all the fore part of the season," lamented President Hammond in a letter to the *Deseret News*, "and now, since the river has fallen, we have nearly as much trouble to keep the water in."[83] They tried to construct wing dams at the head of the ditch to bring the water up in late July.[84] In the end, something of a crop was raised, but it was

---

79. Joseph F. Smith, letter to Francis A. Hammond, March 4, 1886.

80. Francis Hammond recorded in his journal that night that the letter was about holding "not Bluff in particular but San Juan County and all the region round about." See Hammond, Journal, April 4, 1886.

81. Hammond, Journal, April 6, 1886.

82. Hammond, Journal, March 30; May 23, 25, 31; June 4, 11, 29, 1886.

83. Francis A. Hammond, "Interesting from the San Juan Country," *Deseret News*, August 11, 1886, 479.

84. Walton, Diary, July 1886.

to the newcomers "a very dear one."[85] Seeing these struggles to tame the river for the second time only confirmed in the stake president's mind the importance of bringing "cheap and permanent water" onto White Mesa as soon as possible. Yet that undertaking was soon abandoned as well. The same low water levels that had bedeviled the [172] diggers at Bluff also hurt the chances and increased the expense of getting water onto White Mesa. President Hammond had to conclude when he vis-ited the project in July that it was "too heavy a job for us to carry through for the present."[86] But when he continued up to North Montezuma, he found that place promising enough to try to occupy in the near future.

If the Mancos Mill and White Mesa pieces of President Hammond's regional planning failed, other parts went very well in the spring and sum-mer of 1886. Hammond and a few other Bluff stockmen, though not the bishop, summered their herds on Elk Mountain for the first time. But Jens did have a hand in the cooperative dairy that was started up at Dodge Point near the Blue Mountains. It was operated by Willard and Julia Butt, and it was supplying very good butter and cheese by the Pioneer Day cele-brations on July 24. In fact, Mormon efforts in that part of the country went so well in 1886 that outsiders once again charged foul play, claiming that the Mormons had an unfair advantage with the Indians.

Cooperation

Internal relations among the Mormons in 1886 were still not as coor-dinated as they seemed to outsiders, and in the end it was external pressure at least as much as internal principles that led the stockmen of Bluff to cooperate. In August, the leaders of the ward were still wran-gling with the problem of "how to get all our temporal matters orga-nized into a system of cooperation."[87] But as winter approached, the rumors and then [173] the reality of vast outside sheep and cattle herds occupying nearby ranges alarmed them. For the third straight winter, at least forty thousand sheep, many from a New Mexico interest, and perhaps eight thousand cattle, many from the LC Company, stripped

---

85. See Lemuel H. Redd, "San Juan Stake Conference," *Deseret News*, October 20, 1886, 627; Hammond, Journal, June 29, 1886.

86. Hammond, Journal, July 17, 1886.

87. Hammond, Journal, August 8, 1886. See Bluff Ward, General Minutes, August 15, September 5, 1886.

the grass around Bluff.[88] The town's leaders were unable to reach any accommodation with those who ran this stock. Their only alternative seemed to be to compete with them economically, but Bluff's stockowners continued to struggle with how to combine to do this.

Finally, in late November, they found a way. During business meetings after the quarterly stake conference, purchasing sheep and "the securing of our stock ranges etc. w[ere] talked up."[89] Those present decided to expand the Bluff Co-op Store into the "San Juan Mercantile, Stock Raising, and Manufacturing Company." As this title suggested, the new enterprise hoped to increase the size of the old co-op to allow it to undertake more diverse ventures over a larger area. Perhaps President Hammond hoped to imitate the variety of the prototype co-op in Utah, the one started by Lorenzo Snow in Brigham City in the 1870s, not far from Hammond's Huntsville home.[90] [174]

Regardless of whose idea it was, the new San Juan Co-op would continue the dual principles of the old Bluff cooperative: to be a financial embodiment of the Saints' spiritual commitment to be one with each other in all their affairs. Those who bought shares were investing in the hope of future earnings and also casting a vote for cooperative principles. Not only men but also many of the town's women and children cast their votes with the dollars they could pull together.[91] Still, the San

---

88. Hammond, Journal, December 4, 17, 1886; February 11, 20, 1887; Francis A. Hammond, "From San Juan County," Deseret News, January 19, 1887, 32.

89. Stake conferences were not only useful for spiritual growth, but also for economic discussions and planning. As William S. Abruzzi points out in "Ecology, Resource Redistribution," 650, the quarterly conferences "occurred during critical junctures in both the agricultural and seasonal cycles: prior to the planting season (February–March), after the spring runoff (May–June), following the intense summer rains (August–September), and subsequent to the fall harvest (November–December)."

90. See Arrington, Fox, and May, Building the City of God, ch. 6, for the details of this institution. It did the usual mercantile and livestock businesses, but also encouraged a variety of home industries, including a dairy, tannery, woolens mill, furniture shop, and hat factory among its forty departments. A series of setbacks and disasters did away with most of the home manufacturing branches by 1880, but under the co-op, Brigham City had come closer to self-sufficiency than any other place.

91. By the end of 1887, for example, Kirsten Nielson owned $66.00 in stock, Elsie had $43.00, and even Joe's oldest boy, Eddie Nielson, had $5.00. See San Juan Cooperative Association, Ledger, manuscript, Church History Library.

Juan Company was at least as corporate as it was cooperative. It was a merging of capital, and the dividends were paid to shareholders, not consumers.[92] Except in the unlikely event that all bought equal shares, some Saints would profit from their joint economic activities more than others. But more immediately, this capitalistic arrangement would put the profits back in the hands of those who would help Bluff compete with outsiders more effectively: the large stockholders. In spite of the inconsistencies, the expansion of the co-op was the common ground the Bluff Saints had sought over the previous year. Bishop Nielson enthusiastically embraced the plan and was elected president of the enterprise in December. When the San Juan Cooperative Company, as it was officially named, became a legal entity on January 1, 1887, the bishop was one of the largest stockholders.[93]

The co-op swiftly used its increased presence to coordinate Bluff's business [175] ventures. It tried to plan livestock ranges and brought pressure on those with separate businesses, such as Joseph and Amasa Barton, to be united with the rest of the Saints in Bluff.[94] If everyone came together, the cooperative company would not only fulfill the objectives of the old store but also pay larger dividends and fund new projects. It was a convenient merger of interests: their faith required them to cooperate; their interests also impelled it.

The first project of the new company may have been the one that urged its swift incorporation. The people in Bluff had to do something about the sheep that were devouring their countryside. They had almost bought three thousand of the woolly invaders the previous March but could not agree on the terms.[95] Now they entered discussions with a

92. See Arrington, Fox, and May, *Building the City of God*, ch. 5; Peterson, *Take Up Your Mission*, 148–52, for the mix of cooperative and capitalist principles in various co-ops in the Mormon settlements.

93. Hammond, Journal, November 11–23, December 13, 1886; San Juan Cooperative Association, Ledger. By the end of 1887, Jens Nielson owned $1,250.76 in stock, third only to the Barton brothers. Joe Nielson owned $792.00 in stock, Jens Peter had $448.00, while Francis had $111.00. There was a total of $14,793.25 in stock by that time, and the company listed $25,847.27 in assets. This was well below the authorized capitalization of $100,000 but a promising start nonetheless.

94. Hammond, Journal, December 19, 1886.

95. Hammond, Journal, March 23, 1886.

Mr. McCallister about buying four thousand of his herd. During a meeting at the bishop's house on December 28, they closed the business of buying the flock for six thousand dollars. They did not have anything close to that amount in cash, so they bought on credit, most likely through banks in Durango, at "a fair bargain considering all circumstances."[96] The buyers would pay no interest if they retired each of the three notes when due on August 1. If they could not, then they would pay 10 percent interest per year thereafter. The sheep were quickly voted into the San Juan Cooperative Company as stock, and their herding would be managed cooperatively.[97] [176]

Buying these sheep served at least two purposes. First, the animals were an investment and one that many stockmen were beginning to view as more sound than cattle. Sheep exacted a lower initial expense, brought quicker profits, and could yield both wool and meat, giving more security since it was rare for both markets to plummet at once. Although cattle were more mobile, now that the railroad ran through Durango that was less of a concern.[98] As the sheep herd increased, profits could be paid to stockholders through the co-op, sometimes in cash, sometimes in merchandise, and sometimes in increased capital stock in the company. Also, these sheep could be ranged in strategic spots, such as west of the Recapture, where the pressure from outside herds was greatest. In all, the deal furthered Bluff's immediate economic purposes of holding off the outsiders so they could make a living here, while at the same time doing it in a way, similar to the co-op itself, that would unify the Saints in their temporal affairs.[99]

---

96. Hammond, Journal, December 28, 1886.

97. Albert R. Lyman in *Indians and Outlaws*, 71, and *Lemuel Hardison Redd, Jr.*, dramatizes this story greatly, having the bishop making almost the entire decision to buy the flock at extortionate prices. According to these accounts, the bishop decided to "dream on" the purchase overnight. The next morning, he announced definitively, "Ve vill puy de sheep." According to Francis Hammond's contemporary journal, while the bishop was a key figure, perhaps *the* key figure as ward leader and president of the co-op, many were involved in the decision and negotiation of terms. The price of the sheep, $1.50 for graded and $1.25 for ungraded ewes, was not far out of line with other sheep prices in those years. The credit terms also seemed fair enough to those entering into them.

98. See Jensen, "Historical Study," 75, for these advantages of sheep over cattle.

99. The formidable increase in the number of sheep in San Juan County in these years parallels the growth throughout Utah in the 1880s and 1890s. In 1880, Utah

Cattle were another matter. Each individual continued to own and operate his own herd. The various owners tried to coordinate ranges, and Bluff cattlemen generally all sold together. But from time to time, someone would act in a way the others deemed harmful to the common good. Church leaders then had to remonstrate with the offender [177] to act in a more cooperative fashion. In this way the Barton brothers were brought back into the fold, and so was Lemuel Redd when he independently negotiated a big contract in Durango in March 1887.[100] This informal discipline generally worked out most of the problems, but the principles of unity and cooperation, as well as the competition on the ranges, pushed them toward a more formal association.

Mixed Blessings

On December 6, 1886, a team and wagon returned from Colorado with a bell for the Bluff meetinghouse. Among other consequences, this event meant that Charles Walton and his bugle could retire as the official heralds of public celebrations. As usual, those who heard the bell peal had mixed feelings on living in its vicinity. In many ways, the people of Bluff defined themselves by who they were not. They were glad they were not Indians, and they hoped to persuade these neighbors to live more as they did. They were certainly glad they were not like the unattached cowboys who worked for the outside cattle companies. The more successful the sheep and cattle herds of Bluff were, the less they would have to put up with these sorts of characters. The members of the Bluff Ward also felt protected from other problems. The remoteness and marginal nature of their farmland limited rivalry for its use. No one in Bluff ever had his town lot or fields jumped by outsiders, as sometimes happened in other locales of the West.[101] And except for their occasional spasms, Bluff residents did not generate the same level of jealousy and [178] misunderstanding as seemed more common in other wards. In spite of the

---

had 230,000 sheep. By 1900 these numbers skyrocketed to 3.8 million. See Alexander, *Utah, the Right Place*, 225–26.

100. Hammond, Journal, March 10, 1887.

101. See Hammond, Journal, December 8, 1886, for a report of the "jumping" of the Stevens ranch in La Plata, New Mexico, by "three outlaws." Since Alma and Joshua Stevens had killed two of the outlaws, they hid out in and around Bluff for a few years after the conflict.

disagreements in his ward, Bishop Nielson did not have to endure constant "murmuring and complaining" against himself, nor did either of his counselors resign in protest as happened in the Moab Ward to the north. His Bluff Ward, while not perfect, appeared very united by contrast.[102] Lem Redd pointed out another advantage when he spoke in church the first Sunday after the bell came. He had visited the older settlements in Utah, where "he found much derision, ... and the young growing up in carelessness respecting the gospel." After such sights he "was glad to be home again."[103]

But Bluff's citizens could not help taking notice of other things they were not. By living in their forlorn outpost, their standard of living was much lower than that of their relatives and friends in other towns. Salt Lake City "never looked so beautiful" to President Hammond when he visited after living in Bluff for awhile.[104] Every new development in streetcars, or lighting, or communication was something to marvel at, but from a distance, since not even the railroad was ever going to come to Bluff. The settlers were relegated to a backwater at a time when cities were swiftly starting to become more modern. Bluff's roads and fences were sometimes in poor repair in the midst of weeds that were, in the summer, taller than the people. Their log homes continued to grow larger and nicer as rooms, flooring, doors, and windows were added onto the original frames. But the dwellings were "a very inferior class of log cabins" to any outside [179] eyes.[105] They still had the permissive dirt roofs, and their walls could not entirely stop the potent San Juan wind from blowing in heat or cold, dust, grit, and moisture in their seasons.

The only stone home in Bluff was built by Joseph T. Johnson, who had arrived with Francis Hammond in 1885. With imported lime and shingles, he put together a two-room cottage that was soon bought by President Hammond when Brother Johnson moved away. A wide-eyed Bluff girl once "asked her mother if all the houses in Salt Lake City were as good as President Hammond's house."[106] This was the sort of

---

102. Hammond, Journal, October 3, 1886.

103. Hammond, Journal, December 12, 1886.

104. Hammond, Journal, October 5, 1886.

105. Hammond, Journal, November 14, 1887.

106. Albert R. Lyman, "History of San Juan County," 49; see Hammond, Journal, January 11, 1886, for the origin of the house.

provincialism to which the settlers had been called. Spiritually, Bluff was a good place to make Saints, reckoned by Brigham Young's traditional standards. Materially, as the folks of Bluff were reminded every time they traveled elsewhere, it was behind the times.

But making a virtue out of necessity was always a part of the San Juan Mission. Bishop Nielson did the best he could when he confronted the health of the town late in the year. People got sick often, and many babies continued to be born. As most people in small towns did, Bluff's Saints helped each other as well as they could, using a combination of loving care, herbs, traditional cures, and Indian advice. To these home-spun methods they added their faith through frequent prayers and priesthood blessings for the sick. In merging traditional cures, pragma-tism, and spiritual power, the [180] settlers at Bluff resembled their Indian neighbors more than they would care to admit.[107]

Sometime in 1886, Sister Haskell, the leading midwife, moved to Colorado. So Bishop Nielson issued a Church calling to Jody Wood, to be the town's doctor. She and her husband, Samuel Wood, had lived across the street from the Nielsons in Cedar City a few years before. Now she was understandably panicstricken by this medical assignment. "I am as green as a cucumber," she protested to the bishop, "and I don't know how babies are born." But Jens knew her capabilities well. She had a lively personality tempered with the compassion of having lost two of her own children in Cedar City. And furthermore, Samuel Wood had married a second wife, Emma, the year before, meaning that Jody would have help caring for her own children when she had to leave home. So the bishop called her despite her concerns and promised she would be guided by the Lord. Notwithstanding, she sent away for some books then studied and prayed.

Her first delivery came just before the meetinghouse bell arrived. On December 3, Joseph Barton's wife, Harriett, was about to give birth. Jody asked her husband for a priesthood blessing and then asked the bishop to go with her to the delivery. The baby came out with the cord wrapped around her neck. Jody heard someone tell her what to do, and she saved the baby. "I thought Bishop Nielson had spoken to me," she recalled, "but

---

107. See McPherson, *History of San Juan County*, 268–75, for more specific com-parisons made between Ute, Navajo, and Mormon medical practices.

when I turned to look at him, he was not in the room. I knew the Lord had blessed [181] me, telling me plainly what to do."[108]

It did not take long for "Aunt Jody" to become something of an institution. Bluff's children started wondering if she brought the babies in her black bag. Bishop Nielson helped with some other deliveries, but his daughter Mary Jones assisted Aunt Jody frequently. "It was Aunt Jody and Aunt Mary to all, with their herbs and hot poultices, etc., together with their old time jokes and funny stories."[109] Sister Wood's "jolly, kindly disposition worked psychological wonders among the sick," Kumen Jones remembered, "likely as much or more than the packs, poultices, or herb teas she used."[110]

While Aunt Jody's bedside manner and unquestioned dedication were admired by everyone, complicated cases still caused serious problems. Francis Hammond later wrote how his daughter-in-law was almost "murdered" and the baby "butchered" because of "the ignorance of those sisters who have acted as midwives," and how "our sisters are becoming very nervous as the time approached for their confinement." While he may have been referring to midwives in other towns in the stake as well as in Bluff, and doctors of the time might not have done much better, there were limitations to what Bluff's medical team could do. When it came time for Aunt Mary herself to give birth, she called in a midwife from Salt Lake City to try to ensure everything went smoothly.[111] [182] For all but the most difficult cases, the midwives did well. Aunt Jody

---

108. Quoted in Albert R. Lyman, "Josephine Catherine Chatterley Wood," in Carter, *Our Pioneer Heritage*, 19:272–73. For background information, see Noall, "Mormon Midwives," 127–33; and Hoopes, "Birth Records of 'Aunt Jody.'"

109. Kumen Jones, "Writings," 151.

110. Kumen Jones, "Writings," 202.

111. Hammond, Journal, October 13, 1889, for the quotes and the outside midwife for Mary Jones. The record in Bluff doesn't seem unusually severe for childbirths at that time. Of the thirty-one babies born in Bluff by the date of Hammond's entry since Jody Wood started in December 1886, four died within a year. Only two of these died within a week of birth. One mother died soon after giving birth, and President Hammond's daughter-in-law suffered serious complications. Hammond might have also been thinking of the very difficult delivery of Charlie Redd, which any doctor would have struggled with, and none would have stayed the next week as Aunt Jody did, helping to care for the infant as well as cook, clean, and do laundry, all for the usual $5.00 fee, payable in kind. See Arrington, *Utah's Audacious Stockman*, 36.

certainly did well enough by Bishop Nielson when she delivered two of
his grandchildren in two days late in 1886. On December 19, Julia Butt
delivered a girl she named after her mother, Elsie May. And the next
day, Joe's wife Ida delivered a boy, Jens Lyman, who in time would start
toddling around with Jens's oldest grandson, Eddie, born the year before.

Christmas in 1886 was not just festive for the enlarged Nielson family
but for the whole town as well. As was usually the case with any public
event, a committee planned the celebrations. By Christmas Eve the committee members had set up a large tree, decorated with presents on the
branches, the first time such a thing was seen in Bluff. President Hammond played the role of Santa Claus and merrily passed out the presents
to the town's children. Then there was a dance for the youth until almost
midnight. At two o'clock the next afternoon, two large tables creaked
under the food for a public dinner, which fed close to three hundred
people, including about a hundred Indians who had been invited for the
occasion. In the evening, after "they were stuffed like the turkey," they held
a "grand dance," and quite a few outside cowboys attended and behaved
themselves well. Over the next few days various families and organizations continued to throw parties, dances, and dinners, and the whole
week witnessed ball games, horse races, foot races, and whatever other
sports and games the revelers could imagine. All these diversions were a
welcome break dividing the labors of the past year from those of the [183]
next.[112] Bluff might have been lacking in technology and physical amenities, but its residents were determined to make up for such limitations
with their own warmth and merrymaking. For this reason, Christmases
were usually a time to remember in Bluff.[113] The whole holiday season
rejuvenated the town and prepared its residents to once again confront
their "difficulties ... of no common character."[114] [184]

---

112. See Walton, Diary, December 25, 1886, "It being Christmas I spent the day
in idleness."

113. See Hammond, Journal, December 14–January 1, 1886, for holiday festivities;
Hammond, "From San Juan County," 32.

114. George Q. Cannon, letter to Francis A. Hammond, January 1, 1887.

Competition, 1887–1890

Besieged

"The Raid"

Congress, reflecting the moral outrage of its constituents and utilizing the coercive methods it had recently used during Reconstruction, increased its pressure on polygamy. This was exactly what Jens Nielson feared when he advised his daughter Mary to permit Kumen Jones to take a second wife. In 1882, the Edmunds Act amended the Morrill Act of 1862 to make it easier to punish those practicing plural marriage in United States territories. While convicted polygamists could still be fined five hundred dollars and imprisoned for five years, now the new crime of "unlawful cohabitation" was created. Adults found living together without a legal marriage could be fined three hundred dollars and imprisoned for six months. Cohabitation was much easier to prove than bigamy given the difficulty of finding marriage records and the common-law precedent barring spouses from testifying against each other. Furthermore, men and women living in polygamous marriages were declared ineligible to hold elected or appointed government office.[1] Some plural families started colonizing in northern Mexico and southern Canada to avoid [185] this law. The new restrictions also kept Jens Nielson from running for reelection as a county selectman in 1883, a job he had grown accustomed to holding in Cedar City and Bluff.

---

1. Alexander, *Utah, the Right Place,* 192.

As 1887 dawned, more alarming news came from Washington, D.C. On February 18, President Grover Cleveland allowed the Edmunds-Tucker Act to become law without his signature. This congressional hammer threatened to break Mormonism on the anvil of what its members believed was God's law. All Church property over fifty thousand dollars was confiscated, women's suffrage was repealed, common-law strictures forbidding wives to testify against husbands were waived, public records of marriages were required, and territorial probate judges had to be appointed by the President of the United States instead of elected locally.[2]

In the wake of these acts, the First Presidency counseled the men of the Church to live with only one wife under the same roof. Bishop Nielson followed this counsel in Bluff, building a separate two-room log home for Elsie by the time she arrived again in 1885.[3] But federal marshals actively pursued those they suspected of unlawful cohabitation. As more Church brethren were hauled into court, the shock waves rippled out to Bluff. The Saints there subscribed forty dollars to the legal defense fund for [186] fellow Church members defending themselves against these charges.[4]

As "the raid" on polygamy became more severe, the news reported to Bluff became more alarming. The President of the Church, John Taylor, operated out of hiding. When Francis Hammond tried to see him in Salt Lake City in mid-1885, the visitor had to call at the tithing office and leave a note. The next day he returned for the answer, which arranged a personal visit with President Taylor in a private residence more than two miles outside Salt Lake City.[5] Many other Church authorities went into "exile" to avoid the marshals. The next year, the Saints in Bluff read with great suspense about the conviction of Elder Lorenzo Snow and

---

2. Alexander, *Utah, the Right Place* 195.

3. Kirsten's youngest daughter, Caroline, recalled years later, "Wherever they lived father provided separate living quarters for his families." This, however, could mean separate wings of the same house, as it did in Cedar City, but Jens eventually owned two two-room log cabins in Bluff. He most likely built the second in anticipation of Elsie's arrival either this year or when she had come previously. See Kimmerle, "Little Visit," 234.

4. Hammond, Journal, July 12, 1885.

5. Hammond, Journal, July 30 and 31, 1885.

the arrest of the First Counselor to President Taylor, George Q. Cannon, on a train in Nevada. Old friends from Iron County, such as Stake President Henry Lunt and Bishop Christopher Arthur took to the mountains. More alarming still, young Edward Dalton, the son of their visitor in 1881, was shot and killed by a federal marshal in Parowan who was trying to arrest him for unlawful cohabitation. To the Saints it was "cold-blooded murder," and they were further outraged when the shooter was not convicted. "Thus is the law and order trampled upon."[6]

Bluff's residents had to worry about more than just distant news, however. Although they lived in a remote corner of the territory, they grew more suspicious of strangers. Cowboys "might be U.S. Marshals in disguise." Two prospectors who rolled [187] into town with a cart and horse were just as suspect.[7] Bluff's ward members were instructed to report all strangers to their Church leaders and told "not to know too much about other people's business."[8] But no real marshals appeared. Refugees "on the underground" from the marshals did appear with increasing frequency in Bluff. The First Presidency, from their own places of hiding, confirmed they felt Bluff "a most excellent hiding place" for these purposes, and these political fugitives were the most consistent source of population growth for the town in the late 1880s.[9] Some of these "cohabs" on the "u.g." came from a distance, such as Winslow Farr, who arrived with President Hammond from northern Utah in 1885. More local men, such as Hiram Taylor of Moab and Bishop Burnham of the town named after him in New Mexico, also came through from time to time. And the raid persuaded some old friends to visit Bluff in their difficulties. Herman Daggett Bayles, both the father of Bluff resident Hanson Bayles and the husband of Kirsten Nielson's younger sister in Parowan, lived out his final year as an exile in Bluff. Platte Lyman was persuaded by the presence of marshals and a vigilant apostate across the street from him in Scipio to start spending some of his time running cattle in the more obscure parts of San Juan

6. Hammond, Journal, December 30, 1886. See also Seegmiller, *History of Iron County*, 86–87.

7. Hammond, Journal, March 26, 1886; February 12, 1888.

8. Bluff Ward, General Minutes, February 12, 1888.

9. John Taylor and George Q. Cannon, letter to Francis A. Hammond, March 25, 1887.

County again.[10] The raid made those in Bluff feel even more distinct from
their neighbors. On a visit to Colorado, Francis Hammond [188] found,
"The sentiment out here is that if we would give up polygamy all would be
peace with us and the world; we know quite differently from that."[11] Such
persecution was instead a sign of their peculiarity. "The raid is upon us
because God desires to prove us," President Hammond told the members
of the Bluff Ward. In fact, he "was pleased that the devil was at work. It
was a good sign to the saints."[12] More "good signs" were on the way.

Removal

On April 7, 1886, the evening mail "brought the news that San Juan
County is about to be turned into an Indian reservation."[13] This was
not the first that San Juan colonists had heard about this possibility. As
soon as the Weeminuche Utes went onto their reservation in the southwestern corner of Colorado in the 1870s, many found it unsatisfactory.
Its long, rectangular shape made it both inconvenient for the Indians
to travel to the agency and inviting for outside cowboys and miners to
intrude upon. The Utes became increasingly uncertain of their future
in Colorado, whose politicians desired to resolve the issue in a way that
would benefit their enterprising constituents. Homesteads along the
La Plata River granted in severalty to the Indians were rejected as a
solution in the early 1880s, and the Coloradans continued to search for
other answers. Some spoke of moving these southern Utes to the Uintah
Reservation in Utah as they had [189] done with the northern Utes after
the Meeker massacre in 1879, but the Utes in question quickly denied
any desire to go there. Perhaps as early as 1882, some started discussing
the creation of a new reservation in a land the Utes already knew, one
with few white settlers on it: San Juan County, Utah Territory.[14]

---

10. See Platte D. Lyman, "Diary," September 27, 1886; January 4, 1887; and
Albert R. Lyman, Summaries of Each Year, 1886, book 1, p. 29.

11. Hammond, Journal, July 2, 1885.

12. Francis Hammond, in Bluff Ward, General Minutes, February 12, 1888;
March 6, 1887.

13. Walton, Diary, April 7, 1886. Cattlemen had filed eleven claims under the
Desert Land Act of 1877, but that law did not apply to the town site.

14. Thompson, "Unwanted Indians." See also Peterson, *Look to the Mountains,*
71–73; "Bluff Ward Manuscript History," 1882.

These rumors were discouraging not just because they threatened the settlers in Bluff with eviction. The possibility of losing their land also dissuaded the settlers from making substantial improvements to the town. "No one felt like making permanent improvements while the specter of having to pick up and move on again stared them in the face."[15] Those who had the means to build more comfortable homes in Bluff could not take the risk. Furthermore, Bluff's settlers could not file any claims on their lots because the federal government had never done an official survey. In the face of the rumors, they found themselves squatters in their own homes.[16]

In 1885, the rumors materialized. Senator Henry Moore Teller of Colorado filed a bill to remove the Southern Utes to an unspecified location. His colleague, Senator Thomas Bowen, followed up in early 1886 with Senate Bill 1916, which proposed removal to San Juan County. Ute leaders, including Ignacio, were sent to Washington, D.C., to testify in favor of the bill. By April, Bluff's negotiations with the Indian [190] Winchester over disputed claims to Elk Mountain stalled since it appeared more probable that the government was going to turn all the county into a reservation.[17] Amid the doubts, Bishop Nielson encouraged the members of his ward to plant their crops and trees "as though we intended to stay here."[18]

Within days of receiving the alarming letter on April 7, William Halls spearheaded the drafting of a petition to Congress against the bill. Bishop Nielson, Charles Walton, and Lemuel Redd also prepared a list of the improvements colonists had made to the county so they could be reimbursed in case the bill passed. Those in Bluff soon found out the First Presidency of the Church was also opposed to the removal plan, urging Utah's delegate to Congress, John Caine, to do all in his power to defeat the bill. As it turned out, the bill died in committee that year. But the issue was not dead. The Indians were unsettled by it, and Colorado newspapers continued to write strong editorials in favor of removal, urging their congressmen to try again.

---

15. Kumen Jones, "Writings," 188.

16. Hammond, Journal, October 16, 1888; November 25, 1889; McPherson, "Ute Invasion of San Juan County," 48.

17. Hammond, Journal, April 3, 1886.

18. Bluff Ward, General Minutes, April 11, 1886.

Differences

Removal still hung over Bluff when a more immediate threat struck in the summer of 1887. It came out of a clear sky, since relations with the local Indians had continued to improve. When others accused Mormons of having an unfair advantage with the Indians, they were not entirely wrong, though Henry Mitchell continued to go too far when he accused Mormons of colluding with Indians to murder Gentiles like himself.[19] [191] The Durango press and the Carlisles claimed Mormons and Indians were banding together to keep stock off Elk Mountain, though even that exaggerated the matter.[20] But there was an undeniable difference in how the Indians treated Mormons and Gentiles, and it showed the continued success of Bluff's diplomacy. Francis Hammond exaggerated somewhat himself when he claimed the Ute Winchester was "a terror to the cowboys but a fast friend of the Mormons," though he was not far off in his assessment.[21] Visiting authority John Morgan left Bluff with the impression that "the Indians themselves easily detect the difference between the 'Mormon' and the 'American' settlers, and always speak of the former as their friends, and trust implicitly in their honesty." This was largely due to the fact, Morgan felt, that Mormons told the truth, did not get drunk, and did not interfere with Indian women, in contrast to some of the cowboys in the county.[22]

Despite this distinction the Mormons achieved with the Indians, both sides still had problems with each other. Bluff residents maintained their very low opinion of some of the "dirty, lazy, lousy, begging, thieving Utes."[23] But they also perceived the main complaint the Utes had against them: "Poor creatures, they have a hard time ... since the white man has come with his immense herds of stock, the game which was formerly plenty is now very scarce, and the poor Indian is hard pushed to obtain a living."[24] Utes [192] and Paiutes still resented the two- and four-legged incursions on their land, but visited Bluff regularly, especially in

---

19. Hammond, Journal, July 8, 1885.

20. Hammond, Journal, March 24, 1886.

21. Hammond, Journal, March 10, 1886

22. John Morgan, "Correspondence," *Deseret News*, October 17, 1883, 611.

23. Francis A. Hammond, "Another Letter from the San Juan Country," *Deseret News*, February 16, 1887, 66.

24. Hammond, Journal, November 28, 1887.

winter, sometimes to work and sometimes to beg for their livelihood. The Saints continued to admire the Navajos more than the Utes and Paiutes and worked more closely with them. But each side in this relationship also had grievances.[25] All were worried that so many cattle and sheep were devouring the range. The bishop often organized delegations to persuade Navajo herders to take their flocks south of the San Juan.[26] Those in Bluff came to admire the skill of the Navajo women who wove blankets that took up to a year to make and cost a hundred dollars to buy.[27] But some of the high dividends the co-op store paid came because "the poor Indian sells his wool too low and pays too high for his goods."[28]

Bluff's policy also came to include seeking "the better members of the different tribes," and "when all the best ones were won over to our side this gave us the advantage when trouble arose."[29] When Bluff's residents or their cattle wronged their neighbors, the settlers tried to deal justly with them.[30] The bishop continued to send his delegations to work with close allies when problems arose, and once an agreement was reached, Bluff settlers were surprised to find that even renegade Utes and Paiutes kept their word.[31] [193]

Feelings were never better between the Mormons and their Native American neighbors than in early 1887. The previous year was unusually peaceful, the first year in which no livestock were raided. Church leaders finally felt comfortable enough to release Thales Haskell, chief Indian interpreter, so he could rejoin his family in Colorado.[32] Relations with the Indians had become so good, in fact, that Bluff felt it was ready to more fully pursue its mission, which was "largely in the interest of the Indians, to try and civilize them and prepare them in due time to

---

25. See, for example, Kumen Jones, "Writings," 170–72.

26. See Hammond, Journal, January 27, March 9–10, 1886; January 20 and 23, 1887.

27. Hammond, Journal, December 19, 1892.

28. Hammond, Journal, March 29 and April 4, 1886.

29. Kumen Jones, "Writings," 147.

30. Hammond, Journal, June 5, 1888, mentioned an incident when some Bluff cows crossed the San Juan and ate Navajo corn. "We have to pay the damage, which is quite right," ruled the stake president.

31. Kumen Jones, "Writings," 218, 147, 135–36.

32. See Charles E. Walton, "San Juan Items," *Deseret News*, December 29, 1886, 787; Smith, *Thales Hastings Haskell*, 51.

receive the gospel."[33] Now that it seemed the Indians had been taught
"to cease to shed the blood of any one, ... [and] to cease their stealing," it
was time to teach them how "to cultivate the ground and to become like
the white man." All of this would be "preparatory to their receiving the
Gospel."[34] Four men were called as missionaries to the Indians to teach
them how to improve their physical lives. They failed to persuade Utes
and Paiutes north of the San Juan to farm, but as summer approached
in 1887, the residents in Bluff continued to feel "quite satisfied with our
Navajo neighbors" to the south.[35] Until June 1887, an important part of
that satisfaction consisted in the fact that while at least thirty whites
had been killed by [194] Indians in San Juan County since 1880, not one
of them was Mormon.[36]

Nightmare

On June 9, 1887, two Paiutes on horseback pounded into town. They
immediately delivered a scrawled note:

> Come quick someone Amasa is shot in the head in two places and
> Ma and I are alone For the sake of us do hurry....
>   Send for Jo. A Navajo did the shooting Amasa had no gun The
> bullets are lodged near the surface and can be removed do come as
> many as can the bishop, Platte and as many as will and do have faith....
>   Feenie Barton[37]

Platte Lyman and Kumen Jones raced out first, and the bishop and others followed soon after. Sister Parthenia "Feenie" Barton had sent her desperate message from the trading post her husband, Amasa, and her family
operated at Rincon, where Comb Wash flowed into the San Juan, about
ten miles below Bluff. She was the daughter of William and Angeline

---

33. Francis A. Hammond, letter to Capt. D. M. Edwards, June 14, 1889.

34. See Hammond to Capt. D. M. Edwards, June 14, 1889; and Hammond,
"Another Letter from the San Juan Country."

35. The four missionaries were Kumen Jones, Joseph Lyman, Silas S. Hammond,
and Ernest Hyde. The quote is from Hammond, "Another Letter from the San Juan
County." See Hammond, Journal, January 10, March 11, 1887; Charles E. Walton,
"San Juan Stake Conference," *Deseret News*, June 8, 1887, 327.

36. Kumen Jones, "Writings," 203.

37. Albert R. Lyman, *Indians and Outlaws*, 90–91.

Hyde, and the store at Rincon was one of the Hyde family's many trading outfits along the river. Soon after she and Amasa Barton married, just after the floods of 1884, they resettled at this important crossing on the San Juan, where they raised livestock and ran the store. The bishop had tried to discourage Brother Barton from living in so isolated a place unless there were at least ten families down there, reminding him it was against counsel to live outside the settlements, but the newlyweds went [195] anyway.[38] They were joined by Parthenia's mother and at times her two brothers, Ernest and Frank Hyde. The "Jo" in the note was Amasa's brother, Joseph F. Barton, also a partner in the business. Amasa and Feenie had two little boys; the second had been born just three weeks before. The Barton brothers had been called in the February stake conference to open a ferry at "Moquise crossing of the Colorado River" by March, but apparently had not relocated yet.[39] Now came this desperate message.

When the men arrived at Rincon, they found that Sister Barton's note was gruesomely accurate. Amasa had been shot in the head and was unconscious. Old Eye, the Indian who tried to throttle Barton with a rope while another shot, was killed when Barton's struggles put Old Eye's heart in the path of a bullet. Sister Barton and her mother tried to help but were threatened and thrown out at the point of the pistol. Some nearby Paiutes did nothing despite the supplications of the frantic women. The other Navajo then put his pistol to Brother Barton's head and pulled the trigger. He checked on his fallen partner, then he returned and put another bullet in Amasa's brain. He loaded Old Eye's body into a boat with the help of a bystander Paiute and crossed the river. Six other Indians came over after the shooting and ransacked the store, but they left when Platte Lyman and Kumen Jones arrived. The threat did not seem to be over yet, as many [196] Navajos appeared on the cliffs across the river overlooking Rincon. From what the Bluff men could find out, the whole affair had been about three

---

38. Francis A. Hammond, letter to John Taylor and George Q. Cannon, June 19, 1887; Kumen Jones, "Writings," 206. Charles S. Peterson in *Look to the Mountains*, has the Bartons being assigned to Rincon in spring 1887 as part of Bluff's offensive against outside livestock interests, but Francis Hammond's journal for January 9, 1887, has them already located there with the Hydes. Peterson's account does not mention the Church leaders' concerns about the isolated families at Rincon, nor does it mention the Bartons' call to settle at Moquis Crossing on the Colorado.

39. Hammond, Journal, February 27, 1887.

dollars worth of beads that the shooter had pawned at the trading post a few days before.[40] Most of the Bluff men stayed in Rincon overnight to help the distraught Sister Barton watch over her unconscious husband and protect them from any further attacks.

Meanwhile, rumors of what might happen flew to Bluff. The vague fears of extermination by Indians that had remotely haunted the settlers since the beginning leaped forward now. Peter Allan was the only man left in town, and he stood guard over all of the women and children, who gathered in Kirsten Nielson's two-room log home that night.[41] There they kept their tense vigil throughout the dark hours. Jody Wood "washed and dressed her children in their best clothes, the better to find them dead in."[42] No attack came.

When Bishop Nielson returned to Bluff, he assured the townspeople they had nothing to worry about; Church authorities had promised them protection from the [197] Indians.[43] More Bluff men came in from the range to watch over both Rincon and Bluff. After a few days, Tom Holliday, a large and trusted Navajo, came across the river and expressed his desires to have no more violence, but the more sullen attitudes of other Indians left the matter unsure.[44] Meanwhile, Amasa Barton lived his last few days under the influences of morphine and delirium.[45] He opened his eyes once or twice and seemed to recognize people in the

---

40. Jens Nielson, letter to Francis A. Hammond, June 15, 1887; "Murder of A. M. Barton," *Deseret News*, June 29, 1887, 377. The bishop's letter notes that Sister Barton had to pay the two Paiutes sixteen dollars to get them to deliver her frantic message to Bluff. The bishop also had this to say about who shot whom: "They [Navajos] claim Amasa shot the Indian first, but the Paiutes said positively the Indian did it in mistake, but later we hear the Paiutes claim that Amasa shot first. I think the Navajos have hired them to say that in case Amasa dies."

41. Reeve, "Lucinda Diantha Nielson Hyde," 203.

42. Albert R. Lyman, "Josephine Catherine Chatterley Wood," in Carter, *Our Pioneer Heritage*, 19:296. Mary Perkins Wilson, who was thirteen at the time, recalled that this happened more than once: "On several occasions we would all gather at the home of our Bishop Jens Nielson, and huddle in the house and wait for daylight before daring to go home." See Wilson, "Personal History," in "Utah Pioneer Biographies," 30:80.

43. Albert R. Lyman, "History of San Juan County," 53.

44. Kumen Jones, "Writings," 207.

45. Jens Nielson, letter to Francis A. Hammond, June 15, 1887.

room but died on June 16.[46] He was buried in the hill at Bluff the next day with the whole town present, eulogized as "one of the most substantial and reliable members of the mission."[47] But he was also the first to die violently at the hands of the Indians, and his killing revived dreads that had never been entirely put to rest.

In the days after the funeral, the crisis apparently over, most of Bluff's men again dispersed to the range or wherever else they were working. But one morning, close to one hundred Navajo warriors rode into town, their faces painted black. The townspeople barricaded themselves in their homes. Caroline Nielson, twelve at the time, peeked out of the curtains and saw the warriors, their horses, and their guns and felt she might be killed.[48] Mary Jones, clerking at the co-op store, quickly summoned her husband and her father. The two of them, along with John Allan Jr., were the only men near town at the time. Kumen Jones and the bishop hurried toward the war party, which hurled threats and [198] grievances against them. Jens, through his son-in-law, who had already served two missions to the Navajos, told the war party to put down their weapons and talk as friends; they wanted peace. A few of the older Indians did so at once, but most of the younger warriors were reluctant. Finally, the bishop told them that "fighting was not in our line," but they could send for soldiers if that was what the war party wanted. Immediately Navajo hands went up in protest; they knew that if it came to this they would not win. Eventually they descended from their horses, put down their weapons, and sat down to talk. The bishop then reminded them why Bluff was there, and what its citizens had suffered in leaving their former homes. His earnestness and lack of fear, as well as the fact that he had a fat steer butchered and supplies brought over from the co-op, turned the war party's purpose. The meal was followed by a peace pipe and "a general hand shaking, and the war was over."[49]

---

46. "Murder of A. M. Barton," 377.

47. Platte D. Lyman, "Death of A. M. Barton," *Deseret News*, July 6, 1887, 388.

48. L. Wayne Redd, "Jens Nielson Family," 65.

49. Kumen Jones, "Writings," 207, is the only account from someone who was there. Albert R. Lyman, "History of San Juan County," 53, and "Bishop Jens Nielson," 13, mostly follow Jones's account. But Lyman's *Indians and Outlaws*, 95–100, presents the dramatic story with many embellishments, and makes the episode a major turning point in relations with the Navajos. Lyman was seven at the time, and was living

At no other point in his life did the bishop show so poignantly his "indomitable courage."[50] To him it was a natural product of faith. Being true to priesthood authority meant not just obeying what Church leaders had asked but also believing what they had said. As [199] he had told those huddled in Bluff a few days before, they had been promised they would be protected from the Indians. Personally, Jens had been promised in a blessing that "thine enemies shall not harm thee.... Thy days shall be prolonged until thou shall desire to lay thy body down to rest."[51] He believed these promises, which allowed him to limp up to the overwhelming band of warriors and do whatever else this mission required of him without fear.[52]

This showdown did not end all the troubles. President Hammond returned to Bluff from Colorado soon after and held another council with "quite a few of the Navajo Indians," reemphasizing the peaceful purpose of Bluff's mission and reminding them that one white was dead as well as one Navajo; therefore, there was no need for further violence.[53] But some Navajos continued to be "insolent" and "hostile" after the Barton murder, and so, on his return trip to Colorado, President Hammond stopped at Fort Lewis and, for perhaps the only time in Bluff's history, requested troops be sent to protect them. A short time before, a cowboy and camp cook from the LC Cattle Company had been killed farther

---

in Scipio. But he probably heard some of his additions from those who were there after he returned to Bluff in 1891. He also reported that the Navajos called Bishop Nielson "kagoochee," meaning "crooked feet." See "Bishop Jens Nielson," 13. There is no specific date for this incident in any of the sources. It almost certainly happened before Francis Hammond returned from Mancos at the end of June. It may have happened the day after the shooting of Amasa Barton. Jens Nielson, letter to Francis A. Hammond, June 15, 1887, mentions that "The Indians came back the next day and did not want to fight (swam the River as boat is lost)." This seems to refer to Rincon, however, and there is no other mention of an incident at Bluff occurring by the time the bishop wrote the letter, making the most likely window from June 15 to June 27.

50. Lemuel H. Redd Sr., Autobiographical Sketch, 1902.

51. Egler, "Blessing." Kirsten was also promised in a blessing just before the Hole-in-the-Rock expedition that "thou shalt live until thou art satisfied with life."

52. See Hyde, "As I Recall Grandfather Jens Nielson," 26. This belief is an odd parallel to the vision the Chiricahua Apache known as Geronimo had, in which he was told no bullet would ever kill him. His belief in this message made him fearless in battle.

53. Hammond, Journal, June 27, 1886.

north, so two companies of infantry came to the county: one to Bluff, where they were was stationed on the Recapture, and another to Soldier's Springs, near the Blue Mountains. As usual, this caused the Navajos to withdraw from their northern border. When Brigham [200] Young Jr. drove across the reservation a few days after the troops arrived, he found the Indians "feeling quite uneasy."[54]

But the Saints in Bluff also felt "depressed … and somewhat unsettled" by the recent events. These feelings again welled into vital questions about their town's viability. Quite a few, mostly relative newcomers, moved away within a week of Amasa Barton's funeral. President Hammond was more convinced than ever that the mountains to the north were "about the only points in the county where settlements can be sustained."[55] The bishop wondered aloud in church, "There are but few men to stay and too much to do. What are we to do?"[56] So when Apostle Young arrived at the end of July, he once again found the town at the edge of extinction. Steadfast as always in his beliefs on Bluff, he preached once again that their mission to the Lamanites "was of great moment, [and] must not be abandoned." He recognized that it was hard to attract new settlers since "people turn pale at hearing of this ditch and San Juan." But Bluff was also the "nursing mother" and "foundation" for the other Mormon settlements in the stake; if it failed, the other towns would be weakened, and San Juan County could be dissolved by the legislature. Then, reminiscent of what Joseph F. Smith had told the settlers in 1884, he promised, "The people who stay here will be able to buy out those who leave here." He closed by encouraging them to "make your foundations strong. The Lord will not permit these [201] Lamanites to hurt you."[57] As the bishop said the next week, this unequivocal counsel was "just in accordance with his feelings."[58] To help them continue, Thales Haskell was once again retained to serve on the San Juan.[59]

---

54. These events can be found in Hammond, Journal, July 15–29, 1887.

55. Francis A. Hammond, letter to John Taylor and George Q. Cannon, June 19, 1887.

56. Bluff Ward, General Minutes, June 25, 1887.

57. Hammond, Journal, July 31, 1887.

58. Hammond, Journal, August 7, 1887.

59. Wilford Woodruff, letter to Francis A. Hammond, August 11, 1887; Bluff Ward, General Minutes, August 14, 1887.

But the bitterness brought by the murder persisted. The Navajos were not a threat while the troops remained, but Bluff settlers had to tame their own feelings toward the Indians. In late November, President Hammond had to caution the Saints against harboring a spirit of revenge; such feelings might lead to a general massacre. At the precise moment these words left President Hammond's mouth, Frank Hyde shot at a stray cow in his field, startling the congregation and adding some unexpected excitement to the ominous prediction.[60] Frank Hyde, Amasa Barton's brother-in-law, was one of those who most needed to hear his leader's advice, since he and his brother Ernest continued to threaten Navajos who came to town. Even in January of the new year, the bishop and stake president had to talk with those who felt it was proper to whip an Indian caught stealing rather than try to reform him through persuasion. Some Navajos held grudges as well, refusing to let Bluff men cut cedar posts on the south side of the river.[61] Finally, early in 1888, Bishop Nielson and President Hammond got the Hyde brothers to promise not to go after the five surviving Navajos who took part in the murder and robbery. After this, Navajos returned in large [202] numbers to trade in Bluff again.[62] Once more a substantial physical threat had menaced Bluff's survival, but the threat to their mission had been at least as great. And once again, it had been overcome enough so that Bluff's settlers could persist where they were and justify their existence.

How to Continue

Evolution

During these difficulties, more settlers passed through the San Juan sieve. Earlier in 1887, the older settlers once again offered to share some of their southern fields closer to the ditch to satisfy the newcomers who did not like their locations.[63] But once again, the ditch and the other hard facts of life in Bluff disheartened almost all of the recent arrivals. Meanwhile, President Hammond continued to promote the region both

---

60. Hammond, Journal, November 27, 1887.
61. Hammond, Journal, January 3, 1888.
62. Hammond, Journal, January 23–26, 1888.
63. Hammond, Journal, January 13, 1887.

through the *Deseret News* and by writing directly to stake presidents, urging them to send settlers. "Your letters to the *News* are interesting," commented President John Taylor and his counselor George Q. Cannon, "and give the public a very good idea of the country; it has been much misrepresented and therefore been dreaded."[64]

Even for the stalwarts, the ditch continued to be their annual dread, bringing each year a new list of necessary repairs and improvements to keep at least the hope of water coming to the town. The bishop often provided the inspiration, admonishing the ward [203] members from the pulpit to "take hold of the ditch as it is not a big job."[65] The few remaining regulars such as Hyrum Perkins provided the prodigious annual labor: he "traveled on the trot and never tired," according to a fellow digger.[66] And every year the results continued to be about the same: the daunting work somehow got done, the first stream of water flowed to town amid jubilation, then it surged, often too much, until late July, when nature's spigot twisted shut, then the bishop rallied whoever was there (five town men and two Indians in 1889), and some crop was salvaged. Only about a hundred of the seven hundred available acres were harvested in a given year, though the number of available acres was beginning to drop into "Walton's Slough" as the river began to gnaw away at the land south of town. The settlers usually raised enough corn and potatoes to feed themselves, but still depended on flour from Colorado. Fortunately, the price had dropped to only $3.25 per hundred pounds, from almost three times that back in 1880.[67]

It was still incredible to people like President Hammond that such labor be expended, and he migrated to Mancos for most summers.[68] This absence might explain why he commented less on the ditch over the next few years, but it might have also had to do with the fact that if Bluff

---

64. John Taylor and George Q. Cannon, letter to Francis A. Hammond, March 25, 1887.

65. Bluff Ward, General Minutes, March 6, 1887.

66. Albert R. Lyman, "History of San Juan County," 50.

67. See Hammond, Journal for these years; Albert R. Lyman, "History of San Juan County," 58; and regular stake conference reports to the *Deseret News* for regular updates on the ditch and the crops during the late 1880s.

68. Bluff Ward, General Minutes, September 11, 1887, lists him as President Francis A. Hammond, "of Mancos, Colorado."

had to be held, as Brigham Young Jr. had said, then someone had to do it.
Wilford Woodruff, the presiding authority of the Church after John [204]
Taylor died on the underground in 1887, continued to insist that "it is of
great importance to keep it up," especially to keep political control of the
county. Having people relocate to Colorado would not fulfill "the object
of having them go to that region."[69] The Church authorities promised
more help in the form of more bodies, but if new people simply got discouraged and left the area, then the objective was not served either. The
leaders in Bluff had to find some way to hold souls to this hard country.

Offensive

Bishop Nielson and his counselors met at President Hammond's home
on February 27, 1887, just after the regular meetings of their quarterly
stake conference. What they discussed changed the mission. A few days
earlier, they had failed to come up with a mutually acceptable division
of the nearby range with Brooks, the foreman of the LC Cattle Company. That outfit was moving another thousand head of cattle closer to
Bluff, to go with perhaps three thousand more head of "outside" cattle,
plus forty thousand sheep.[70] And so, in their meeting, Church leaders
agreed that they would call certain families from Bluff and Mancos to
make new settlements on the North and South Montezuma creeks. The
plans were announced in a special meeting the next day.[71] Clearly this
was an attempt to extend the San Juan Stake of Zion to better hold the
resources and ranges in the county against the Gentiles. But the settlements would further [205] constrict the Utes who chose not to live on
the reservation and the Paiutes, who still had no reservation on which
to live. The Church leaders may have discussed other consequences of
the move in their meeting. The new areas might be more dependable for
farming, allowing the Saints to diversify what they produced and buy
grain from each other rather than "from Babylon."[72] They seemed to be

---

69. Wilford Woodruff, letter to Francis A. Hammond, October 3, 1887.

70. Hammond, Journal, February 11 and 21, 1887.

71. Hammond, Journal, February 27 and 28, 1887.

72. See Abruzzi, "Ecology, Resource Redistribution," 642–55, for the advantages
of multihabitat settlements in the harsh environment on the Little Colorado River
in Arizona. Bluff and Monticello did not develop the same institutionalized system
of tithing redistribution, but they eventually aided each other in different ways.

more desirable places to live than Bluff, solving most of the problem of dissatisfied settlers fleeing the county altogether. It had to be a difficult choice for the bishop, since it consigned those who remained at Bluff to their annual purgatory of ditch digging with meager numbers. But this was the compromise position between the bishop and the stake president: Bluff would not be abandoned, but it would be weakened for the good of the mission.

F. I. Jones was called in 1887 to preside over the North Montezuma settlement, and a number of Bluff residents, including Jens Peter Nielson, were called to help establish it that summer. They were specifically instructed. First, they should be careful what they wrote about the mission: far too many negative reports in newspapers had made people reluctant to come to the county in the past. Second, they had to find out exactly what the Carlisles claimed up there. They should stay together that first year and try to avoid difficulties with cowboys. "We expect Carlisle & Co. to make some objections to our locating on these streams," President Hammond wrote. He also wrote a preemptive letter to the British brothers, informing them of the impending settlements. [206] Sure enough, Brother Jones soon reported he had been "warned off" the property by Harold Carlisle. Still, when President Hammond met with the Carlisles in Colorado, some cordiality remained despite the Carlisles seeming "a little sore over the matter." But President Hammond also consulted an attorney on the issue, who advised him to keep possession of the area.[73]

Meanwhile, the Mormons went to work on their new towns. One of the reasons so few men were in Bluff during the confrontation with the Navajos in June was that many of them were digging a ditch on the North Montezuma. F. I. Jones, the Charles Waltons (Sr. and Jr.), Parley Butt, and the Adams brothers were all up north. Originally their settlement was to be named "Hammond," but when the object of that honor objected, Charles Walton proposed "Monticello," after Jefferson's "little mountain."[74]

It did not take long for the Carlisles' stranglehold on the land and water to weaken. A former Carlisle cowboy named Fritz filed a quit-claim deed

73. Hammond, Journal, April 3, May 13 and 17, June 8, 1887.

74. Albert R. Lyman, "History of San Juan County," 54–55.

on behalf of the Mormon settlers. Then President Hammond met a woman in Colorado who claimed she owned half of the Carlisles' North Montezuma ditch. A Mr. Carpenter owned the other half. It appeared that the Carlisle brothers, English citizens that they were, might not own title to any of their land personally. The first season at Monticello ended in triumph for its residents. The wheat crop did very well, and Edmund Carlisle failed to show up at a hearing to defend his water rights.[75] The Monticello pioneers folded back into Bluff for [207] the winter, but made bigger plans for 1888.

One day that next spring, the Waltons were almost completely surprised by the flock of people and the quantity of food that descended on them. They were packing up to be the first family to permanently settle in Monticello, and almost all of Bluff came to send them off. The young gave recitations, the old gave speeches, and everyone sang until a late hour.[76] Bluff would miss the actor/bugler/teacher/fiddler and his family. Farewells, with or without the party, would be repeated often in the years to come. What built Monticello directly diminished Bluff. But Bluff's bishop now understood that his town could not do everything alone. This conclusion was apparent in his own family's movements. Soon after the Waltons departed, Kumen and Mary Jones, as well as Jens Peter, went to Dodge Springs for the summer to run the "Nielson's & Co." dairy, where they used common range cows to produce at least fifty pounds of "very good" cheese a day.[77] Willard and Julia Butt split time between the dairy and South Montezuma (later named Verdure), where Willard and his brother Parley operated a sawmill. Joe, France, and Jens Peter were often out on the range with the herds, and Joe was running a store on the San Juan above the abandoned town of Montezuma.

As a whole, the county prospered. Monticello already superseded Bluff in some ways. Some of its new homes were shingled, and its farmers raised another good crop of wheat, oats, and vegetables, in spite of the cowboy who told Charles E. Walton Jr. that [208] "you'll have to draw your gizzard up pretty small if you live on farming in this country."

---

75. Albert R. Lyman, "History of San Juan County," 54–55; Hammond, Journal, August 9, November 15, 1887.

76. Hammond, Journal, May 14, 1888.

77. Hammond, Journal, July 24, 1886, June 11 and 21, September 14, 1888; Francis A. Hammond, "The San Juan Country," Deseret News, August 22, 1888, 499.

Monticello hosted its first stake conference in its new meetinghouse (shingled, of course) in August 1888, but Bishop Nielson did not attend for some reason.[78]

Not everything was perfect, though. Just after the town's Fourth of July celebration, the Carlisles turned the water out of North Montezuma Creek and put an injunction on the claims of the Blue Mountain Irrigation Company, the organization of Monticello water owners. President Hammond had to again engage in personal diplomacy with the brothers to get at least some water sent back down, and the legal issues would take years to fully untangle. Furthermore, that first conference in the Monticello meetinghouse was disrupted by a cowboy riding through town firing his pistol, a sign of ugly incidents to come. And the eight families that braved the winter of 1888–89 in Monticello were snowed in for six weeks.[79]

But on the whole, President Hammond's bold venture onto new land with questionable water rights worked. Even some residents of Bluff bought fields in Monticello to farm in the summer. All of this was good for the mission: the Mormon presence in San Juan County was significantly increased. But it left Bluff a lonelier place. When Brigham Young Jr. stopped by Bluff after the Monticello Conference to count how many men were still settled there, he found fourteen.[80] Platte Lyman felt "there are but eight families here who are not interested in making a place somewhere [209] else."[81] Yet the bishop and his remaining few soon found some compensating advantages in staying where they were.

Flocks and Herds

By the fall of 1887, President Wilford Woodruff had heard regarding Bluff that "the families who are there are making means more rapidly than double the same number of families in any other settlement."[82] When the bishop wrapped up his year as the first president of the San Juan Co-op,

---

78. The quote and the events are in Albert R. Lyman, "History of San Juan County," 58–59.

79. For these difficulties, see Lyman, "History of San Juan County," 58–62; Hammond, Journal, April 20 and 24, September 3, 13, 15, and 20, November 17 and 18, 1888.

80. Hammond, Journal, September 4, 1888.

81. Albert R. Lyman, "History of San Juan County," 66.

82. Wilford Woodruff, letter to Francis A. Hammond, October 3, 1887.

his report confirmed the town's prosperity. There was a bounteous crop of nearly five thousand lambs, and the store, small tannery, and shoe businesses also did well. This meant that the shareholders would gain a thumping 40 percent dividend on their initial investments. Francis Hammond was elected as the new president, while Jens Nielson was chosen as one of four directors to try to continue the bonanza.[83] This was why the co-op was organized, to help the Saints prosper through cooperation rather than competition. But the cooperation did not last uninterrupted for long.

Under the co-op arrangement, shareholders could submit bids to herd the collective sheep. The bishop had a particular interest in the well-being of this flock, since an increasing fraction of it was the ward's tithing herd, paid to him as the sheep multiplied. He and his sons also hoped they could profit from doing the herding. To [210] pursue these ends, they put in a bid that was accepted by the co-op board for the next two years. The Nielsons posted a fifteen thousand dollar bond for security, which was standard procedure for anyone undertaking a corporate or public trust. But everything changed after a heated meeting on Saturday, January 28, 1888. Francis Hammond, the new president of the co-op, reversed the board's decision. Hanson Bayles had pointed out to him that the bishop and his sons were already bonded for more than they were worth. Joe had taken out bonds for his position as county selectman, and the family might also have been in debt for some of their business ventures. Technically Hammond was correct on this point, and he felt it was part of his duty as president to reject the bid. But the bishop was furious, since this also appeared to be a lack of trust among men and Saints who had worked so closely together. Jens was still upset at church the next day. President Hammond approached him on the stand and offered his hand, but Jens refused to take it. Hammond was stunned; nothing like this had ever happened to him before. For his part, the bishop had never been so upset at a priesthood leader. The ward could not help but notice the split. On Monday, the two men tried to restore unity by talking "at length" over the issue, as they knew they must, but agreement still escaped them. Francis Hammond, looking at the letter of the law, was not conscious of having done any harm. In the

83. Hammond, Journal, December 27, 1887; San Juan Cooperative Association, Ledger, 274.

spirit of the matter, Jens still felt the wound and proposed submitting the affair to the ward's teachers for resolution.[84] [211]

Sister Mary Ann Bayles, Hanson's wife, had given birth to a baby girl the same Sunday the bishop refused to shake the stake president's hand. The delivery did not go well, and Sister Bayles was very ill. President Hammond and William Adams visited her and had just finished giving a priesthood blessing, when they were summoned to Charles Walton's home. Brother Walton was in charge of the teachers quorum of the ward, and he requested President Hammond to come answer charges filed against him by the bishop, his two oldest sons, and Parley and Willard Butt regarding the bid for herding. After some discussion, the group decided the matter most properly belonged to the co-op's board of directors, so the teachers were dismissed and a special session of the board was called. After only minutes of this meeting, an urgent summons came to again administer to Sister Bayles since she seemed to be nearing death's door. Some men went to do this, then they returned and resumed the meeting. It was again interrupted by another call to administer, followed swiftly by the message that Sister Bayles had died. The meeting adjourned, and as the men left they found Brigham Young Jr. had arrived just in time to be with Sister Bayles at the end. All discussion about things such as flocks and herding was suspended for the evening as the ward mourned the death of this twenty-six-year-old sister. The next day the weather was as unsettled as the ward. The bishop and the stake president shared the stand in the packed meetinghouse as they commemorated the late Sister Bayles. There was both snow and mud on the ground as the house emptied to march up to the cemetery. Lemuel Redd dedicated the grave, and a choir sang "White Robes Are Waiting for Thee." [212]

Brigham Young Jr. was in business with his brothers-in-law, Alma and Joshua Stevens, who had made some improvements up Butler Wash

---

84. See Hammond, Journal, January 28 to February 12, 1888, for the whole episode about the herding bid and Sister Bayles. See also Jensen, "Historical Study of Bluff City," 72, for additional details. President Hammond continued to insist that proper bonds be filed. When Judge Barton failed to post the six thousand dollar bond required for his position in early 1889, Selectman Hammond protested. When Barton did post the bond later, Hammond still protested, since Barton had assumed the duties of his office before posting the proper amount. See San Juan County Minute Book, March 5, 1889.

and on Elk Mountain. So Elder Young decided to take a trip with his partners to look things over, and Jens Nielson accompanied them. They were gone for three days, until Monday, February 6, so Bishop Nielson did not have to confront President Hammond on the stand again on Sunday. It also gave him a chance to talk the matter over with Elder Young and get some distance from it.

The night they returned, the co-op board met again to review the issue. Not only did the Nielsons' bid lack the proper bonds, but so did all the others, so all were nullified. Then, "after a long labor with each other it was agreed to mutually ask each others' forgiveness and shake hands and try and do better in the future." Jens confessed he wished he had not brought the matter up in the first place. After midnight the meeting broke up, as the issue, which had been a public spectacle, was laid to rest—almost. There was one last thing to say, and Jens said it. The next Sunday, the bishop stood before the ward and asked forgiveness for refusing to shake President Hammond's hand two weeks before. The requested favor was swiftly granted, and good feelings were officially restored. The bishop, who normally helped resolve these clashes of interests and personalities, was reminded how swiftly they could destroy his ward and himself if he were not faithful and careful.

Jens and the rest of the co-op board had plenty to deal with for the rest of the year. They continually tried to improve their original Navajo and Mexican stock by [213] crossbreeding them with French merino rams.[85] Herding continued to be a problem. They arranged as well as they could after the bid fiasco, but the summer herding was not done well. Many sheep were lost, and many others developed scab. Rain was scarce in the late summer and fall, and they knew in the winter they would have to successfully hold their range against perhaps a hundred thousand outside sheep, many of which came in from Colorado for a winter range that charged lower taxes. Indian trade dropped at the store because the supervisor, Joseph F. Barton, "was not qualified to win the Indians' good feelings."[86] Perhaps he was not yet over the murder of his brother. And the widow Barton, along with her mother and brothers, wanted to withdraw their substantial four thousand dollar investment from the company, more than a quarter of the

---

85. Jensen, "Historical Study of Bluff City," 71.
86. Hammond, Journal, April 26, 1888.

total stock. The corporation could ill afford to let this amount go, since they still owed four thousand dollars to the Durango banks from their large sheep purchase more than a year before. The co-op board hoped to pay this off with the profits from the fall wool clip, but when wool sold for only twelve cents a pound, they could not cover the whole amount and had to pay the 10 percent interest on the balance. At the end of 1888, with all these difficulties, the co-op paid no dividend. Early in 1889, many stockholders talked about dissolving the San Juan Co-op altogether.[87]

Meanwhile, the cattle owners of Bluff continued to try to unite. Across the [214] western United States, range wars blazed between sheepherders and cattlemen. Bluff experienced few such difficulties, largely because the same person usually owned both types of stock. If conflicts did break out, the Church provided both the incentive and the forum to work them out. In May 1888, for example, the bishop appointed Hyrum Perkins to smooth some friction between the two interests.[88] Most of the Bluff cattlemen summered their herds somewhere near Elk Mountain. Their winter ranges extended from Lake Pagharit, close to the Colorado River, down to the washes surrounding Bluff. But some of this range had been preempted by a herd of two thousand Texas longhorns that grazed around the abandoned outpost at Rincon in the fall of 1887.

The competition from the Texas outfit, as well as the Carlisles and the LC cattle companies, finally drove Bluff's stockmen to cooperate. Just before they left to take their herd onto Elk Mountain for the summer in 1888, most reached an agreement and hired herders for a "Bluff Pool" of cattle. But they were also pressured by the poor cattle market in 1888. Complaints of monopolies controlling the eastern markets echoed through Bluff as well as the rest of the country.[89] By pooling and selling together, the Bluff cattle raisers hoped to cut herding costs and improve their negotiating power, though each member would continue to control his own brand and calves. But the pool was not watertight yet. Disagreements kept some from joining and caused contention among those already in. "Through selfishness

87. For these troubles, see Hammond, Journal, April 26, June 6, September 5, November 11, 1888, February 1, 25, 1889. See also Lemuel H. Redd Sr., letter to family, January 22, 1889; Hammond, "San Juan Country."

88. Jensen, "Historical Study of Bluff City," 78; see also Jens Nielson, letter to Francis A. Hammond, June 15, 1887.

89. Hammond, "San Juan Country."

we cannot unite," lamented President [215] Hammond, who later shipped some of his stock east with the LC Company.[90] Poor prices and the parched range made most stockmen nervous about the upcoming winter. In a year in which "cattleman in the West were all overdrawing their bank accounts," when Durango bankers offered to help the pool buy out the troublesome Texas herd, the pool declined.[91] Jens Nielson, though, was well off enough that he could buy some new stock toward the end of the year.[92]

Business turned up the next year. The San Juan Co-op took a hard line with its debtors and started to charge them the same 10 percent interest the company had to pay the Durango banks.[93] They made a better contract with Durango businessmen for their wool, and they brought back Indian trade to the store by hiring Thales Haskell as the salesman. By August the co-op was out of debt.[94] The cattle multiplied and fattened as well, even though the range was still dry. Just after Thanksgiving in 1889, the quarterly stake conference was held at Bluff. President Hammond announced that all the wards had been blessed financially during the past year, but Bluff especially had prospered. When the San Juan Co-op declared its dividend at the end of the year, it was 40 percent again, a return that would be repeated for the next three years. As the town approached its tenth anniversary in 1890, all were satisfied with the co-op, and the cattle [216] pool held together.[95] In spite of its annually undermanned ditch digging and its permanent "dry camp" status, Bluff was prospering financially.[96]

---

90. Hammond, Journal, August 5 and November 20, 1888.

91. Hammond, "San Juan Country"; Tennity, "Elk Mountain Cattle Company," 16–17.

92. Hammond, Journal, September 30, December 12, 1888.

93. Hammond, Journal, February 25, 1889.

94. Hammond, Journal, May 27, July 6, August 5, 1889.

95. See Martha Hammond, letter to Francis A. Hammond, December 11, 1889, Francis A. Hammond Papers, Perry Special Collections.

96. Peterson, Look to the Mountains; and Alexander, Utah, the Right Place, 208, declare Bluff's livestock either a carefully planned offensive or deliberate war against the other cattle companies. Alexander even refers to "several lamentable killings" that occurred over the Montezuma water controversy. I agree that the Mormons aggressively expanded onto the range, and quite a few of these activities were coordinated by Francis Hammond. But it was not as deliberate and aggressive as both authors make it sound. Many times the Mormons worked for and cooperated with the other cattle companies, and President Hammond's exchanges with the Carlisles as well as Brooks, the LC foreman, were always at least civil. Both authors also use the

If Leonard Arrington's assertion that "the building of the Kingdom was partly a process of turning disasters into windfalls" is true, then Bluff was a prime example during these years.[97]

Bluff Life

Cowboys

Prosperity brought its own problems. The cowboy lifestyle was not very conducive to building a community. The men were gone for weeks at a time several seasons of the year, and this was hard on their families. One Bluff girl recalled the often-repeated farewells. After kissing their father goodbye, "we'd stand there and wave as [217] long as we could see him. Oh that was sad.... We sure hated to see Dad go."[98] In the absence of the men, the prayers of many Bluff women continued to be, "Bless the Indians that they may have no power over us."[99] The cattlemen had to ride hundreds of miles to round up and move the herds to their summer and winter ranges, go after strays, brand calves, and drive the cattle to market. Sheep had their own demands. They had to be herded perpetually, bred properly, sheared once or twice a year, and dipped just as often to fight scabies. They also had to be driven to their winter and summer ranges and marked or docked for identification.[100]

---

term "Bluff Tigers" to refer to the town's cattlemen. This nickname goes back to John Riis's book, *Ranger Trails*, 51, in which he, a newly arrived forest ranger around 1907, declares "Bluff City Tigers" the name by which "the cowmen from that section were called." This name was probably not used until the 1890s or early 1900s. The "vigorous and almost ruthless self-interest" referred to in Peterson's and Alexander's works and echoed in McPherson, *History of San Juan County*, is overstated. Bluff expanded vigorously to secure a range, carved out a basic working arrangement with the other companies, and maintained usually cordial relations and open communications throughout. The drought and depression of the 1890s forced the big companies out more than Mormon aggressiveness. Since the Mormons were rooted in the country, some were happy to buy the companies when they left. The "Bluff Tigers," in fact had plenty of trouble forming and holding together their own cattle pool.

97. Arrington, *Great Basin Kingdom*, 38.

98. Quoted in Lambert, "Al Scorup," 312.

99. A. J. Redd et. al., "A Short Biography of Lucy Zina Lyman Redd," in Amasa Jay Redd, *Lemuel Hardison Redd, Jr.*, 189.

100. Albert R. Lyman's journal gives excellent details about the life of a San Juan cowboy. Platte Lyman's diary and Wayne Redd's journal also give some good

Life on the range was not particularly pleasant: saddle sores and bowed legs were just the beginning. Camps were often unsanitary.[101] "Every trip had its peculiar thrills and interesting features, but they all included riding, riding, choking, starving, driving cattle, branding calves, drinking water alive with wigglers and pollywogs and meeting with drenching rain or stinging hail."[102] The cowboys ate a lot of bread, beef, and beans in their camps and were lucky if they had bottled rice or stewed peaches for variety. These staples, along with the jerked beef on the trail, sometimes "bred nausea and thirst [218] and cramp."[103] The long rides with only cows for company became monotonous: "I sang, preached, recited, lectured and yelled to pass the time," one cowboy remembered of a long ride back to Bluff.[104] Stationary life in camp often was not much better, as Joe Nielson lamented to his family one summer, "There is nothing to write about. I believe it will be more lonesome for me this summer than last. I hope some of you will write often. Tell the boys to write."[105] Still, nothing made the men appreciate Bluff more than a trip to "the Lake" or some other forlorn place. "Bluff seemed like a green garden compared to the country I had just come from," wrote one homesick cowpuncher.[106]

There were also the occupational hazards of the job. Bluff's men were very fortunate in these early years not to have any serious accidents or deaths on the trail. No one had yet lost fingers in a suddenly constricted lariat like the Carlisles' foreman Latigo Gordon. But the risks were always there of this or some worse accident, and the stock was often in danger as well, sometimes from Indians, sometimes from storms or droughts, and sometimes just from themselves. An unknown cause started the Hydes' sheep stampeding in 1889, for instance, and they did not stop until about two hundred had plunged over a one-hundred-foot cliff.[107]

---

information about this subject. See also Jensen, "Historical Study of Bluff City," 73–75.

101. Albert R. Lyman, Journal, July 9, 1897.

102. Albert R. Lyman, Summaries of Each Year, 1892, book 1, p. 73.

103. Albert R. Lyman, Summaries of Each Year, 1894, book 1, p. 98.

104. Albert R. Lyman, Journal, October 7, 1901.

105. H. J. Nielson, letter to Ida Nielson, July 1, 1902, 165.

106. Albert R. Lyman, Journal, June 18, 1904.

107. "A Disastrous Stampede," *Deseret News*, August 16, 1889, from Journal History, August 16, 1889, 2.

The cowboy life hid spiritual dangers as well. Men out on the range could not [219] attend Church meetings. They might start neglecting their prayers. Sermons were frequently given on the subject of not cursing or beating the poor, dumb cattle, but out on the range with the wayward cusses the temptation could easily become too great. Bishop Nielson also warned the youth against branding stray cattle as their own.[108] Especially when working for gentile companies or with outside cowboys, there was the strong temptation to mix in with their profane ways. Platte Lyman not only disliked the hard country and life of the cattleman, but found it sad how even Mormon boys would sometimes mock anyone who tried to uphold his virtues on the range.[109] The drinking, smoking, and tobacco chewing prevalent among gentile cowboys were also too readily adopted by Bluff cowboys.

The allure of the cowboy was too much for Bluff boys to resist. At their age and place they could not help but admire the lariats, wide hats, fine boots, pearl or ivory handled revolvers, the "short rifle under the fender," and especially the attitude: they "did not give a damn for nothing."[110] Some Bluff men tried to protect their boys against this influence. When Platte Lyman found Texas outfit cowboys in the same area where he needed to work for a few days, he sent his son, Albert, on a fifty-mile ride back to Bluff alone rather than be around those men. The Nielson boys seemed to have more contact, being older and working sometimes for the outside cattle companies, though at times Church authorities [220] counseled against such employment.[111] Bluff's young men had been taught well against the vices of the cowboys, but even young Albert Lyman, who had once scrawled, "I would much sooner make shoes than be a wretched cowboy," admitted an unconscious admiration for them and later on bought himself a six shooter because he liked the look of it.[112] For other Bluff boys the admiration was much more determined. Francis Hammond pled "for mercy and charity to be shown towards our wild boys." "Gain them by love," he urged.[113] There

---

108. Hammond, Journal, March 10, 1889.

109. Albert R. Lyman, "Experiences and Impressions," 1:51.

110. Lyman, "Experiences and Impressions," 1:120.

111. Hammond, Journal, September 9, 1888.

112. Lyman, "Experiences and Impressions," 1:51; Albert R. Lyman, Journal, 2:6.

113. Hammond, Journal, May 26, 1889.

was something of a reformation in early 1889. Boys and young men such as Jens Peter Nielson "expressed their desires to do better in the future than they had in the past" and declared their testimonies of the gospel more often in meetings.[114] Still, as Martha Hammond contemplated matches for the Hammond girls, she was unimpressed: "You know the boys that are here in Bluff as well as I do are not a fit companion for the girls."[115]

If the Bluff cowboys were not fit, outside cowboys were even less so. Bluff's dances were a magnet for range-weary men. Their attendance was acceptable as long as there were not too many of them and they behaved themselves. Those who played instruments were particularly welcome now that Samuel Cox and Charles Walton had taken their fiddles elsewhere. The cowboys had to respect the authority of the floor [221] manager, dance only when their numbers were called, remove their spurs, and not smuggle in alcohol and firearms. When they first started showing up in early 1887, "they behaved like gentlemen," and a few even stayed around to attend Church meetings the next day.[116]

But real trouble broke out at the dance that closed the quarterly stake conference in March 1888. Bluff boys invited some cowboys to attend. The word spread, and the cowboys came in such large numbers that some were refused admission to the dance. This did not go over well, and the bishop and stake president tried to make some explanations to them. But those who were "disposed to cause trouble" tried to force their way in. In the fracas, some of the cowboys and some of the Bluff boys went for their guns and serious trouble seemed imminent. But since there was no liquor and enough chivalry was "possessed by a good percent of the otherwise rough cowboy element," both sides compromised and violence was averted. The disgruntled cowboys who could not get in "only shot off their mouths," even muttering some threats against the Church leaders, until the end of the dance, when they rode out of town at a gallop shooting off their guns in the streets of Bluff. There was "a great panic for a few moments," but everything was calm by 1:00 AM. A few of the cowboys were ashamed the next day, but others were still contemplating

114. Hammond, Journal, January 6, 1889.
115. Martha Hammond, letter to Francis A. Hammond, January 21, 1890.
116. Hammond, Journal, January 1, 1887.

action against Bishop Nielson and President Hammond until Kumen Jones gave them a dressing down in camp a few days later. "May the Lord give us wisdom … to keep ourselves from contamination with the wicked," hoped [222] President Hammond.[117] "Keep your daughters from the society of the *cow boys*," was a common theme in church.[118]

Part of the situation improved soon after. Cowboys kept attending dances, but behaved better. Most of the concern in dances was directed toward Bluff's youth. Girls dressed too extravagantly, in the opinion of their Church leaders, and boys and girls alike would not give up their closed-position round dances, such as the waltz. Church authorities preferred the called quadrilles, similar to square dances, in which the partners were not so close. An epistle from the Apostles in 1877 recommended that no more than one or two waltzes be permitted in an evening.[119] The bishop tried to set the example. When a dance was ready to start, he asked the musicians if they were ready and willing, then called on someone to open with prayer before turning over direction of the dance to the floor manager for the evening. Despite his twisted feet, he danced some respectable figures, such as the quadrilles, speed the plows, and Scottish reels, but he never danced the waltzes. He called for the closing prayer before it got too late.[120] But there were still problems. On one occasion a young man successfully bribed Joe Nielson and Kumen [223] Jones, the floor managers, to add another waltz. "The priesthood must be firm," lamented their stake president.[121]

Once again, though events in Bluff were sometimes alarming, the town looked good by comparison. Monticello, closer to the Carlisles' base, had more frequent ruckuses and Bishop F. I. Jones had to deal with more threats. On one occasion he may have missed being dragged up and down the town's streets when he decided at the last minute not to attend a dance. Mons Peterson, the storekeeper, imported liquor "for

---

117. See Hammond, Journal, March 6–11, 1888; Kumen Jones, "Writings," 210–11; Albert R. Lyman, "History of San Juan County," 56–58.

118. See Hammond, Journal, November 15, 1888.

119. Shumway, "Dancing the Buckles Off Their Shoes," 197, 215–16; Arrington and Bitton, *Mormon Experience*, 219.

120. Albert R. Lyman, "To the Family of My Dear Bishop Jens Nielson," September 21, 1965, 48.

121. Hammond, Journal, December 6, 1887.

medicine," which, once stolen by cowboys, fueled them in a furious spate of riding and shooting around town. Latigo Gordon and Tom Roach were two cowboys who married Mormon girls. At least in Monticello, Church authorities kept a tenuous grasp on the reins of authority. In Moab the cowboy element was in charge. Killings were frequent, and even the schoolteacher was beaten out of town by a cowboy.[122]

Domestic Concerns

Dances were not the only occasions that caused Bluff's leaders to consider the town's safety. Leaders always worried and sometimes spoke about the danger of leaving the women and children exposed to insults and violence from Indians and "wicked whites." "Our families are worth more than the cattle on a thousand hills," President Hammond admonished.[123] Often there were only two or three men in town, and [224] occasionally the bishop was the only one left. Jens was still one of the few men who could stay in town most of the time, thanks to his older boys, who could care for the livestock and look after the dairy. Joe was thirty by 1890, and his family had grown to four children by then. He had taken over for his father in civic responsibilities, serving as a county selectman from 1885 through 1889. As such, and as someone who traveled often from Verdure to Bluff and Colorado, he helped to extend and improve county roads north to the border with Emery County and east to Colorado. Jens himself contracted with the county court in 1888 to build a section of road on the north side of Devil Canyon, leading toward Monticello, and his sons undoubtedly did a lot of the work.[124] Joe continued to be his open, cheerful self, and he was so hospitable that his wife, Ida, never knew whom he was going to bring home for dinner.

Jens Peter, at twenty-eight, was not married, but was a giant of a man at six and a half feet and over 250 pounds, capable of loading four fifty-pound sacks of flour at a time.[125] Kumen Jones felt he "did more hard work than any one man."[126] His altitude became a unit of measure, as

---

122. See Albert R. Lyman, "History of San Juan County," 65, 68; also *Indians and Outlaws*, 102–8; Hammond, Journal, October 25, December 14, 1888; April 4, 1890.

123. Hammond, Journal, October 20; May 26, 1889.

124. See San Juan County Minute Book, December 31, 1884–August 6, 1889.

125. Jennie R. Nielson, "Memory Gems of Jens Peter Nielson," 170.

126. Kumen Jones, "Writings," 192.

children claimed the water in their swimming hole in Cow Canyon came up to Jens Nielson's neck.[127] But he always had something childlike about him and was full of mirth and jokes. France was twenty-two, a little less shy than he once was, and rode the range for the pool. The unmarried boys worked for the family's [225] prosperity "without compensation."[128] Jens's sons-in-law also helped in the family businesses. Kumen Jones, Willard Butt, and, after Margaret married him in 1888, John Ernest Adams added to the manpower that allowed the bishop to remain with his ward in Bluff. Julia's husband, Willard, was also appointed the constable for the Bluff Precinct in late 1888, and his title was later revised to that of sheriff. Soon after his appointment, law enforcement in the county was upgraded when the county court approved the expenses for four pairs of handcuffs and two pairs of shackles.[129] Julia was often the hostess to travelers and to arrested criminals passing through Verdure and won a reputation as being hospitable to everyone, regardless of the time of day or the misdeeds of those she was hosting.[130]

The prolonged absence of the men meant that much of the time Bluff's society was dominated by women and children. The women not only nurtured their faith in divine protection but also developed a "sturdy self-assertiveness."[131] It was a difficult life their church asked them to live. As one outsider noticed later, if the men "worked hard on the range and in the fields, the women toiled twice as hard at home."[132] They ground away at the tasks that occupied most of a woman's time throughout the West. A great [226] deal of Monday was devoted to washing, assaulting the soiled clothes with the washboard, tub, boiling water, and homemade soap.[133] Regular meals, bread, cheese, candles, and clothes were other items most were expected to produce, and many also

---

127. Albert R. Lyman, "History of San Juan County," 84.

128. *Utah Since Statehood*, 4:688–89.

129. See San Juan County Minute Book, December 28, 1888; September 2, 1890; and December 30, 1891.

130. Ellertson and Ellertson, "Julia Ann Nielson and Willard (Dick) Butt," 134.

131. Albert R. Lyman, "History of San Juan County," 66.

132. Riis, *Ranger Trails*, 44.

133. Some had early washing contraptions, but they were still hard work, as Albert Lyman indicated when he boasted, "I turned thirteen hundred licks on the washer." Albert R. Lyman, Journal, August 6, 1895.

had to care for vegetable gardens and domestic livestock. Spring cleaning was particularly difficult, with the yards of stained factory cloth added to all the other items that needed to be purged. A woman living in another frontier settlement in Arizona summed up the labor this way:

> I will just write my morning chores. Get up, turn out my chickens, draw a pail of water, water hot beds, make a fire, put potatoes to cook, then brush and sweep half inch of dust off floor and everything, feed three litters of chickens, then mix biscuits, get breakfast, milk besides work in the house, and this morning had to go half mile after calves. This is the way of life on the farm.[134]

This was the life Jens's wives lived. Elsie continued to quietly burn daylight making life more comfortable for all around her. Her more limited abilities in the English language made her radius smaller than that of her husband and Kirsten, but within that arc she was well esteemed. She was particularly well loved by Katrine's children, one of whom felt that "Aunt Elsie" was the "best, kindest woman on earth," treating him "like his own mother would have."[135] She spent a lot of time on a little, green chair with rawhide straps across the seat in front of the fireplace. But she was always busy, always [227] industrious, like most Bluff women, her fingers were always working on some project. "She was one woman that could do anything she wanted done."[136] Kirsten also continued to carry out her demanding domestic role. She had been trained as a seamstress in Denmark and used these skills to good effect in Bluff, making her family's clothes out of cloth from Durango or the mail-order catalogues. She also traded for tanned buckskin from the Indians and made scores of gloves and other articles.[137] Like many Bluff women, Elsie and Kirsten often hired Indian women to help with the burdensome chores, particularly the washing. Jens's wives also participated in the quilting and sewing and rag bees to socialize through these long tasks. Elsie and Kirsten continued to get along like sisters, helping each other when it was possible. As one of Kirsten's daughters recalled, "I have never seen

---

134. Lucy Hannah Flake, Diary, May 16, 1896, quoted in Peterson, *Take Up Your Mission*, 255–56.

135. Uriah Nielson, "Elsie Nielson," 80.

136. Meo, "Uriah and Annie Butt Talk About Elsie Rasmussen," 82.

137. Reeve, "Lucinda Diantha Nielson Hyde," 201.

a polygamous family who had less friction than our family had."[138] Jens
ate breakfast and supper with Elsie and dinner, the big mid-day meal,
with Kirsten.[139]

While "just living was so time consuming," Bluff's women had to
continue to live knowing that their lives would be easier elsewhere.[140]
Frequently they and their children had to care for the farms during their
husbands' and fathers' long absences. And they [228] were approaching
ten years of living in log cabins, some still with dirt floors. They might
be driven out of even these if the government decided to do it, and some
secretly hoped it would happen. Martha Hammond confided to her
husband, "It is amusing to me to hear the sisters talk. They all hope and
pray that this place will go in to Indian Reservation. I tell them I hope
it won't go as it would be such a disappointment to the men. But if I am
not mistaken I think that the sisters are only telling what the men would
like."[141] Reflecting on the situation, Kumen Jones mused he was glad he
was not born a woman.[142]

On top of all this, Bluff's women also fulfilled the obligations of
their church and civic organizations. When Jane Walton left with her
husband to settle in Monticello in 1888, Kirsten Nielson was called
by her husband to be the president of the Relief Society in the Bluff
Ward. As such, she held weekly meetings, looked after the women in
the ward, engaged in projects to help the Saints and Indians, such as
making carpets and quilts, and looked after the small sheep herd owned
by the group. Her home was often where visiting Church authorities
stayed. And like all women in the town, she visited the sick and afflicted
with small tokens of her good wishes, such as bullberry jam or loaves of
bread.[143] Elsie was a champion of the older teachings of self-sufficiency:
she faithfully kept her beehives and tended her mulberry bushes. Both
women spoke in the quarterly Relief Society conferences that were held
just after the stake conferences. Whether they [229] were referring to their

138. Reeve, "Lucinda Diantha Nielson Hyde," 200.

139. Kimmerle, "Little Visit," 226.

140. See Perkins, Nielson, and Jones, *Saga of San Juan*, 112–13, for a description
of women's life in Monticello.

141. Martha Hammond to Francis A. Hammond, December 11, 1889.

142. Kumen Jones, "Writings," 188.

143. Gabbart and Redd, "Brief History of Kirsten Jensen Nielson," 138.

spiritual or language limitations, each said "she felt her weakness in trying to say anything" to the group or instruct the Saints. But both grew
more confident with time and always expressed strong testimonies "in
all Revelations and principles of the gospel" as well as in their mission.[144]
Both were also diligent students of the Bible. The Church and the community added more work to do but also eased the physical and mental
burdens these women always carried, and Jens was present to help more
than most men of the town.

Jens could also spend more time with his younger children, though
they were no longer so young. The boys were old enough to start riding
the range in the summer, and all the children went to school in the fall and
winter, taught by Charles Walton, J. L. Young, and A. P. Sorenson in these
years. The day sessions were supplemented by special spelling schools,
debates, and presentations held in the evening. They also had their round
of Primary and youth association meetings, programs, and activities. Even
though the county collected taxes to support public education, the bishop
was at least partly responsible for the quality of the schools.[145]

But Jens's oldest daughter, Mary, needed particular attention. She
continued to help care for the sick in town while harboring her own
inner grief. She had consented for Kumen to take a second wife in 1882,
but her father's promise of a child of her own remained unfulfilled.
She visited the temple in St. George sometime in these years and [230]
received a special anointing in which she was once again assured she
would bear a child. She conceived after returning to Bluff, but her hopes
were dashed when she miscarried. In 1889 she was expecting again and
with guarded hopes guessed the baby would be a girl. On November 6,
the long-awaited infant was delivered, and it was a boy. "Why I was
expecting a girl baby," Mary told her father. Jens replied, "Did you ever
hear of a literal child of promise being a girl?"[146]

Jens could be proud of the work his children were doing to build the
Church and fulfill their mission. Mary was first counselor in the ward's
Young Ladies Mutual Improvement Association. Julia was the president
of the stake Primary organization for children. Margaret was president of

---

144. San Juan Stake Relief Society Records, March 22, November 27, 1886;
December 4, 1887; November 27, 1888; June 12, September 30, 1889; May 25, 1890.

145. See Walton, Diary, March 25, 1886.

146. "'Aunt Mary' Nielson Jones"; Albert R. Lyman, "Bishop Jens Nielson," 12.

the ward's young ladies association and also assisted Julia with the stake Primary. Joe worked in the ward's Sunday School, France worked with the deacons, and Uriah had just been ordained a deacon. The older boys spent much of their lives on the range and were subject to the temptations out there. They made some mistakes but also showed contrition for their errors. Jens must have been proud to hear all of his older boys, Joe, Jens Peter, and Francis, tell their testimonies of the gospel in the same meeting during the drive to reform the young men in early 1889.[147]

Jens had plenty of work to do himself. When he was not busy looking after the members of the ward, going to meetings, urging ward members yet again to keep their livestock out of the corn fields, caring for the tithing yard, raising his family, dandling [231] grandchildren (six of them by 1890), contracting for work on county roads, or inspiriting whoever happened to be home to repair the ditch, the bishop looked after his gardens and fields. As he approached his seventieth birthday, he may have started to feel, like Francis Hammond, that while his capacity to do manual labor was diminishing, he could "direct as well as ever."[148] He probably put in tomatoes, cabbage, beans, beets, onions, carrots, cucumbers, and perhaps another crop or two in the vegetable gardens around the house, and grew corn, potatoes, and maybe some sorghum out in the fields. There were occupational hazards at home as well as on the range. Jens was laid up for a few days in early 1887 when he ran a sunflower snag into his foot. The flu got him for a couple of weeks in 1890. At times like these, papers such as the Deseret News, which was "found in nearly every household, and ... read with interest" were particularly welcome.[149] Jens also loved good horses, taking great care in breeding them and great pleasure in riding them.[150] And there were frustrations as well: since

---

147. Hammond, Journal, February 24, 1889. Each of the older boys was rebaptized sometime from 1885 to 1889. This may have been prior to accepting a new calling or office in the priesthood, but it may also have been to show repentance and rededication following a period of waywardness.

148. Hammond, Journal, April 27, 1888.

149. Charles E. Walton, "San Juan Quarterly Conference," Deseret News, January 13, 1886, 831.

150. See Albert R. Lyman, "Bishop Jens Nielson," 13; also Lemuel H. Redd Sr., letter to family, January 22, 1889, for the recollection of a fun horse ride the bishop took with one of "Pap" Redd's daughters.

Bluff still had so many tall weeds, finding domestic stock could be infu-
riating. Platte Lyman once searched for two days up Recapture Creek
for a cow who was all the time roaming in the stinkweeds at Bluff.[151]

Occasionally the bishop traveled, which was much easier once the
Denver and Rio Grande ran through Thompson's Springs, north of
Moab. In late March 1888, he took a [232] trip to general conference in
Salt Lake City, with the added pleasure of accompanying his daughter
Margaret to her wedding in the Logan Temple. After a weeklong wagon
trip through Monticello and Moab to Thompson's, they bought confer-
ence-rate, round-trip tickets for $13.95 apiece. The train left at 10:40 PM
and delivered them to Salt Lake City at 8:00 the next morning. Kirsten's
brother, John Lollin, lived in Salt Lake City. While he had lapsed from
the Church, making part of his living operating a saloon, he stayed in the
family, failing to disown his sisters, as he had once threatened to do, for
entering polygamous marriages. The Nielsons probably stayed with him,
as they did on other trips, at his home on the first or second block of
South Main Street. They may have also seen the great Shakespearean
actor and brother of Lincoln's assassin, Edwin Booth, play at the Salt
Lake Theater during his engagement there at that time.[152] They certainly
noticed the amenities available in some city homes: "heating by steam
from the basement to all the rooms above, lighted by gas, and hot and
cold water in the rooms."[153]

After the wedding on April 4, the Nielsons attended conference.
Many of the General Authorities were either in hiding or exile from federal authorities, but Jens heard those who remained, including Lorenzo
Snow, John Henry Smith, and Heber J. Grant, speak on the principles of
the gospel, mission experiences, and relations with Gentiles. Jens, Mary,
and the newlyweds returned to Thompson's on April 13 and were back
in Bluff by April 21. The next day in church, the bishop, along with other
ward members [233] who attended, gave the first reports of what was said
in conference to the Bluff Saints.[154]

---

151. Hammond, Journal, March 28, 1887; February 26, 1890; Albert R. Lyman,
"History of San Juan County" for the year 1889.

152. Hammond, Journal, March 28, 1888.

153. Hammond, Journal, October 18, 1892.

154. See Hammond, Journal, March 28–April 22, 1888, for details on this trip.

Church authorities continued to visit them in Bluff as well. Apostle John Henry Smith came twice in 1889 and left a strong impression, bearing "one of the most powerful testimonies I ever heard come out of the mouth of man," in the opinion of Francis Hammond.[155] In his first visit, he helped organize a high council for the San Juan Stake, a group of twelve men called to assist the stake presidency. In the second visit, Elder Smith dedicated the Moab meetinghouse. With the addition of the Moab Ward, President Hammond now had a loop of seven hundred miles to cover in his buggy, which he faithfully endeavored to do every quarter, true to his namesake, the long-traveled Methodist circuit rider Francis Asbury.

Jens and Kirsten also attended the October 1889 general conference. They crowded into the full sessions in the "Big Tabernacle" on Saturday. Wilford Woodruff was still in hiding, but they heard from other authorities. Many discussed the difficult situation of the Church, particularly in Salt Lake City, where the non-Mormon Liberal Party threatened to beat the orthodox People's Party at the polls and seize control of the city as they had previously done in Ogden. While in Salt Lake, the Nielsons loaded up on items they could not conveniently buy in Bluff. Sometime after the conference, they visited with Church authorities about their son. Joe had been called in March to be the first missionary from Bluff. He was excused from the call, however, due to "the unsettled [234] affairs of the people at Bluff," largely related to the proposed Indian removal.[156]

Continuing Problems

Removal, Part II

Sometime in late 1886 or 1887, an amendment to a bill in the U.S. Congress authorized a three-man commission to negotiate with the Utes in southwest Colorado for the surrender of their reservation lands. When the commissioners arrived at the reservation in mid-1887, however, their negotiations proceeded poorly. Ignacio, Mariano, Buckskin Charlie, and some of the other leading Utes who had favored removal when Senator Thomas Bowen introduced his bill back in 1886 were now suspicious. Would the new land be any better? There was no large river running

---

155. Hammond, Journal, February 3, 1889.
156. Hammond, Journal, October 2–13, 1889.

through the middle of the proposed new reservation. The land in Utah was not as good for farming. What was to prevent stockmen in Utah from causing the same sort of trouble as those in Colorado? How long would it be before the government chose to remove them from this land, too? What would happen to the other Indians in the area?[157] The commissioners returned the next summer to tour San Juan County with the Utes, try to satisfy their questions, and again forge a treaty.

In the meantime, life in San Juan County continued as it had. Utes and Paiutes kept clashing with settlers on the lands they traditionally wandered, particularly in the [235] narrow McElmo Canyon.[158] The Mormons in Bluff increased their efforts to teach the Utes "to raise their own living" rather than live "by the chase and begging." Twenty to thirty Indians joined Thales Haskell in Allan Canyon. They grubbed the land, dug a ditch, fenced the fields, and put in some wheat, corn, and potatoes. But on the whole, Haskell did not think the experiment was going too well since the Indians were not much help. Bluff held a large celebration for the Utes in early June. Benow and Red Jacket led a "grand dance," and the town gave the Indian two cows and a lot of flour, sugar, and coffee. The few Navajos who were present seemed jealous of this increased attention to the Utes.[159]

But during a social party on November 28, Jens and most of the other people in town found that their situation on the San Juan had become precarious again. Francis Hammond showed them a letter from the Southern Ute Commissioners that confirmed they had made another treaty with Ute leaders. The thousand Utes affected would receive almost all of San Juan County, five thousand dollars a year for ten years, and twenty thousand dollars in sheep. The negotiating chiefs also received five hundred dollars apiece. An Indian agency would be established in San Juan County, and the Indians could also hunt on the unoccupied areas of the La Sal Mountains. The commissioners now wanted to know what sorts of compensation the settlers expected for their improvements. Bishop Nielson and Hans Bayles were appointed to help President [236] Hammond appraise the place.[160]

---

157. McPherson, "Ute Invasion of San Juan County," 47–48.

158. See McPherson, *History of San Juan County*, 146–48.

159. Hammond, Journal, February 1, April 29, June 5, 1888.

160. Hammond, Journal, November 28, 1888; Thompson, "Unwanted Indians," 196; Peterson, *Look to the Mountains*, 73.

Over the next two weeks, they looked over what they had built. Between Bluff, Monticello, and outposts at Verdure, Dodge Springs, Indian Valley and Rincon, there were just over two hundred Mormons in about thirty families. They had constructed over sixty log cabins and a handful of rock homes, President Hammond's still being the only one in Bluff. There were two schoolhouses, a store building, and a shoe shop. Twelve hundred acres of fields had been fenced, as had almost all of the town lots. There were seventeen miles of ditch. They had spent twenty-seven thousand dollars on roads, from Bluff and Monticello to Colorado, and from Bluff to the Colorado River and to Moab. Only seven thousand dollars of this amount had been paid for by the territorial legislature. There were a lot of corrals, a few good orchards, and a lot of lucerne hay fields that yielded three crops a year. The bishop and Brother Bayles added in the double cabin headquarters of the Carlisles and whatever other improvements the cattle companies had installed. The bishop looked over what his people had wrought in a little more than eight years and valued the lot at seventy-five thousand dollars.[161]

While he was doing this, President Hammond went to Colorado, where he attended a celebration held at the Ignacio Agency and a large party of the commissioners at the Stratton Hotel in Durango. He found the people and papers of Colorado jubilant at reclaiming the two million dollars worth of land on the reservation about to be reopened [237] for their use. There was enough farmland for two thousand farmers to settle on 160 acres each, to say nothing of the rangeland. On both occasions President Hammond expressed his opinion that this was a "blessing to all concerned": the Indians were removing to a land "better adapted to their wants than the one they are leaving." Furthermore, he could speak with authority when he said the large, broken land in San Juan County was "such as the average white man will not covet." If the Mormons could get a fair valuation for their improvements, they could move to a better place, making it a good deal for everyone.[162]

---

161. I am assuming not too much changed between this survey and the numbers reported to the governor the next year. See Hammond, Journal, October 10, 1889; Francis A. Hammond, "Indians and San Juan," *Utah Enquirer*, October 15, 1889, in Journal History, October 15, 1889, 9.

162. Hammond, Journal, December 3 and 5, 1888; November 25, 1889; "Indians En Route to Utah," *Utah Enquirer*, December 14, 1888, in Journal History, December 14, 1888, 5.

He may have been surprised when he returned to Bluff to find that the settlers there did not agree with him. "The people are much exercised over the prospect of our removal from this county." They hoped that if the removal order came, the government would allow them to remain to live among and work with the Indians, but they realized this was not likely. Wilford Woodruff and the other authorities of the Church also assumed there was not much left to do but plan for removal. Utah Territory was on the short end of the political stick, with only a delegate to the U.S. House of Representatives against Colorado's full delegation to the House and the Senate. On several occasions Church authorities counseled the Saints to get the best deal they could out of the government but not to give up their mission. They should rather continue to live close to and work with the Indians from places in Colorado and New Mexico.[163] This was a difficult prospect, because by this time most ranges were already full, and "the stock the [238] people own are their wealth." "The Lord only knows where they would go if this place was to go to the Indians," one settler lamented.[164] As Bluff stockmen moved their flocks and herds south to their winter ranges for perhaps the final time, President Woodruff hoped for blessings on "all the Saints who are thus deprived of their hard earned homes, and make your present inconvenience light to you."[165] Meanwhile, the Ute commissioners headed toward Washington, to deliver their work to Senator Bowen, who would translate its provisions into another removal bill. Eager Indians headed directly for San Juan County assuming the deal was already done.[166]

These new arrivals increased the burdens on those in Bluff. Not only were there more Utes in the county, but 1888 had been a hard year for crops and herds. The Indians had already grown more "insolent" in the fall, and things got worse in winter. Some Utes were always in town and increased their begging, sometimes helping themselves to what they wanted in the settlers' homes. They detained travelers and in some instances even covered them with their rifles from a distance. The Navajos were also upset at

163. Hammond, Journal, November 9, December 15, 16, and 19, 1888; Wilford Woodruff, letter to Francis A. Hammond, December 11, 1888.

164. Lemuel H. Redd Sr., letter to family, January 22, 1889.

165. Wilford Woodruff, letter to Francis A. Hammond, December 11, 1888.

166. Thompson, "Unwanted Indians," 196; "Indians En Route to Utah."

the strengthening of their traditional rivals, and they also increased their demands on the settlers and their stock.[167]

In early 1889 Bluff did its best to plan for an uncertain future. Church authorities counseled settlers to put in crops as usual, but hold off from making more substantial [239] improvements until their future was better known.[168] Kumen Jones and the Allan brothers explored the lower Mancos River as a potential new home but returned with a negative report.[169] The townspeople vigorously rejected Commissioner T. S. Child's allegation to Congress that the Bluff canal was an unusable failure that had been swept into the river.[170] The co-op's members, whose unity was already cracking the year before, held a meeting until midnight and finally voted to sell their sheep and "wind up the affairs of the company" on April 18.[171]

Maybe they heard rumors in the interim, but they did not dissolve the San Juan Co-op. By late May those in Bluff heard the news that Bowen's bill, though it passed the Senate, had been defeated in the House. Removal would not happen that year. Utah's delegate John Caine deserved some of the credit for lobbying hard against a bill that passed the Senate in a form that did not give the San Juan residents fair compensation.[172] But more powerful forces had coalesced to defeat the bill. Cattle companies such as the Carlisles and the Pittsburgh outfit on the La Sals were mostly opposed to losing their ranges. The Pittsburgh Cattle Company found an effective ally in its home state: the Indian Rights Association was headquartered in Philadelphia.[173] This group was opposed [240] to the reservation system altogether and had been instrumental in passing the Dawes Act in 1887, which allotted homesteads to individual Indians instead of reserving large parcels for tribes. They saw the Bowen bill as a backward step in their drive to assimilate Indians to American culture and agriculture. The association had potent connections and lobbyists. They sent two inspectors to the San Juan, who returned reporting the improvements in the

---

167. "Indian Trouble Feared," *Utah Enquirer*, September 7, 1888, in Journal History, September 7, 1888, 4; Hammond, Journal, December 29, 1888; February 23, 1889.

168. Hammond, Journal, May 8, 1889.

169. Hammond, Journal, February 23, 28, March 6, 1889.

170. Hammond, Journal, February 26, 1889.

171. Hammond, Journal, March 18, 1889.

172. Hammond, Journal, May 30, 1889.

173. Peterson, "San Juan in Controversy," 52.

county were worth double the seventy-five thousand dollars the bishop
had assessed. This amount gave other members of Congress, particularly
empathetic westerners, more pause. Finally, those in the government of
Utah Territory used whatever influence they had against the bill, feeling
the area had too many Indians in its borders already.[174] If Martha Hammond's earlier appraisal was right, when news arrived of the bill's defeat,
the stockmen cheered while their wives quietly mourned through their
pallid smiles.

Bluff's troubles on this issue were far from over, because many of
the Utes were understandably furious. In August, Amelia Hammond
reported them singing, dancing, and shooting every night. "Brother Jones
said he never knew them to act so saucy before." The Utes stole watermelons, dug up potatoes, and frightened the women and children in general,
especially when they arrived at sundown and lurked into the night.[175]
The settlers were "really in danger because of the restless condition of the
Indians, they [241] regarding the white people as trespassers."[176] With only
six men in town, once again the bishop's faith was all he had close at hand
to withstand perhaps 250 Indians.[177] Furthermore, the Coloradans were
not going to be stopped short of victory; the bill was sure to be reintro-
duced. When Utah's governor asked President Hammond for another
assessment of the county's improvements, the bill went up. The canals
themselves were now worth a hundred thousand dollars, and everything
in the county was worth two hundred thousand dollars. According
to this second assessment, the government should either pay the settlers
this windfall or reopen the county to white settlement and build some
reservoirs as part of the bargain.[178]

The threat was still imminent enough that President Hammond did
two more dramatic things. First, he arranged to buy a new home for the
soon-to-be displaced saints of Bluff. He visited Manassa, Colorado, and
was impressed with the town, now with over a thousand residents, a large

---

174. Thompson, "Unwanted Indians," 196.

175. In Adamson, *Francis Asbury Hammond*, 98.

176. Francis A. Hammond, "Indians and San Juan," *Utah Enquirer*, October 15,
1889, in Journal History, October 15, 1889, 9.

177. Francis A. Hammond, "Indians Getting Mad," *Deseret News*, August 23,
1889, in Journal History, August 23, 1889, 4.

178. Hammond, Journal, October 10, 1889.

co-op store, and a flourmill. In the same valley, he set his sights on a twenty-one-thousand-acre ranch on the Zapato River. It was impressive enough that he, in consultation with Silas S. Smith, put seven thousand dollars down and arranged financing for the twenty-three-thousand-dollar balance over the next five years. "Altogether it is the finest country for saints to make ready homes in I have ever [seen] in these mountains."[179] But he also went to Washington, D.C., in December. Delegate Caine felt it would be beneficial to have a [242] representative from San Juan County in the capital, and Hammond was the logical choice. "The sentiment is strong on the part of the saints here," he recorded before he left, "to be let alone in their homes, but if forced to move make a strong effort to obtain full compensation for our claims."[180] Jens Nielson, Platte Lyman, and John Allan were appointed to draft a strong protest to Congress and also revise their list of claims in case the protest did not work. Instead of finishing the job, though, they later wrote President Hammond telling him they would leave the business to him.[181]

The people in Bluff received periodic updates on President Hammond's activities in the East, mostly through letters written to Lemuel Redd. Although Washington was "a very wicked and corrupt city," it had many impressive buildings, museums, and theaters. He shook the hand of President Benjamin Harrison, though as a Republican, "his form and looks did not strike me very favorably." Hammond toured Mount Vernon, and when he got back they could see the magnolia leaves and coffee beans he had bought from an "old negro," who assured him they came from trees planted by George Washington himself. They eagerly read President Hammond's accounts of New York and Philadelphia, in which he told tales of buildings that were fourteen stories high and of a contraption that talked and sang and made him "*roar* with *laughter*, it was so natural."[182] In the latter city he conferred with the Indian Rights Association before returning to the cloakrooms and corridors of the nation's capitol. Senator Dawes, head of the Indian [243] Affairs Committee, "seemed every inch a gentile," but arranged a subcommittee hearing on removal. In his conversations, testimony, and lobbying, Hammond held to his position that the settlers wanted either two

179. Hammond, Journal, November 1–14, 1889.
180. Hammond, Journal, September 4, November 25, 1889.
181. Hammond, Journal, November 29, 1889.
182. Hammond, Journal, March 26, 1890.

hundred thousand dollars or an opportunity to perfect their own claims on the county. In spite of his efforts, the bill that was reported out of the House committee and looked likely to emerge from the Senate committee appropriated only fifty thousand dollars for the residents of the county. From Bluff, these residents reported back to President Hammond that the Colorado newspapers continued to incite the issue and the Indians, who were extremely impatient with the long delays.

When President Hammond returned to Salt Lake City in April 1890, he was convinced removal could not be stopped. "Colorado State is too powerful for us to oppose," but he also believed the representatives and senators from that state would help the San Juan settlers get more money for their claims to help pass the bill. As it turned out, however, the same combination of forces that defeated removal the first time succeeded in doing it again in 1890. Once more, however, the government refused to open the land to white settlers, and the issue remained alive for future Coloradans to agitate and future Congresses to consider.[183] For the time being, at least, the ranch on the Zapato River would not be occupied by those leaving Bluff, though President Hammond and Silas Smith continued to try to acquire more land for the future.[184] [244]

The Raid, Part II

The people in Bluff had other pressures to worry about during these times. The raid against polygamy continued, and intensified leading up to 1890. Grover Cleveland, the Democratic president, "was as good as he dared to be" to Utah, even favoring statehood. But when he lost to "the cold-blooded Presbyterian" Harrison in 1888, the Mormons in Utah looked for "an increase of the persecuting spirit that we have contended with for the past four years."[185] Church leadership discouraged the open

---

183. Hammond, Journal, November 30, 1889–April 10, 1890; June 10 and November 12, 1890; "The San Juan Claimants," *Salt Lake Herald*, December 11, 1889, in Journal History, December 11, 1889, 4; "Dispatch from Durango, CO., Dec. 25," *Deseret News*, January 4, 1890. On June 5, 1890, the Church's General Tithing Office still advised the co-op to cash out on their sheep for 75 percent of their value. See Francis Hammond's Journal for this date.

184. See Hammond, Journal, June 10 and 11, October 10, 1890; Silas S. Hammond, letter to Francis A. Hammond, February 12, 1891.

185. Hammond, Journal, November 7, 1888; March 4, 1889.

preaching of plural marriage. Refugees continued to come. Platte Lyman spent significant time in San Juan County, moved his second wife, Annie, to live there, and prepared to bring his other wife, Adelia, and children back to Bluff as well. In late 1890, he was called to serve as a counselor in the stake presidency to Francis Hammond, to replace William Adams, whose health was not good. Lemuel H. Redd's father, "Pap" Redd, was tired of being a fugitive, "never feeling safe to spend one night under his own roof."[186] So in 1887, he brought some of his family, his cattle, and his horses to Bluff "for the purpose of bettering his financial affairs as well as to escape the persecution of the law."[187] Although Pap was sixteen years Bishop Nielson's junior, the two men enjoyed each other's company, sharing good humor and keen judgment of people as well as livestock and horses. When Pap returned to Bluff with one of his wives in 1889, he wrote back to a daughter that Jens [245] was "the same old comic boy he was when you saw him."[188] The raid also caused Ben Perkins to return to San Juan County with the wooden hat rack he had made during his five months in the state penitentiary.[189] After moving around the stake, he settled the younger of his two wives, Sarah, in Bluff, and lived most of the time with his first wife, and Sarah's older sister, Mary Ann, in Monticello. Jens was of great help to detached families such as this one: "The dear old bishop was such a comfort to me," recalled Sarah, "he came so often to know our wants."[190]

Those in Bluff heard of how tight things were around the perimeter of the county. Brigham Young Jr. came through from time to time with reports of how narrowly he had escaped rigid antipolygamy enforcement in New Mexico, where he had a home and family.[191] Bishop Christopher Arthur of Cedar City, as well as Bishop Stewart of Moab, finally turned themselves in by 1889 rather than subject their families to further harassment.[192] The newspapers informed Bluff's residents that the government

---

186. Lemuel H. Redd Sr., Autobiographical Sketch, 1907.

187. Lemuel H. Redd Sr., Autobiographical Sketch, 1902.

188. Kumen Jones, "Writings," 191; Lemuel H. Redd Sr., letter to family, January 22, 1889.

189. Riis, *Ranger Trails*, 43.

190. Albert R. Lyman, "Notes on the Life of Sarah Williams Perkins," 10.

191. See Hammond, Journal, February 1, 1888.

192. Hammond, Journal, September 8, 1888.

had confiscated over a million dollars in Church property and that Idaho Territory had started to disfranchise polygamists under the Edmunds-Tucker Act.[193] Women, who had voted in Utah Territory since 1870, also lost the vote. The Supreme Court ratified these actions in [246] 1890, and Congress was considering the Cullom Bill, which would take the vote away from all Mormons. The "political world is *hot* towards *us*," as President Hammond saw it.[194]

The federal marshal for San Juan County was Joe Bush, and he was generally very competent in tracking down train robbers, horse thieves, and the like, often with the assistance of sheriffs and deputies from Bluff such as Willard Butt, Hyrum Perkins, and Hans Bayles. But the townspeople continued to be skittish of any mention of marshals coming to town. When a Mr. Wolcott showed up in June 1888 claiming to be investigating the year-old shooting of Amasa Barton, many agreed that "he is here more to see and learn how many are here that he could have arrested for *cohab*."[195] The bishop counseled with his ward members on when and where to hide. Sometimes suspect men would hole up in other ward members' houses for a few days.[196] Sometimes the wives of polygamists, such as Lucy Redd or Ida May Jones, went on the underground somewhere else in the stake for a few months.[197] In August 1889, Nephi Bailey rode into town, Revere-like, a few minutes before midnight, to warn that the marshals were coming. He hustled all the prosecutable men with their blankets out of town to sleep. In the morning they found the federal officers were only after train robbers.[198] Pap Redd, used to intense interest from law enforcement officials, was amused by this. "The people here are quite excited just now [247] about marshals. One of them sent a letter unexpected which makes some think everything isn't right in Rome. I haven't got very bad excited yet as I have been used to such scares."[199] In the end he was right. Marshal Bush endeared himself to the San Juan Mormons by showing little interest in catching cohabs. It

---

193. Hammond, Journal, December 16, 1888.

194. Hammond, Journal, May 31, 1890.

195. Hammond, Journal, June 3, 1888.

196. Martha Hammond to Francis A. Hammond, January 21, 1890.

197. Hammond, Journal, July 20, 1890.

198. Adamson, *Francis Asbury Hammond*, 99.

199. Lemuel H. Redd Sr., letter to family, January 22, 1889.

was a good thing, too, because when it came to other kinds of criminals, he usually got his man.[200]

Although removal and the raid were largely beyond their control, San Juan Mormons kept control of county government. Their numbers were not overwhelming, especially after the restrictions of the antipolygamy acts, but in the 1880s the Mormons in Bluff voted solidly for the pro-Mormon People's Party to elect local officials, territorial legislators, and the territory's delegate to Congress.[201] Joseph Barton was usually chosen as county judge. This voting solidarity, as well as the Mormons' more solid communities, allowed them to hold all of the county offices, though the gentile cattle companies paid most of the taxes.[202] A time or two, enough Gentiles showed interest in voting to make those in Bluff nervous, but never in sufficient numbers for the gentile Liberal Party to win a county position.[203] Election day in August 1889 brought out ten to twelve voters in Bluff and only twenty in the whole county. Concerns that the Liberal Party would win in Salt Lake City were so high that, [248] despite their own feeble numbers, Jens Nielson and other Bluff officials talked about sending men to Salt Lake to vote in next February's elections.[204] In the end, the Liberals took Salt Lake, "a dark day for the Saints." But in San Juan County, the People's Party had little trouble holding power due to the transient nature of the cattlemen. In 1890 there were thirty registered voters, none of them Liberals. Emissaries were sent from Bluff to Monticello and onto the range to fetch voters to give all the support they could to John T. Caine as territorial delegate to Congress over C. C. Goodwin, publisher of that scourge, the *Salt Lake Tribune*. Twenty-four of the thirty voted; Caine stayed in Congress, and Mormons stayed firmly in control of the schools, roads, and tax rolls of San Juan County.[205]

Anniversaries

On April 6, 1890, Jens Nielson and those who were still in Bluff could look back on ten years by their muddy, unpredictable stream. The town

---

200. Austin and McPherson, "Murder, Mayhem, and Mormons," 45–46.
201. Platte D. Lyman, "Diary," November 7, 1882; Hammond, "San Juan Country," 514.
202. See Bluff Ward, letter to President John Taylor, May 19, 1884.
203. Hammond, Journal, December 20, 1885.
204. Hammond, Journal, August 5, November 25, 1889.
205. Hammond, Journal, October 31–November 4, 1890.

still was not much. C. L. Christensen, an Indian missionary, came looking for it later in the year. He traveled up the "roughest road [he had] ever
seen" from Rincon. "When I got there near the old cottonwood church I
asked when we would be to Bluff City; I looked for 400 inhabitants or
more. Some one answered this was it. A sure surprise!"[206] The Bluff settlers did not have the steam-heated, gas-lit, well-plumbed homes of the
more prosperous Utah settlements. But they had survived, which was
saying something. Their stock prospered, [249] and they were becoming
wealthy. Still, it was a precarious prosperity that could be toppled at any
time by the weather, the raid, Indian removal, or the Indians themselves.
But the settlers were sticking to their mission. They had the good will of
some Indians, they still clutched political control of the county, and they
prevented gentile cattle from overrunning the ranges.

On the worst days, when it was mercilessly hot, the water was out of
the ditch, and the wind blew the dirt and grit relentlessly into their irri-
tated eyes and defenseless homes, they could still congratulate themselves
for being different. They were not like the Carlisles or the Coloradans or
the Liberals in Salt Lake, and they could fire their salvoes from a distance
that the city under the Liberals was "the paradise of thieves, burglars,
foot pads, and all classes of the vile and ungodly."[207] And they were also
different from the Mormons in Cedar City or even Mancos. They could
rail against Saints in Salt Lake and Ogden selling out their inheritances
to Gentiles under a spirit of speculation; they were holding theirs.[208]
What was easier to see at a distance was harder, though not impossible,
to see at home. As President Hammond was in Alamosa negotiating the
purchase of the Zapato Ranch, he noticed, "The world seems on wheels
traveling to and fro seeking wealth and pleasure—all in commotion and
a state of unrest."[209] Bluff residents rode all over the county in pursuit
of their herds, and they still wrestled with keeping enough men in town
to protect their families despite their leaders' [250] repeated admonitions.
But they had been promised blessings if they stayed, and though their
homes did not show it, and they were threatened on many sides, they
felt they were blessed. If they had stayed in Cedar City or Parowan, each

---

206. Christensen, Diary, typescript, 162.
207. Christensen, Diary, January 22, 1891.
208. Christensen, Diary, March 30, October 20, 1889.
209. Christensen, Diary, July 25, 1890.

of which had almost a thousand people by 1890, they would have been more comfortable. But they stuck it out by the San Juan despite such enticements.

In the early afternoon on April 25, the bishop walked toward the schoolhouse, summoned on some pretext or another. The cheers that greeted him from the murky, lamp-lit interior could not have been a complete surprise given that his seventieth birthday was the next day, a Sunday, and not another soul was to be seen on the streets of Bluff. All of them, about fifty adults plus their children, were packed into the schoolhouse, awaiting their bishop. The Nielson women outdid themselves with "a most bountifully prepared feast." President Hammond was asked by the family to make a short speech on their behalf, at the close of which Joe presented his father with a new suit, and the stake president gave him a silver-headed cane. Then came the singing and dancing by all, and more dancing for the adults in the evening. "A real nice time was had." A few cowboys came, by invitation, and behaved themselves. The weather was fine.[210] [251]

---

210. Christensen, Diary, April 25, 1890.

Golden Years, 1890–1893

Assimilation

Manifesto

When Francis Hammond returned to Bluff in late October 1890 after his trips to Washington, D.C., Salt Lake City, and Huntsville, he had more to tell than tales of phonographs, skyscrapers, and the other wonders of the East. Bishop Nielson called on the stake president almost immediately to discuss what Hammond had heard in general conference a few weeks before. President Wilford Woodruff, under tremendous pressure from the federal government and in danger of losing even the temples of the Church, issued a manifesto discontinuing plural marriage. The document received a unanimous sustaining vote (though some Saints abstained) from those at the conference as a revelation from God. But now all those in plural marriages had to ratify the decision in their own minds, hearts, and homes.

Bishop Nielson and his wives had struggled to accept the principle over thirty years before and practicing it under pressure had increased their conviction. Now they had to let it go and doing so was one of the greatest trials of Jens's faith in Church [253] leadership.[1] He was not going to disavow either of his wives, and the Manifesto did not require it. But after decades of constructing a faithful fortress around the doctrine of plural marriage within himself, it was difficult to demolish it at a blow. It

---

1. See Hyde, "As I Recall Grandfather Jens Nielson," 26.

was a quiet, personal struggle. Sometime between when Jens first heard of the Manifesto and this meeting with President Hammond, he had made up his mind to again reconcile himself to obey priesthood authority even now that the doctrine was different. The "brethren are disposed to accept and endorse the action of our leader and the conference," President Hammond recorded after that evening's discussion on "the spirit of the times, and the action of the Church at our late conference."[2]

Many felt they had no choice. Laws like the Edmunds-Tucker Act were constricting the political, financial, and even religious life out of the Church, which was nearly bankrupt by the confiscation of so much of its property. As President Woodruff said, this was the only course open to secure the "temporal salvation" of the Church. In this light it worked. "A short time ago," President Hammond later observed, "it seemed we would be crushed to atoms by the political power of the government. Today a great change has come over the nation and a time of peace seems to have set in."[3] Bluff had been fortunate in its draw of federal marshals during the raid, but now many men in town could rest easier knowing they would not have to head into the hills with every rumor. [254]

Some in Bluff were not entirely reconciled to the conditions set up by the Manifesto. The bishop still insisted on the importance and accuracy of the revelation to his congregation over a year later. Pap Redd, John Allan Jr., and a few of the other refugees who had lived in Bluff went to the Mormon colonies in Mexico in the early 1890s, after the Manifesto was issued. Down there they could live with both their wives instead of slighting one or more. Some, thoroughly converted to the necessity of plural marriage in order to receive the highest level of salvation, continued to contract multiple marriages south of the border in the years following the official declaration.

Partisan Politics

Even though the Manifesto brought greater peace with the Gentiles, it threatened greater disunion among the Saints. In the wake of the announcement, Church leaders wondered if it was not time to do away with the old party system and embrace the national parties. It could only help the territory's

---

2. Hammond, Journal, October 26, 1890.

3. Hammond, Journal, May 1, 1892.

chances for statehood if they did away with the People's Party, which would most likely force the Liberal Party into extinction as well.[4] When he received a feeler on this issue from Franklin S. Richards on June 3, 1891, President Hammond was fully in favor of it, seeing it as a sign that "the old issues of hate are dying out."[5] In the afternoon meeting of church two weeks later, the main subject was politics. Platte Lyman, now in Bluff full-time, announced that two great parties were being organized. The Lord was teaching them political science, he felt. [255] Francis Hammond quickly followed, proclaiming that the Saints must "act as a leaven in politics as well as in religion and so reform the world in all things." Bishop Nielson bore his testimony to end the meeting, most likely endorsing what the other two had said.[6] It was the most harmonious political meeting the town would have in some time. Before too long, Platte Lyman would be the head of Bluff Republicans, while Francis Hammond would champion the Democrats.

But the Democratic and Republican clubs springing up in counties around the state stayed out of San Juan for the time being. The main concern in Bluff was holding county government safe from the outside cowboys. So at a political meeting held at the bishop's house on July 9, 1891, Church members felt it was not yet wise to divide into the two national parties, since Gentiles could exploit the division of so few voters and control the balance of power. Therefore, the Mormons agreed to support a "Citizens'" ticket for county officers, probably modeled after the transitional Citizens' ticket in Salt Lake City, which fused Mormon and gentile candidates.[7]

Many who went to vote in early August were surprised to find an alternate slate under the old "People's Party" name. The bishop's son Joe ran for selectman in place of the Citizens' candidate. Some placed the blame on Monticello, whose citizens, they felt, were trying to draw the county's government into their orbit more than Bluff's. Cowboys could not be far away from such intrigue either. It was a "farce election," and the next Sunday Church leaders denounced these factions that turned brother against brother and [256] would "expose ourselves to our political enemies."[8]

---

4. For the general political trends in the territory, see Alexander, *Utah, the Right Place*, 200–4.

5. Hammond, Journal, June 3, 1891.

6. Hammond, Journal, June 20, 1891.

7. Hammond, Journal, July 9, 1891.

8. Hammond, Journal, August 3, 5, and 9, 1891.

One thing almost everyone could agree on was that women should be allowed to vote again. Utah's females voted from 1870 to 1887, before they were disfranchised by the Edmunds-Tucker Act. Two energetic women from the Relief Society in Salt Lake City, Sister Elizabeth Anderson Howard and Sister Mary Ann Freeze, toured Bluff in April 1892 to drum up support. They organized a Bluff suffrage association, with Adelia Lyman as president, Martha Hammond, Mary Jones, and Ann Bayles as vice presidents, Harriett Barton as secretary, and Calistia Hammond as treasurer. While Kirsten and Elsie Nielson did not hold office, they paid the fifty-cent fee to become members alongside their husband, who spoke after the Relief Society sisters in favor of the vote.[9]

Church authorities understood that joining the national political parties could be done only if substantial numbers of Mormons joined each party. If they did not, regardless of the names of the parties, they would fall back into the pro- and anti-Mormon axis of old. But more Mormons leaned toward the Democrats for a number of reasons. That party generally favored less federal government and more state control, a welcome plank to Utahns. Furthermore, the Democratic President Grover Cleveland had been more restrained in prosecuting polygamists, while the Republicans, since their start in the 1850s, were the party that wrote the antipolygamy laws and more energetically enforced them. It looked increasingly as if the Utah Democrats would turn into a People's Party by another name. This suspicion was confirmed by the results of the 1891 election, which saw [257] twenty-four Democrats, twelve Liberals, and zero Republicans elected to the territorial legislature.

Many prominent Church leaders, such as Joseph F. Smith, Marion Lyman, and John Henry Smith, swiftly came out in support of the Republican Party and recruited new members. George Q. Cannon switched from Democrat to Republican. Other leaders resented this emphasis on the one party and countered strongly in favor of the Democrats. Moses Thatcher, an Apostle, gave a partisan speech reinforced by dogma: Jesus was a Democrat, he thundered, because he was for a diffusion of government, while Satan was Republican, since he stood for centralization of decision making. Republicans, especially Joseph F. and John Henry Smith countered almost as strongly.

---

9. Hammond, Journal, April 21 and 22, 1892.

Bluff stayed aloof from national parties in name only in 1892. The Citizens' and People's tickets were again on the ballot, but county citizens were quickly becoming Republicans and Democrats. Francis Hammond was chosen as the county's representative to the territorial convention, and he struggled with the idea of parties in a unified Church. He returned from the convention in Provo in October and surprisingly urged San Juan Saints to vote for the Republican F. J. Cannon for Congress, instead of the Democrat J. L. Rawlins. Delegate Hammond had met privately with the counselors in the First Presidency of the Church, Joseph F. Smith and George Q. Cannon, who persuaded him that it would be better for the Church and the state if Cannon were elected and good relations with the national Republicans were cultivated. Not surprisingly, Cannon won eight of the twelve ballots cast in San Juan County, but lost in the overall election. "Quite a feeling is apparent in politics in our midst," mourned President Hammond. He [258] hoped instead that the Lord would "overrule all for the good of his saints," both in Bluff and in the whole territory.[10]

Ditch and Stock, 1890–1892

Ditch

The relaxation of outside political pressure in 1890 did not mean the San Juan River relented that year. The water rose, as it almost always did, to break the banks of the canal in the spring. "Men all at work repairing break in canal," lamented President Hammond. "It has been much trouble this season so far—break, break, *break*."[11] It did not get any easier. The next year the people were "almost discouraged" a number of times. They were swept with a mania for fruit trees in the spring, some planting almost three hundred seedlings and cuttings of peaches, plums, and grapes. But early in the season, the river took "a course to leave and [has] gone to [the opposite] bank."[12] It took ten or so teams of animals and their owners almost a month to enlarge and prepare the ditch. Under the bishop's direction, they located the headgate farther

---

10. Hammond, Journal, September 24–November 15, 1892.
11. Hammond, Journal, May 22, 1890.
12. Hammond, Journal, April 11, 1891.

out than usual to capture the water, and the spring floods almost took it away. The few men in town flung themselves into fixing the perpetual breaks through May and June and tried to protect the headgate and the road nearby. Water dropped earlier than usual in July, but a lot of rain saved them from disaster late in the month. By the end of August the ditch committee quit. They turned the matter over to the bishop for ten days, to see if he could get the [259] water back in after the river sank below the head. His efforts salvaged a respectable fruit crop, though the town's farmers lost most of the corn.[13]

The bishop became frustrated by the secularization of the county court. Since the improvements put in near the headgate also protected a county road, he felt the court should reimburse the irrigation laborers for part of their efforts. Road supervisor and county selectman Hans Bayles had collected almost $250 the year before for reinforcing the banks above town. But when the bishop put in for $50, the motion was denied. At the end of 1891, Bishop Nielson and eighteen others requested $150 for their labors but were again rejected. To be reimbursed, it appeared the job had to be done through the county road supervisor rather than through the ward's bishop.[14]

The next year, Cottonwood Wash flooded in February, threatening to carry a few homesteads downriver. The bishop, Joe, and a number of other farmers brought their teams to rescue these fields, yards, and homes. They "riprapped" the banks, something they had done with increasing frequency on the San Juan. This meant they piled brush and stones on the slope to prevent erosion. They got a good deal done before many of the men had to go find their cattle on the range. But the practice they got working on the Cottonwood served them well, since the San Juan came back to its northern bank with a vengeance, threatening to carry more Bluff soil with it. Going out on the range grew more enticing as the year went on, because it meant not having to hew the ditch. It also [260] meant stockmen might be able to cash in on the ten-dollar bounty offered by the county court for any cougars they bagged, rising with the increased threat from

---

13. Hammond, Journal, August 27 and 28, 1891.

14. San Juan County Minute Book, June 3 and September 2, 1890; December 29, 1891. When a bill for riprapping was submitted the next year by the road supervisor, it was once again accepted. See San Juan County Minute Book, July 28, 1892.

three dollars the year before.[15] But after the usual superhuman efforts of the few who remained, the water stayed in almost all summer. By late August, President Hammond recorded almost incredulously, "Water is still in the ditch; we have been blest in this beyond any season the people have been here."[16] More blessings came as well.

Stock

The wealth of those living in Bluff rose dramatically in the early 1890s. Some of it was connected to their efforts on the ditch. The molasses wrested from sorghum cane in John Allan's mill brought in a good price in Colorado, as did some of their fruit. But mostly it was the caravans of wool-laden wagons and the herds of cattle and sheep that rolled and trotted into Colorado that brought such rich returns. The Nielson boys each did some of everything, but each also had his specialty: France ran the cattle, Joe minded the sheep, while Jens Peter was the farmer.[17]

The San Juan Co-op still managed the sheep herd, and the Bluff Cattle Pool continued to hold together from year to year.[18] The two enterprises complemented each other well. In 1890, for example, when it was difficult to sell beef, sheep sold nicely.[19] [261] Jens, Joe, and increasingly France played important parts in the pool, though Fletch Hammond, Lemuel Redd, and Hans Bayles were usually the directors during these years. There was some temporary trouble with the Carlisles when the British brothers fenced across the new county road north of Monticello, but accommodations were quickly made by both sides to resolve the conflict.[20] Besides that, outright disputes with the Carlisles had dwindled as fights over water rights moved to the courts, and Mrs. Carlisle even attended a quarterly stake conference in Monticello in 1890. She also had girls from the town out to the company's double-cabin headquarters for days at a time and would teach them crocheting and other types

---

15. San Juan County Minute Book, December 29, 1890; July 8, 1891.

16. Hammond, Journal, August 26, 1892.

17. Floyd Nielson, "Francis and Leona Nielson," 191.

18. See Hammond, Journal, April 27, 1890; January 13, 1891; for annual organizing meetings of the pool.

19. Francis A. Hammond, "Accidents in Bluff," *Deseret News*, December 6, 1890, 789–90.

20. San Juan County Minute Book, December 30, 1891; June 6, 1892.

of needlework.[21] But the Texas herds still ran around Rincon, and the LC Company still occupied lands to the east of Bluff.

Since at least 1890, Bluff's stockmen contemplated buying out the Texas herd, owned by two men named Crosby and Gallagher. Doing so would rid them not only of the intrusive longhorns stripping so much of their winter grass, but also eliminate the unruly cowboys the outfit tended to employ. But it was too big for them until late in 1892, and even then they almost could not do it. Finally, though, they bought the two thousand head and fifty horses of the Elk Mountain Cattle Company, as the Texas outfit was officially called, for twenty thousand dollars. It was a huge commitment, since they would pay five thousand down and four thousand for each of the next four years, at 8 percent interest. It also meant they would have to mortgage the cattle they already owned, which made some [262] flinch. But at less than ten dollars per head, even if they were inferior longhorns that they would try to sell off as soon as possible, it was hard to pass up. Add to this the fact that Bluff's stockmen would have much tighter control over their range, and the purchase was irresistible. By early 1892 they concluded the deal, and the bishop and his sons bought at least an eighth of the company, which was reorganized under the same Elk Mountain name and was managed separately from the Bluff Cattle Pool.[22] Bluff cattlemen also bought a partial interest in the LC Company.[23] By 1892, they were the preeminent cattle interest in the south end of the county. Their sons could work for their own cattle outfits instead of hiring out to gentile companies. Herding cattle still was not any easier, and there was not much rain at the end of 1892, but these animals were starting to make a lot of money for many of the people in Bluff.

Unraveling

As fortunes swelled in Bluff, so did individual aspirations. The San Juan Co-op grew as much as the cattle herds did. The company continued to

---

21. Roring, "Leona Jane Walton," 195.

22. See Hammond, Journal, April 27, 1890; July 22, September 26, November 2, December 29, 1891; January 18, March 7, 1892; for details of Elk Mountain Cattle Company purchase.

23. See Hammond, Journal, October 23, December 13, 1890; January 16, 1891; February 24, 1892; for hints of this purchase.

pay 40 percent dividends every December from 1889 to 1892.[24] Livestock thrived in a booming national market, and wool prices rose under the high protective duties of the McKinley Tariff, passed by the Republican "Billion Dollar Congress" in 1890. The sheep generated most of the profits, and the store did well, too. Various people clerked in the store, but Kumen [263] and Mary Jones often had a hand in it.

In March of 1891, however, the venture caused a significant rift in town. Kumen Jones felt the prices were too high. If this was true, then at least some of the windfall dividends paid to shareholders came from gouged consumers. Since most Bluff residents, like Brother Jones, were both shareholders and consumers, they felt both the loss and the profit.[25] Still, some resented the capitalist organization of the co-op, through which, they felt, "the big fish in the store are eating the little ones and the board who runs it are cheating the people."[26] Furthermore, as one of the settlers who worked closely with the Indians, Jones resented the fact that some of Bluff's good fortune was extracted from the Navajos and Utes, who held no shares in the co-op. So he intended to open his own store, which, by underselling the cooperative store, would bring in financial and moral profits. Hyrum Perkins and Phil Sorenson agreed with him. James Decker, another director of the co-op, announced he was preparing to open a store as well.[27]

Bishop Nielson and President Hammond quickly countered this plan in the strongest terms. As a practical matter, the town should stay united in trading with the Indians. They urged Brother Jones to remember what had happened to Amasa Barton when he separated himself from the group. But spiritually, they must be united. "I claim it will divide the people and cause strife if we divide up the store," the bishop reproved. [264] "A division of the sheep will come next and a division in every thing."[28] President Hammond then reinforced these traditional community values: "We have two natures, spiritual and temporal, and

---

24. San Juan Cooperative Association, Ledger, 276–83.

25. Hammond, Journal, March 20 and 26, 1891. See Peterson, *Take Up Your Mission*, 151–52, for a similar situation in the settlements on the Little Colorado in Arizona.

26. Bluff Ward, General Minutes, March 22, 1891.

27. Hammond, Journal, April 21, 1891.

28. Bluff Ward, General Minutes, March 22, 1891.

as yet I have not found anyone wise enough to separate them. Some of us claim the bishop has no right to interfere with our private temporal affairs, but as Latter-day Saints we cannot afford this."[29] Furthermore, the store, as a main point of contact with the Indians, was a "question of vital importance." It had to help "create an influence with them looking to their welfare and preparing them to receive the Gospel." But that was exactly what Brother Jones felt the store was not doing. The bishop's spiritual advice was not strengthened by his position as the co-op's second largest stockholder, though in his mind this was a result of his support for the cooperative principle as much as it was an investment.[30]

Kumen Jones relented in part. He agreed to follow the counsel of the bishop, but he maintained that he was right on the issue. A moving testimony meeting on Sunday, March 22, also helped. Many testified that they were willing to follow the counsel of their priesthood leaders. Just after the meeting, Bishop Nielson, President Hammond, and Lemuel Redd worked on Kumen Jones some more. His depth of feeling was great on this issue. President Hammond found this "a great surprise to me as I have looked upon him as one of the best men in the ward and a full-hearted, counsel-supporting and abiding [265] man." The leaders opened up again in the afternoon meeting. Bishop Nielson gave "an earnest appeal to the saints for union in our temporal as well as spiritual matters." He recited the history of Bluff, reminding them of their struggles and how the Lord had blessed them in temporal matters through the principle of cooperation. He exhorted them to see the folly of multiplying stores in dealing with the Indians. They must continue to cooperate. President Hammond followed for an hour endorsing what the bishop said. They were not like the rest of the world, but rather "our situation and condition is very peculiar." The safety of themselves, their wives and children depended largely on this policy. They should correct the evils of the co-op or turn the business over entirely to others. Those who wanted to start stores should go into some other industry, such as fruit canning. The issue was finally resolved in the reverberations of this unequivocal

---

29. Bluff Ward, General Minutes, March 22, 1891.

30. San Juan Cooperative Association, Ledger, shows the accounts of almost all the stockholders booming from 1890 to 1892. Jens Nielson's stock rose from $2,092 to $3,657. The value of all the shares in the co-op rose from $14,968 in 1890 to $20,484 in 1892 and to $30,802 by the end of 1893.

counsel. Brother Decker agreed to try his hand at canning. Kumen Jones, if not entirely satisfied, at least did not open his own store.[31]

After such effort to restore unity on such an important issue, the bishop was disappointed to see his own son tear it open again. Joe Nielson had long been interested in trade. He and William Hyde had operated a trading post above Montezuma by at least 1886, and in 1888 Joe had leased the store outright from Hyde.[32] In 1890, he had gone in with Willard and Parley Butt on a store in Verdure. In January 1892, Joe had decided that he should open his own store in Bluff. He might have operated on the same principles as his brother-in-law Kumen did the year before. He might have been tired of riding the range [266] or roaming among his many other ventures in the region and felt this would let him live a more sedentary life. Whatever his reasoning, his father was opposed and said so publicly in church soon after. He and President Hammond recited their counsel from the previous year with little effect. Joe's action reopened the town's strong emotions on the subject as "some considerable feelings [were] manifest concerning the matter." Jens was especially direct in insisting on obedience to religious leaders even in economic matters: "I have broken up my home six times because I have been counseled to," he reminded his oldest son and any others who were of the same mind. "If we think we are right in our undertakings and the priesthood is wrong, it is safer to wait awhile and take counsel on these matters before taking steps."[33] But by April, just as the co-op opened a branch store at Rincon now that the Texas cattle outfit was gone, Joe opened his store in Bluff. Not long after, though, he relented, due to either failure or contrition. In July, the co-op bought out the renegade store's stock, and union, at least in appearance, was restored. Unlimited individualism, the strongest threat to their spiritual foundation, was rebuked, but its causes were not entirely denied. The co-op store experienced some cash shortages soon after, as it started paying higher prices to the Indians for their sheep and probably for their other commodities as well.[34] [267]

---

31. Hammond, Journal, March 18–23, 1891.

32. See Hammond, Journal, November 17, 1886; November 30, 1888.

33. Bluff Ward, General Minutes, January 31, 1892.

34. Hammond, Journal, January 5, April 22, July 20, August 5, 1892.

Youth

Growing Up in Bluff

"Our greatest hope is with our children," Bishop Nielson once reminded his ward members.[35] In many ways, Bluff was a fun place for children to grow up, and each year had a regular rhythm. Holiday festivities usually trickled into the first week of the New Year as the younger residents continued to dance, race on foot or on horseback, and play baseball, sometimes for fun, sometimes for a candy pulling, and sometimes for a canned oyster supper. After the holidays, it was back to school, where they learned "reading, writing, spelling, arithmetic, grammar, history, hygiene, etc."[36] On Valentine's Day, the older schoolboys developed a custom of throwing little valentines inside President Hammond's outer door, then knocking and running. They usually got to celebrate Washington's birthday soon after with the usual programs, recitations, and songs. One boy one year proclaimed with pride that in a parade of marching states, "I was Texas."[37]

Dainty pink and blue cliff flowers bloomed and gave off their first fragrance in late February or early March, and the blossoms of the apricot and peach trees followed soon after in town.[38] This was the sign that it was time to plan picnics. The children might go out to Sand Island on the Cottonwood or follow Primary President Jody Wood barefoot up Cow Canyon.[39] There they played games and climbed the cliffs up to the [268] caves, one of which, with a particularly good echo, was known as Primary Cave. The young men and women dubbed another aperture "Dance Hall Cave."[40] Throughout the year, daring spelunkers and climbers plumbed the caves and scaled the cliffs north of town, "in wild hazard of harm, but having a big time."[41] The bishop now owned the field south of town, which was the home of another popular attraction. Townspeople often traipsed down the "fenced-in lane, bordered by poplar trees, wild rose bushes, wild plum trees and strawberry bushes"

---

35. Bluff Ward, General Minutes, July 10, 1887.

36. Hammond, Journal, January 16, 1891.

37. Albert R. Lyman, Journal, February 22, 1897.

38. Albert R. Lyman, Journal, March 26, 1901.

39. Elliot, Diary, April 13, 1900.

40. Albert R. Lyman, Journal, February 17, 1901.

41. Albert R. Lyman, Summaries of Each Year, book 1, p. 160.

toward the river and the "Old Swing Tree." Groups assembled under its enormous boughs for picnics and socials, couples came to hold "dual conferences," and individuals stopped to think as they sat next to its trunk or on the swing suspended from its lofty branches.[42]

As the weather continued to warm, many looked forward to traveling longer distances to a quarterly conference or riding along with a freighting trip to Durango. There they could stay in a hotel, shop somewhere that was not the San Juan Co-op, and maybe even have their pictures taken.[43] Whenever conference was held in Bluff, it meant a lot of dinners and parties and a lot of out-of-town guests. But first it meant a lot of work. Houses were scoured, bedding aired, yards mended and tidied. Bathed, scrubbed, and combed children scurried up the bluffs to watch for the arrival of visiting authorities, [269] especially Bishop Burnham with his wagon full of apples.[44] Whether their family was putting up Saints from other wards in the stake or Church dignitaries from farther away, it often meant the children were turned out of their beds to sleep outside, sometimes on haystacks. Girls, according to Jennie Wood, were "hung on nails" to make room for the visitors.[45] A favorite trip to take, especially with conference guests, was to the "Big Cave" five miles up the San Juan River from Bluff. The cavern was three hundred feet high and about the same expanse from side to side and from front to back. There were sixteen rooms of ruins in the back, and President Hammond thought they were built by the Gadianton robbers, infamous marauders described in the Book of Mormon.[46]

Bluff residents of all ages could not help but notice the great quantity of ruins and relics around them, which at times gave them a forlorn sense that they were only a recent, small band compared with the former residents of the land. It was hard to go far in their travels on the range without encountering some artifact of past occupants of the country. Jens Peter Nielson and Charles Lang, a recently arrived, multi-talented young man from Pittsburgh, took particular interest in these

---

42. Roring, *Beautiful Bluff*, 26; Albert R. Lyman, Journal, April 29, 1901.

43. Mary Kisten Adams, "Life of Margaret Adams," 181–82.

44. See Marion G. Nielson, "Apostle on Horseback," 248–51, for a charming description of the preparations and expectation that came before each conference.

45. Quoted in Hoopes, "Josephine Catherine (Jody) Chatterley Wood," 38–39.

46. Hammond, Journal, September 3, 1891.

relics, exploring Grand Gulch sometime before 1890. They also helped guide the McLoyd expedition from Durango in 1890 and 1891. Platte Lyman and Samuel Wood showed an interest in the artifacts as well, sometimes taking along Hans Bayles and the Perkins brothers. None of them knew much [270] about the relics or how to excavate them, usually labeling them all Aztec ruins. But they uncovered a lot of interesting items. Lyman found a mummy in Allan Canyon, wrapped in a fabric and feather blanket. For a time, the withered corpse was stored in his cellar and dubbed the "King of Blue Mountain" by those children who dared to peek in at him.[47]

Late spring and summer brought a steady succession of celebrations. Founder's Day, the bishop's birthday, the Fourth of July, and Pioneer Day were festive occasions, often with a children's dance in the afternoon. The kids could have "a rowdy time" complete with "candy and apples."[48] They might even be lucky enough to get ice cream on Independence Day, if there was still snow in the Blues and someone was willing to go get it.[49]

Summer meant more excursions. Sometimes groups of youth traveled to the cattle camps on Elk Mountain for a few days. The Nielson children spent some summers up at the family dairy at Dodge Point with Uncle Willard and Aunt Julia Butt, helping with the chores but having "a glorious time."[50] They even got to keep their share of the profits. Throughout the year every young man and woman in Bluff had to tend and herd the livestock around the house and in the hills surrounding the town. Learning to ride was as much taken for granted as learning to crawl and walk. Their horses, mules, and [271] milk cows became to them like so many more ornery or amenable relatives, whose characters became well known through long experience together.

The fruit came in late summer. First the raspberries ripened, followed by apricots, plums, peaches, grapes, melons, and apples.[51] "I am gorged on watermelon half the time," commented young Albert R. Lyman

---

47. See Blackburn and Hurst, "Charley Lang," 5–13; and Hurst, "Colonizing the Dead," 2–13, for details on these expeditions. See also Hammond, Journal, April 2, June 8 and 18, 1891.

48. Albert R. Lyman, Journal, April 3, 1896.

49. Elliot, Diary, February 25, March 1, 1900.

50. Reeve, "Lucinda Diantha Nielson Hyde," 202.

51. See Albert R. Lyman, Journal, August 3, 1895; July 3–October 14, 1901.

approvingly.[52] Often these melons were consumed at parties for that purpose, and with any luck these occasions would wind up with a rind fight.[53] Scaffolds to dry peaches went up and were heavily laden in September and October. "We dried peaches as if our lives depended on it," which left "the whole place stinking with them."[54] The smell of molasses also wafted through town as the youth helped with the difficult process of transforming sorghum cane into something sweeter in John Allan's mill.[55] The scent was not entirely pleasant for the older children, since it was the result of a lot of hard work stripping cane. To the younger ones, though, it was the signal that there was a big pile of springy and slippery "pummy" stalks from the sorghum cane to play on.[56]

By November the children were back in school. They could go through only the eighth grade in Bluff, but Mancos had a good secondary school. Some of Bluff's children were starting to be packed off to the Brigham Young Academy in Provo for secondary [272] education. But they had other educational opportunities as well. The bishop, impressed by his daughters Caroline and Cindy's singing performance at the conjoint youth meeting the week before, reminded Bluff's children of how fortunate they were. He spoke in Sunday School in early 1891 of "the difference between the manner of raising and training children when he was young in Denmark, and the way our children are supplied with advantages for culture."[57] Children and youth were encouraged to read, memorize, recite, sing, and act in their Church groups and schools. They played what instruments they could (some boys even started a harmonica band), but skilled training was scarce. David Edwards, the brother of one of the Hole-in-the-Rock pioneers, arrived sometime in the early 1890s and started teaching music lessons in town. Sometimes the Bluff Ward Choir would serenade families in the evening. Jens managed to send for two organs, one for each of his homes, by mail order, and the young people in town would often gather around one or the other to sing.[58]

---

52. Albert R. Lyman, Journal, August 29, 1895.

53. Albert R. Lyman, Journal, August 25, 1895.

54. Albert R. Lyman, Summaries of Each Year, book 1, p. 159.

55. Albert R. Lyman, Journal, October 2, 1895.

56. Reeve, "Lucinda Diantha Nielson Hyde," 200.

57. Hammond, Journal, January 24 and February 1, 1891.

58. Reeve, "Lucinda Diantha Nielson Hyde," 201.

Finally, the big celebrations arrived around Christmas and New Year, which would start the whole cycle over again. Throughout it all Indians came to town and were a perpetual source of wonder and the willies, fights, and friends for the young. Between the regular festivities, the assorted animals, the mysterious landscape, and the exotic neighbors, Bluff's children had plenty that could break the routine of their studies and chores.

Jens's younger children enjoyed all this growing up in Bluff, and most of them had [273] graduated from childhood in these surroundings. Cindy was eighteen, and Caroline, Kirsten's youngest child, turned sixteen in 1890. Katrine's three survivors, Annetta, Uriah, and Freeman, were fifteen, thirteen, and eleven. Annetta, or "Nettie," was shorter and quieter than the average Nielson child. She did not socialize as much as most Bluff youth but had a solemn reservoir of faith.[59] Uriah and Freeman were more rambunctious, and sometimes these boys may have wondered if they were lucky to have their father around so much, since he did not neglect discipline. After Jens spanked Uriah a few years before, the father looked down at the angry boy and announced, "Now what do you tink, I know what you tink, you tink, 'Damn you old Dad,' now I'll spank you for that."[60] Freeman was also an energetic lad, "an entertainer, he was magnetic; he was a chief among the boys."[61]

Troubles Right Here

"We should take more interest in our young," Bishop Nielson announced from the pulpit in late 1890. "There is a great labor to perform in this respect."[62] On another occasion he warned his ward, "We will be to blame if our children do not grow up in the path of right as we have few bad influences to contend with in this land."[63] But there were enough contrary influences and instincts in Bluff to make raising so many children [274] and young adults difficult, not just for the parents, but for the whole town. Some of the youth had turned the pleasures of childhood into vices. They started betting more than canned oysters on ball games

---

59. Johnson, Autobiography, 208.
60. Maxine Nielson, "Grandpa Uriah Nielson History," 249.
61. Albert R. Lyman, "Experiences and Impressions," 1:26.
62. Bluff Ward, General Minutes, November 6, 1890.
63. Bluff Ward, General Minutes, November 6, 1887.

and horse races. One race put several hundred dollars at stake before it was called off by alarmed authorities. Parties became too frequent. "Two social parties this evening, one in the school house and one at a private house," mourned President Hammond at the end of an extended holiday season. "This spirit of frivolity among the young is running wild, and the Lord is not pleased with it."[64]

There were other examples of taking their fun too far. The bishop scolded the deacons at their weekly meeting for their "rude behavior at the singing school last Tuesday evening."[65] Soon after that the parents were reminded in church that since Bluff had the blessing of being free from saloons, their children should be better for it, but there were fears they were not. Dancing, within its proper bounds, uplifted the spirits of the town and helped keep the youth content.[66] But outside these limits it became a menace. The leaders exhorted the ward "to put a check upon these everlasting dances, and turn the hearts of the young into a more elevating channel."[67] The youth were urged to spend more time seeking a knowledge of the gospel in prayer and in the scriptures. The young men were given more responsibilities in the ward. Bishop Nielson, perhaps mindful of his episode with Uriah, instructed the ward, "We should exercise kindness towards them [275] and not drive them from us by harsh treatment."[68]

In some ways the Bluff Saints were paying the price for their frontier existence and for turning from agriculture to livestock. Young boys were often left in town without their fathers, who were out on the range or freighting co-op merchandise to Colorado. Older boys were out on the range themselves, sometimes with and sometimes without their fathers, far from regular families and church meetings. These older boys were turning into "the rough character" of the cowboy. The boys in town not only picked up coarse manners from older boys, but also some of their habits. The bishop and other leaders increasingly reproved the young men for drinking whiskey. On the Fourth of July in 1891, a number of Bluff boys celebrated too much and shot up the co-op store, and on the

---

64. Hammond, Journal, January 9, 1891.
65. Hammond, Journal, January 26, 1891.
66. See Riis, *Ranger Trails*, 45.
67. Hammond, Journal, January 26, 1891.
68. Bluff Ward, General Minutes, August 23, 1891.

fifth the sobered young men were reprimanded by their bishop and stake president in church.[69]

The outside cowboys continued to hang around, "a low-lived set generally, [with] a few exceptions."[70] Bluff had fewer of them in town than Moab or Monticello, but the rough outsiders still showed up at dances. "They always manage[d] to find out when our parties are held."[71] A group tried to crash a dance late in June 1891. The bishop refused to let them in; they took offense and rode through town firing their guns. The Bluff girls were to blame, not just for attracting the cowboys, but for poor judgment. Regarding the cowboys, Martha Hammond wrote her husband that "most of our girls seem to think as [276] much of them as they would of a boy of good standing in the church."[72] President Hammond agreed that "our girls are much too fresh in company with the outside element."[73] But Bluff's young men also put off marriage until a later age, leaving some of the young women to look elsewhere. Many of these problems came together to mar Bluff's Pioneer Day celebration on July 24, 1891. Some cowboys came to the dance along with some liquor, and once again the night was brought to a conclusion by the sound of gunfire racing through the streets.[74]

The worried Bluff parents soon found out, however, how fortunate they were. At nine o'clock the next morning, Willard Butt arrived in town after riding all night. He brought grim news: Jane Walton was dead. She had been the president of the San Juan Stake Relief Society for almost as long as it had existed and had been esteemed as "a very kindly disposed woman, full of charity and sympathy, abounding in deeds of practical piety."[75] She had just been in Bluff two weeks earlier at a Relief Society conference, where she advised the young women to learn useful crafts so they could support themselves. This would give them the independence to "refuse marriage to the unworthy."[76] Now, as

---

69. Hammond, Journal, July 4 and 5, 1891.

70. Hammond, Journal, June 22, 1891.

71. Hammond, Journal, August 21, 1893.

72. Martha Hammond, letter to Francis A. Hammond, February 26, 1890.

73. Hammond, Journal, October 23, 1890.

74. Hammond, Journal, July 24, 1891.

75. Hammond, Journal, July 26, 1891.

76. Hammond, Journal, July 7, 1891.

Butt told his stunned listeners, she had been shot accidentally by an inebriated Mormon boy confronting a drunken cowboy. [277]

Immediately Bluff mobilized. The bishop and most of the older settlers, who knew the Waltons well from their eight years in Bluff, formed a wagon train that set out for Monticello soon after noon. When darkness came, the procession was still two miles away from Mustang Spring, but some of the men went ahead with torches to pick out the road. Rain started falling. Bishop Nielson's wagon slid off a muddy grade and tipped over. Luckily, no one was hurt, the wagon was righted, and the column slogged on. After camping for a few hours, they were on the road as soon as light broke, arriving at Monticello by eight o'clock in the morning.[77]

There they found a "dense cloud of gloom on the whole ward." The Waltons were in "great grief," their two daughters, Magnolia and Leona, were "almost inconsolable." The citizens also found out the details of the tragedy, which had been caused by troubles all too familiar to them. Someone in Monticello had sold whiskey to cowboys and Mormon boys before the Pioneer Day dance.[78] Tom Roach, a Carlisle cowboy who lived across the street from the Waltons, was well-liked when sober but dangerous when drunk. He had killed an Indian in a squabble a few years before, and he had appeared late at the Pioneer Day dance in a similarly soused state, upset with the Mormons for the trouble he thought they had been causing between him and his Mormon wife.[79]

The fatal chain of events commenced close to midnight when Roach insisted on [278] dancing out of turn and tried to shove Nephi Bailey off the dance floor. Frank Hyde intervened, and Roach gashed him in the back with a knife. Hyde and some others grabbed Roach, and they were about to tie him up when a friend said he would look after the troublemaker. But Roach got a gun and started threatening the whole house. Bill McCord, another cowboy friend, tried to coax the gun away, but Roach shot him dead. Then he threatened to kill anyone who left the building. Frank Adams, a nineteen-year-old Mormon who had also had

---

77. Hammond, Journal, July 25 and 26, 1891; Albert R. Lyman, "History of San Juan County," 72.

78. Hammond, Journal, July 26, 1891.

79. The account in this and the next paragraph comes from Hammond, Journal, July 26, 1891; Reeve, "Lucinda Diantha Nielson Hyde," 203–4; and Perkins, Nielson, and Jones, Saga of San Juan, 106–7.

too much whiskey that night, escaped through a window. He ran to the Waltons' nearby home and grabbed Charles Walton's rifle. By the time he returned, the ruckus had moved outside the meetinghouse. The drunken Mormon called on the menacing cowboy to lay down his weapon. A gun thundered, and Jane Walton fell dead, shot "just under the arms killing her instantly."[80] Roach's wife cried out and flung herself over the body of the fallen woman. Roach seemed to believe that he had killed Sister Walton and became distraught. He collected money from his captives so he could get away then contritely returned it and let everyone go. He found a horse, left town, and had not been seen since.

The funeral was held at two o'clock in the afternoon the day the Bluff Saints arrived. Just as the party made ready to leave the Waltons' home and proceed to the church, a shroud of rain and hail, heavier than many had ever seen before, dropped three [279] inches of water on the ground in half an hour. The six young pallbearers waded through the muck and brought the casket to the church. Jens Nielson and the other leaders did their best to assure the congregation, "Saints do not mourn without hope as do the wicked." Then those at the funeral loaded into wagons and carriages, drove to the cemetery east of town, and made Jane Walton its first occupant, "laid away until the resurrection day."[81]

Sister Walton's death was tragic by any measure, but more so because it would not have happened if the members of the San Juan Stake had listened to their leaders. If only Mormon boys had not imitated and associated with cowboys so much, and Mormon girls had not invited them to their dances through words or demeanor, this could have been averted. President Hammond trusted it would teach this one lesson:

---

80. Walton, Diary, July 24, 1891, tells what Jane's husband saw firsthand. Walton wrote that while Roach started the row and killed McCord, the drunken Frank Adams "accidentally shot" his wife. Francis Hammond also recorded in his contemporary journal that Adams fired the fatal shot, since Roach had killed McCord with the only bullet in his gun. But see Bluff Ward, General Minutes, August 2, 1891, in which President Hammond implicates Roach for the killings of both McCord and Walton. Either some new evidence came to light, or, as Allen, "Killing of Jane McKechnie Walton," 13–15, concludes, the settlers shifted the blame to Roach to keep the community, the Waltons, and young Brother Adams from further suffering over the accident.

81. Hammond, Journal, July 26, 1891; the quote is from Walton, Diary, July 26, 1891.

"That those who are not for us are against us."[82] The mission to control San Juan County was not just on the borders against outsiders but
within their own wards and homes.

Church leaders stepped up the fight. After the stake conference in
August, the high council voted to ban cowboys from social gatherings
and disfellowship any Church members who either sold alcohol or drank
it and disturbed the peace. Those in the stake were especially vigilant for
the rest of the year. Many of the younger men in Bluff, including Joe,
Jens Peter, and France Nielson, were confronted with their drinking and
asked forgiveness from the assembled ward members.[83] Problems with
the youth did not [280] end with this episode. Young men continued to
misbehave in church, drink occasionally, and persist in round dancing.
Church leaders even had to ferret out the young men who stole apples
from Bishop Burnham's wagon after a stake conference, then ferret out
feelings of contrition from them. But authorities continued to preach
to them and enforce regulations on dances in the wake of the disaster. The stake conference in February 1892 concluded with a "priesthood
dance," in which all the Saints were on their best behavior. "We enjoyed
ourselves much, the Spirit of the Lord was present, no whiskey, no mis-
conduct." To the leaders, at least, it was "the best party ever had in this
stake."[84] They continued, amid their rising fortunes, the fight without
and within: to save the county, their children, and themselves from the
influences of the Gentiles. Meanwhile, the six hundred dollar reward for
Tom Roach remained unclaimed.

The Peak, 1893

One of the parties of the 1892 Christmas season was a dinner thrown
by Jens Nielson in honor of his son's wedding. France had grown swiftly
from the quiet boy who had helped herd cattle on the trek to Bluff to a
six-foot-two-inch, sandy-haired, twenty-four-year-old bridegroom. He
was a major part of the Nielsons' financial ventures, spending time on
the range, at the dairy, and in Verdure, and he was stepping up in his
religious duties as well, having just been made a counselor in the ward's

82. Hammond, Journal, July 26, 1891.

83. Hammond, Journal, November 21, December 27, 1891.

84. Hammond, Journal, February 22, 1892.

young men's organization. He had married Leona Jane, or "Lone," Walton, the younger daughter of the departed Relief Society president, a month before in the Logan Temple. Now, nearly [281] the whole ward came by to offer their congratulations and have a good time. Nearly the whole ward, in fact, would have a good time, not just that night but for the next six months, as the fortunes of Bluff continued to rise to the highest point they had yet reached. To start, they found themselves in the middle of a gold rush.

Boom

Various and scattered groups had tried to extract precious ore from San Juan County before 1892, but their efforts had always been ultimately unsuccessful. When reports came out of Monticello that prospectors found gold and silver in the Blue Mountains, most in Bluff assumed it would be over quickly. They were surprised to learn that more miners were coming in September 1892, and by early December some had discovered gold on the San Juan River, eighty miles west of Bluff. As Christmas approached, the *Deseret News* proclaimed the "New Gold Fields" and announced the Denver and Rio Grande Railroad had discounted rates from Salt Lake City to Thompson's Springs.[85] Bishop Nielson took time on the day of France's reception to huddle with other Church leaders about how to handle the traffic to the mines. Two days before the New Year, Bluff was being transformed: "A constant stream of people are daily passing through our little town, nearly every house is being turned into boarding houses, and our people are being excited over the changed conditions."[86] Reports from the fields fed the rush, claiming large nuggets were being found and that Utah would be bigger than the Black Hills and [282] "scaling up close to early California" in gold production.[87]

The ward tried to meet the influx together. On New Year's Eve, the leaders gathered at one of Jens Nielson's homes and agreed to encourage a stagecoach company by building stables next to the tithing lot. They also concluded that the co-op ought to build a hotel near the store to accommodate and capitalize on all the visitors.

---

85. "The New Gold Fields," *Deseret News*, December 22, 1892, in Journal History, December 22, 1892, 3.

86. Hammond, Journal, December 30, 1892.

87. See reports in Journal History, December 29, 1892, 5; December 30, 1892, 6.

But this opportunity was also an invasion, and Church leaders tried to strengthen their ward members against dangerous influences. Francis Hammond told about his sobering experiences in the California gold fields years before and recalled how Brigham Young had stated that "we are not a mining people." Bishop Nielson reminded his flock that the principles of the gospel were better than gold and silver, and he encouraged the ward teachers to visit the homes of the Saints more frequently than usual.[88] Forewarned by their experiences with the cowboys, the biggest concern was about the youth: the girls should treat the miners "courteously, and let them pass on." The young ladies should, under no circumstances, paint their faces, "as some had done lately." Mothers should "set a double watch over children."[89]

The rush continued to swell. By January 4, one reporter guessed some seven hundred miners had started their diggings just below Bluff and worked the fields 250 miles down the San Juan and up the Colorado River. While that estimate was probably too high, the streets of Bluff were crowded with wagons, pack animals, and their owners. [283] More arrived daily on the stage set up from Dolores, Colorado, to Bluff, which deposited its first passengers in town on January 2, and the *New York Sun* even sent an expedition. The residents in Bluff were already starting to mine the miners by feeding and lodging them and their animals. Signs popped up all over the town, advertising such services as hotels, "meals at short notice," laundry, and "bread for sale."[90] The co-op ordered thirty thousand board feet of lumber to build their hotel. From the demands of the town and the miners, Willard Butt's sawmill at Verdure did outstanding business. France Nielson and Wayne Redd went down to the gold fields to check into the wisdom of opening a meat market for the miners. Fast meeting on Thursday, January 5, was devoted to the town's guests. The Saints were counseled to act as such and treat the visitors fairly, without charging exorbitant prices or losing sight of their duties in their haste to get rich. Instead, the miners should leave impressed with their honesty. The meetinghouse was packed full for Sunday meetings, with over fifty strangers present.[91]

---

88. Bluff Ward, General Minutes, March 5, 1893.

89. Hammond, Journal, January 1, 1893.

90. Francis A. Hammond, "Report from San Juan," *Deseret News*, April 1, 1893, 470–71.

91. "The San Juan Gold Fields," *Deseret News*, January 4, 1893, in Journal History, January 4, 1893, 5; Hammond, Journal, January 5, 1893.

The initial bubble burst by the second week in January. France returned discouraged about supplying meat to the miners. J. Clayton Nichols, a geologist and banker from Grand Junction, brought back negative reports about the quality of gold in the fields. It was too fine and therefore too expensive for individual miners to retrieve.[92] But all sorts of people kept arriving, "bankers, mechanics, farmers, merchants, black-legs, [284] and tramps, [and] one or two preachers."[93] Most of them did not go on to the gold fields, however, once they heard the latest reports. Some went up to Monticello, but many tried to sell their equipment and get out altogether. Honest and gouged profits kept coming to those in Bluff, as did a lot of merchandise sold cheaply by disillusioned miners. Some of the town's old residents may have remembered all the effort the early Bluff settlers had expended in exporting their labor to Colorado. Now Coloradans and other outsiders were conveniently coming here to deposit their wealth.

But the fortunes for Bluff were not unalloyed. John Morton Wood, the fourteen-year-old son of Samuel and Jody Wood fell and bruised his knee while playing baseball on New Year's Day. For the next three weeks, all through the big days of the rush, he lay in bed in great pain, at times unable to eat. On January 18, as the number of miners waned, he died. Perhaps it was blood poisoning or some other type of infection, but this was a particularly strange and sad funeral for Bluff. Uriah and Freeman Nielson helped the other boys carry their fellow deacon's casket into the log meetinghouse.[94] Jens Nielson, Platte Lyman, and Francis Hammond tried to console the living with the hopes of the resurrection before they lowered the coffin into the hill. John's mother had promised the boy a birthday party that year. On June 5, even though John was no longer there, she had one anyway, inviting his friends over for more of a commemoration than a celebration. At the occasion she handed out black-edged cards reading, "Absent but not [285] forgotten: John M. Wood."[95]

Hopeful miners continued to drift in throughout the year, but the boom was over by February. The gold on the San Juan was mostly "flour gold," of such small particles that it was almost impossible to extract

92. Hammond, Journal, January 3, 1893.

93. Hammond, Journal, January 9, 1893.

94. Hammond, "Report from San Juan," 470; Albert R. Lyman, Journal, January 18, 1893.

95. Albert R. Lyman, Journal, June 5, 1893.

profitably without expensive machinery.[96] For a time, Bluff dealt with the backwash. Many of the miners were not only disappointed, but destitute. Some of them panhandled in Bluff, but others could do more than mine. Melvin Dempsey, for example, taught music lessons, and a number of the other miners had skills in masonry, stonework, and carpentry that would soon be useful in town.[97]

Bluff's hopes for itself died with the boom. The hotel was never built. The stage lines quickly quit operation. The Southern Rio Grande never went beyond inquiries in extending a line to Bluff. But if the boom did not fulfill the dreams of the town, it did not realize its nightmares either. In fact, compared with the cowboys, the miners were choirboys. There was one lethal fight among about forty miners down by the diggings but no violence near Bluff. Some worried about the influence of miners on certain Bluff boys, but on the whole the town's youth behaved themselves.[98] Some boys drank a little whiskey on New Year's Eve, some girls were too fresh in blatantly choosing miners as their dance partners, and there was one fracas between two of the miners at one of the [286] dances. But that was about it. Since the town could not prevent a saloon from opening, the co-op bought two loads of whiskey from those planning to do so and locked it all in the store.[99]

Instead, the biggest worry was about their land. Since the government still had not conducted an official survey of their town, the residents had no legal claim to it. Fearing that the gold seekers might stake claims not just down the San Juan but also on their homes, lots, and fields, Bluff's leaders organized a mining district comprising the whole town. It caused some inconveniences to meet the requirements of doing so, but it was the only way to secure their land, which had already cost them, "if labor be counted in, at least one hundred dollars per acre."[100] On the whole,

---

96. Jensen, "Historical Study of Bluff City," 106–7.

97. Albert R. Lyman, Summaries of Each Year, book 1, p. 93. Dempsey was a part-Cherokee, part-black miner of wide interests who stayed in Bluff a few years before the gold bug took him to Alaska by 1898.

98. Hammond, Journal, February 18, 1893.

99. One resourceful miner reportedly memorized where the barrels were located and drilled through the floor into them to get what he was after. See Lyman, "History of San Juan County," 78; Hammond, Journal, January 7, 1893.

100. Hammond, "Report from San Juan," 471.

President Hammond's wish from the height of the boom came true: "We hope the excitement will soon pass over and leave us."[101] Mining companies continued their attempts to extract significant amounts of the precious ore on the San Juan and in the Blue Mountains for the next decade. Despite names like the Gold Queen and Dream mines, they did not do well.

The main bounty the gold rush yielded to Bluff was in goodwill, just as the leaders had hoped. Although the townspeople did make significant profits and the ward teaching did not get done as frequently as the bishop had wanted, most miners left with a good impression. "Strangers generally seem surprised to find such good order prevailing in our [287] midst," according to President Hammond, "and they have many words of praise for us, and acknowledge how their prejudice is removed by visiting us at our homes."[102] Bert Loper, who came later with a mining company, gave a strong example of such feelings:

> During my sojourn in Bluff I lived with a Mormon family by the name of Kumen Jones—his wife was the daughter of the Mormon bishop. "Aunt Mary" was one of God's own people, and during my time here on earth I have never met a finer woman. I believe she took just as good care of us "gentiles" as she did her own people. Her father was just the same kind, and I really believed that he died without an enemy—loved by all.[103]

Far more miners showed an interest in Mormonism than the cowboys ever had. Up to sixty attended meetings on Sundays, and "without any exception they have behaved like gentlemen."[104] President Hammond defended the Manifesto as more than a political expedient on a couple of occasions, especially to Dr. Bull, a visiting Episcopalian minister. Despite the visitor's skepticism on this issue, he was given the pulpit on Christmas Day and returned the favor by saying "nothing but what all saints could endorse."[105] After his remarks, Jens Nielson contrasted the contentions among other churches and their trials of logic to the plainly revealed

---

101. Hammond, Journal, January 7, 1893.
102. Hammond, Journal, December 26, 1892.
103. "Bert Loper and the Gold Rush of 1893," 25–26.
104. Hammond, "Report from San Juan," 471.
105. Hammond, Journal, December 24, 1892.

truths of Mormonism. "Our souls have peace concerning all doctrines," he concluded.[106] Five miners were baptized into the Church in 1893, and possibly a sixth in 1894. While the first convert, German professor and gold seeker Jacob Schuessler, left town soon after his confirmation into the Church, [288] Charles Sitzer, William Nix, and A. L. F. McDermott stayed and raised families in the county. The gold rush also attracted some Mormons who remained. David John Rogers had married one of Walter Stevens's daughters in New Mexico but was attracted to Bluff by the boom. Ezekiel Johnson, son of Joel H. Johnson, an associate of Joseph Smith, had herded cattle and wandered aimlessly in geography and beliefs. He also came with the gold boom, but his bishop in Arizona introduced him to Jens Nielson on his recommend in this way:

> To whom it may concern: This is to certify that when Brother Johnson came to this ward he had with him a good recommend, but while here he paid no tithing and tinkered with the gospel but very little. But he is of a good family and faithful parentage and would be a power for good in a ward if he would apply himself. Try him; he is all right.[107]

Perhaps twelve hundred miners rushed through Bluff in late 1892 and early 1893, and these few were the sediment who stayed.

Dedication

If the gold rush meant the Saints in Bluff had one foot on earth in early 1893, they tried to place the other somewhere closer to heaven. They were preparing for something transcendent. When the ground was broken to start construction of a temple in Salt Lake City in 1853, the earth was frozen so hard that a pick had to be used in place of a shovel. It seemed the same pace continued throughout the construction. Between filling in the temple's foundation when Johnston's Army approached in 1857 and completely rebuilding it so it would be more solid starting in 1862, it took fourteen years [289] to get the structure to ground level. The enormous difficulties and expense of custom carving every stone for the structure occupied most of the next twenty-five years.

---

106. Hammond, Journal, December 24, 1892.
107. Johnson, "Autobiography," 207.

Jens and Kirsten Nielson attended general conference in Salt Lake City in April 1892. After the sessions, they joined perhaps fifty thousand others who thronged around the temple for the long-awaited capstone ceremony. They sang "The Capstone March," then watched eagerly as President Wilford Woodruff pressed a button, which caused a current of electricity to operate the apparatus that lowered the top half of the round ball on the center east spire into place. Great cheers and shouts of "hosanna" erupted. The gold statue of the Angel Moroni, trumpeting the gospel to the world, was then placed on top of the ball. But the building was not complete. The interior of the temple still needed three more years of solid work to be finished. At the end of the capstone ceremony, however, Elder Francis Marion Lyman challenged Church members to have the temple completely ready for dedication in only one year.[108]

The Saints in the San Juan Stake endeavored to do their part. They had already given over five hundred dollars to the cause in 1892 when they were assessed another six hundred dollars in November. By the end of February in 1893, they exceeded their quota and sent in over seven hundred dollars, with the Bluff Ward contributing more than four hundred of it. The last two hundred were donated in April, perhaps in an informal tithe of the gold rush bounty.[109] Church members also tried to get their ward and themselves in order before the great event. They made sure [290] their organizations were fully staffed and running smoothly. Individuals straightened out their lives so they would be worthy to have a recommend to attend the dedication ceremonies.[110] They also endeavored to rid themselves of any hard feelings they had toward each other.[111] All who could go to the ceremonies were exhorted by their leaders to do so. About one hundred people from the San Juan Stake took the Denver and Rio Grande to Salt Lake in early April.[112] But Bishop Nielson stayed in Bluff. Perhaps the ward needed minding with so many strangers still in town. In any event, he did not see the dedicatory ceremonies

---

108. Hammond, Journal, April 6, 1892.

109. Hammond, Journal, April 2, October 4, November 13, December 26, 1892; January 25, February 28, 1893; also a list of temple donations on end page after March 16, 1893, entry.

110. Hammond, Journal, March 6, 1893.

111. Hammond, Journal, February 17, 1893.

112. Hammond, Journal, April 3, 1893.

the whole Church had so long awaited. He learned of the events as he did much of what was going on in the world outside his own experience—from the *Deseret News* and other papers as well as from those who were there.[113]

The reports the bishop received were as good as he had hoped. In the enthusiasm of the moment, Francis Hammond may not have felt he was exaggerating in the least when he proclaimed the dedication of the Salt Lake Temple "the greatest event ever transpired on the earth since the advent of Father Adam." Most Saints felt heaven came close to earth during the week. Many from Bluff attended general conference sessions first and heard the Church authorities reflect on the miraculous progress on the temple, but also on how the Church had been divinely led through its trials to this time of peace. The temple was actually finished at noon on April 5. That afternoon, an open house was held for [291] about six hundred prominent Gentiles. Even C. C. Goodwin of the *Salt Lake Tribune* wrote a beautiful description of the striking structure.

The next day, April 6, Church leaders were given a tour of the temple, from the life-sized oxen in the baptistry to the "heavenly grandeur" of the celestial room. Then the first dedicatory session was held in the assembly hall in the temple, which could hold 2,250 people. The choir sang an anthem, then President Woodruff offered the dedicatory prayer. For forty minutes he recounted the history of the Church and of the temple and then dedicated the specific parts of the building. Lorenzo Snow then led the Hosanna Shout, and it seemed to some as if "the heavenly hosts had come down to mingle with us." Through their tears of joy, the congregation sang "The Spirit of God" as the choir performed the "Hosanna Anthem." Joseph F. Smith "sobbed and wept like a child before the assembled hosts of Israel" as he tried to speak. President Woodruff then proclaimed the temple and the people of the Church accepted of the Lord. Those who were disposed to look for signs found them in the gale that assaulted the temple during the ceremonies or the flock of about one hundred seagulls, not seen around Salt Lake City for years, hovering around the spires despite the gusts.[114]

---

113. Bluff Ward, General Minutes, April 2 and 9, 1893, shows Jens was present in meetings at Bluff on both of these Sundays, so he was not in Salt Lake City for the dedicatory sessions.

114. Hammond, Journal, April 6, 1893.

It was a great time of rejoicing for the Saints. The temple, so long delayed and so recently surrendered into the hands of the government, was now completed and dedicated. The First Presidency sent around a circular letter, urging the members of the Church to keep the same spirit they had had at the time of the Salt Lake Temple dedication. They should begin by fasting, praying, repenting of their sins, and putting their own households in order. Then their [292] influence would spread throughout their wards and stakes. Bluff's leaders encouraged the ward to follow this counsel.[115]

More Dedications

Bluff Ward members also had their own dedication to attend to. After the afternoon church meeting on May 14, 1893, they hiked out of the old log meetinghouse "a few rods west and north." There, President Hammond laid the southeast cornerstone for a new stone church. The ward had thought about building such a structure for a long time but put off plans out of uncertainty over how long they could stay in the county. In 1892, however, Platte Lyman "alluded to our poor, old log house where we worship at Bluff" and expressed his desire for a place of worship dedicated solely for that purpose. A few months later, Brother Lyman, the bishop, and a few others were appointed as a committee to investigate the building of a new structure. The gold rush provided a number of skilled men who, in the absence of gold, contracted to do the work. President Hammond did not like the idea of Gentiles building their church, but his concern did not last long. John Lumpkin, the stonecutter and mason, as well as all three carpenters, Charles Sitzer, Alfred Johnson, and William Nix, were baptized by the end of the year. A stone quarry was started near Bluff, teams took turns hauling the rocks, and by mid-May they were ready to start. Bishop Nielson stood atop the cornerstone and offered the dedicatory prayer for the new meetinghouse.[116] [293]

In these flush times, the town also started building a sandstone schoolhouse. At 50' by 25', it was five feet narrower than the meetinghouse but could accommodate up to one hundred pupils. Together these

---

115. Hammond, Journal, May 14, 1893; Bluff Ward, General Minutes, April 23, 1893.

116. Hammond, Journal, February 21, July 18, 1892; May 7, 12–14, 1893; Lyman, "History of San Juan County," 79.

buildings would cost over six thousand dollars, but that seemed easily possible in the bounties that were pouring in from the range, from the pockets of the miners, and seemingly from heaven. When the bishop reported his ward to the quarterly stake conference a week after the meetinghouse dedication, he had many reasons to be satisfied. The ward's meetings were well attended and its members had paid full tithing and contributed more than their share for the Salt Lake Temple, plus they were building a solid church and schoolhouse as monuments to their determination to remain in the settlement. Jens had one more reason at that conference that made him swell with justifiable pride.[117]

Joe was going to be the first missionary from Bluff. He had been called with four other members of the stake the previous November but almost did not make it. During the gold rush, Joe again could not resist some sociable whiskey and gambling. But he confessed fully and was forgiven at the February stake conference. Now he spoke of his eagerness and expectations to work in the Northern States Mission. It would be difficult to leave Ida and his five children, the oldest of which was only seven, but there were plenty of family members on both the Nielson and Lyman sides to help in his absence. A collection was taken in the ward to help him on his way, and Joe departed before the end of May.[118] [294]

While on his mission, Joe might have been able to visit the spectacle of the century, the Columbian Exposition in Chicago in 1893. If he did, with the other visitors he would have marveled at the magnificent neo-classical structures of the "Great White City" and been astonished at the technological wonders they housed. He might have even ridden the ferris wheel or eaten some cracker jack. If he did go, he was not the only representative from San Juan County.

In 1892, the First Presidency expressed its desire to send an exhibit of ancient Indian artifacts to the exposition. In December, the San Juan County Commission appropriated two hundred dollars to ship items to the fair. The next February, two officials coordinating Utah's contributions to the fair arrived in Bluff. They decided to ship Charles McLoyd, who had collected relics with Jens Peter Nielson and Charles Lang in previous years,

117. Francis A. Hammond, "Report from San Juan," 471; "Bluff Ward Manuscript History"; San Juan Stake General Minutes, May 20, 1893.

118. Charles E. Walton, San Juan Stake Conference Report, *Deseret News*, November 19, 1892, 788–89; Hammond, Journal, November 24, 1892; February 18, 1893.

along with his whole collection to Chicago. But the commissioners also agreed to send some of Platte Lyman's artifacts as well, along with some Navajo blankets. Then they roamed up and down the San Juan, taking pictures of various Indians, ruins, and relics.[119] By the time Joe visited the fair, he could have communed with all these items from home.

The great exposition represented more to the people in Bluff than regional pride. They noted with interest the triumphant tour of the Tabernacle Choir under its conductor, Evan Stephens, through the Rockies and Midwest en route to the fair. The choir was even lauded by a kindly mob at Independence, Jackson County, Missouri, a place from which Mormons had been expelled fifty-five years before. The choir performed to similar acclaim at the Columbian Exposition, taking second prize and a [295] thousand dollars, with conductor Stephens earning a gold medal. It was a refreshing change in the winds of public opinion. "All seem now to vie in doing us honor," Francis Hammond observed.[120] As the Church changed to become more like the outside world in its marriages and politics, outsiders were finding new ways to look at the Mormons.

But the other side of this coin was hinted at near the end of the fair by a young historian from the University of Wisconsin. Frederick Jackson Turner noticed that the supervisor of the Census declared after the 1890 enumeration that "the unsettled area [of the United States] has been so broken into by isolated bodies of settlement that there can hardly be said to be a frontier line."[121] This "end of the frontier" also meant that even as Gentiles began to praise rather than condemn Mormonism, they continued to crowd in around it. Mormons had been a distinctive people largely because they could live beyond American culture in the western wilderness. But now the world was closing in on them. With no new places of refuge, the main bodies of Mormons had to live amid a growing population of Gentiles.[122] "The benefits of frontier isolation" were disappearing for the Mormons, but they were also beginning to enjoy the glow of inclusion after the Manifesto.[123] The obligation to be

---

119. Hammond, Journal, February 15, 16, and 27, 1893; Platte D. Lyman, "Diary," March 1893.

120. Hammond, Journal, September 9, 13, and 19, 1893.

121. Turner, "Significance of the Frontier."

122. These ideas are found in Ridge, "Mormon 'Deliverance,'" 140.

123. Ridge, "Mormon 'Deliverance,'" 152.

socially, economically, and politically distinct from the outside world was also fading, and anyone who tried to preach the old principles of [296] cooperation and self-sufficiency had a harder time of it.

Professor Turner also believed that up until 1890 "the existence of an area of free land, its continuous recession, and the advance of American settlement westward, explain[ed] American development."[124] In this light, much of Bluff would make sense to Turner: the resolution of sturdy pioneers to tame a wild land, the pragmatism in the face of adversity, the sense of dominion over available resources, and the incredibly hard work were all there. But beyond these traits, Turner would have been frustrated with Bluff, because its residents did not do what he predicted. Instead of improvising new institutions and becoming more democratic, they had carried with them a predetermined pattern for their settlement and tried to become more orthodox, even when they had to modify their practices. Religious faith had little place in the young professor's landmark historical thesis. But Bluff's citizens soon found the opportunity to write that element into their own history.

Church historian Andrew Jenson visited the town in November of 1893. Jenson stayed with Bishop Nielson for two days and received "a full-hearted reception." Ward members took Jenson up the river to tour the big cave, and he attended their Sunday meetings, during which he urged the people to keep journals. As John was told on Patmos, "What thou seest, write in a book."[125] Then the Bluff Ward amazed him before he left:

> After the evening meeting, Bishop Nielson surprised me by handing me $11.00 in cash, which he had collected for me to help bear my traveling expenses, and be it [297] here said to the credit of the good saints at Bluff, that this was the first time that the presiding officers in any of the settlements of the saints had taken steps to raise means to assist me on my travels. God bless Bishop Nielson and the saints in Bluff for their generosity.[126]

---

124. Turner, "Significance of the Frontier."

125. Albert R. Lyman, Journal, 1:87. This message found fertile ground with thirteen-year-old Brother Lyman. From then on he kept a conscientious and observant journal, rarely missing a day.

126. Jenson, *Autobiography*, 212. Jenson added another reason why he was so grateful: "I really needed the money, as I had not wherewith to bear my traveling expenses from Mancos to the San Luis Stake of Zion, where I had to go by rail."

The bishop then called David Edwards on a special mission to take Brother Jenson on to Burnham.

It must have warmed the Bluff Saints more to read the Church historian's account of them in the *Deseret News:* "I have seldom, if ever, in my visits to the settlements of the saints in the Rocky Mountains, found a more open-hearted and appreciative people than the saints at Bluff."[127] But they also were glad to see he published what they told him. After the 1884 floods, they reminded him, Elders Erastus Snow and Joseph F. Smith visited what was left of the town. President Smith promised that those who left would be blessed, but those who remained would be doubly blessed. Now, nine years later, Brother Jenson wrote, "A number of the present inhabitants of the place whom I have interviewed during my visit here are very anxious that I should state as a historical fact that the words of President Smith have had a literal fulfilment."[128] *[298]*

---

127. Andrew Jenson, *Deseret News,* November 19, 1893, 748, in "Bluff Ward Manuscript History."

128. Jenson, *Deseret News,* 748.

7 Decline, 1893–1897

Depression

Sliding Finances

Even before the town's residents bid Andrew Jenson a cheerful farewell at the end of 1893, their economic outlook had become less rosy. Bluff's dependence on livestock had made the town dependent on national markets. This attachment had brought the bonanza of the previous years, but when the national economy started sliding, so did stock prices in San Juan County and Colorado. Although the gold rush bounty and spiritual glow of 1893 delayed and obscured the fact, Bluff was following the nation into depression.

A year before, in late 1892, the outlook was as bright as ever. The San Juan Co-op had delivered another 40 percent dividend to its investors, and the Bluff Cattle Pool had yielded a 15 percent profit. In the early months of 1893, President Hammond began to negotiate with the Carlisles about buying large chunks of their land claims. But at the same time, Bluff's stockmen saw troubling signs. The profits of earlier years had brought too many cattle and far too many sheep to their ranges. At the same time, the grass was thinned by what was beginning to look like a drought. Cattlemen lost more stock over the winter of 1892–93 than they ever had before, possibly as much as one quarter of their herds. The sheep survived better, but when the co-op's directors returned from the Salt [299] Lake Temple dedication, they discovered that some of the herders they had hired from New Mexico had sold or gambled away a substantial number of their sheep to Navajos. Their spring wool clip sold for only eight cents a pound, half the price of a few years before. Their supposed disaster insurance, the mutton market, was low as well. The U.S. Congress did not help either. The Democrats, who regained control in the 1892 elections, passed the Wilson-Gorman Tariff in August of 1894, lowering wool tariffs.[1]

Forebodings turned to gloom as the pool and co-op boards met after Pioneer Day in the summer of 1893. Fletcher Hammond could barely get payment for the four hundred head he had sold for the pool in Omaha. He reported the banks of Denver were closed and confirmed that Bluff was not just struggling with its own troubles but with a "general panic in financial matters."[2] The co-op was eight thousand dollars in debt, owing to the loss of sheep, lax management, and too much profit seeking during the boom. The individuals in Bluff as well as its companies found themselves in debt at a time when credit had fled and past obligations pressed down with more weight than ever. On one occasion, for instance, Platte Lyman had to borrow change from his children to meet an interest payment.[3] Few in town had cash to spare, the rates for day laborers plummeted, and [300] herders were taking as little as fifteen dollars per month.[4]

The decision to build a school and church at the same time in Bluff began to seem less than wise. Church headquarters was in the same, strapped situation, having a hard time paying its monthly expenses. The Presiding Bishop urged all the wards to put off improvements that were not absolutely necessary and to forward any cash they had on hand or any they could get by selling tithing in kind to Salt Lake City.[5]

Some looked to the county court to help ease their burdens by reducing taxes. Instead, Bluff tried to steal a march on Monticello. San Juan County had matured to the point where it needed a county courthouse,

---

1. Francis A. Hammond, Journal, September 23, 1892; January 22, February 1 and 25, April 27 and 29, May 26 and 27, June 8, July 4, 1893; Francis A. Hammond, "Report from San Juan," *Deseret News*, April 1, 1893, 470; Albert R. Lyman, Summaries of Each Year, 1893, book 1, pp. 84–85; Lambert, "Al Scorup," 309; Peterson, *Look to the Mountains*, 104.

2. Hammond, Journal, July 23, 1893.

3. Albert R. Lyman, Summaries of Each Year, book 1, p. 137.

4. Hammond, Journal, January 15, 1895.

5. Hammond, Journal, July 23, 25, and 28, 1893; William B. Preston to Francis A. Hammond, July 1, 1893.

and the boom leading up to early 1893 encouraged the county court to discuss it. But the two main towns could not agree on its location. Bluff was the older town and the traditional county seat, but Monticello was more centrally located, and it seemed to have the momentum of future population headed its way. So Judge Joseph F. Barton and some Bluff members of the county court tried to settle the matter by decisive action. They passed a quick resolution, perhaps loaded by the absence of councilmen from Monticello, that named Bluff as the location for the courthouse. Then ten teams and wagons from Bluff went for lumber in Cortez, Colorado, instead of their usual source, the Butt brothers' sawmill near Monticello. Word got to the Monticellans, who were just as disjointed with the hard times as were the people in Bluff, and they loudly protested the sly attempt to make Bluff the de facto county seat by conjuring a courthouse. Those in Monticello were joined in their objections [301] by other taxpayers who thought this was the worst time to build a courthouse. Finally, in mid-August Judge Barton and the court had to withdraw their plans, having succeeded only in antagonizing county residents instead of relieving them.[6]

Division

Under the heat of the drought and the pressures of depression, the unity of the Bluff Ward began to crack as well. In the crisis, "nearly every man wants to be the manager or 'top sawyer,'" which only added to the confusion. Some almost came to blows. Judge Barton seized Lemuel Redd by the throat, accusing him of lying about whose turn it was to ship freight for the co-op. Hyrum Perkins got involved in a scuffle as well. To make matters worse, too many teams were traveling on Sunday, breaking another commandment. The stake president felt that in these trying times "the priesthood is set at naught and counsel trampled under foot."[7]

Soon, however, the priesthood leaders were at each others' figurative throats as well, though the cause was not entirely clear. It might have been the courthouse. Or under these circumstances it might have been

---

6. Hammond, Journal, July 17 and 20, August 9 and 14, 1893, hints at this, from which I have put together the plot. Francis Hammond may have tipped off the Monticellans, traveling there in early August.

7. Hammond, Journal, July 29, September 3, 1893, give both the quotes and the incidents; Albert R. Lyman, *Lemuel Hardison Redd, Jr.*, 56.

as trivial as Bishop Nielson resenting the stake president for telling him he could not punish people who rang the meetinghouse bell without authorization because bishops had no civil authority. Or Jens might have had enough of the president's constant quibbling about building the new [302] meetinghouse and school. Whatever the reason, the men had another falling out. With everything stewing in the ward, these disagreements took a full month to fully resolve, but after an extended series of meetings, conferences, and free discussions, the tensions were cut at the Thursday afternoon fast meeting on September 7. The bishop went first, confessing his sins and then asking forgiveness of the ward. Francis Hammond, Platte Lyman, the stake high councilors in town, the bishop's counselors, then "all the elders and saints with very few exceptions" followed. This "glorious time" again cleared the air, and more importantly to those involved, made them "more acceptable before the Lord" and more likely to "obtain forgiveness from him." Still, it did not help President Hammond collect the money Judge Barton owed him when he needed cash to get to general conference.[8]

As it turned out, the bishop would need more peace and strength than any of them. Soon after the purging fast meeting, he became seriously ill. Jens had lived with chronic inflammation in his nose and throat for years, probably from "catarrh," or the drainage of sinus infections, but now the pain in his head became unbearable. He could not attend meetings, and on September 16, a number of the ward's leaders gave him a priesthood blessing. But soon after, he was so much worse that his family sent for a doctor. Francis Hammond, Platte Lyman, and Kumen Jones administered to the bishop again. The doctor arrived from Cortez on the twentieth and immediately removed a polyp from the suffering man's nose. Two days later, fluid started running out of his ears as the infection spread. Jens's temperature rose and his strength declined even more. Visitors found him "very [303] weak" and "dangerously ill." His fever broke the next day, but the doctor did not yet consider him out of danger. When the physician finally left on the twenty-fifth, his bill in those cash-strapped days was $175.00, what a cattle hand earned in seven months on the range. But the infection still rumbled around in Jens's ears, nose, and throat. In October, it gathered strength again, and the bishop suffered a

---

8. Hammond, Journal, July 30 to September 25, 1893.

relapse. He was bedridden throughout the month, and at seventy-three, it was uncertain if he could muster the strength to survive. By November 1, though, he felt up to attending Francis Hammond's birthday party, and by December, he was completely recovered. It was the closest he had come to moving onto Bluff's cemetery hill.[9]

Deeper Down

While the bishop was ill, the schoolhouse was finished. He missed its jubilant first social at the end of October. They also held some Church meetings in the school as the rock meetinghouse was still being built. All were not entirely pleased with the new building: at first its main room seemed too tall, too dim, and too noisy. But a curtain dividing the primary and secondary students made a big improvement, and it was a triumph to have the building finished.[10] The rest of the news Jens heard in his illness was bad. Wool prices were so low that the co-op had decided not to shear the sheep, and now they had scabies. Despite the hard times, the ward had to continue assessing its members for the continuing costs of their new church.[11] [304]

For the first time since 1888 the co-op declared no dividend since it still owed four thousand dollars. And for the first time since the early days of Bluff, children worried if they would get anything for Christmas.[12] The holiday season proceeded with less verve than usual. Church leaders were happy that the youth put on two plays, one about an ostracized Jewish maiden and the other a farce titled "The Mischievous Major." These replaced some of the dances of which the young were too fond. But the leaders were disappointed when some of the young men got drunk at the Christmas Day Ball, one so badly that he had to be carried

---

9. Hammond, Journal, September 16 to December 9, 1893. My understanding of this medical episode was greatly aided by Dr. Peter Sundwall Sr.

10. Hammond, Journal, October 27, 1893; January 7, 1894.

11. Hammond, Journal, December 12 and 14, 1893.

12. Thirteen-year-old Albert R. Lyman's journal for December 24, 1893, reads, "It is Christmas tomorrow but I do not expect any presents as the money panic is all over the United States, and it deprives us of the rights we would have with out it. Tonight is a very gloomy Christmas Eve. It is the only time I have wished that there was no Christmas." The next day brought him two apples, a bunch of raisins, a package of candy, silk handkerchiefs, and a map of Colorado.

from the hall. The bishop was particularly disappointed that two of the culprits were his backsliding sons, Jens Peter and France. They confessed their sins later in church, but it still did not remove the fact that his sons were cowboys in more than their occupation.[13]

Jens had cause to be concerned about Freeman as well. Always energetic, the fourteen-year-old was devoting some of his energy toward bullying and mischief. Albert Lyman, his former friend, mourned the treatment he had received from Freeman and his gang: "There are no boys in this town to sling at me and curse me because I am a Mormon as they did in Scipio, but they treat me just as bad on other principles."[14] On a Saturday in late January, just after the opening hymn had been sung in the 2:00 PM session of stake [305] conference, Calistia Hammond burst in to the meeting announcing Freeman had been shot. The meetinghouse emptied as the congregation rushed to the boy. It turned out he had been loafing on a haystack while Frank Hyde was shooting at some birds, and two small shot grazed Freeman across the eyelid and forehead. There was no lasting damage, and the meeting resumed, though there is no record of what consequences came later at home.[15]

Caroline, however, gave Jens more reason to celebrate. Wayne Redd had come to Bluff with his father, the polygamist exile Pap Redd, in 1887. When Pap went to Mexico in 1891, Wayne stayed, partially because of this Nielson girl. They got married in the new Salt Lake Temple in late November 1893. "It was time, too," according to a Bluff boy, "because he was twenty-three."[16] When the newlyweds returned to town just after the New Year, despite the hard times, Jens threw them a "sumptuous dinner" at his home. Wayne, rejoicing at his good fortune, threw everyone a party in the new schoolhouse.[17]

The drought and depression continued unquenched in 1894. The town was amused when a man with a phonograph came through, and they paid to hear it "sing songs, preach negro sermons, recite pieces, etc."[18] But the rest of the news was not as entertaining. The rain did not fall, the streams

---

13. Hammond, Journal, December 25, 1893, to January 1, 1894.

14. Albert R. Lyman, Journal, December 5, 1893; January 6, 1894.

15. Hammond, Journal, January 27, 1893.

16. Albert R. Lyman, Journal, November 28, 1893.

17. Hammond, Journal, January 3, 1894.

18. Hammond, Journal, January 16, 1894; Albert R. Lyman, Journal, January 15, 1894.

were nearly parched by mid-April, and the range dried out earlier than ever before. Some Navajos felt their flocks were only a year [306] away from ruin and speculated that "God is either dead or he has moved a long way off."[19] It was particularly difficult to try to prepare the ditch for such low water, and much of the watering of garden plots and orchards had to be done by hand if it was done at all. The generally depressed economy and the failure of the co-op to pay a dividend echoed in the meager tithing amounts the bishop could forward to Salt Lake City.[20]

Many cashed in their relics. Platte Lyman sold his four Native American mummies for one thousand dollars. Those who had laughed at him when he first started digging stopped laughing and started digging. Jens Peter Nielson and Robert Allan ("Rollicky Bob" to his friends) sold some of their collection for twelve hundred dollars. Jens Peter had less success on a relic-hunting expedition with Joseph Hammond in which they not only came home empty-handed but minus Jens's pack mule as well, which Hammond had inadvertently shot.[21] In essence, however, even though they lived on the land and made no secret of their activities, these hunters were ransacking the relics. While they added some pieces to museum collections, their amateur methods made it impossible to properly evaluate many of the items they found once they had wrested them from their earthen strata. Soon, some people in Utah and even San Juan County itself would be wondering if the state needed legislation to protect its antiquities.[22] [307]

The adversity of the times seemed to bring some humility as well. "There is a silent reformation going on in the midst of the people," felt President Hammond. Some members of the ward, mostly women, began holding a class to study the Doctrine and Covenants at President Hammond's house. By the end of the year, there was some kind of Church meeting or class going on every night of the week.[23] The

---

19. C. L. Christensen, "Direct from San Juan," *Deseret News*, December 22, 1894, 826.

20. San Juan Stake General Minutes, February 18, 1894.

21. Hammond, Journal, January 15, 1894; Albert R. Lyman, Journal, January 2, 1894.

22. "Utah Should Do Something," *Deseret News*, February 9, 1895, in Journal History, February 9, 1895, 2–3; Hammond, Journal, March 9, 1897. Hammond proposed a law that would set San Juan County apart as a reserve "to prohibit people from resorting here for Indian relics and curios."

23. Hammond, Journal, December 20, 1894.

baptized builders of the previous year made progress on the buildings and their faith in the gospel. Brothers Sitzer, Nix, Johnson, and Lumpkin were all ordained deacons in the Aaronic Priesthood in February, making for a quorum with members from ten to fifty years of age.[24]

But peace did not last long in these difficult days. The ward watched and fasted in pity and apprehension as John Allan Jr. was checked in and out of the asylum in Provo twice, claiming "he was troubled by evil spirits" due to family problems.[25] Then John Adams, Margaret Nielson's husband, assaulted Judge Barton over some business of the Bluff Pool. This caused "quite a feeling" in the ward, and Adams was later found guilty by Bluff's justice of the peace and fined twenty-five dollars plus court costs.[26] Pettier problems also came out as the Bluff citizens jostled against each other in their hardships from day to gritty day. The co-op ran a meat market, which was supplied with beef by its patrons when they needed to pay up their accounts. Beef was butchered one to three times a week. But to get the premium cuts, customers lined up early, meaning the "most [308] aggressive hog" got the best beef. The cows went in cooperatively but went out competitively, causing hard feelings among the losers in the carnivorous derby.[27] The bishop took his own knock when a vengeful post he was pulling down whacked him, decorating his forehead with a nasty gash.[28]

Despite all the troubles, the Bluff Ward was still the strongest in the stake, "presided over in a very efficient manner by Bishop Jens Nielson and his very worthy counselors."[29] This competence was more of an achievement than it seemed, especially in hard times, as the bishop of the Mancos Ward could testify when he became unpopular. One sympathetic ward member felt this sniping at bishops was "a natural failing all over Zion; he is the target for all to shoot at."[30] Bluff could also take cold comfort from

---

24. Hammond, Journal, January 29, February 26, 1894.

25. See Hammond, Journal, April 11 and 20, May 3, November 15, 1894; April 17, 1895.

26. Hammond, Journal, March 3 to 12, 1894.

27. Albert R. Lyman, Summaries of Each Year, 1894, book 1, p. 98; Albert R. Lyman, Journal, February 20, 1896; Hammond, Journal, February 20, 1896.

28. Hammond, Journal, June 30, 1894.

29. Francis A. Hammond, "Homes in San Juan," *Deseret News*, June 2, 1894, 763.

30. Silas S. Hammond, letter to Francis A. Hammond, July 25, 1892.

the Moab Ward, which was reduced to a branch because of much strong opposition to its bishop and because it was "so mixed with gentiles and Jack Mormons and apostates that it is not a desirable place to live in."[31] During the depression, Bishop Nielson continued to preach traditional Mormon values to his ward. He urged his people to cut back on their expenses and cooperate more during these hard times. But no preaching could stop the wind from blowing up the dry dirt and sand into "genuine San Juan blinders" throughout the summer or halt the sun from glaring off the rock walls around them or add life to the [309] dry range, which "was never known to be in a so poor a condition as it is at the present time."[32] Nor could the bishop force his followers to get along. The main advice they received in the July stake conference was to settle their difficulties with each other without dragging them before the high council. Christians should need none but the parties concerned to reconcile their differences.[33]

Bluff did have two things to look forward to despite the depression. On July 17, 1894, Grover Cleveland, in his second term as president, signed a bill that provided for Utah to be admitted as a state in the near future. The good feelings that had developed after the Manifesto and continued through the temple dedication and the Columbian Exposition had reached the nation's capital. And as a more local source of pride, Bluff's rock meetinghouse was almost finished. The project was still several hundred dollars in debt, as was the new schoolhouse, but at least it would be completed. When the choir tried it out in September, they liked its acoustics.[34] The Bluff Ward would have a place to worship for decades, provided its members were still there to do the worshiping.

----

31. Hammond, Journal, April 17–18, 1894.

32. Albert R. Lyman, Journal, June 1, 1895. Peter Allan, "San Juan Stake Conference Report," *Deseret News*, August 4, 1894, 210–11. Albert Lyman reported a sandstorm so thick in 1893 that he could not see a rod (16.5 feet) in front of him. See Albert R. Lyman, Journal, December 14, 1893. He also described a span of difficult days in March 1869 in this way: "Sun. 1. S[unday] S[chool] and meeting. It blowed all day and the sand blew. Mon. 2. School. Sand blew. Tues. 3. School. Sand blew.... I answered Joseph's letter and sent for a pair of goggles."

33. Allan, "San Juan Stake Conference Report," 210–11.

34. Hammond, Journal, July 27, September 16 and 19, 1894.

Indian Affairs

Upbringing

By the 1890s most of the children in Bluff had been born and raised there. They saw Indians [310] almost every day and got to know them fairly well. For some, this familiarity did not help. "Luella is wonderfully nervous frightened of Indians," President Hammond reported regarding his daughter, "and in a state of terror all the time."[35] Previous killings reminded the settlers there was danger, but most of them had more personal interactions with the Native Americans around them. In addition to seeing them when they traded at the store, Bluff men and women often hired Indian men and women to work for them. Sometimes they would work for cash, but "some of them are quite willing to work for something to eat, especially this season of the year when they cannot hunt for game."[36] And as Bluff children worked alongside Indians, they got to know each other a little better. "I shoveled with Tom Navajo," Albert Lyman wrote about a day at the ditch, "he learned me some of the language he spoke and I learned him some of my language."[37] But there was a mental hierarchy, and Bluff's children inferred they were on the higher rung, as the same Brother Lyman realized indirectly while a young man. He was working for the Wetherills in Mancos, and he noticed "such pride and class … and such style as they maintained made me to feel that I was getting exactly the kind of reception that we gave to Indians when we had them in our service."[38]

Bluff youth also knew Indians thought higher of Mormons than of "Americans"[39] and that as second-generation missionaries they still had an [311] obligation to teach the Indians something. On one occasion one of Platte Lyman's horses got away and an Indian found it and returned it. "We gave him some cloth afterwards to pay him for his kindness and to learn him to be honest."[40] On another occasion, Albert loaned his pocketknife to Manito's wife to open a can of fruit. At sundown, Manito came back to return it. "I believe if anyone will trust an Indian and the Indian

---

35. Hammond, Journal, September 17, 1892.
36. Hammond, Journal, February 29, 1892.
37. Albert R. Lyman, Journal, July 23, 1895.
38. Albert R. Lyman, "Experiences and Impressions," 1:142.
39. Albert R. Lyman, Indians and Outlaws, 100.
40. Albert R. Lyman, Journal, 1:30.

knows they are trusting him, he will not steal."[41] Sometimes, the lessons were harsh, such as the time Mike Moancoppy was snared in a double wolf trap when he kept removing wool from a chink in the wall of the co-op warehouse.[42] But Bluff's settlers also learned it was better to avoid some Indians if they could. When an Indian named Posey accidentally shot his wife, all of his and Aunt Jody's efforts could not save her. He cremated her corpse west of town, and some Bluff boys had to go see. Posey, understandably upset at this intrusion, yelled at the terrified boys and chased them a long way toward town.[43]

On the whole, relations with the Indians were more stable than they had been just a few years before. There were few enough troubles in the early 1890s that Thales Haskell, the Indian interpreter, was once again released from his assignment in Bluff to rejoin his family in Manassa, Colorado. By this time, Christian Lyngaa Christensen, a Dane nicknamed "Lingo" for his ability to interpret, had been called to live in Bluff. "The Indians are very [312] much like other human beings," he opined, "they are easy to be led, but slow to be driven; and if there were more interpreters and fewer soldiers it would soon work a reformation."[44] The worse the season, however, the more Indians could be counted on to leave their reservations and come into towns for help, he cautioned. The drought starting in 1892 hit the Indians as hard as it hit Bluff. This made the situation more precarious, but the settlers were used to it. "While it is not impossible to have some trouble with Indians on our borders," Christensen noted, it was usually outsiders who caused it and Indians who got blamed for it.[45]

Still, the danger could be real. In 1893, Clark Field, a Gentile traveling alone, was shot in his sleep by a Navajo after Field tried to warn them away from his camp with his gun. His end would have remained unknown, but

---

41. Albert R. Lyman, Journal, April 26, 1894. On occasion the tables were turned. Once when Lemuel Redd was on North Elk Mountain and could not find his sheep camp, Posey made him chop wood before he would give the disoriented man some food in his camp. See Arrington, *Utah's Audacious Stockman*, 31.

42. Albert R. Lyman, "History of San Juan County," 67.

43. Albert R. Lyman, Journal, 1892 summary; Albert R. Lyman, "History of San Juan County," 75.

44. C. L. Christensen, "An Interpreter's Experiences," *Deseret News*, October 30, 1892, 657.

45. C. L. Christensen, letter to editor, *Deseret News*, May 20, 1893, 674.

his grieving mother from Boston persisted in finding out his fate.[46] As the drought grew worse, so did Indian begging and demands. Benow, a Ute, brought his band to Bluff in August 1893, but the settlers had little to spare. Some Indians began to steal crops as well as turn their ponies loose into fenced fields to feed. Bluff's leaders worried that violence might break out if one of the "rash brethren" lost his temper.[47] By September the Indians were "here almost every day begging, and we feel it is better to feed than fight them. The game is almost gone and they are very destitute."[48] *[313]*

Final Removal

Behind all this, the issue of Indian removal to San Juan County had never entirely died. Every once in a while there were rumbles from Congress about the treaty made with the Utes back in 1889, but nothing came of them. Francis Hammond again wrote to Senator Henry Teller of Colorado in early 1891, pressing him to either pass the bill or reopen the land for settlement, "for we are in great suspense."[49] But when the removal bill failed to pass the Senate again that year, President Hammond and Silas S. Smith sold their Zapato Ranch land in Colorado to the First Presidency. "I lose $1,000 and a good deal of time," the stake president lamented, "but I could not handle it unless the government should buy us out for the Indians in San Juan County."[50] Left in suspense, the settlers in Bluff received varying signals from their religious leaders. Brigham Young Jr. urged "the people of Bluff to go to and build and improve and not wait for the settlement of the Indian question," and "the Lord will sustain them."[51] But George Q. Cannon later felt it was unwise to build public buildings on unsurveyed lands that might be confiscated.[52] While the school and church were being built, settlers waited for a resolution before they hazarded building better homes.[53] "If the Ute removal question was

---

46. Albert R. Lyman, Journal, vol. 1, pp. 36, 47, c. June 1893.

47. Hammond, Journal, August 4 and 25, 1893.

48. Hammond, Journal, September 12, 1893.

49. Hammond, Journal, February 11, 1891.

50. Hammond, Journal, October 20, 1891.

51. Hammond, Journal, February 21, 1892; November 11, 1893.

52. Hammond, Journal, August 15, 1893.

53. "Bluff Ward Manuscript History," 1893.

settled," felt "Lingo" Christensen, "San Juan County would soon fill up, and still add [314] wealth and population to blessed Utah."[54]

In early 1894, Colorado people and papers were once again agitating to get a bill through Congress. President Hammond consulted with the bishop and other ward leaders and forwarded the customary request for compensation, though now the bill had risen to three hundred thousand dollars, to Utah's delegate John Rawlins and Senator Teller of Colorado. Toward the end of February, however, Bluff's leaders read a copy of a telegram sent by Delegate Rawlins to Utah's governor, Caleb West, alleging that the Coloradans had sunk to new depths. The Utes were now being incited to come to Utah and drive out the settlers themselves. Immediately the bishop and his counselors met with Francis Hammond and Platte Lyman. This was an alarming prospect, but the danger would not really arrive until the grass grew tall enough to feed the Indians' ponies.[55]

In March, reports came in from the range that twenty to thirty Utes under Red Jacket had killed up to forty Bluff sheep. In early April, Delegate Rawlins informed the settlers that the Senate committee reported favorably on the removal bill. By May, however, things were quiet enough that President Hammond advertised in the *Deseret News* that he considered removal "a dead issue; they will not come now."[56] But Red Jacket and a band of Utes did come into Bluff a week later, and the Ute leader was upset. He told the residents he wanted to live in their homes already, and they could find a place somewhere else. The Utes, he continued, would even let the Mormons settle on the [315] western part of their new reservation.[57]

A very unsettled summer followed. Impatient Utes continued to raid Bluff's livestock. Navajos came into town in large numbers in mid-July "and acted very strange."[58] Some were stealing fruit, and by the end of the month the town's "danger from them and the Utes was never greater."[59] One day, Mike Moancoppy struck at Bishop Nielson with a quirt, but

54. Christensen, "Interpreter's Experience."

55. Hammond, Journal, February 10 to 20, 1894.

56. Francis A. Hammond, "Homes in San Juan," *Deseret News*, June 2, 1894 (written May 6, 1894), 762.

57. Hammond, Journal, May 13, 1894.

58. Hammond, Journal, June 11, 1894; Albert R. Lyman, Journal, July 15, 1894.

59. Hammond, Journal, July 26, 1894.

Lemuel Redd stopped him with a kick to the midsection.[60] Bluff's leaders "counseled the people to be very careful in their treatment of the Indians, for they are *mad*."[61] The town leaders wrote to David Day, the Indian agent at the Southern Ute Reservation in Colorado, requesting that he hold his Utes there.[62]

Bluff's agitations with the Indians declined as the heat of summer fell, but other problems failed to wane with the season. A diphtheria scare in August forced the bishop to suspend meetings for a week. As fall came, Bluff's citizens were left to contemplate how they could hold their dry range against the huge anticipated number of sheep that would be brought for the winter. Just to be certain of their helpless situation, President Hammond confirmed at the territorial land office in Salt Lake City that since they lived [316] on unsurveyed land, "if a cowboy turns his stock onto our fields we have no legal redress."[63] But some events made even these problems look small. The whole town mourned the sudden and striking death of President Hammond's twenty-one-year-old daughter, Hannah, in November. She was seized by convulsions soon after a bath and "expired in a few moments exclaiming, 'Let me go, let me go—kiss Pa and Ma good bye for me.'"[64] Jens sent Freeman out with fresh horses to help bring the Hammonds in from Colorado, and with the other town leaders did everything he could to console the stunned parents.

When Jens attended stake conference in Monticello in late November, there were a lot of Utes around, more, in fact, than he had seen before. They were belligerent when questioned, insisting that they had more right than the whites to be there. Some even felt that if the settlers tried to stop them, the militia would come to help the Indians. Scores of Navajos also came north from their reservation, invited, rumors said, by the Utes. It was not surprising that the talks of the conference focused on "kindness, patience, and all other necessary virtues towards the Indians," since "any

---

60. Albert R. Lyman, "History of San Juan County," 67. Moancoppy then demanded one hundred dollars in damages, which he never received.

61. Hammond, Journal, July 26 and 29, 1894.

62. Hammond, Journal, June 29, 1894.

63. Hammond, Journal, October 19, 1894.

64. Hammond, Journal, November 11, 1894.

hothead could start a fight in the county," which, given their numbers, would go much better for the Indians than the colonists at first.[65]

Another rumor that spread through the conference was that the Indian presence was a deliberate plot by the Southern Ute Indian agent, David Day. The Indians near [317] Monticello repeatedly explained that Day had told them to come. According to his reconstructed calculations, one of two things could happen. The Indians might be allowed to stay, and this would give the necessary shove to ratify the removal treaty. Or, war might break out. Either way, the Indians would be out of Colorado. To the Utahns, this was "a nefarious scheme of some of the people of Durango, Colorado, who are conspiring with the present unscrupulous Indian agent, Mr. Day." For the San Juan settlers, it was an alarming situation. They could probably control their own people, but who could tell what some cowboy might do? Jens's son-in-law Willard Butt, the sheriff of the county, sent off a petition from county citizens and an alarming telegram to Governor Caleb West, requesting state militia to protect the settlers and stabilize the situation.[66]

As Jens returned to Bluff after the conference in Monticello, more Navajos streamed by, heading north into the county. Their sheep were stripping the range from Bluff's already famished stock. If it came to violence, he and the other old men who were usually in town, Francis Hammond, William Adams, and Father John Allan, would not last long. As always, Jens had faith it would not come to that. But when he got home, he had other things to do. Cindy had apparently forgiven Frank Hyde for shooting Freeman earlier in the year, because the two were going to get married after "running together" for five years.[67] They were not traveling to a temple to do it, which was surely a letdown for the devout bishop, but it was a festive occasion nonetheless. Jens gave the couple some words of advice on [318] marriage, being the veteran of three such relationships himself, then President Hammond performed the ceremony. A big party

65. C. L. Christensen, "Direct from San Juan," *Deseret News*, December 22, 1894 (written December 2, 1894), 26–28; Willard Butt, "The Indian Invasion," *Deseret News*, December 8, 1894, 795–96.

66. Christensen, "Direct from San Juan," 26–28; Seymour B. Young, "The San Juan Situation," *Deseret News*, December 15, 1894, 825–26; Butt, "Indian Invasion," 795–96; "The Indian Invasion," *Deseret News*, December 15, 1894, 804–5.

67. Reeve, "Lucinda Diantha Nielson Hyde," 201.

was thrown for Cindy four days later, as the newlyweds prepared to move to Monticello.[68] This meant all of Kirsten's children but one, the thirty-two-year-old holdout Jens Peter, were safely wed.

Not long after, on December 6, Brigham Young Jr. came in from Durango and lodged with the Nielsons. He had spoken with Agent Day, who had seen nothing wrong with the current Ute situation. Of course he had ordered the Utes off the reservation, Day affirmed, since they could not leave without his permission. But the Utes had always wintered their stock in Utah, so this was nothing unusual. The cowboys could protest, but since the county had been withheld from settlement since 1888, they were the trespassers. Since white cattleman in Colorado had robbed the reservation of forage, people could hardly expect chiefs such as Ignacio and Mariano to simply stay there and let their stock starve. If there was any trouble, the agent continued, it would come because the cowboys started it. Day suggested that "Messrs. Hammond, Nielson, Jones, Lyman, and others who lived in the county … send him a written statement of the facts, and he would forward the same to Washington." Elder Young had also consulted with Ignacio and other chiefs and agreed they had a right to be in Utah. Ignacio had been in Washington, D.C., again the previous winter. When he told various congressmen that he had always wintered in Utah, no objection was made. In fact, some unofficially encouraged him to return this year. Young urged the Bluff leaders to write the letters to Agent Day and the Secretary of the Interior of the United States, Hoke Smith, to express their view of the [319] situation.[69]

On December 11, notice came that a meeting was going to be held the next day in Monticello. Governor West would meet with Agent Day personally. The governor had not sent troops, but he had sent weapons and ammunition. He was furious at Day, not only for his "nefarious scheme" but for an "impudent and blackguard" telegram Day had sent him, insisting that it was the Indians who required protection from the cowboys.[70] President Hammond raced up to Monticello for the meeting, and all the people in Bluff could do was wait.

---

68. Hammond, Journal, November 30, December 3, 1894.

69. Hammond, Journal, December 6, 1894; "The Indian Trouble," *Deseret News*, December 6, 1894, in Journal History, December 6, 1894, 5–6; "The Indian Invasion," *Deseret News*, December 8, 1894, 796; "Indian Invasion," *Deseret News*, December 15, 1894, 804–5.

70. "Indian Invasion," *Deseret News*, December 15, 1894, 804–5.

The news that arrived in Bluff a few days later was the best possible for the settlers there: the Utes were returning to Colorado. President Hammond and Samuel Wood told the ward how it happened in church the next Sunday. Many of the Indians were determined to stay when they got to Monticello, some saying they would not leave for anyone, not even the United States. President Hammond attended the 10:00 AM meeting with the governor and representatives from the towns, cattle companies, and mining interests. Agent Day had not yet arrived, but Governor West showed those who were there his trump: a telegram from Secretary of the Interior Smith ordering the Indians to move back to the reservation immediately. When Day arrived after lunch, there was little need for discussion. All agreed to help get the Indians back, and they sent a telegram to Denver requesting troops to assist them. [320]

At 3:00 PM the Indian leaders were brought into the meeting, along with "Lingo" Christensen, the interpreter. Governor West, Agent Day, and President Hammond, among others, told them their fate. Ignacio, Mariano, and Benow replied for the Indians. The consensus was that the Indians "could be cut up and eaten by us if we were hungry, but they would not go back." At this impasse, the chiefs were told to think about it until the morning. During the evening, weapons were distributed among the settlers and a guard was set for the night.[71]

The next morning dawned much brighter. The chiefs said they would return if they were given hay for their horses and supplies for themselves. The appropriate amount of beef was promptly butchered, and the hay was quickly brought. In the evening the settlers held a picnic and a meeting. They commended Governor West for his decisive role in the crisis. Agent Day grumbled that it was all a great noise without real danger. The disappointed Utes returned to the reservation as soon as the harsh season permitted. There was still the question of what to do with Benow's band of Utes, who had never been on the reservation, as well as the eighty or so Paiutes who roamed around San Juan. But the largest question of what to do with the 1,140 reservation Utes was closed.[72]

71. Hammond, Journal, December 12, 1894; "Indian Invasion," Deseret News, December 15, 1894, 804–5.

72. Hammond, Journal, December 13, 1894.

The next time C. L. Christensen came by Bluff, he probably explained his role in lubricating the settlement. He knew Ignacio felt he was right in the debate; after all, he had been in Washington and had even sat in Grover Cleveland's chair. This had come out [321] clearly during the discussions of the first evening. Ignacio interrupted often, particularly battling President Hammond on every point. Christensen did what he could to reduce the tension by not translating some of the more angry phrases. Then he stayed up with the Indians all through the night. He reminded them that the whites were as numerous as the grains of sand, something he knew Ignacio had seen in the East. Early in the morning, when he told the weary Indians that black troops were coming to remove them, the chiefs capitulated.[73] Lingo's nocturnal diplomacy had helped avert an explosion. Colonel Williams, the Navajo agent, helped get his charges back on their reservation in the days to come, and when several returned to Bluff for the Christmas feast, they did not seem threatening in the least.[74]

Bluff's citizens could afford to be amused by how the event fell out in the newspapers. The *Deseret News* editors mocked Colorado for their failed attempt in the "dumping business." David Day aired his frustrations against Governor West and the San Juan settlers in the Colorado papers, and even chastised the *Salt Lake Tribune*.[75] A few hundred reservation Utes lingered in the county through the winter, but the hopes of those [322] urging removal departed with these last Indians.[76]

Permanence

The winter in early 1895 turned severe, alternating between heavy rains, subzero temperatures, and snows of up to a foot. Every roof in town leaked. Francis Hammond had the option of shifting his bed into the

---

73. Christensen's recollections are quoted in McPherson, "Ute Invasion of San Juan County," 49.

74. Eventually a bill passed Congress over Secretary Smith's objections that allotted the Southern Ute Reservation to the Indians in severalty. This was carried out in 1899, but Ignacio and some others refused to do it. So the Ute Mountain Ute Reservation was created out of the western end of the previous reservation. See Thompson, "Unwanted Indians," 196.

75. "Utes in San Juan," *Deseret News*, December 22, 1894, 5; Hammond, Journal, January 10, 1895.

76. See Jensen, "Historical Study of Bluff City," 94.

stone and shingled section of his home, but everyone else had to deal
with the dripping. They did not mind it too much, though. The kids got
the rare chance to go sledding. But the adults had something to make
their eyes bright also. They had been living in their log homes for over
fourteen years. As always, "the women folks were the hardest hit" by
such primitivism.[77] The biggest hindrance to improving their homes had
been the possibility of removal hanging over their heads. Now, finally,
removal itself had been removed. As soon as Secretary of the Interior
Hoke Smith reopened the county to settlement, which he did before
1895 was out, the settlers could begin to build something better.[78]

The first physical symbol of their newfound permanence, the stone
church, had been finished in February. At the 10:00 AM dedicatory service held on February 23, the choir sang "Lord We Come Before Thee
Now," and Platte Lyman offered the invocation. Jens Nielson, as head
of the construction committee, gave a brief history of how their new
church had been built over the previous two years at a cost of nearly
four thousand dollars. It was quite a change, he reflected, from [323] their
log meetinghouse. In place of the old, rough-hewn furniture, the new
podium, secretary's desk, sacrament table, and benches were well-made
and smoothed to a satin finish. Instead of looking up at leaking factory cloth sagging from the ceiling, the Saints could gaze out of stained
glass windows. The steeple had a bell, and after the schoolhouse bell
was hung a year and a half later, the two could sound simultaneously
for special occasions.[79] Next on the program, Lemuel Redd described
how the Bluff Ward members "responded admirably in this matter" of
paying for the building, even during their difficult financial times. There
was, in fact, a small surplus in the treasury.[80] Brigham Young Jr. offered
the dedicatory prayer on the building, so long in coming. It was to be
used only for strictly religious meetings. To close the quarterly conference meeting held after the dedication, Francis Hammond noted that
the Bluff Ward paid more tithing in 1894 than they had the year before.

---

77. Kumen Jones, "Writings," 188.

78. "San Juan Reopened," *Deseret News*, November 7, 1895, in Journal History,
November 7, 1895, 2.

79. Albert R. Lyman, Journal, November 2, 1896; Roring, *Beautiful Bluff*, 10.

80. Hammond, Journal, February 21 and 23, 1895.

His words, echoing up toward the spire, signaled "that the Saints were on the improve."[81]

Disunion

Politics

Political winds blew through Bluff with increasing force in the mid-1890s. Back when the only choice was Mormon versus Gentile, voting was easy. But the time had come for voters in Bluff to decide if they were Republicans or Democrats, and [324] voters in San Juan County, Mormon and Gentile alike, fought for control of the county as the population on the northern end increased. When Grover Cleveland restored full civil rights to all Mormon males in early 1893, the bishop and other Bluff polygamists could once again take active part in the elections. But Bishop Nielson regarded the parties with the same suspicion he had for all outside influences. As seen from the First Presidency down, party politics could easily become a wedge to divide the Mormon bloc and turn brother against brother. Therefore, he kept his distance from these new partisan divisions, only helping to heal breaches as they occurred.[82] "We are required to take sides with the political parties of the day and mix up with those who are not of our faith," he warned. "But it will require all of our faith to keep us from partaking of their evil ways."[83]

---

81. San Juan Stake General Minutes, February 23, 1895; Roring, *Beautiful Bluff*, 3; Report of San Juan Stake Conference, *Deseret Weekly*, June 14, 1895, 805.

82. It is hard to tell if Jens leaned toward the Republicans or Democrats, though there are clues both ways. Francis Hammond lamented that many Democrats in the county could not vote due to the Edmunds Act. Father John Allan and William Adams were two who fit that category, so it may or may not have included Jens Nielson. On one occasion "Jens Nielson" gave a prayer at a local Democrat primary, but that is no guarantee he was a registered member. Also, his son Jens Peter was a Democrat, and sometimes he was referred to without his middle name, making it difficult to decide if it was the father or the son. Joe and Uriah Nielson were also Democrats. On the other side, the bishop probably subscribed to the *Denver Republican*, a partisan paper, and his son Francis became a strong Republican. See Hammond, Journal, July 1, 1893; September 18, 1896; September 1, 1898; Maxine Nielson, "Grandpa Uriah Nielson History," 241.

83. Bluff Ward, General Minutes, July 19, 1891.

Bluff's other leaders also tried not to let political divisions run too deep. Francis Hammond energetically worked to organize the Democrats in 1893. Late in the year, however, he resigned from his party posts on the advice of the Church's First Presidency, so that priesthood leaders could "be free to counsel without bias the saints in political [325] matters."[84] His informal survey at Bluff's polls that year showed eight Republicans and eight Democrats, though a few more Democrats stayed home.[85]

Early in 1894, Bluff was divided when President Hammond circulated a petition for Joseph F. Barton to be removed as county judge, a position still appointed by the president through the U.S. Attorney General under the provisions of the Edmunds-Tucker Act. His reasons might have been political, since Barton was appointed by a Democratic administration, but now, perhaps, showed himself to be more of a Republican. In any event, Platte Lyman, the most prominent Republican in the county, came to Judge Barton's defense. Harsh charges were leveled, wounding both sides. A council including the bishopric and Apostles Brigham Young Jr. and John Henry Smith decided Hammond should ask Barton's forgiveness in the matter. The stake president was reluctant to do so, but finally both sides apologized in Church meetings on April 15, and Hammond rescinded his petition.[86]

In the 1894 elections, the Democrats again felt betrayed. The citizens of Bluff had agreed before the election to run a nonpartisan convention to nominate candidates to begin the process of drafting a state constitution. They also had agreed to shake free of any sort of People's Party and run under the national party labels. Instead of holding to this, however, the Republicans ran under a Citizens' ticket, perhaps hoping to draw more gentile votes to put their party over the top. There was also a Democrat ticket, but the [326] "Citizen" ploy worked well, winning most of the races.[87]

Everyone in the county could be proud, or at least amused, by how Francis Hammond represented them at the state's constitutional convention in early 1895. He could not help but speak often and became noted as "the funny member from San Juan" and "the most popular member

---

84. Hammond, Journal, July 1, September 2, October 13, 1893.

85. Hammond, Journal, November 7, 1893.

86. Hammond, Journal, April 14, 15, 27, 29, 1894.

87. Hammond, Journal, September 3 and 24, November 3 and 6, 1894.

of [the] convention."[88] He was one of the 107 delegates who worked for sixty-six days under John Henry Smith on the document, which reinstated women's suffrage. In the end they all signed it and looked ahead to popular ratification in November. But the partisans in them also anticipated capturing control of the first state government in those elections, as well as winning the first full delegation to the U.S. Congress.

Politics in San Juan County were hot leading up to the elections in 1895. Republican Platte Lyman and Democrat A. P. Sorenson stumped around the county for the office of state legislator. Both were Mormons, but there were more differences between the two than their personalities or their parties. Sorenson lived in Monticello, which, on the strength of its surging population, was ready to seize control of the county government after fifteen years of Bluff control. Judge Barton's failed courthouse coup in 1893 may have accelerated the process. In early 1894, the Pittsburgh Cattle Company, operating in the La Sal Mountains on the north end of the county, petitioned the territorial legislature to detach the top twenty-five-mile strip of the county and annex it to Grand County to the north. It was simply too hard to travel clear across the county to the seat in [327] Bluff to transact business. Platte Lyman was dispatched to lobby the legislature against such a loss, and it helped that Francis Hammond's old friend from Huntsville, David McKay, was chairman of the committee that considered the bill. Even though the cattle company's attempt had failed, it highlighted the existing inequity.[89] Within a few months, Monticello citizens presented a petition to move the county seat from Bluff to their town, and it became an initiative that would be decided on the 1895 ballot.

The political and religious aspects of the election became superheated in the final weeks. In the October general conference of the Church, Joseph F. Smith made comments in the priesthood meeting that were endorsed by George Q. Cannon and that made it sound as if the Church wanted the Republicans to win. Democrats quickly reconvened their state convention, including their own General Authorities, such as B. H. Roberts and Moses Thatcher, to declare politics should be free

---

88. Hammond, Journal, May 2, 1895.

89. Hammond, Journal, January 7, 9, 13, February 7, 1894; Platte D. Lyman, "Diary," January 13, 1894.

from Church dictation. Elder Smith later softened his comments in the *Deseret News*, but the exchange still caused great commotion, even in the far corner of San Juan County. The persistent depression did nothing to improve the feelings of Bluff's residents toward each other either. Fifteen-year-old amateur cobbler Albert Lyman tried unsuccessfully to dun his neighbors for accounts receivable and "felt so disgusted, I went off by myself and swore a bit."[90] Still, relations among the Saints at Bluff remained good enough that nearly the whole ward united in regaling President Hammond until midnight on his seventy-third birthday a few [328] days before the election.[91]

When the results from the contests came in, there was something for everyone in the county. The Utah Constitution passed comfortably, though many Gentiles were impelled to vote against it by the Church's recent insertion into politics. The document passed in San Juan County by a margin of 82 to 12, an even larger majority than the 80 percent of the vote it had won in the whole state. But the county's ninety-four voters were less than one quarter of one percent of the entire electorate in the state.[92] The Republicans won a majority of the state legislature, causing resentment among the Democrats for the slanted comments of Smith and Cannon. But the northern part of San Juan County also won, approving the transfer of the county seat and electing all the county officers but Commissioner France Nielson and Assessor and Collector Hans Bayles from the northern end of the county. Lyman, though a Republican, lost the state congressman race to the northern Democrat, Sorenson. Bluff had lost command, though the Mormons had not: they held all county positions but one. Still, shifting control of the county to the north was a victory Gentiles were poised to exploit.[93]

The Church straightened its own house after statehood by announcing what came to be called the "Political Manifesto" in April 1896: no Church officer should accept a political office without consulting Church leaders. Moses Thatcher, the lone holdout from sustaining this measure, was eventually dropped from the Quorum of Twelve Apostles. [329]

---

90. Albert R. Lyman, Journal, September 7, 1895.

91. Hammond, Journal, November 1, 1895.

92. Palmer and Lisenby, "First Woman Elected," 41.

93. Hammond, Journal, November 5 and 16, 1895.

Utah became as excited as the rest of the country over the major elections in 1896. There were no organized Populists in San Juan County, but the Democrats in the cash-poor region held to the national party standard of free silver and supported its champion, William Jennings Bryan. The plank was so popular in this western area that the Republicans of the county also supported the free coinage of silver, removing an issue that caused intense campaigning in other areas of the country. But there was plenty of local controversy. Many Gentiles in the northern section of the county were nominated as candidates for office by the Democrats. This meant that if a Mormon voted that party's ticket, he would be helping to elect Gentiles to control the county. V. P. Martin, for example, was running for the state legislature against Platte Lyman. A few years ago, Martin would have run on the Liberal Party ticket, and the Mormons would have rallied against him in the People's Party. But now national party politics had weaned many Bluff voters away from such considerations and made it thinkable for them to support someone who did not belong to their faith or champion its causes. Monticello, the largest and most divided town in the county, was where these crosswinds were the strongest.

There was even some mudslinging leading up to election day. Francis Hammond, not running for any particular office, but still a prominent Democrat, was accused of being drunk and speaking ill of Platte Lyman because he was a Republican. In the election, the state and the county turned Democrat. Bluff voted 34–6 for Platte Lyman for the state legislature, but its votes were easily overwhelmed by the county's northern Gentiles. Monticello went 60–30 for Martin, who also won every vote in La Sal, McElmo, and Indian Creek to triumph 109–64 countywide. Two out of the three county commissioners [330] were northern Gentiles, with Cindy Nielson's new husband, Frank Hyde, the lone Mormon. One man from Bluff had won the election as county sheriff, but he resigned in 1897, and Latigo Gordon, who had just opened the Blue Goose Saloon in Monticello, took over the job.[94] Not only had power shifted north, but now it was firmly in the hands of Gentiles, thanks to their successful use of the national parties. Many people in Bluff strongly resented these developments. Platte Lyman's son groused, "Pa ran for the legislature, and we got the word tonight that he

---

94. Hammond, Journal, October 17, 1896; Palmer and Lisenby, "Law, Order, Print and Politics," 66.

is beat. The man that got it was an outsider and elected by Mormons. I am disgusted with some people."[95]

With the county seat more centrally located and more gentile influence in county government, law enforcement became steadily more regular and secular. Misdemeanors were still taken before the local justice of the peace.[96] But felonies went north, though not as far as before when they had to travel to Provo.[97] Instead of that, trials were held quarterly in Monticello when the Utah Seventh District Judge came to town on his circuit. Residents of Bluff were frequently summoned to Monticello for jury duty. In one of the first cases before the newly traveling court in June 1896, Jens, Jens Peter, and Joe Nielson, as well as Kumen Jones and John Ernest Adams were all drawn for the same panel of jurors.[98] Bluff residents, however, often felt they were getting the short end of [331] the legal stick. Some crimes were impossible to prosecute, such as when someone poisoned the nosebags of the Nielson brothers' six-horse team that was hauling wool during a contentious time on the range.[99] Before regular court proceedings in the county, Bluff's Mormons usually did not prosecute many crimes against their property. Now they took more cases of cattle rustling to court, but often felt cheated when the accused were let off for lack of evidence. It was unchristian to haul a Church brother before the law, so generally the cases involving Mormons were suits against Gentiles.[100] France and Joe Nielson filed suit a few times over the next decade and always either lost or settled out of court before trial.[101] The most frustrating case, especially galling given the hard times

---

95. Albert R. Lyman, Journal, November 7, 1896.

96. Albert R. Lyman, Journal, February 22, 1896; December 13, 1897.

97. Peterson, *Look to the Mountains*, 104.

98. Utah District Court (San Juan County), Minutes, June 15, 1896.

99. Albert R. Lyman, "History of San Juan County," 88.

100. See Hammond, Journal, March 9, 1896, in which the stake president tried to get Joe Nielson and Frank Adams to work out the solution to a financial disagreement outside of court.

101. See Albert R. Lyman, Journal, February 2, August 1902, for a case in which an Indian accused of stealing one of Sam Wood's cow's was let off for lack of evidence, and for an account of when Albert Lyman served on a jury in a trial for a sensational murder in La Sal. Also Albert R. Lyman, Journal, February 22, 1896, for the results of a case, probably in Bluff, in which two Gentiles were found innocent on charges of stealing one of Platte Lyman's cows. Adelbert Raplee, a Gentile who

of the 1890s, came after Joe and Jens Peter took a contract to cut and haul five hundred cords of wood for the Gold Queen Mining Company. After the brothers had stacked a prodigious pile, the company did not pay, and Joe took them to court. The defendants hired a Nebraska lawyer who won the case for them, netting Joe and Jens "experience instead of cash." The pile of wood remained as an overgrown monument for at least twenty years.[102] [332]

Departure

Politics were not all Bluff argued about in these years. There were always pesky troubles to be extinguished. When a woman stole Albert Lyman's irrigation water three times in a week, he broke her ditch and hid her shovel for a day.[103] Such frustrations could break out in any village in the state. But beyond the everyday, the Bluff ditch continued to devour labor in 1895. Those sweating out in the sun could not help but think about how well irrigation was going in Monticello that year. Since the San Juan had once again departed for its southern shore, the Bluff Saints had to build dams to funnel water back their way. By July, after a freshet washed the dams away and the crops started burning up, some at the job started talking of selling out and moving someplace else. "It makes me tired to hear such talk," wrote Albert Lyman, "as the town is too notorious small now." But he was not an unqualified booster, either: "I have got the blues and do not intend to make this my abiding place for life."[104]

Neither did his father. Platte Lyman had been back in Bluff full time for four years. He was an important part of the town, laboring diligently with his stock, in his fields, and among the Saints. But the depression hit his interests especially hard, and he was struggling mightily to emerge from debt. He might have been preaching to himself as much as anyone when, on a visit to Fruitland (formerly Burnham), New Mexico, in June, he preached "on the subject of remaining where we are

---

sometimes made his home in Bluff, was the judge in the case. See also Austin and McPherson, "Murder, Mayhem, and Mormons," 49; Utah District Court (San Juan County), Minutes, August 27, 1900; August 1902; April 21 and August 17, 1903.

102. Utah District Court (San Juan County), Minutes, September 27, 1897; Albert R. Lyman, "History of San Juan County," 88.

103. Albert R. Lyman, Journal, April 23 to 28, 1896.

104. Albert R. Lyman, Journal, July, 1895.

called to reside—and not to [333] go roaming around the country seeking good places."[105]

It might have been the new difficulties with the ditch that caused Lyman to reconsider. In the afternoon meeting on July 7, he ruminated on the fact that many fine places had been settled after Bluff. Some of them had more fruit trees in one orchard than existed in all of Bluff. He could not understand why people were held in this place, where it was so hard to make their living. The bishop was up right after. With the situation in the town so precarious, the Saints could not afford to hear such thoughts, logical though they were. Bishop Nielson was perfectly satisfied with his call to Bluff, he said. He emphasized again that this was where he was willing to live and this was where he was willing to die. Francis Hammond tried to soften the confrontation by switching to another topic to close the meeting, but the old positions, held by both men since 1884, had resurfaced.[106] Many people meditated on what Brother Lyman said as the river continued to undermine their efforts on the ditch in the next week. On Sunday a number of them expressed their dissatisfaction with the place. Resentment continued to fester for another week as the ditch absorbed their energy.[107]

To open the afternoon meetings on July 21, William Adams reported his recent visits to Parowan and St. George. He described the prosperity of those two towns, which also had some difficulties getting started, then contrasted their welfare with the fifteen years of trouble on the Bluff ditch. Clearly he was not settled on the wisdom of staying. [334] But then Platte Lyman spoke again. He had obviously thought about the matter considerably over the past two weeks, as had everyone. He might have realized that what he was saying was of the same nature as his reasoned comments of 1883 and 1884. Once again the prospect of being somewhere else was very appealing, but he did not want to leave under the same circumstances as before. So on this day he apologized for his remarks. While he did not concede that what he had previously said was false, he felt his statements had been "calculated to unsettle the people." He asked the congregation's forgiveness for doing such a thing.[108]

---

105. Hammond, Journal, June 23, 1895.
106. Hammond, Journal, July 7, 1895.
107. Hammond, Journal, July 14, 1895.
108. Hammond, Journal, July 21, 1895.

President Hammond spoke next. He also understood what he had to say here, which was difficult since he agreed with his counselor on the insufferability of trying to hold Bluff. But they were held there by Church leaders, and those who were still there obviously respected that authority and would not move without it. "Union is what we need" to master the river this year, he said. But the basic question of Bluff still hung over them: they had to solve the water question or abandon the settlement. In a way, he said, they had been granted an artificial extension of life through their Indian trade and livestock. But they would have to ultimately answer the question sometime.[109]

Bishop Nielson rose last. In response to the questions raised, he defended his course as bishop. Church leaders had called them here, and until Church leaders released them he had to do what he could to make the settlement survive. When he sat down, the issue had been dealt with but not settled. "This subject is a source of constant irritation to [335] the saints here," observed President Hammond.[110]

Declining Stocks

The livestock and co-op which had allowed them to sustain their lives in Bluff also started to dwindle. Much of it had to do with the long depression of the 1890s, the worst the country had ever experienced. Some signs looked hopeful in 1895, but the market retrenched again in 1896. The Bluff Cattle Pool had always been a rather loose herding and negotiating association, and under the pressures of the drought and depression that also reduced competition from other cattle companies, more members chose to fend for themselves. Fletcher B. Hammond, who had often been the foreman of the pool in its earlier years, sold his cattle to the Nielsons, Kumen Jones, and Lem Redd for a total of $2,300. Francis Hammond soon pulled his cattle out of the pool as well, and both Hammonds transferred more of their resources into sheep. A few others withdrew from the pool in the late 1890s, leaving the Nielsons, Perkinses, and Redds at its heart.[111] Francis Nielson became the foreman of the association.[112]

---

109. Hammond, Journal, July 21, 1895.

110. Hammond, Journal, July 21, 1895.

111. Hammond, Journal, February 8, March 26, May 20, June 15, October 22, 1895; March 26, 1896; Albert R. Lyman, Journal, August 14, 1896.

112. Hammond, Journal, June 9, 1897.

The co-op staggered along. It paid a 4 percent dividend at the end of 1894, which was an encouraging increase from the year before. But it was paltry compared to the 40 percents of earlier years. The dividend rose to 5 percent in 1895, still comparatively slim. Some stockholders wanted to withdraw their capital stock to help them through the hard [336] times, but if enough of that were done, it would lead to the breakup of the business. When times turned harder in 1896, the directors jostled among themselves about their future course as they headed toward another dividendless year. As with the cattle, adverse conditions persuaded many of the co-op's investors that they could do better themselves. In October, the co-op decided to divide the sheep among the shareholders and remove them from the co-op stock. This meant the total stock of the corporation would be cut from thirty thousand to ten thousand dollars, and it would be left primarily as a mercantile business. The division was done by 1897. The bishop now had to arrange to take care of his own herds as well as the tithing and Relief Society flocks. Many shareowners, however, preferred owning the paper co-op stock to managing the actual animals. So a reconsolidation of the sheep happened in the following months, as some Bluff men either bought them outright or herded them on consignment.[113] When asked by Lem Redd and Hans Bayles if they ought to contract for over eight thousand of these sheep in spite of the uncertain economy, the bishop advised them to do it. The two men borrowed money in Durango to carry out the plan. Some in Colorado questioned the move, wondering if the bishop's self-interest in the matter had not colored his judgment. But Redd and Bayles believed the bishop when he promised them it would be a profitable investment. At first it did not look so promising, since they could not meet some of their early payments. But the Durango bankers extended the deadlines, based on the men's past trustworthiness, and the [337] flocks were eventually profitable for them.[114] This was yet another example of why ward members asked their bishop's advice and often accepted it. They had come to trust "his sound judgment and his strong sense of justice and absolute fairness."[115]

---

113. Hammond, Journal, January 29, 1897.

114. Hammond, Journal, January 1 and 7, August 1, December 30, 1895; October 21 and 22, December 1, 7, and 8, 1896; Albert R. Lyman, "Bishop Jens Nielson," 11; Amasa Jay Redd, *Lemuel Hardison Redd, Jr.*, 42, 51.

115. Kumen Jones, "Bishop Jens Nielson Sketch," 21.

One problem that went away for the most part was the Carlisles. Over the past few years they had pulled their cattle operations out from the drought-stricken San Juan range and continued to negotiate with various people to sell their land. Some of the old hands, like Sheriff Gordon, stayed in Monticello or moved to Moab.[116] The increasing number of Gentiles, as well as the carelessness of some of the Mormons, made the Monticello Ward increasingly difficult to manage. Cindy Nielson Hyde reported that while she was lying in bed soon after giving birth to her first daughter, two cowboys ran past her window and one shot the other dead. Their dances were still suspenseful since they never knew when cowboys might come in and take over.[117] Bishop F. I. Jones almost resigned at the end of 1896 but instead kept trying to unite his people.[118]

Cowboys continued to pester Bluff as well, even if most of the rival cattle outfits were gone. A plague of horse thieves and cattle rustlers struck in 1895 and 1896. It got so bad that on one occasion Bishop Jones of Monticello proposed to Bishop Nielson that [338] they cooperate with the remaining cattle companies in organizing a vigilante force to rid the county of the outlaws. The bishop declined after getting advice from President Hammond that it was not for Saints to get mixed up in such matters; rather, they should let "the wicked slay the wicked."[119]

The cowboy influence still had a strong hold on the town's men and boys. France and Jens Peter were improving, but the draw of the saloons in Colorado and the rough life on the range were sometimes still too much for their morals. Some Bluff men and boys broke into the co-op twice during the holidays in 1894 to liberate the whiskey stored there from the gold rush.[120] Freeman had helped operate the Grey Goose Saloon in an abandoned house in Bluff, an obvious attempt to imitate the parent institution in Monticello. Alcohol, tobacco, gambling, and even a traveling New York hypnotist found their way into the establishment. Some of the town's girls also started acting too wild for decent opinion, not only riding bicycles and playing baseball, but doing it in

---

116. Hammond, Journal, February 25, 1895; August 23, 1896; "A Trip to Eastern Utah," *Deseret News*, December 19, 1896, 28–29.

117. Reeve, "Lucinda Diantha Nielson Hyde," 204.

118. Hammond, Journal, January 12, October 17, 1896.

119. Hammond, Journal, June 2, 1895.

120. Hammond, Journal, December 22 to December 26, 1894.

bloomers. They were quickly counseled that "modesty in dress and deportment [were] becoming in women."[121]

There were some signs of hope. "Joe Nielson returned home Saturday" from his mission in the Northern States, Wayne Redd wrote to his father in October 1895. "He looks ten years younger than he [339] did when he left.... It sure made a man out of him."[122] The whole town noticed the change in Joe. Jens had already read the difference in Joe's letters and was impressed when Joe requested an extra six months in the mission field to make up for the first six months, spent studying the gospel and converting himself from cowboy to missionary.[123] But the changes were more striking in person, as Joe occupied almost a whole meeting in church with an impressive speaking style, thanking those who had called him to serve a mission. The ward saw the change in how he mingled with the Saints the next evening during the grand reception thrown for him by the young ladies' association. Joe had always been a friendly, open individual, but more than two years preaching without purse or scrip added substance to him. And he was only the first. Even before he came home, Jens's son-in-law Wayne Redd along with Peter Allan and Frank Adams were called on missions. Wayne was up on Elk Mountain herding Bluff Pool cattle when Hans Bayles told him the news. It "made me feel blue for a while, as it looked as though it was impossible for me to get the means to go."[124] But he sold his saddle and enough cattle to meet his expenses, and all those called, with the help of relatives and ward members, found a way to go. Caroline and her baby moved back in with Kirsten when Wayne left.[125] Maybe trying to straighten out a crooked world would straighten out Bluff's range riders themselves.[126] [340]

Bishop Nielson took further comfort when there was no trouble with whiskey in the holiday celebration at the end of the year. The ward held a "leap year" dance in which the girls got to choose and escort the boys to the

---

121. Hammond, Journal, June 2, August 1, 1895; Albert R. Lyman, "Experiences and Impressions," 1:27, 124, 127; Albert R. Lyman, Summaries of Each Year, 1896, book 1, pp. 92, 117–18.

122. Wayne H. Redd, letter to L. H. Redd Sr., October 13, 1895.

123. Albert R. Lyman, "Hans Joseph Nielson," 150.

124. Wayne H. Redd, Journal, September 1895.

125. Alice Redd, "Sketch of the Life of Caroline Nielson Redd," 209.

126. Hammond, Journal, August 26, October 13, 14, 1895.

occasion, but the bishop could live with that much tinkering with tradition. It helped that there were still a few close to his own age with whom he could talk. On December 30, Jens, Platte Lyman, William Adams, Father John Allan, visitor Pap Redd, and their wives sat down for dinner at Francis Hammond's house. All of them were older than the Utah Territory, and they enjoyed "a real old time visit."[127]

Changes

The wizened group may have noticed in the age of bloomers, bicycles, and leap year dances that Bluff had changed. There seemed to be less cooperation, for one. Their labor on the ditch was their ingrained, often futile salute to the traditional principle of self-sufficiency. Beyond that, these senior leaders still insisted that Bluff needed to unite to buy out the Carlisles, spruce up the co-op, and establish milling, tanning, and canning operations.[128] But the opposite was happening. Politics and the depression were pulling the ward members apart, and the pool and co-op organizations were weakening. Fred [341] Adams even opened his own store.[129] Perhaps the younger generation had not been schooled as thoroughly in the principles of cooperation or they had not developed the same instinctive attachment to them as the older pioneers. They mingled more with Gentiles in their business and worried more about the bottom line than the common good. The older settlers were not immune from these impulses, as their many failed attempts at cooperation in the 1870s showed, but at least they tried. Taken together, Bluff's residents were beginning to act more like partisans and capitalists—like Americans, in other words.

The town's population was different as well and had been since the gold rush. "We have scarcely held a meeting for two years," observed Albert Lyman in early 1895, "except we have had some strangers present."[130] More outsiders came through to prospect or hunt relics. Bluff was not

---

127. Hammond, Journal, December 30, 1895.

128. Hammond, Journal, August 24, 1895; March 22, November 9, 1896. See also Albert R. Lyman, Journal, May 28, 1896, in which he recorded that he "mended the bishop's shoes, worked at them nearly all day. They were pretty badly to pieces, but I made them over." The bishop was either practicing what he preached or tightening his belt during the depression. Most likely it was some of both.

129. Albert R. Lyman, Journal, May 27, 1896.

130. Albert R. Lyman, Journal, February 3, 1895.

nearly what Monticello was in this regard and both were far behind
Moab in back-country cosmopolitanism, but the Bluff census and ward
list were no longer identical.[131] There were Gentiles, such as Charles
Lang, Melvin Dempsey, and the photographer Charles Goodman, who
used Bluff as a base for their forays into the hinterland. These transplanted polymaths were accepted as residents in town and were appre-
ciated for their many skills. In addition to Dempsey's ongoing guitar
lessons, Charles Lang led the San Juan Orchestra, and Charles Goodman took pictures of many people and places around Bluff. None of
these men were fully integrated into a town whose life revolved around
a religion they did not share. But Bluff was at least as [342] hospitable to
them as it was to most outsiders; the town might have been clannish but
never exclusive. When Lang moved to Moab in 1898, the people of Bluff
threw him one of their customary surprise send-off parties.[132]

The town itself looked different. Besides the rock church and school,
Kumen Jones and Bishop Nielson began to build more commodious
houses out of sandstone and brick. Others soon followed. These fine
homes, almost mansions in some cases, were a far cry from the crude log
huts that ringed the old fort or the improved cabins they had lived in for
so long. These new dwellings displayed the progress and permanence
the San Juan settlers had improbably attained. They began to bring the
comfort the inhabitants had lived so long without. But they also showed
the increased privacy and affluence its residents had developed, characteristics that were more difficult to reconcile with their missionary goals and
pioneer principles. Bluff was still distinct from other gentile and Mormon
towns, but it was not as different as it once had been. As the old timers ate
together at the end of the year, they might have reflected on the contrast
between their more modern town and how it looked back when it was an
outpost of Zion, holding the fort against the outside world.

---

131. Albert R. Lyman, Journal, February 3, 1895.

132. Albert R. Lyman, Journal, April 1898. See also Riis, *Ranger Trails*, 32–33.
Riis was one of the first Forest Service rangers in the county. When he arrived in
Monticello in 1907, he judged the people to be "clannish mountain folk" at first, and
as a Gentile and government man he was "completely ignored in social functions."
But "in later years I came to know the true worth of those rugged Mormon settlers,
an industrious, law abiding and loyal people whose friendship, once won, was well
worth the price."

Utah finally entered the union a week later, on January 6, 1896. The flag was raised at sunrise in Bluff amid the clatter of guns firing and bells ringing. Jens Nielson served as chaplain over the day's festivities, as the state and town in which he lived [343] entered a new era.[133]

Modern Times

Medicine

Hannah Sorenson arrived in Bluff in August 1896. She had practiced obstetrics at the Royal Hospital of Denmark, which was very useful to her as well as her patients since she had ten children herself. But when she joined the Mormons, her husband abandoned her, and he took all the children with him. Hannah came to Utah, where she continued to study and practice medicine. Her errand in Bluff was to teach its residents about health and the "new hygiene."[134]

Before her arrival, Bluff's makeshift medicine had kept doing the best it could. Aunt Jody and Aunt Mary continued to be marvelous bedside presences in the town. Over the years Aunt Jody had helped almost everyone, and "all Bluff is obligated to her."[135] "It seemed quite unthinkable that anyone could die in Bluff, or be born, or have pneumonia, a broken limb or a broken heart without Aunt Jody being there to bear a generous part of the burden and offer her words of soothing and cheer."[136] Mary Jones received letters from grateful former patients addressed simply to "Aunt Mary, Bluff, [344] Utah."[137]

These women and the people of Bluff continued to use whatever they thought might work for their many injuries and illnesses, whether it came from folk medicine, Indians, or mail-order catalogs. Sage tea might cure colds, or a concoction from the same plant might heal bruises, as might equal parts of turpentine, egg white, and vinegar. Milkweed was good for

---

133. Hammond, Journal, January 6, 1896; Albert R. Lyman, Journal, January 6, 1896.

134. McPherson and Mueller, "Divine Duty," 336–37.

135. Albert R. Lyman, Journal, December 31, 1903.

136. Albert R. Lyman, "Josephine Catherine Chatterley Wood," in Carter, *Our Pioneer Heritage*, 19:275. When Lyman's wife had her first baby years later, the father reported that Aunt Jody "asked only $5.00 but however I got it I thought it worth ten." Albert R. Lyman, Journal, December 31, 1903.

137. "'Aunt Mary' Nielson Jones."

dropsy and cactus poultices helped just about anything. On one occasion
Aunt Jody gave ill Francis Hammond a vapor bath that almost knocked
him out. Melvin Dempsey treated the same man's sciatica with an electric
belt, which drove the pain from his hip to his shoulder. The great discovery
of the late 1890s, however, was the "fountain syringe," or the enema. After
a few bouts with it, President Hammond confessed, "I begin to believe
it almost a panacea for nearly all ills that poor mortals are afflicted with."
Albert Lyman later went one better by ordering a stomach pump.[138] Den-
tistry continued to be agonizing. When Wayne Redd had a toothache, he
burned the tooth all day with hot irons and carbolic acid, while Caroline
applied hot packs. In the evening, Monroe Redd's pliers slipped the first
time he tried to extract the offending tooth, causing Caroline to flee to
France and Leona's home rather than witness more of her husband's torture.
Monroe got the tooth out on the second yank, but Wayne was still sore a
week later.[139] Frontier remedies were not just limited to people. On one
occasion Aunt [345] Jody was summoned to save a bloated cow. She poured
a dose of soda and water down its throat, and the beast survived to moo
another day.[140] Prayers and priesthood blessings continued to be vital com-
ponents of Bluff's medical system.[141] Sadly, none of these saved Harriett
Barton after complications following the birth of a boy. She was the wife
of Judge Joseph Barton and the mother of seven other children, who took
her death "pretty hard."[142] The baby boy died two weeks after his mother.

Everyone in Bluff had plenty to learn about medicine, however, as
did most people in the United States around this time when insects
and microscopic organisms were found to possess more than met the
eye. People in Bluff got their water from shallow wells, they dealt often
with manure, and all sorts of bugs buzzed around their outhouses. It

---

138. Hammond, Journal, June 7, 1892; March 13 to 18, 1894; June 9, 19, 1897.

139. Wayne H. Redd, Journal, December 12 to 18, 1898. Professionals were not
much better when they came. The appropriately named dentist Dr. Pulford came to
town in November of 1905. "Spent the forenoon having the live nerve bored out of
that tooth," Albert Lyman recorded, "and O My it did hurt." See Albert R. Lyman,
Journal, November 16–18, 1905.

140. Albert R. Lyman, "Josephine Catherine Chatterley Wood," 293, 299.

141. See McPherson, *History of San Juan County*, 271–72, for more San Juan
home cures.

142. Albert R. Lyman, Journal, May 29, 1896.

was not a good sign when the custom was "the apostles will soon be here, so every body is burning trash."[143] And so Hannah Sorenson arrived to teach them the "new hygiene." Most of the women in town took her class, which covered midwifery, physiology, hygiene, and the delicate subject of "What Women Should Know" as they approached marriage. These teachings included the idea that "the more sensitive of the two bed fellows will absorb the poison excretions from the body of the other.... Often the languor and nervousness with which certain individuals arise in the morning is directly [346] traceable to the influence of the companion during sleep."[144] But Sister Sorenson also taught important information on cleanliness. "The new hygiene, a subject which we accepted," probably helped avert future tragedies, and earned Sister Sorenson the admiration of most Bluff residents by the time her classes concluded.

Education

Bishop Nielson had plenty to keep him busy in these years. He still supervised the ditch and watering turns.[145] He was also involved in supervising school instruction. Earlier teachers had been drawn from among the settlers, but for a decade now Bluff had usually imported graduates from the Brigham Young Academy's normal school.[146] These teachers lodged with families in town and generally had one-year contracts. The school year started in late September or early October and went for three terms of ten weeks each, unless money ran out first, as it threatened to do in early 1895 and 1896.[147] Despite Bluff's sociability, this could be a lonely time for these teachers, so far away from their families and familiar surroundings. A few of these instructors, however, married someone in Bluff.[148]

---

143. McPherson and Mueller, "Divine Duty," 350; Albert R. Lyman, Journal, November 20, 1897; April/May 1901; Hammond, Journal, June 8, 1888.

144. McPherson, *History of San Juan County*, 271.

145. Hammond, Journal, December 30, 1896.

146. Teachers in Bluff included Ida Lyman, 1880–81; Charles E. Walton, 1885–86; Thomas (J. L.?) Young, 1886–87; Emma Bayles, 1887–88; A. P. Sorenson, 1888–92; Peter Allan, 1892–93; William Allen, 1893–95; Vilate Elliott and Jennie Brimhall, 1895–96; Wilhelmina Isabel Wright, 1896–98 and 1899–1900.

147. See Martha Hammond, letter to F. A. Hammond, March 29, 1895.

148. Emma Bayles married Al Scorup, A. P. Sorenson married Mary Alice Hammond, and Isabel Wright married Joseph Hammond.

Teaching so many students at once was also a difficult job. "Lots of cheating [347] goes on in school," commented Albert Lyman at the opening of the 1896–97 year, "lots of noise and laughing."[149] On the teacher's side, Miss Elliott recorded, "I must introduce percentage tomorrow to my eighth grade. I dread it."[150] So the bishop's job consisted in encouraging the students and teachers alike in making the classes as good as possible. Jens continued to have a personal interest in the schools with five of his grandchildren attending. Sometimes the teachers and pupils could outdo themselves, as on George Washington's birthday in 1897. The boys acted out scenes from colonial days, then forty-five girls represented the states in "a beautiful piece."[151]

When his younger kids had finished the eighth grade in Bluff, Jens sent them to Provo for secondary schooling at Brigham Young Academy. Uriah attended when he was eighteen, and he and Annetta were still going in their early twenties, for the 1898–99 school year, along with sixteen other students from Bluff.[152] While this was expensive for the bishop, it gave these children an above-average education at a time when finishing the eighth grade was considered being well-schooled.

In early 1897 the town lost a landmark. The old log schoolhouse, which had held such a variety of meetings over the years, had no practical purpose anymore. The new stone church and schoolhouse replaced it, so the settlers decided to pull it down. But before the pioneer building came down, Charles Goodman captured it on film. Bishop Nielson, Platte [348] Lyman, Kumen Jones, James Decker, and Francis Hammond stood in front of the old meetinghouse and had their portrait taken, "as a reminder of the style of public buildings in primitive days."[153] The integration of town life was dismantled more slowly than the old building. Bluff's citizens used to learn, worship, and celebrate in the same structure. By 1898, there were two separate buildings for those purposes, and religious instruction could no longer be part of the public school curriculum. So the bishop sat on a new education board that oversaw a forty-five minute religion class taught before the public school day

---

149. Albert R. Lyman, Journal, October 1896.
150. Elliott, Diary, October 30, 1899.
151. Hammond, Journal, February 22, 1897.
152. Hammond, Journal, March 20, 1899.
153. Hammond, Journal, February 11, 1897.

began.[154] As Francis Hammond saw it, "The world is surely moving."[155] Bluff, in some ways, was trailing along behind it.

Drenched and Parched

The ditch was another remnant from primitive days, but still very much a concern. The main difficulty in 1896 was the continued drought. Even though the men got water into the ditch by the third week in March, a new record, it did not stay in. Neither Monticello nor Bluff raised much of a crop due to the dryness. But a ripping thunderstorm in mid-September announced a change in the weather. Hailstones the "size of walnuts, hard as rock" crashed down with sheets of rains, which continued to fall for days. Cottonwood Wash swelled to twenty feet deep and one hundred feet across, stranding Monroe Redd and three others on the far side; townspeople flung peaches and other food over to them. The lower part of Bluff flooded, and the Perkinses had [349] to be evacuated in the middle of the night. Cut corn, hay, and fruit were ruined. Once again land was washed away, roads flooded out, fences pulled down, fields strewn with sand and debris by the torrents in this startling end to the drought. In irony they had seen before, the flood destroyed their ditch. At that section called "the jump," where the cribs had been put in years before, the bank was washed away to the rock cliff again. It looked as if it would cost as much to fix the ditch as it did to build it in the first place. Even people used to annual labor and disappointment felt "very much discouraged about their location here."[156]

The bishop was discouraged as well, but he was not going anywhere. He had finished building a brick home for Elsie. Kumen Jones had finally moved Mary, May, and the children into what was probably the first full-sized rock home in Bluff back in March 1896. A stonemason named Tyndall had constructed it, and only after he finished it did he admit that: "this was the first house I ever built!" Others were progressing on their new houses as well. Elsie's home was finished enough to throw a dance in by October, soon after the floods. And on January 15, 1897, just after a gloomy ditch meeting was held to survey the year's prospects, the bishop threw

---

154. Hammond, Journal, January 24, February 4, 1898.

155. Hammond, Journal, January 16, 1896.

156. Hammond, Journal, September 18 to 24, 1896; Albert R. Lyman, Journal, September 18, 29, 1896.

a party and dedicated the home officially. He gave a short speech about how he had been blessed during its construction, then offered a prayer dedicating every part of it, from yard to foundation through the walls to the roof to serve its purpose. Finally, almost all the adults in the ward sat down to a "bountifully prepared feast." "It was quite an event in our town as [350] there are only a few good houses."[157] Jens was also planning to build another one for Kirsten, this time out of sandstone.

Repairing the ditch in 1897 was just as difficult as everyone thought. People had to clear off their lands from the wreckage of the flood, and also work off a ditch tax of at least six dollars per acre, meaning that the average family needed to contribute about sixty days of labor. Plus they had to look after their stock and move them up to the summer range, and some men, doubting the chance of getting water to Bluff, had to get up to Monticello to put in crops there. The work was overwhelming. They dreamed of all sorts of things to ease their burdens. Charles Sitzer thought a windmill attached to a water wheel could raise the water. Francis Hammond in one of his journeys looked at a "curious kind of engine for pumping water for irrigation," powered by some fuel called gasoline, which might do the job.[158] In the end the intrepid men riprapped at least a mile of the bank to hold it in and blasted through the rock at the jump. They kept their upper lip stiff to the outside world. The happy story in the *Deseret News* was that although the floods had destroyed much of the ditch, "our good, old Bishop, Jens Nielson, who is full of faith in Bluff, rallied the brethren and went to work about a month ago, and now has the ditch about ready for use; estimated cost about $4,000."[159]

The cost estimate was about right, but the harmony was more questionable. Two days after President Hammond wrote his optimistic report, a less optimistic Albert Lyman [351] groused, "The ditch here is pretty badly out of order (water not in yet), and it looks as though Bluff might yet be abandoned. I hope it is."[160] While part of this might have been the frustrations of a teenager, others in the town felt about the same. A quarter mile at the head of the ditch was gone. They could still get about eight

---

157. Hammond, Journal, March 5, 1896; January 15, 1897; Albert R. Lyman, Journal, October 10, 1896.

158. Hammond, Journal, May 6, 11, 1897.

159. Francis A. Hammond, "News from San Juan," *Deseret News*, May 1, 1897, 633.

160. Albert R. Lyman, Journal, April 18, 1897.

inches of water to trickle down to the jump, but then it broke through the channel they blasted and went back into the river. They could try to dump in rock and brush along this stretch to create a channel, but it would take about a hundred wagonloads, and if the usual high waters rose in May, it would be washed away. Understandably, many of the "brethren feel a good deal like giving it up" and more went up to Monticello to plant their crops.[161] There was no promise of anything in Monticello, either. Church leaders sent the townspeople a shipment of seed grain, since their crop had failed the previous year in the drought. The ward was "very careless and neglectful of their duties" as well.[162] But hopefully the new reservoirs of water would make for a better year.

The San Juan writhed back to its southern bank, and for a while the men at Bluff tried to bring water from the Recapture. Their unbelievable efforts over the next three weeks brought one brief watering down to the town. They might get one cutting of lucerne; they would probably get a decent yield from their orchards; but there was little chance of getting anything else. Bluff's inhabitants would have to import all their food beyond what they had stored from the year before. The bishop called for another meeting [352] on the ditch after church on June 13. Somehow the ditch committee was persuaded to go inspect the thing again, and enough men went out to get the water back three days later. But again it drained out just as fast, and residents started watering their trees by bucket. All hope for field crops or even vegetable gardens were gone. One last attempt in July got the water back in, but not a drop made it to town. The ditch was dead.[163]

Dubious Jubilee

Oddly enough it was time to celebrate. While Bluff struggled, most of the state was preparing to mark its jubilee. Fifty years had passed since the first Mormon pioneers arrived in the Salt Lake Valley. The Nielsons and most other adults in Bluff were going to attend the festivities in Salt Lake City. As they traveled north through Monticello and Moab, there were fields of crops, enough to make them at least a little jealous and perhaps enough to make them think about moving.

---

161. Hammond, Journal, April 29, 1897.

162. Hammond, Journal, May 13, 1897.

163. Hammond, Journal, June 13–17, 1897; Albert R. Lyman, Journal, July 19–30, 1897.

Jens and Kirsten arrived in Salt Lake on July 20. The city was indeed celebrating. Main Street was lit up from the corner of Temple Square a half-mile south, "a blaze of sparkling gems of every hue and color, all done by electricity." Many beholders thought it "the best they ever saw."[164] The Brigham Young statue was unveiled, and there were concerts and plays to take in. The Nielsons may have gone out to the Saltair resort on the Great Salt Lake and seen the high-wire act amid the exotic minarets. There was a grand parade on the twenty-first, and over five thousand children marched on the twenty-second, dropping flowers [353] at the base of the Brigham Young statue to a foot deep. The next day, Jens and Kirsten watched with pride as the San Juan float came by in the parade of counties. Charles Lang had helped design it, and it showed cliff dwellers, relics, and Navajo blankets. In the afternoon there was an Indian Ghost Dance, bicycle tricks, hot air balloons, and even a skydiver. On the twenty-fourth, the grand anniversary officially started with a cannon boom from Fort Douglas at sunrise. About one hundred thousand people were in the city to celebrate. The parade started at eleven. The Twenty-fourth U.S. Infantry and the Ninth U.S. Cavalry filed by, followed by Governor Heber Wells and over forty survivors from the Mormon Battalion. President Wilford Woodruff followed in a carriage with Joseph F. Smith, and then the five hundred pioneer survivors filed past, greeted by enthusiastic cheers. The parade also featured a Pageant of Progress in Utah, showing development from wagons to telegrams and beyond. The fireworks were greater than anyone had seen: Brigham Young was portrayed in a thirty by fifty foot explosion. The finale featured hundreds of shells of flowers and diamond chains. The next day was Sunday, and Joseph F. Smith, Brigham Young Jr., and Marion Lyman commemorated the event in their discourses. The choir and congregation closed by singing the pioneer anthem "Come, Come Ye Saints."[165] It was a spectacular celebration, with six parades during the week.

The bigger event for Jens and the other leaders from San Juan happened on Monday, July 26, when they filed into the First Presidency's office. Once again they asked Church leaders to pass judgment on Bluff. Bishop Nielson gave the case for the defense. They were called to settle Bluff City back when the Indians were very [354] troublesome and outlaws were likely to overrun the county. They had followed the advice of Erastus Snow and stayed there,

164. Hammond, Journal, July 19, 1897.
165. Hammond, Journal, July 20–25, 1897; Journal History, July 24, 1897.

in spite of having so little farmland and so little control over the water. Some had left the place, and others felt it was useless to continue trying to hold it. There were twenty-two families numbering about 185 souls still there. The ditch had cost anywhere from six to ten dollars per acre every year, but there had been compensations. Because of the difficulties, they had gone into livestock, from which they had profited about twenty-seven thousand dollars in the past year alone. Jens said "he did not think it would be a good thing to abandon the place, and Elder Brigham Young [Jr.] had promised them in times past that if they would hold the place they should be prospered more than if they moved away." Jens believed "that they had been greatly prospered, notwithstanding the great difficulties they had contended with."[166]

President Hammond stood next to give what he felt was the more reasonable position. He cataloged the hardships, the greatest of which was "the uncontrollable condition of the river." There was only a little good land left. "It was a serious question whether there was sufficient good results to be achieved at so much expense to warrant a continuation of the struggle." Some men had already voted by their actions in securing farms for themselves and their families elsewhere in the county. Kumen Jones spoke next and "supported the bishop's view of the case entirely." Lemuel Redd agreed with President Hammond's position. Bluff had to import their grain and potatoes. There was little land and not enough water even for that, and if a few more settlers made a break "it would demoralize the place." Still, if the Church leaders thought it was wise for [355] them to stay, "he was willing to try it a while longer." The bishop remarked that if a majority of the people felt like Brother Hammond and Brother Redd, they ought to move somewhere else.[167]

Brigham Young Jr. broke in. As someone who had visited the town in its infancy and had passed through often, he felt it was indispensable. If Bluff were abandoned, renegades would occupy it, becoming a menace to the other settlements. Besides, it had become as developed as any other town its size. Its church, schools, and homes were just as good. He would not force anyone to stay, but the sooner Bluff's citizens "settled down to the fact that Bluff was their home, and it was their duty to maintain it, the better it would be for them and that part of the country as well."[168]

---

166. Journal History, July 26, 1897, 2–3.
167. Journal History, July 26, 1897, 3–4.
168. Journal History, July 26, 1897, 4.

George Q. Cannon compared Bluff with St. George and settlements in Mexico and other places. Many original settlers became discouraged and left, but those who stayed enjoyed blessings and prosperity. "He admired the pluck of Bishop Nielson and those who had supported him in the determination to hold on, and he felt that the Lord was pleased with them for their integrity."[169]

Joseph F. Smith asked what it would take to continue to hold Bluff against the river. The bishop answered that if they owned a pile driver, then they could secure the banks. He also remarked that it was not too long ago that President Hammond had gone to Washington, D.C., to keep the land from falling into the hands of the Indians. Now [356] "the same people who made that protest seemed to be willing to abandon the place themselves," in spite of the twenty-five thousand dollars of improvements that had gone in since. Hans Bayles was skeptical that a pile driver would solve their problems. Even if they could pile seven miles of riverfront, the quicksand bottom would not hold, and it would be expensive to keep the machine in repair. Furthermore, the expense of just maintaining the roads was more than they could handle, since the county was almost bankrupt. Gentiles controlled their government because of the partisan voting of the Saints. Still, he admitted that President Smith's promise had been literally fulfilled: they had been doubly blessed by sticking to Bluff. President Hammond reiterated that he was subject to the will of the Church authorities, but if left to himself he would move to Moab.[170]

At this point the bishop offered to step down if the authorities felt a younger man should be bishop. "But he did not wish to shrink nor resign unless it was thought better for him to do so." After such free discussion the authorities decided to consider the matter at the meeting of the First Presidency and Quorum of the Twelve in the Salt Lake Temple in three days.[171]

In that meeting the Church leaders were as divided as they had always been on Bluff. Francis Hammond had sent a letter, which was read, stating that those who wanted to leave were not going to leave the county, just the town. A letter from Marion Lyman urged that those who

169. Journal History, July 26, 1897.

170. Journal History, July 26, 1897, 4–5.

171. Journal History, July 26, 1897, 5.

wanted to go should go. "He did not think that Bluff would go to pieces if all the settlers were given their liberty." Brigham Young Jr. recited how much [357] better the Indians in the area were. The settlers, he felt, were no longer in danger from them. But the meeting deadlocked, and in the end the Church leaders determined to send a commission to the site to determine its fate again.[172]

When Bishop Nielson returned to Bluff, the dry fields told the tale. Many people still talked about moving and were disappointed the bishop brought no final word.[173] It looked as if a fruit crop could be salvaged, but that was all. When Jens reported the condition of his ward at the stake conference in Monticello, he exaggerated when he said Bluff's farmers raised a half-crop.[174] The yields in Monticello and Verdure, on the other hand, never looked better. The farmers there were expecting forty bushels of wheat per acre and up to seventy bushels of oats.[175] Meanwhile the residents of Bluff waited in suspense for the commission of General Authorities to arrive. The visit was delayed, however, due to the heat of the season and the poor health of some of the visitors.

In the meantime, Walter C. Lyman had returned to Bluff after an absence of seventeen years, and Platte's half-brother had a dream. It was about White Mesa, the spot about halfway between Bluff and Monticello that Francis Hammond and others had tried to develop in 1885. Lyman saw a city there and had come south to build it. In September, Walter, Platte, and Jody Lyman, who had returned with his brother, scouted the mesa and staked their claims. Had the Carlisles still been in the county they would [358] have had something to say about it, but the drought of the previous years had driven them out, leaving the land uncontested again. This time the idea looked possible. As Albert Lyman put it, "I am infatuated with it," especially when the alternative was the endless digging in the ditch in Bluff.[176]

The bishop could be comforted that not all the townspeople had given in to the gathering momentum of their impending release. Kumen Jones stood squarely behind him in maintaining the town. And the bishop's

---

172. Journal History, July 29, 1897, 2.

173. Albert R. Lyman, Journal, July 25, 1897.

174. San Juan Stake General Minutes, August 23, 1897.

175. Hammond, Journal, August 21, 1897.

176. Albert R. Lyman, Journal, September 29, November 6, 1897.

son Joe refused to believe the approaching authorities were going to release them. He insisted the Apostles would tell them to stay, "and that is what he was prepared to do."[177]

Finally the days of judgment arrived. Elders Brigham Young Jr., Anton H. Lund, and George Teasdale came to Bluff on Thanksgiving, soon after the quarterly stake conference in Moab, during which most wards reported such splendid crops that the Saints were advised to lay up a surplus. The visitors immediately inspected the ditch and Cottonwood Wash, then celebrated the holiday with the Saints at the schoolhouse. The next day, they called for meetings at two and six o'clock. After the congregation sang "Do What Is Right" to open the early meeting, Brigham Young Jr. looked them over and asked some pointed questions: "Why were the people called here if they were not wanted here? Why blessed and prospered above all other wards in the stake if they were not in the right place?" Their children were better off, he continued, for being raised in so [359] isolated a place with so few outsiders and apostates in it. Then he told them about his father, President Brigham Young, and the persecutions he had faced in his life. He had wanted a colony to be established between the Navajos and Utes, "to make friends with them and prepare them for the gospel when the time came." Then the son taught the cooperative doctrines of his father: there were plenty of industries that could help the people of Bluff sustain themselves, such as a gristmill and a tannery. Some are dissatisfied when they aren't allowed to "roam at [their] own sweet wills." But the Saints were under obligations: if they could not forsake all, their faith was in vain. They would be judged for all their actions.[178] The talk was a strong tonic or a bitter pill, depending on the disposition of those who heard it.

George Teasdale opened the six o'clock meeting with the subject "I want to be where the Lord wants me to be." "You are here," he told the Saints, "because the Lord wants you here. The Lord intended your children to be born here." They should carry out the counsel of their president and bishop. At this point he "broke out and blessed Bishop Nielson for his integrity and blessed his numerous family." "I prophesy ... that those who want to remain at Bluff shall be blessed more than heretofore." Anton Lund told

---

177. Albert R. Lyman, "Hans Joseph Nielson," 149.

178. The accounts of the visit of the Apostles and what they said are in Albert R. Lyman, Journal, November 24 and 25, 1897; Hammond, Journal, November 24 and 25, 1897; and Bluff Ward, General Minutes, November 25, 1897.

them their mission was not a failure: they should look among themselves. There they were, all in the Church, without apostates among them. They were living in a place of refuge, not from persecution for polygamy anymore, but from sinful influences. "You need not fear you will be blessed here in Bluff ... both spiritually and temporally." [360] Brigham Young put the will of the conference into words as gently as he could. Echoing the phrase of his father above the site of Salt Lake City fifty years before, he declared, "This is the right spot." If any wanted to leave, they could go, since no one should be held against his or her will. But Bluff was to be maintained. The ditch was useless, but they should study the issue: maybe a pump would work. "If united you can do all." Then he called for the names of all those who were willing to remain and wrote them down in a notebook. Joe Nielson pinched John Rogers's knee to remind him that was what he had predicted the Apostles would say.[179] All present agreed to stay, some through choking emotions. They may not have liked it, but "there is, however, one consolation. That is that we know it is 'the will of the Lord.'"[180]

Francis Hammond echoed Elder Teasdale's theme. He wanted to be where the Lord wanted him to be. It seems he had been mistaken, he said, about the importance of Bluff. Now he felt converted to its cause. Brigham Young told them not to abandon the place to their enemies, but to raise their children in purity there. The Apostles blessed the congregation in the name of the Lord, the assembled Saints sang "The Spirit of God Like a Fire Is Burning," and so ended the meeting.[181]

Church services the next two weeks were full of vigor. But when the ditch [361] committee met at the bishop's house on the raw, chilly day of December 13, 1897, its members were not very enthusiastic. They still had no solution for their old, intimate problem.[182] [362]

---

179. Albert R. Lyman, "Hans Joseph Nielson," 149.

180. Albert R. Lyman, Journal, November 25, 1897.

181. Hammond, Journal, November 25, 1897. See also Albert R. Lyman, "Bishop Jens Nielson: The Old Wagon," 74. Lyman asserts in later accounts that the Apostles said those who settled on White Mesa were still considered as fulfilling their mission. There is no record of this in the contemporary sources, including his journal, President Hammond's journal, and Bluff Ward, General Minutes.

182. Hammond, Journal, December 13, 1897.

8
Mission's End, 1898–1906

Old and New

The Aged

Bluff was "a good country for the aged," proclaimed Francis Hammond in his latest dispatch to the *Deseret News* in January 1898.[1] Jens Nielson and his wives, along with the Hammonds, Adams, and Allans, were about to experience how kind the country would be to the elderly. The bishop and his families were finally fully settled, with the completion of "quite a commodious rock house" for Kirsten.[2] With all her children grown, Kirsten was often alone in her comfortable new quarters. Some of her offspring lived with her at times, and those who were in town visited her often as the grandchildren scurried about. Jens continued to reside with Elsie in the brick home the next lot over, to satisfy the requirements of the Manifesto. He would usually cut through the gardens and trees to Kirsten's home to eat dinner, the mid-day meal. The red bandanna in his pocket was his napkin, and it matched the red checked tablecloth Kirsten usually set. If it was a particularly good day, Kirsten might have made dumplings. After a leisurely meal, Jens would usually chat with Kirsten for a while before returning to the fields or the tithing [363] yard. The bishop still worked as hard as his health allowed, stumping south to his fields early in the

---

1. Francis A. Hammond, "The Cliff-Dweller Country," *Deseret News*, January 26, 1898, in Journal History, January 17, 1898, 9–10.

2. Journal History, January 17, 1898, 9–10.

morning, pondering the questions of the day in the cool air, but he made the trip less frequently with time.[3]

As always, he was full of advice, practical and spiritual, for the members of his town and ward. "Brother Adams, your alfalfa is too ripe. You need to cut it right away," or "Brother Perkins, you'd better mend your ditch."[4] Sometimes he would be blunt. When one brother tried to explain to the bishop what he wanted to do in a certain matter, Jens replied, "I don't care what you want to do. I want you to do it this way."[5] Some of this was confidence in his own judgment, but it was mixed with great concern for the welfare of those in his ward. Sarah Perkins remembered, "He advised and directed us and knew our affairs as well as we knew them ourselves."[6] When in 1899 Adelia Lyman's ninety-three-year-old mother fell ill in Fillmore, the family summoned Sister Lyman to come and see her mother one more time. She was not sure if she would make it in time, so she asked Bishop Nielson for his advice. He didn't know immediately, but promised to tell her before she started out early the next morning. When the time came, the bishop told her not to go. "You will not see your mother," he told her. "She will be dead before you get there, and your long trip will be in vain." Sister Lyman stayed and the bishop's [364] prediction turned out to be correct.[7]

Kirsten and Elsie also kept as busy as they could. Kirsten was still the president of the ward Relief Society, and Elsie was the treasurer. The members of the organization continued to take care of each other through their compassion and frequent visits. They collected cloth to make sheets, quilts, and pillows and some of their funds went to the poor among them. They also saved to build a Relief Society hall with the members' small contributions as well as from the revenue generated by their sheep herd, which was on consignment with Lemuel Redd (paying them $21.20 in the year 1900).[8] Elsie still tended her beehives. Her children and grandchildren helped turn the extractor and pack the

---

3. Leland W. Redd, "Bishop Jens Nielson," 32.

4. Hyde, "As I Recall Grandfather Jens Nielson," 24.

5. Albert R. Lyman, "Bishop Jens Nielson," 13–14.

6. Albert R. Lyman, "Bishop Jens Nielson," 14.

7. Albert R. Lyman, "Bishop Jens Nielson," 14.

8. See Amasa Jay Redd, *Lemuel Hardison Redd, Jr.*, Appendix 1, 79–82.

honey into the five-gallon cans Elsie distributed throughout the family and the community.[9]

Bluff was still far away from the railroad, but the world continued to get smaller. People in Bluff could order all sorts of items, from books to guns to stomach pumps, from Montgomery Ward. Newspapers came with the mail three times a week and, with their "telegraphic dispatch," continued to make "the whole world a kind of a neighbor."[10] Jens often discussed world events as he and others waited for the rider to come to the post [365] office on Tuesday, Thursday, and Saturday evenings.[11] He might also find other people, particularly Francis Hammond, John Allan, and William Adams, at the co-op or Adams's stores and opine on the explosion of the U.S.S. Maine in February, the government's declaration of war with Spain in April, or the General Authorities' advice to show patriotism by helping with the war effort. Local boy Henry Wood answered the call and packed supply mules toward Santiago, Cuba, later in the year.[12] The town was proud of his performance, as well as that of the country, which showed itself to be "one of the first class nations of the earth in every particular."[13]

While American imperial power swelled during 1898, politics continued to diminish Bluff's position in the county. The Gentiles' hold on county offices didn't last long, as they lost control of most posts in 1897 and 1898. The Bluff Mormons helped elect Lemuel Redd as representative to the Utah Legislature in 1898 and again in 1900. But Monticello kept its suzerainty over San Juan County. When the county elected its first female official, Kate Perkins, as clerk in 1898, her victory was almost entirely due to the northern influence, which supported her 113–80. Those in Bluff futilely backed their man, Peter Allan, by a margin of 41–10.[14]

The broader world continued to come to Bluff a visitor or two at a time, as [366] miners, oil prospectors, or relic hunters.[15] May 1898 brought

---

9. Meo, "Uriah and Annie Butt Talk about Elsie Rasmussen," 82.

10. Francis A. Hammond, Journal, February 15, 1897.

11. Riis, Ranger Trails, 45.

12. See Hammond, Journal, January 20, 1899.

13. Hammond, Journal, August 25, 1898.

14. Palmer and Lisenby, "First Woman Elected," 41.

15. See Hammond, Journal, January 23 and 25, 1897, for one of these groups of "rich men's sons" from the East, guided by Richard and Clayton Wetherill of Colorado in their hunt for relics.

one of the most exotic: a man named Sidhi Mahomet Taciber arrived with his traveling companion, a Miss Peabody. He presented a letter to the bishop from President Hammond, whom he had met in Colorado, explaining his past and why he was in Bluff. He had been born to English parents in India but then orphaned and educated in Indian schools. He came to the county to study the ethnography of the ancient Indians, and Charles Goodman helped him excavate extensive ruins just north of Bluff and others in Comb Wash. The visitor stopped into town from time to time over the summer and gave lectures on India. The Bluff congregation was curious about and courteous to his philosophy and took up a collection for him when he left for Salt Lake City in September.[16]

The land showed its age as well. The settlers had stripped nearby banks of their cottonwoods and by 1898 foraging for wood meant a major expedition, sometimes occupying a whole day. If they were lucky, they might find some driftwood in Cottonwood Wash; otherwise, they had to travel increasing distances to find any trees. This was not only an inconvenience for the settlers, but an invitation to the rivers to wander more than they previously had. The San Juan banks had eroded more in the years since the settlers arrived than they had in the previous centuries.[17] The river meandered from bank to bank in 1898, and it continued to eat away at the bishop's hay field and [367] other acres of farms south of town. But there was one good sign early in the year. U.S. government surveyors were finally starting to officially measure the land, even if there was less of it to measure. At long last Bluff settlers started preparing their applications for the land that most of them had been living on for almost twenty years.[18]

Temporal Affairs

On the whole, Bluff's spirits stayed high in early 1898. There was a brief flash when some thought oil discoveries downriver would go far in "redeeming that section from the scorn with which many would-be wits and real ignoramuses have spoken of it," but the boom collapsed quickly.[19] Bluff's men decided to try something new on the ditch: this

---

16. Hammond, Journal, May 10–September 29, 1898.

17. Aton, "River, the Ditch," 17.

18. Hammond, Journal, January 25 to December 15, 1898.

19. "San Juan Petroleum," *Deseret News*, February 15, 1898, in Journal History, February 15, 1898, 5–6.

would be the year of the pump. The jump was the only section upriver where the San Juan hadn't left its northern bank, so along the site of the old cribs the townspeople tried their technology. A man named Morris Posthelwaite, known to everyone as "Posty," came to engineer the pump. A few wagons brought the contraption to town in late January to great acclaim, and by early March the steam engine was chugging along, to the delight of the children who went out to take a look. But by mid-March it was obvious the thing was not working: the boiler was too small. France Nielson helped haul in a larger one at the end of April, but when the first of June came, the expectant town still had not celebrated the first trickle in the ditch. It turned out the muddy waters of the San Juan were as hard on the large boiler as they had been on the small. [368] When the river went down in late July, the experiment was abandoned. The year of the pump turned into another year of measly yields: some orchard fruits, but very few vegetables, and only half a crop of hay. At least the pump failed convincingly enough to persuade them not to try it again. The next year the laborers unleashed their full traditional arsenal: digging, scraping, cribbing, riprapping, and damming the river, without much more success.[20] Reports from New Mexico that there were five thousand acres of unsettled land that could be irrigated for $1.50 an acre only galled them further.[21]

The range was in better shape. France Nielson was still the foreman of the pool in 1898. Heavy snows in the winter of 1897–98 had forced the cattle down to lower levels and made it easier for enterprising cowboys such as Al Scorup to round up the strays. The pool and other cattlemen gained more stock this way than they lost to the continued operations of horse thieves and cattle rustlers, some of whom operated out of the notorious Robbers' Roost in Emery County. Bluff residents continued to appeal to the government for help. Governor Wells put out rewards for the outlaws, but they would take time to be effective.[22]

The co-op board of directors decided that their store should look as nice as the new homes in town, so they authorized building a larger stone structure with a dance hall on the second floor. And after so many years,

---

20. Hammond, Journal, January 13–July 28, 1898; Albert R. Lyman, "History of San Juan County," 95.

21. Wayne H. Redd, Journal, November 20, 1900.

22. Wayne H. Redd, Journal, April 12, 1898; Lambert, "Al Scorup," 316.

a gristmill was coming to the county, but [369] to Monticello, not Bluff. A few Bluff men who also farmed in Monticello, such as Hans Bayles and Joseph Barton, invested in the project. Hopefully this would bring down the price of the imported flour on which Bluff always depended. It was hard on Bluff residents that they now also had to depend on outside hay for the winter or let their domestic animals forage. But overall the heavy snows made for a fine year for cattle. Francis Nielson increased the pool's stock by buying over sixteen hundred head late in the season even though prices were high. Francis Hammond dubbed it the "most prosperous season for cattle and sheep" since he came.[23] Although the pump failed, their stock continued to sustain them.

But prosperity was no proof of unity. In fact, it might have made cooperation more difficult. The Bluff Cattle Pool broke apart at the end of the year. The cold snap in early December 1898 might have been the last straw. Temperatures hit fourteen below zero, and though Bluff's children were delighted at the chance to skate or slide on the frozen San Juan or play in almost a foot of snow, the intense cold killed some cattle and convinced many of the pool's participants that they could care for their herds better themselves. But in larger terms, the outside pressure from competing cattle companies, which was a major reason the pool was formed in the first place, had diminished. The Pittsburgh Cattle Company was the last big "outside" outfit left, but it operated far to the north, and it was getting smaller. Fewer outside herds invaded Bluff's ranges during the winter. Without these threats to Bluff's stock raisers, men who once had cooperated for the common good now went their [370] separate ways. Many sold their cattle to the Scorup brothers.[24] The Nielson brothers continued to operate the family's interest and also ran some of their sheep together with the increasing flocks of Lemuel Redd. Individual ranchers began to fence their own pastures on Elk Mountain.[25]

---

23. Hammond, "Cliff-Dweller Country."

24. Lambert, "Al Scorup," 311.

25. Platte D. Lyman, "Diary," August 11, 1901. An ordinance had been passed by the county court in 1892 requiring all private lands to be enclosed with a fence at least four and a half feet and four barbed wires high. Bluff's stockmen seemed to be privatizing their lands with their fences, even though they couldn't claim legal title yet. See San Juan County Minute Book, September 5, 1892.

All continued to support cooperation as a principle, but their practices were fraying from that ideal.[26]

As competition continued to replace cooperation, Bluff stockmen employed more Mexican herders to watch over their stock. A few worked as herdsmen, tending twenty-five hundred to three thousand head apiece for eight to ten months before returning home to spend a few months with their families in the winter. As many as fifty would converge on the large sheep camps during the spring and fall shearings.[27] These migratory laborers had been used since at least 1890 and usually remained anonymous to Bluff's residents, who hired "a Mexican" just as they hired "an Indian." Not only did these herders have experience with stock, they could be hired for less, generally getting twenty-five dollars a month, instead of the thirty dollars paid to boys or men from Bluff.[28] Sometimes D. J. Rogers would teach the deacons a lesson in "Mexican," and some boys picked up enough of the language to allow them to converse basically. [371] Every once in a while, especially among the younger generation in Bluff, a laborer would distinguish himself by name. Albert Lyman became good friends with a young worker named Jose Aragon and later traveled to New Mexico to meet his family.[29] Lemuel Redd developed close relationships with some of his herders.[30] But more often these workers were noted only for their tragedies, such as the poor man who fell off a heavy wagon and was crushed to death by its wheels. Bluff held a funeral for the man, but did not know his name or where he lived. Writing of him, Albert Lyman lamented on the lonely life of these workers: "He says he (I should say said) had a grown up family. I feel sorry to think they do not know where their father is tonight."[31]

---

26. Albert R. Lyman, Journal, March 9, 1901, relates Brother Lyman's feelings for these old-time principles through a pair of spurs he had just made: "They were rather rough looking things, but my mania for home industry blinds my eyes to all their imperfections."

27. Gonzalez and Padilla, "Monticello."

28. Francis A. Hammond, letter to David M. Edwards, October 22, 1900.

29. Albert R. Lyman, "Experiences and Impressions," 31–33.

30. See Redd, *Lemuel Hardison Redd, Jr.*, for examples.

31. Albert R. Lyman, Journal, March 16, 1897. For other incidents and interactions, see Hammond, Journal, March 17, 1897; March 18, 1898; April 19, 1899; Albert R. Lyman, Journal, November 9, 1896; November 19, 1898; February 14, 1901; also Albert R. Lyman, Summaries of Each Year, 1900, 184.

Drought returned in 1899 and continued through the next year. The San Juan actually dried into puddles in the summer of 1900, a sight those at Bluff had never seen before.[32] While it was a novelty to cross the river dry-shod and it was easy to pull fish out of the pools, the drought once again brought serious consequences to the county. Bluff didn't raise any grain in 1899 or 1900. Stock continued to suffer on the range, but did well enough to allow the town to survive. Once again though, Bluff looked good by comparison. The drought seriously hurt the crops in Monticello as well, forcing people there to look for outside work. Church leaders now had to counsel the Saints in [372] Monticello, much as they had done in Bluff in its early years, not to move about without consent from their Church leaders. The downturn caused the owners of the new gristmill to be in danger of defaulting. Bluff's livestock allowed its owners to raise the three thousand dollars needed to keep the mill.[33] Bluff's cattlemen were fortunate in other ways: none of them, despite countless close calls, had been seriously injured or killed on the range. Bert Stevens came closest in 1901, sleeping through a stampede that would have trampled him if the panicked cattle had fled down the gulch instead of up.[34]

The drought increased another problem that already existed. Since at least 1895, the county had perpetually been on the brink of bankruptcy. Roads were still the greatest expense, and many Bluff men who planned on spending a day as they wanted were collared by the road supervisor to work off their road tax instead. When the Gentiles took over county government in 1896, they lowered property and liquor taxes dramatically and increased expenditures, making the deficit worse. By 1897, some spoke of annexing the almost insolvent county to Grand County, which was understandably reluctant to absorb San Juan's debt.[35] When Mormons, albeit mostly Monticellans, took back most county offices in the following years, they had no solutions either, and petitions for annexation were sent to the Utah Legislature again in 1899 and 1901, failing

---

32. Wayne H. Redd, Journal, August 31, 1900.

33. Hammond, Journal, August 8, September 15, October 9, November 11, 1900; Redd, Journal, March 4, 1901.

34. Albert R. Lyman, Summaries of Each Year, 1900, 185.

35. Peterson, *Look to the Mountains*, 105; Francis A. Hammond, "Cliff-Dweller Country."

both times to win a [373] majority in each county.[36] San Juan County's government continued to drag along as well as it could until better times returned.

Bluff hung on as well. The completion of the two-story, rock co-op store symbolized how its trade and livestock kept them afloat. But by the time the physical co-op building was finished, the principle of coop-eration was practiced less in Bluff than ever before. Bishop Nielson and President Hammond continued to preach the principle, sometimes in sharp terms, condemning the "lack of faith by failing to carry out counsel given us in our temporal matters. Cooperation seems to be lost sight of by many of us."[37] But besides these admonitions, there were no new cooperative ventures. Bluff was not alone in abandoning the practice of these principles. As Bluff stockmen were losing their distinctive coop-erative organizations, Utah as a whole was becoming more like the Gentiles in financial matters.

Other long-time residents followed Kumen Jones and the bishop's lead in building substantial homes. Joe Nielson joined Lem Redd, Hans Bayles (no longer a widower, having recently wed Eva Lyman, Albert's older sister), and James Decker in putting down foundations for homes in 1898 and 1899.[38] But some were also pulling them up. Francis Hammond, who emerged from debt in 1897 and prospered during the boom year of 1898, left his stone cottage on "Vinegar Hill" and moved to Moab in 1899, after obtaining permission from Church leaders. Although Moab was still a town of three [374] whiskey saloons, two blacksmith shops, a large dance hall, and one small Mormon church, President Hammond felt it was a better place for him to be as he approached his eighties.[39] He could continue his exhausting quarterly tours of the stake but would also be closer to the railroad at Thompson's Springs for his frequent visits to Salt Lake City and Ogden. His son Fletcher was already in Moab, and he and his large family would be a comfort to President Hammond and his wife in their older years. At his farewell party in Bluff, the ward gave him twenty-one dollars, which they said he should use to buy an easy chair in which to

---

36. McPherson, *History of San Juan County*, 320.

37. H. M. Taylor, San Juan Stake Conference Report, *Deseret News*, June 25, 1898, 57:46.

38. Hammond, Journal, April 20, November 4, 1899.

39. Hammond, Journal, June 22, 1899.

rest his old bones.[40] President Hammond and Bishop Nielson said their farewells on mutually good terms, despite their past differences.[41]

Spiritual Matters

Missionaries

Bishop Nielson declared in early 1899 that he "never heard bad counsel" from his Church leaders, a remarkable declaration given what he had been through as a result of that counsel.[42] The young men were still known to disregard that counsel, however, and make "asses of themselves" when they found the saloons in Durango at the end of their cattle drives. Sometimes they didn't have to go that far, as at the reception in honor of Henry Wood's return from the Spanish-American War, where "most of the boys were [375] intoxicated, and the doings wound up with an attempt at murder."[43] The effort to reform "our careless young men" was accelerated in 1898 and 1899 with a wave of home missionaries, Joe Nielson being one of them, called to travel around the stake, paying particular attention to teaching the young men in the wards.[44] "Never in the history of our stake," exclaimed Lemuel Redd, "has there been as much union and interest in attending the meetings of the different organizations. Many who have laid dormant for years are waking up and showing signs of life."[45] At an evening meeting soon after the fracas at the Wood reception, old William Adams spoke in tongues, prophesying, upon translation from the thrilling and strange language, that soon a large number of young men from Bluff would be called on missions.[46] The trend, in fact, had already started.

---

40. Hammond, Journal, June 18, 1899.

41. Hammond, Journal, July 10, 1899.

42. Hammond, Journal, January 8, 1899.

43. Albert R. Lyman, Summaries of Each Year, 1898; Albert R. Lyman, Journal, February 10, 1899.

44. The description comes from Hammond, Journal, January 6, 1899.

45. L. H. Redd, San Juan Stake Conference Report, *Deseret News*, March 19, 1898, 430.

46. Albert R. Lyman, Journal, February 12, 1899; Albert R. Lyman, Summaries of Each Year, 1899, 170; Hammond, Journal, February 12, 1899. This was the only instance of someone in Bluff speaking in tongues, aside from two female visitors from Salt Lake City. For that instance, see Elliott, Diary, September 24, 1899.

In early 1898, Church authorities had requested stake presidents to submit as many names as they could for missionary service.[47] President Hammond had probably done so, but the next missionary called from Bluff surprised even him. Platte Lyman received a letter on October 5 from P.O. Box B in Salt Lake City, the address of the First Presidency of the Church. Lorenzo Snow had just been sustained to succeed Wilford Woodruff as the prophet. Platte Lyman had been called to become the [376] president of the Church's European Mission. It was astounding to Platte Lyman himself and to the whole town, and they took it as a collective compliment that someone from their remote location would be asked to assume such great responsibilities. To President Lyman personally it meant vindication for the years since 1884 when he had felt outside the confidence of the Church authorities. But this mission would be difficult for his family, since he had just inched out of debt in 1898. The bishop loaned him some money for his expenses to Europe and on Tuesday, October 18, 1898, the Bluff Ward threw a party for the departing dignitary. At the end of the program, Elder Lyman "made a speech that brought tears to many eyes," and two days later he left.[48]

Within a week, Wayne Redd returned from his diligent service in the Southern States Mission. Caroline was, of course, ecstatic to have her husband home, and the rest of the ward was again impressed with what a difference a mission had made on a man. Scarcely a month after he returned, Elder Redd was called to fill Platte Lyman's place as a counselor to Stake President Hammond.

In that cold December of 1898, soon after the "holiday amusements began in dead earnest," another letter came from Box B. France Nielson was holding a dinner with Wayne Redd and other recently called or returned missionaries when they were interrupted by France's little boy Lisle, who came in with the letter. France had been called to the Southern States Mission, where Wayne had just served. Before Francis left in April, Jens Peter, Uriah, and seven other young men from Bluff were "endorsed as missionaries," in some cases to their great surprise, in the Bluff Stake Conference in [377] February. Albert Lyman was among them; he was to join his father in London. Most of the others, including

---

47. First Presidency Bulletin.

48. See Platte D. Lyman, "Diary," October 1898; Albert R. Lyman, Journal, 1898.

the Nielson boys, were called to the Southern States Mission along with Francis. They were typical of the many different types of missionaries Church leaders had called at the time: Jens Peter was, besides Peter Allan, the town's most recalcitrant bachelor at age thirty-seven; France, at thirty, left his wife with three small children; Uriah was twenty-two and attending Brigham Young Academy when he heard the news.

The next months saw a string of missionary preparation classes, parties, collections, and farewells for the departing proselytizers. Francis left in April, Jens Peter and Uriah in October. The letters they wrote home reminded those in Bluff how much faith was required of missionaries traveling without purse or scrip, especially in the southern United States. Mobbing was increasing in the wake of the B. H. Roberts hearings in Congress. Roberts had been elected to the House of Representatives from Utah but was accused of being unfit since he still had more than one wife. Eventually he was refused his seat, and widespread suspicions that Mormons were still practicing polygamy were taken out on the Church's representatives. Two missionaries from the San Juan Stake had been beaten in Tennessee already in 1899.[49] So the Nielson boys knew what might be coming.

Families and friends in Bluff followed the missionaries' reports eagerly. The trip to the mission was fascinating if they had never traveled to Omaha or Chicago to sell stock before. The immense cornfields on the Great Plains were astonishing, while the [378] enormous grain elevators and massive factories in Kansas City and St. Louis were at least as impressive. Somewhere along the line the greenhorn missionaries bought a new suit or two and sent their old clothes home.

Once they arrived at their field of labor, which was usually rural, they found a new brand of hard work. They got blisters the first week, often walking over ten miles a day through dust or mud and usually over two hundred miles in a month. San Juan men were used to roads like these but not the walking; in Bluff they had horses to cover such distances. And there were other unfamiliar things: "prickly heat, seed ticks, and red bugs" among them.[50] At times the missionaries bathed themselves

---

49. Hammond, Journal, September 19, 1899.

50. Wayne H. Redd, Journal, August 22, 1896. The following description of life in the Southern States Mission is based on Wayne Redd's detailed journal of his mission a year or two before this batch of missionaries left.

and washed their clothes in secluded creeks and ponds. The people they encountered were sometimes even more rural than they were: "These are good, piney woods people. They do not know their ages, and all chew tobacco," including a girl who might have been six.[51] If the missionaries couldn't get dinner, they walked through the afternoon on empty stomachs, unless they happened on some berries. And it was often discouraging as they tramped late into the night, through many refusals, until someone would give them "entertainment": food and shelter for the evening. They came to appreciate quickly and keenly the luxuries of a good bed and filling food. They didn't travel on Sunday, so every week they had to find someone willing to give them two nights' entertainment. The sweetest words in the world were those some people used to invite them back for another [379] night's lodging if they ever wanted it.

It was a sobering and sometimes intimidating experience as each missionary bore his testimony for the first time in front of strangers, especially when some of the listeners were "old, hard-shelled Baptists" who had strong beliefs and traditions of their own.[52] The Mormon preachers gave away thousands of tracts and held hundreds of "gospel conversations" and scores of meetings, but they sold few books and were fortunate if they found people willing to take them seriously for very long. Every so often a letter from home would find them in their wanderings, and sometimes these had contributions in cash or in the prized commodities of envelopes and stamps. It was unusual to see so many Black Americans. In some parts of the mission, the missionaries were marching through the country "visiting the white people which were scattered amongst the Negroes."[53] Even if the missionaries didn't baptize a single soul, their experiences made them think about their own beliefs and their home in Bluff.

All of these missionaries gave old Bishop Nielson much more to do. He had more duties as the father of his family now that three of his sons were gone at once. Joe would also have to carry more of the load of the family's enterprises, and his oldest sons, Eddie and Jens Lyman, were just old enough at fourteen and thirteen to be of some use. The bishop also had more to do looking after the families of the other seven missionaries

---

51. Redd, Journal, February 6, 1897.
52. Redd, Journal, June 11, 1896.
53. Redd, Journal, April 28, 1896.

who went out with his sons. Monroe Redd left behind a wife and six children. The Redds were having a particularly hard time doing without their husband and father and were [380] about to call him home. The bishop visited them and told them what to do to keep Monroe in the field. They did it, and he stayed out until he finished his mission.[54] Sometimes good news came from afar. When President Lyman visited Denmark, he wrote Bishop Nielson about it, and Jens enthusiastically replied.

The people of Bluff were still on their own mission, though its goals slowly changed. In recent years Bluff sent few missionaries to the Indians to convert them either to agriculture or Mormonism. C. L. Christensen, their most experienced Indian missionary, relocated to Monticello over the objections of Bishop Nielson in 1897. The attitudes of many in the town became more frustrated and impatient, especially toward the Utes and Paiutes. Francis Hammond felt as early as 1896 that "the seventy-five or a hundred renegades with which they had been afflicted for years" should be "given a small reservation of their own or be settled by the government," since "the settlers had cared for them about long enough."[55] Now, Bluff residents and Church authorities seemed satisfied to maintain peace and encourage trade and friendship without looking for anything more. A Navajo fair was held in Bluff on September 21, 1899, for these exact purposes.[56]

For the first time, the San Juan Mission had competition for Indian converts. Howard and Evelyn Antes, Methodist missionaries, moved in twenty-five miles upriver from Bluff to a place they named "Aneth" after the Hebrew word for "answer." In 1899 they opened a school to educate Navajos from their "heathen superstition." The Antes couple considered the reservation a "cesspool of ignorance and superstition and immorality." Bluff's residents had little to do with the Antes effort, though it may have been a painful [381] reminder of what they once aspired to do.[57]

Howard Antes also assumed the role of advocate for the Navajos, and one of the groups he felt he needed to protect them from was the Mormons. He was not worried as much about theology as about land rights. Navajo herders had brought their flocks off the reservation to

---

54. Albert R. Lyman, "Bishop Jens Nielson," 14.

55. Francis A. Hammond, "From Sunny San Juan," *Deseret News*, April 11, 1896, 539.

56. Lucinda Alvira Pace Redd, Journal, September 21, 1899.

57. See McPherson, "Howard Antes and the Navajo Faith Mission," for particulars on this effort. The mission lasted until 1907.

the land east of Bluff more often in the past few years. The drought had been hard for them, and they sought better pasture for their herds. But Bluff needed that range as well and allowing the Navajos to use it "would starve out our people."[58] Bluff's stockmen considered this a violation of their traditional boundary along the San Juan and aggressively negotiated to keep the Navajos south of the river. Antes, however, was able to win concessions from federal officials for the Navajos to graze their herds north of the San Juan. He then assumed the power, reminiscent of Henry Mitchell, to write passes for Navajos wishing to do so.[59] Bluff's stockmen felt the pinch, and Bluff's residents might have felt the sting of being the rivals of a people they had worked so long to befriend.

Tithing

If the Mormons in Bluff could not make much headway in their original mission to their Indian neighbors, they could be satisfied with their ward's record in comparison with that of other Church units. The Bluff Ward continued to sponsor the full program of the [382] Church despite its limited numbers. Its members took great pride in having sent out so many missionaries, even though this caused hardship at home. As friends and neighbors helped out, the sacrifice was shared by the community and so was the sense of achievement. In this informal way, the cooperative principle endured. Bluff Ward members diligently sought to have a good record in other areas. When a Brother Lambert came to town in early 1900 "in the interest of the *Deseret News*," he had little work to do, since everyone already subscribed to that paper and the *Juvenile Instructor* as well, and almost everyone took the *Improvement Era*.[60]

Bishop Nielson and his ward also did their best to help the Church out of its financial difficulties. By 1898, Church headquarters found itself $2.3 million in debt, with less than $1 million in tithing coming in per year.[61] President Wilford Woodruff was disappointed in his desire to retire the debt during his life, and when Lorenzo Snow succeeded him

---

58. See Hammond, Journal, November 13, 1900, for an example of Navajo pressure north of the river.

59. Aton and McPherson, *River Flowing from the Sunrise*, 76.

60. Wayne H. Redd, Journal, February 20, 1900; Hammond, "Cliff-Dweller Country."

61. Alexander, *Mormonism in Transition*, 5.

in 1898, the new president felt the same urgency. George Q. Cannon wrote to his old friend "Frank" Hammond, "There should be a disposition shown by every member of the church, and especially by the officers of the church, to do all in their power to reduce expenses and help clear off the load of indebtedness."[62] The First Presidency urged bishops to care for the tithing items as well as possible: "Nothing should be allowed to waste or decay for lack of care and attention." They should also [383] send in tithing cash at least monthly and liquidate whatever they could.[63] As had been the practice for years, bishops were entitled to 6 to 7 percent of the ward's tithes in return for their efforts, and stake clerks 3 or 4 percent.[64] In May 1899, after receiving a revelation on the subject while visiting St. George, President Snow felt that he must teach the principle of tithing more powerfully to the Church. A solemn assembly in Salt Lake City in July 1899 impressed on the leaders that the principle of tithing had to be from henceforth "faithfully and fully kept."[65]

Bluff also did well in this crusade. Its members had paid a full tithing for some years already, even during the difficulties of the drought and depression of the early 1890s.[66] Still, J. Golden Kimball was sent from Salt Lake City to the San Juan Stake in November 1899. "His special mission is to preach tithing," Wayne Redd recorded, "but he hits us on all sides and speaks with a great deal of power."[67] Both the visited and the visitor were impressed with each other. All who recorded their thoughts were struck by the force of Elder Kimball's remarks, not only on tithing but on kindness toward the Indians and on the evils of round dancing and allowing Gentiles to dance with Mormon [384] girls.[68] Bluff gave Elder Kimball the full treatment, taking him up the river to the big cave

---

62. George Q. Cannon, letter to Francis A. Hammond, February 2, 1898.

63. Snow, Cannon, and Smith, Circular Letter, December 1, 1898.

64. Hammond, Journal, January 1, 1891; September 25 and November 21, 1899. Stake presidents were also paid a Church salary of about four hundred dollars a year for their expenses in administering their stake, and their counselors received about half that much, though these amounts changed over time. See First Presidency, "General Bulletin," June 6, 1888. See also Hammond, Journal, February 26, 1897.

65. Francis M. Lyman, letter to Platte D. Lyman, July 3, 1899.

66. See, for example, Hammond, Journal, January 14, 1891.

67. Wayne H. Redd, Journal, November 5.

68. Hammond, Journal, November 6, 1899.

and holding a social at Joe Nielson's before he left. At this event they presented him with a collection of forty-two dollars to defray his expenses,
a sum, according to the town's schoolteacher, "that seems wonderful for
such a little place."[69] Elder Kimball was as impressed with the Saints
in Bluff as Church Historian Andrew Jenson had been six years earlier,
remarking that he had never visited a ward with less inequality or more
kindness in all his travels among the Saints.[70] All together, as Kumen
Jones later calculated, Bishop Nielson's talents led his ward to establish "a
record in church activities, as well as temporal affairs, that brought com-
mendation of church authorities and surprise from friends of our little
colony."[71] Of course the bishop had great amounts of help. Kumen Jones
had been counseling him the whole time and Lemuel Redd for almost all
of the time Nielson had been bishop. Jody Wood had been the Primary
president for sixteen years in addition to her calling in the medical field.

Twenty Years at Bluff

As Bluff entered the year 1900 and its residents debated with some
vigor which century they were in, they marked twenty years in San Juan
County.[72] The actual anniversary was celebrated with a "very pleasant"
picnic social on April 6 and [385] commemorative speeches at church two
days later.[73] The speakers and the occasion invited the citizens to reflect
on what they had done and why they had done it.

They had survived, and as the years ticked by, this became an increasingly impressive accomplishment by itself. Their feelings toward their
home were still mixed, however. At its best, Bluff could be idyllic, such
as for Albert Lyman one day in the spring when he was courting his
future wife: "Had a big sleep in the afternoon, and fixed our field for
the water. The sky is somewhat cloudy tonight. Water still in the ditch.
Everything is green. My cattle have all come back."[74] At its worst, it was

---

69. Elliott, Diary, November 8, 1899; Lucinda Alvira Redd, Journal, November 8,
1899.

70. Lucinda Alvira Redd, Journal, November 8, 1899.

71. Kumen Jones, "Writings," 142.

72. Wayne H. Redd, Journal, December 31, 1899.

73. Lucinda Alvira Redd, Journal, April 6, 1900; Elliott, Diary, April 6 and 8, 1900.

74. Albert R. Lyman, Journal, April 27, 1901.

a purgatory:"Today I hauled manure, the wind blew, and it was a dismal day."[75] But those who were at the celebrations had somehow endured everything so far.

In a way, Bluff had prospered. Its 193 residents were the same number as lived in Bluff and Montezuma combined back in 1880, but only three more than lived in Bluff in 1890. The mostly Mormon communities to the north also had significant numbers: Monticello had 161 occupants and Verdure had 32. Close to 60 percent of Bluff's population was still under twenty years old, but everyone had moved up in the brackets. There were far more teenagers than toddlers now, and many more adults in their forties and fifties than before. The young couples in their twenties during the Hole-in-the-Rock trek, such as Kumen and Mary Jones, Lemuel and Eliza Redd, and Hyrum and Rachel Perkins, were now in their forties. The babies born back in 1880 were now seriously [386] considering marriage. Bishop Nielson had been there all along. He was still the oldest person in town, though the recent "Old Folks" dinner put Aggie Allan "just a little behind."[76]

By their own spiritual reckoning the citizens of Bluff had prospered more than their numbers indicated. As a stake clerk recalled toward the end of 1900, the few who remained after the floods of 1884 "commenced to prosper from that very time and have done exceedingly well ever since. Many of those who moved away were unsuccessful in their new endeavors to make homes and most of them are poor financially to this day (1900) while those who stayed on the San Juan with their children are well off at the present time and could buy out all those who went away twice over."[77] While most had done well for themselves, they still had to justify their existence as a mission. Given the limits and frustrations they found in recent years in their politics and with the Indians, Bluff's residents increasingly found justification for their mission in its effect on themselves and their children.

Bluff still had a distinctive identity, forged largely from what they lacked, as President Hammond wrote his nephew in 1899: "We have no doctor, no lawyer, no gambling houses, no poor that need support in

---

75. Albert R. Lyman, Journal, April 9, 1896.

76. Wayne H. Redd, Journal, December 31, 1899.

77. "San Juan Stake Manuscript History," December 21, 1884.

our midst; we are free from such things as afflict most all communities."[78] They had not converted many Indians, but they had converted some miners, and at the end of 1900 even the "infidel" and "avowed atheist" [387] Edward Thompson, a Scottish stonemason who had constructed many of their homes, was baptized.[79] Despite the town's peaks and valleys, President Hammond declared in November that "this is the richest ward in the stake and a good people."[80]

By then the Nielson family had grown richer as well. Jens's youngest daughter, Annetta, married the former miner, Ezekiel Johnson, on October 9, 1900. Nettie only measured up to Zeke's shoulders, but, as he put it, that was high enough to reach his heart.[81]

Dark Times

There had been surprisingly few deaths in Bluff during the previous four years. That changed swiftly with the new century, and the daily labors of those in Bluff were again interrupted by tragedy. Aggie Allan died in April, but she was a respected woman who had lived a full life and died naturally. President Hammond's departure was different. After his visit to Bluff in November 1900, his relentless schedule took him to a conference in Bloomfield, New Mexico. While pulling up to the home of a Church member, the top of President Hammond's buggy hit a wire clothesline. The horses took fright, dashed forty feet, and overturned the buggy "with great force" against an adobe granary with a rock foundation. President Hammond was crushed against the hard stones. He remained unconscious for a day before he died. His funeral was held in Mancos, and his body was shipped back to Huntsville for burial. In Bluff, Bishop Nielson presided [388] over the ward's memorial service "in honor of this sad affair" on December 2.[82]

---

78. Francis A. Hammond, letter to D. H. Edwards, January 1899.

79. Hammond, Journal, November 6, 1898; Wayne H. Redd, Journal, December 6, 1900. The arguments of Annie Allan helped convince Mr. Thompson. The two were married early the next year.

80. Hammond, Journal, November 13, 1900.

81. Rose, "Annetta Nielson," 234.

82. Hammond, Journal, November 25, 1900 (President Hammond's counselor William Halls wrote a postscript in the journal explaining these events); Wayne H. Redd, Journal, November 25–December 2, 1900.

The bishop and the stake president may have been too much alike in their vigorous personalities, and they collided with each other about Bluff and other issues, but each admired the other's faith and good works. President Hammond had done his best to build up the mission under cooperative principles, and the mission would be much less without his character and contributions.

The bishop himself almost went next, succumbing to a severe "cold in the head." At his age, despite his vigor, any illness was dangerous, and it caused a "sudden gloom" to fall over Bluff. Jens's sickness continued into 1901, which "dawned upon us clear and cold."[83] He gained strength through the next few weeks, and on January 27, 1901, he returned to Church with fervor. From the pulpit he assured doubters "he did not think our mission here in Bluff had been in vain; a great deal of good has been accomplished with the Lamanites and yet much is yet to be accomplished in the future." Then "with much warmth" he predicted, "There are many of us who will live to see a temple built in this part of the land and administer the ordinances of the Lord's house to many of the Lamanites."[84] [389]

For the time being, however, Bluff's woes continued. The entire town rallied in support of Lem Redd's eleven-year-old son Charlie, stricken by pleurisy in his lungs. The Primary children fasted for him, the choir sang to him, and the bishop and elders administered to the endangered boy often. His parents finally took him to Salt Lake City, where Church authorities repeated the promises made to the boy in Bluff, and a surgeon tried to drain the infection. The town rejoiced together when the energetic lad returned home just after his twelfth birthday in May.[85]

---

83. Lucinda Alvira Redd, Journal, January 1, 1901. For the illness, see Albert R. Lyman, Journal, January 11, 1901; Wayne H. Redd, Journal, January 1, 1901; and Lucinda Alvira Redd, Journal, January 11, 1901. Jens suffered from a similar sickness in the later winter and early spring of 1900. This, along with his advanced age, probably prevented him from attending the festivities in Salt Lake City for the Scandinavian Jubilee in June 1900. See Eliott, Diary, April 1, 1900; Hammond, Journal, June 14 to 17, 1900.

84. Bluff Ward, General Minutes, January 27, 1901; Albert R. Lyman, Journal, January 27, 1901.

85. Albert R. Lyman, Journal, March 7, 1901; Arrington, Utah's Audacious Stockman, 45–47.

But smallpox came back to Bluff as well. The town was quarantined on the first day of summer, and the bishop suspended Church meetings for almost a month. Kirsten was stricken by the illness, and her daughter, Caroline Redd, was in mortal danger.[86] Jody and Sam Wood lost another child at an early age, their seven-year-old daughter Bernice, but the other families were spared.

France Nielson returned and reported his mission just before the outbreak. His presence began to relieve some of the burden on the bishop to care for his family. Platte Lyman also returned, called back from Europe to again assume the stake presidency, and the Saints welcomed him as well as they could in the middle of the quarantine. Soon after it was lifted, they threw him a party in the upper level of the co-op store and presented him with a check for $22.50 to help him get reestablished in Bluff.[87] [390]

President Lyman was not well, either. He hoped to build a more comfortable home for his wife, similar to the impressive structures that had appeared in his absence. But he couldn't start on that yet. Soon after he was set apart as stake president on September 1, he and Adelia left for Salt Lake City. He had noticed an increasingly large and painful growth under his arm, and it needed to be removed.[88] While the Lymans were gone, William Adams's failing health gave way. The Irish patriarch of two large families, who had lent his practical wisdom to both Bluff and Monticello over twenty years, died on September 30.

Platte Lyman returned in October, when "the wind [was] blowing sad and lonely as it does in the fall."[89] Although surgeons had tried to remove the tumor, he was not cured. Once again, the town rallied its spiritual resources. The bishop declared a fast in late October, followed by a special priesthood meeting and blessing for President Lyman.[90] The doctor came from Cortez over the next few weeks but could do little to heal his patient or reduce his suffering.

---

86. Lucinda Alvira Redd, Journal, July 3, 1901; Albert R. Lyman, Journal, July 24, 1901.

87. Platte D. Lyman, "Diary," July 9 and 26, 1901.

88. Platte D. Lyman, "Diary," September 1, 1901; Albert R. Lyman, Journal, September 7, 1901.

89. Albert R. Lyman, Journal, September 23, 1901.

90. Albert R. Lyman, Journal, October 25–27, 1901.

More misfortune rained down on the stunned town. Caroline's husband, Wayne Redd, suffered a serious accident. He was driving down the dugway near Dolores, Colorado, with a "four horse load," when the brake lever broke. Wayne was caught by the rope tied across the front of the wagon and dragged close to eighty feet downhill; when he was found a few minutes later, he had a broken arm and a badly bruised head. Wayne [391] was flat on his back in Durango when Caroline got the news, and she rushed off see him at once.[91] In all the history of Bluff, with all the traveling and freighting its residents did on uncertain roads, it was surprising that this sort of accident didn't happen more often. Yet the timing of this wreck could not have been worse.

Platte Lyman's agony became awful in his final days. His cries could be heard through much of the town; his family and neighbors were "horrified at his torture." On November 13, the travail was so terrible that he requested that the bishop gather some elders to bless him for death. After this ordinance, Platte's children and neighbors gathered about his bed for his final words. President Lyman, between groans, spoke to each person present and instructed all to "stay with the church and stand by each other. Listen to the advice of the bishop." When Jens came in, Platte grasped his hand and told him, "Oh bishop, you have been a true father to me."[92] As night descended, the suffering man extended his arms and pleaded, "O pray the Lord to let me go!" Suddenly, the house swayed back and forth, rocked by an earthquake. Soon after, life finally slipped out of Platte Lyman. Jody Wood explained that "Brother Lyman is passing to the great beyond and the heavens are opening to receive him."[93] Lucinda Redd felt that "the elements were taking part in his departure."[94]

The bishop and ward members helped the Lymans as well as they could. Albert [392] Lyman was left in charge of the family, and in the coming years he worked hard to build the house that his father could not. The Nielsons were cheered when Uriah and Jens Peter returned home in the weeks after President Lyman's funeral. But little pure happiness came to Bluff in 1901, and the worst was yet to come.

---

91. Wayne H. Redd, Journal, November 2–December 13, 1901.

92. Albert R. Lyman, "Bishop Jens Nielson," 15.

93. Hoopes, "Josephine Catherine (Jody) Chatterley Wood," 36.

94. Albert R. Lyman, Summaries of Each Year, 1901, 189; Albert R. Lyman, Journal, November 13, 1901; Lucinda Alvira Redd, Journal, November 13, 1901.

The day Jens Peter returned, December 15, in spite of prayer meetings called by Bishop Nielson, five-year-old Lynn Decker died of diphtheria. The bishop presided over the memorial meeting that afternoon, though the little body could not be brought into the meetinghouse for fear of infection. The next day, James Bean Decker, whom everyone had known since the Hole in the Rock, and his fourteen-year-old daughter, Gertrude, died also, no more than three days after showing symptoms. The ward members, aghast, did what they could. One large grave was dug. The quarantined surviving family members, along with Jody Lyman and Joseph Barton, who were also quarantined as nurses, went to the grave site first, then returned home as the those in town not isolated held a memorial service. More families were quarantined as the illness spread to other households. Dogs seen playing around the Deckers' home were killed. Church meetings, then school, then all public meetings were suspended after the bleak new year began. When the postmaster fell sick the mail was shut off as well. Seventeen-year-old Horace Decker and nine-year-old Clare Decker died in late January. Sister Decker, having lost her husband and four of her eleven children within six weeks, was "nearly driven to distraction" within the confines of her home. "This is the most terrible plague [393] that Bluff has ever known, and we wonder what the end will be."[95]

As it turned out, the diphtheria epidemic ravaged only the Deckers. Although other people developed symptoms, no one else died from it. Public meetings resumed at the beginning of March, though a few more homes showing signs of scarlet fever were quarantined after that. Still the awful chain of misfortune had one last link. At 3:30 A.M. on April 17, the town was awakened by the pealing of the church bell. The home of John Larson was on fire. Larson, a former sailor, had come to town during the gold rush in 1892 and had been baptized. Within the last month, the fifty-four year old man had married sixteen-year-old Lenorah Hadden of Parowan. When the flames flickered out, searchers were terrified to find the charred remains of Sister Larson in her bed. Enough of her remained to determine that before the fire she had been brutally assaulted with an ax, and the fire had been ignited to cover the crime. This grisly sight haunted many who were there forever after.[96]

---

95. Albert R. Lyman, Journal, December 15, 1901–February 14, 1902.

96. Albert R. Lyman, Journal, April 17, 1902.

Some suspicion fell on Brother Larson, since he had not been entirely stable before the event occurred, though many later professed it was done by a tramp who had been in town that day but who had left before the evidence against him came to light.[97]

Throughout these mortal distresses, life continued. The men at Bluff returned to the "nasty hard job" of scratching out the ditch, breaking only occasionally for wrestling [394] or racing contests and the demanding routine of herding their stock.[98] The fruit came in plentifully in 1901, but there was continued wrangling with cowboys in Monticello over the fences the men in Bluff were building on Elk Mountain.[99] Lemuel Redd's imposing home was completed, France and Leona Nielson were starting to build one of their own, and Kirsten was proud that the ward finally finished its Relief Society hall.[100] The renewed drought continued to make their lives precarious, yet despite their struggles, residents also saw the advantages of where they lived. When Joe Nielson wrote to Ida from Colorado in the waning summer of 1902, they both agreed, "I am glad my home is in Bluff. I feel something like you say you do—would not change home with anyone even if it is so far from civilization."[101]

Posterity

Legitimacy

Bluff's struggle to survive and prosper exacted a heavy price from the settlers themselves, but it also was hard on the land from which they extracted their living. At the quarterly stake conference in February 1903, a committee was appointed to look into dry farming.[102] At Bluff, however,

---

97. Albert R. Lyman, "History of San Juan County," 97. It is impossible to say what really happened. It is possible the town blamed the tramp to close ranks around one of its citizens and put the awful event behind them. Larson remarried the next year and remained in Bluff for at least another decade.

98. Albert R. Lyman, Journal, August 5, 1901, February 18, 1902.

99. Platte D. Lyman, "Diary," August 18, 1901; Albert R. Lyman, Journal, September 23, 1901.

100. Roring, *Beautiful Bluff*, 14, 24; Albert R. Lyman, Journal, January 29 and December 31, 1902.

101. H. J. Nielson, letter to Ida Nielson, September 14, 1902.

102. Albert R. Lyman, Journal, February 14, 1903.

the farming was in danger of being too wet. The San [395] Juan River continued to eat into the land below Bluff at Walton's Slough, which meant
the toilers of Bluff now had two contrary tasks. Upstream they endeavored to coax the water into town, while at the same time below Bluff they
had to keep the water away from the fields. In 1903 they began to build
a dam across the slough, using all of their old tricks and also some new
ones. The men reinforced the dirt with rocks, logs, and riprap, and they
also used a pile driver. They strengthened "the dam work," as they came
to call it, the next winter.[103] Between this and the renewed drought, it
seemed to some that the county was "going to the dogs" and was "hardly
the miserable ghost of what it used to be 11 years ago."[104]

Regardless of how they felt about the land it finally became theirs.
Even as the river was carrying away Bluff's fields, the town's inhabitants finally secured their claim to what remained. By early 1903, the
government surveyors had finished their work and the necessary notices
had been published in the newspapers. On April 21, all those occupying land in Bluff appeared before the traveling judge of the Seventh
District Court and at long last became landowners in the eyes of the
United States Government. It was a satisfying day for the bishop and
all those who had spent so much of themselves on this ground for so
many years.[105]

Soon after Bluff won its land, it lost some range. Navajo herders
continued to spread their flocks north of the San Juan on land Bluff
stockmen considered part of their [396] own pasture. Jens summed up
the charitably impatient attitude of his ward members in church on one
such occasion when he declared that while he respected the rights of the
Navajos, "we also desire them to respect our rights."[106] He continued
the old diplomacy of sending delegations across the San Juan to negotiate removal of the Navajo herds to the south side of the river.[107] But
these intrusions happened more often as the drought continued, acutely
increasing competition for the scarce grass to the east of Bluff. Perhaps

---

103. Albert R. Lyman, "History of San Juan County," 96.
104. Albert R. Lyman, Journal, February 13, 1904.
105. Utah District Court, San Juan County, Minutes, April 21, 1903.
106. Bluff Ward, General Minutes, January 27, 1901.
107. See, for example, Wayne H. Redd, Journal, January 14, 1901. Redd reported,
"The Lord is with us, and we persuade them to leave immediately."

to ease the pressure on the range, Lemuel Redd and other people in Bluff sent a petition requesting that the government help the starving Navajos along the San Juan. A commission headed by Jens Nielson, Howard Antes (the Methodist missionary at Aneth), and Samuel Shoemaker (a government demonstration farmer), would distribute any aid allocated. But when the Indian agent investigated, he found no starving Navajos. Antes accused the Mormons of devising the plan to increase business through their co-op, but he had no proof. A year later, however, with the lobbying of Antes and William Shelton, the respected superintendent of the Shiprock Agency, the Navajos won a further extension of their reservation. By executive order 324A, President Theodore Roosevelt added the Aneth Area to the Navajo Reservation in 1905.[108] Just as the Mormon mission had grown in numbers and expanded successfully to the north, so had the Navajos, but at the expense of the Mormons. [397]

The Utes and Paiutes remaining in the county had little to console them as they continued to struggle to survive in traditional ways on dwindling resources. The Paiutes had been added to the rolls of the Southern Ute Agency in Colorado in 1895, but those who lived there at all did so for only part of the year. Resources on the reservation were not much greater than those in San Juan County, even adding in the inconsistent rations. So many Utes and Paiutes continued to live "out of the blanket" most of the time. This was increasingly more difficult, since Monticello and Verdure, along with the wide-ranging livestock, severely constricted the land and game the Indians had to live on. As the pressure grew, so did the conflicts.[109] By now the Mormons were less likely to patiently suffer thefts than they had been in the early years. The Indian Posey was arrested in 1903 for stealing a horse but escaped before his trial ended, despite being wounded in the leg. Facing a grim echo of what had happened to Native Americans across the continent, Posey began to wonder how to push back the white settlers. Meanwhile, the opinion of those in Bluff and Monticello toward him continued to

---

108. McPherson, "Howard Antes," 17–18. The Greater Aneth Oil Field was under the Aneth Addition, and it would generate millions of dollars in income for the Navajo tribe when it was discovered and leased in the 1950s. See McPherson and Aton, *River Flowing from the Sunrise*, 77, 124.

109. See McPherson, *History of San Juan County*, 150–53, for the difficult situation of the Utes and Paiutes.

decline: "Posey has murder in his heart," wrote Albert Lyman at the time, "and his advantage over us is that he has no conscience and would not scruple to shoot us in the back if he could conceal his guilt, but we would not kill him but in self defense."[110] The difference between how Mormons treated these Indians and how other "Americans" treated them grew narrower. [398]

Father and Grandfather

The year 1903 was a festive one for the Nielsons. In January and October, Freeman and Uriah married the Perkins cousins, Maggie and Beatrice. Jens performed the earlier ceremony in Bluff, and Rye and Bea traveled to the temple in Salt Lake City. In between, however, a miracle happened. Forty-one-year-old Jens Peter Nielson married Martha Jane "Jennie" Roberts in Farmington, New Mexico. Now all of Jens's children were married, and the next generation came in force.

By the end of 1903, Jens had thirty-six grandchildren, and they all lived in Bluff. The oldest was Joe's boy Eddie, who was eighteen, and the youngest were infants: four of them had been born within the past year. These grandchildren often visited Jens's homes, which were surrounded by fruit trees and berry bushes. Despite Elsie's occasional stern warnings to them about staying out of the raspberries, Jens let the children eat what they wanted. While they did not fully understand his traditional maxims, such as "Eat what you can and can what you can't," they enjoyed the bounty anyway.[111] They might have figured out these sayings had something to do with the stories their grandfather had told them about his handcart ordeal, how adults got only a small teacup full of flour per day and children even less. Some starving pioneers, he told his small audience, would beg the leaders to press down the flour in the cup so they could have more.[112] Jens was kind and understanding with his grandchildren, but they were bothered by how one side of his [399] beard was a little longer than the other. They also remembered the sore that never healed on his nose and his extremely long prayers: "By the time he got around to blessing the General Authorities for the third time, we knew he was almost finished."[113]

---

110. Albert R. Lyman, Journal, July 28–August 2, 1903; February 12, 1904.
111. Hyde, "As I Recall Grandfather Jens Nielson," 24.
112. Leland Redd, "Bishop Jens Nielson," 32.
113. Hyde, "As I Recall Grandfather Jens Nielson," 25.

Jens was also the patriarch of Bluff. He and the score of families who chose to stay came to know each other intimately through all their celebrations, mournings, endeavors, and arguments during the generation they had lived together. As bishop, he had done so much for so many of its citizens that "we all felt that he was a father to every one."[114] He helped the town develop the contrasting characteristics that most impressed outsiders: dogged tenacity and kind hospitality. Walter Lyman "said he had never met a person who was as active and full of energy as Bishop Nielson was who had made as few enemies as he had."[115] He was also a grandfather to the town. The ward's children looked up to him as their white-haired bishop, as much a part of their landscape as the red cliffs. He was something of a literal grandfather to the town as well. Out of the fifteen nine- and ten-year-old children in Albert Lyman's Sunday School class in 1905, five of them were Jens's direct grandchildren, and he was related through the marriage of his children to seven others.[116]

If he were disposed to make such connections as he surveyed his long life, Jens might have noticed its similarity to that of the biblical patriarch Abraham. Both men [400] were called out of a foreign land, were willing to sacrifice their firstborn, took other wives after the first was barren but had children by all of them, and were blessed with prosperity and great posterity, they believed, due to their faithfulness.[117] Now, as Bishop Nielson approached the last years of his life, his family was gathered around him. His children had caused him great concern at times in their lives, but they had become, if not exactly what he hoped, a credit to his name and good citizens in the county.

Enduring to the End

Jens Nielson's trials were not over, though he had one last happy night. On December 8, Bluff threw a reception for Jens Peter and Jennie, and the dancing and dining went on until one in the morning. No future joy in Jens's life would be as complete. Just before Christmas, his son Joe caught typhoid pneumonia. Almost too fast for his family to hope it did not

---

114. Lucinda Alvira Redd, Journal, December 30, 1900.

115. Bluff Ward, General Minutes, April 25, 1906.

116. Albert R. Lyman, Journal, February 5, 1905.

117. Caroline Lane, a descendant of Jens Nielson, pointed out this connection.

happen, Joe died on Christmas Eve. He was forty-three years old and the
father of eight children, the youngest boy had just been born in September. The funeral on Christmas Day was "indeed a sad occasion," despite
the efforts of the ward to decorate the meeting hall and provide beautiful
music. Joe was the son who was most like his father, "large and well built,
… a man full of faith and good works, [who] made friends wherever he
went," as Albert Lyman eulogized him in his journal. "He is Brother or
Uncle Joe to the Bluff folks, and if he is called only Joe it is not through dis-
respect, but rather through love."[118] He was also widely respected among
his friends and business [401] associates in Colorado, "the most honest and
liberal man in this part of the country."[119] C. L. Christensen reflected on
"the gloom [it] cast over the whole community," wondering why "such men
are not spared to do good as these kind of men are very scarce."[120] Jens
wondered that as well. He tried to comfort the family by explaining Joe
had "gone to prepare a place for us," but the survivors felt "our sorrow is
more than we can bear."[121] Kirsten fell ill for the next two weeks after her
dear son's passing. Although he did not know it at the time, Jens had been
speaking to himself four days before Joe's death when he told his ward, "All
will have to be tried to see that we are on a sure foundation."[122]

The heart of the old bishop never entirely recovered from this hardest blow of all. He carried on through the first difficult days, thanking
the ward members the next Sunday for their kindnesses and reminding
them to settle their tithing if they had not already.[123] In time, his spirits
revived. During the May quarterly conference he returned to his foundation of optimism and obedience. "Keep your plate right side up," he
told the assembled Saints. "Be careful about your duties and agencies."[124]
The next year on the same occasion he proclaimed, "I feel thankful for
the blessings we enjoy in this part of [402] the land.… I have no reason to

---

118. Albert R. Lyman, Journal, December 24 and 25, 1903.

119. Kirsten Nielson, letter to Mr. and Mrs. John Lollin and Family, January 10,
1904, on "Jens Nielson History," CD-ROM, 142.

120. C. L. Christensen, Diary, January 1, 1904.

121. Kirsten Nielson, letter to Mr. and Mrs. John Lollin and Family, January 10,
1904, 142.

122. Bluff Ward, General Minutes, December 20, 1903.

123. Bluff Ward, General Minutes, December 27, 1903.

124. San Juan Stake, General Minutes, May 7, 1904.

complain."[125] But at the same time, when he heard or sang the hymn he loved so much, "When Joseph His Brethren Beheld," it brought more melancholy than before.[126]

The San Juan River did not relent. Efforts to control its waters continued, and as usual, enormous efforts won only small success. The river had washed away "a good many acres of the Bluff field" in the previous years, and in 1905 it swept away much of the dam meant to keep it away.[127] The high river that summer also continually broke through the banks of the ditch, making it difficult to irrigate, which in effect extended the drought.[128] The men of Bluff had to do fifteen hundred dollars of riprapping in the first two months of 1906 to try to save what was left of their fields.

Once again, many Bluff residents found a more desirable place to live. Walter Clisbee Lyman's vision of a village on White Mesa had come true. Difficulties with irrigation and Lyman's two-year mission had caused the plans to be delayed until 1903, when Albert Lyman and his wife, Lell, became the first residents in the settlement, eventually named Grayson.[129] Jody Lyman bought the old LC Ranch in the area. In 1904, at a meeting held on top of a pile of wood, the Grayson Branch was organized subsidiary to [403] the Bluff Ward. By 1905 the town was a growing concern, and Grayson farmers were planting, among other things, wheat and oats, "crops not heard of in Bluff."[130] Jens Peter Nielson was skeptical. At first he quipped that he would not give his corn patch in Bluff for all of White Mesa. "The San Juan, however, annexed that corn patch," and Jens Peter later put in a "fine field" on White Mesa and built the first "real house" there.[131] In future years, as Bluff continued to diminish, Grayson, later called Blanding, absorbed most of the exodus.[132]

---

125. San Juan Stake, General Minutes, March 4, 1905.

126. Albert R. Lyman, "To the Family of My Dear Bishop," September 21, 1965, 46.

127. Albert R. Lyman, Journal, May 31, 1905.

128. San Juan Stake General Minutes, July 29, 1905.

129. Albert R. Lyman, "History of San Juan County," 91–92; Shumway, "Blanding." The name of the town was the maiden name of Joseph Lyman's wife.

130. Albert R. Lyman, Journal, July 27, 1905.

131. Albert R. Lyman, "History of San Juan County," 106, 108.

132. The name was changed in 1914 when a wealthy easterner promised a thousand-volume library to any town that adopted his name. The Utah town of Thurber took his last name, Bicknell, but Grayson gave itself his wife's maiden

The bishop's health declined along with the population of his ward. He still limped out to his fields some mornings and pulled an unfortunate weed or two, but that was about all the work he could do anymore.[133] In February 1905, Albert Lyman sent away for an "ear drum outfit" for the aging bishop.[134] Jens's old afflictions continued to bedevil him, and his body swelled with dropsy. By the end of the year it became difficult for him to do anything but sit in a large rocking chair in Elsie's house. After twenty-five years, Jens felt he could no longer perform the duties of bishop. He quietly presented his resignation to his stake president, Walter Lyman, who sent it on to Salt Lake City for [404] approval.[135] From his post in the rocking chair, Jens continued to follow the fortunes and misfortunes of his growing family. Caroline lost another baby after merely a month of life. France's oldest boy, Lisle, died at age eleven due to complications after a broken leg.[136] But Jens also performed a few final ordinances for his grandchildren, confirming three of them into Church membership in the late summer and fall of 1905.

In meetings of the Bluff Ward conference on January 6 and 7, 1906, "Bishop Jens Nielson, owing to his advanced age and failing health [was] tendered his release." It had been approved, as he had insisted all along, by the First Presidency and his stake presidency. Jens had held the position from the first autumn in Bluff, when Erastus Snow called him before the old log meetinghouse was built. Lemuel Redd now became the bishop, with Kumen Jones remaining as first counselor. Francis Nielson was called as the second counselor in the Bluff Ward. Jens told the congregation that the new bishopric was "perfectly satisfactory to him. They were men who had always been faithful to their mission." He recalled some stories from the ward's history then told the Saints in his melodic Danish voice that "he laid down his labors as bishop with a great deal of satisfaction.... He exhorted the saints to be humble and faithful and sustain those called to preside over them."[137]

---

name, Blanding. The two towns split the books, many of which were outdated and abstruse, and kept the names. See McPherson, *History of San Juan County*, 23–24.

133. Leland Redd, "Bishop Jens Nielson," 33.

134. Albert R. Lyman, Journal, February 23, 1905.

135. Bluff Ward, General Minutes, January 6, 1906.

136. Albert R. Lyman, Journal, September 5, 1905.

137. Quotes and facts from Bluff Ward, General Minutes, January 6 and 7, 1906.

As Jens's last days ran out, he remained in the big rocking chair, unable to sleep lying down. His mind stayed lucid to the end. Although confined to the northwest room of [405] Elsie's red brick house, "he seemed to know all that went on in town."[138] Some of it was horrible. May Jones, Kumen's second wife, died from burns she suffered trying to save her home and children from a fire caused by an overturned oil lantern. Mary Jones became the mother of May's eight children, in addition to her own son.[139] But these griefs had to be salved by younger men now.

Jens's mind swept back across his past and found "genuine satisfaction" in how he had converted to the Church in Denmark, crossed the plains, "how he had helped build towns and grown old as a pioneer."[140] The dying man also peered into the future. He seemed ready to find out what came next, speaking "rationally and calmly about the expected change."[141] When Joe's oldest boy, Eddie, visited before leaving on his mission, Jens told him, "Before you return, I will be on the other side, and I will never see you again in mortality. I hope I am good enough to see the Prophet Joseph Smith and some of the other leaders."[142] But his thoughts had not entirely left the earth. A few days before the end, he wondered to those present if there were enough men in town to bury him.[143] As Jens's family gathered about him on his last day, he reviewed his life one more time, "telling them again how the gospel had come to him in his native land, and how he had embraced it and cherished it always through tribulation." He repeated his conviction that [406] Joseph Smith was a prophet of God through whom the gospel had been restored.[144] Jens Nielson died on April 20, 1906, a few days before his eighty-sixth birthday.

Long before, two weeks prior to when he volunteered to be called to the San Juan in 1879, Jens opened the Cedar Ward's fast meeting. He said he was thankful for his association with the Saints of God. He declared "the Lord will have a tried people." "We must school ourselves in the

138. Albert R. Lyman, History of San Juan County, 97.

139. Kumen Jones, "Writings," 46, 151; Gwen Jones, "Kumen Jones."

140. Albert R. Lyman, "History of San Juan County," 97.

141. Albert R. Lyman, "History of San Juan County," 97.

142. Leland Redd, "Bishop Jens Nielson," 33.

143. Albert R. Lyman, "History of San Juan County," 97; Albert R. Lyman, "Bishop Jens Nielson," 15.

144. Albert R. Lyman, "Bishop Jens Nielson," 15–16.

principles of the gospel," he continued. In order for any to do well, "we must observe the counsel of the holy priesthood."[145] These were the same principles he maintained so tenaciously in Bluff. They were what he had learned when he escaped the snows of the Rockies and made a solemn promise he never forgot. "How far I have come short of this promise," he wrote his son Uriah forty-five years later, "I do not know, but I have been called to make six new homes, and, as far as this goes, I have fulfilled my promise."[146] Soon after Bishop Nielson died, his ward members carried his body to its final home in Utah on the hill overlooking Bluff. His will requested a burial lot at least a rod square with a "respectable fence" and "a suitable and respectable headstone or monument."[147] The obelisk marking his grave rises out of Bluff's sandy soil and points toward heaven. [407]

---

145. Cedar Ward General Minutes, January 2, 1879.

146. Jens Nielson, letter to Uriah Nielson, March 20, 1901, 28.

147. Utah District Court, San Juan County, Probate Division, "Probate Records and Register of Estates, 1888–1966," book A, p. 219.

Conclusion

By many accounts, Jens Nielson kept busy after he died. Kumen Jones saw him "in a vision that was so real and so impressive that I can never doubt or deny it, which seemed to cement a friendship of a lifetime."[1] Albert Lyman told of an "unforgettable dream" he had many years before he wrote his history of Bishop Nielson in 1936. The bishop signaled toward symbols representing his sons and impressed on Lyman an obligation for the spiritual welfare of his children.[2] A few days before Elsie died in 1914, she refused to get out of bed. She felt fine but announced that her husband had visited her the night before, and he said he was coming back to get her a few nights later. Sure enough, on the date Elsie indicated, she died from no obvious cause.[3] Kirsten had passed on in 1908.

Five months after Jens Nielson died, Bishop Lemuel Redd and the presidency of the San Juan Stake met with the First Presidency and some of the Quorum of the Twelve in Salt Lake City to discuss Bluff one last time. "It was decided to abandon that place."[4] [409] A month after this often-awaited, unconditional release, the property owners in Bluff met and appointed Bishop Redd, Kumen Jones, Francis Nielson, Hyrum Perkins, and Hanson Bayles as a committee to appraise the town and, if possible, sell it to the United States government as an Indian school. Superintendent William T. Shelton of the Shiprock Navajo Agency and

---

1. Kumen Jones, "Bishop Jens Nielson Sketch," 21.
2. Albert R. Lyman, "Bishop Jens Nielson," 10.
3. Meo, "Uriah and Annie Butt Talk about Elsie Rasmussen," 81.
4. White, *Church, State, and Politics*, 574.

Senator Reed Smoot of Utah seemed supportive of the idea, but the Senate never made the appropriation, and the sale never occurred.[5] The San
Juan River finally claimed the Old Swing Tree during floods in 1907.[6]

The town did not die, though most of the original settlers and their
children left within a decade of Bishop Nielson's passing. Kumen Jones
became bishop after Lemuel Redd was made the stake president in 1909.[7]
An oil boom a few miles down the river in 1908 brought a swell of settlers, but it subsided by 1912.[8] Mormon refugees from the turmoil in the
Mexican colonies came to the county but settled mostly in Blanding and
Monticello. Tourists kept using Bluff as a base camp for their expeditions
to see relics [410] and natural wonders.[9] Federal rangers of the new La Sal
National Forest stepped in to manage and rehabilitate the range.[10] The
Bluff ditch, which had cost at least $150,000 in materials and labor and
an inestimable amount of grief and faith during its precarious existence,
quietly fell into disrepair.[11] Some in Bluff tried to raise lucerne with a
ditch from Cottonwood Wash, but by 1920, less than two hundred acres
were being farmed, and soon after only a few families remained. Many

---

5. See "A Meeting of the Property Owners of Bluff," Minutes, November 7, 1906;
William T. Shelton, letter to Lemuel H. Redd, January 7, 1908; Reed Smoot, letter
to Mr. L. H. Redd Jr., Kumen Jones, and Francis Nielson, December 20, 1907; all
in Lyman, *Lemuel Hardison Redd, Jr.*, 95–102. The town meeting did decide that if
the sale happened, "a substantial fence around the graveyard" would be constructed
from the proceeds before the money was distributed to the landowners.

6. Ross, "I Have Struck It Rich at Last," 31.

7. Bishop Jones served until 1918, making for thirty-eight years straight in the
Bluff Ward bishopric.

8. The 1910 Manuscript Census shows 268 residents in Bluff, more than ever
before. Some of the old settlers were still there, and there were some new Mormon
families. But most of the newcomers were connected with the oil boom and did
not stay long. See McPherson, *History of San Juan County*, 249–51, for the boom.

9. Perkins, Nielson, and Jones, *Saga of San Juan*, 287–92; McPherson, *History
of San Juan County*, 347. Jens's son-in-law Zeke Johnson was the first custodian for
Natural Bridges National Monument after that site northwest of Bluff was set aside
by Theodore Roosevelt in 1908.

10. Albert R. Lyman, "History of San Juan County," 101; Perkins, Nielson, and
Jones, *Saga of San Juan*, 281.

11. Albert R. Lyman, "History of San Juan County," 105.

of the sandstone homes built by the past generation "were left vacant to fall in ruins."[12]

Still the town survived. Automobiles, better roads, clean water, and telephones came to Bluff soon after Jens Nielson died, and eventually even electricity arrived along with a new burst of settlers during the uranium-mining boom in the 1950s.[13] All these things brought a way of life scarcely glimpsed by Bishop Nielson, who had lived in Bluff when it was a mission with pioneer conveniences. Jens threw his whole soul into the town during the last years of his life, and the force of his personality and conviction carried many with him in the uncomfortable determination to stay. But for what ends?

Bluff succeeded partially in the objectives that caused its creation, though all its [411] successes came with a cost. The town held a corner of Zion for Mormon settlement, but was sacrificed in the process. Disappointments with the ditch and competition for the range caused the settlers to spread out, and Bluff became the parent settlement for Monticello, Verdure, and Blanding. But their prosperity came at the parent's expense as population and political power shifted north. The Mormon communities' deeper commitment to the county allowed them to outlast most outside cattle companies and gentile settlers from Colorado. But the Mormons' success in holding the country devastated it as well. The range and its riverbanks were ravaged from overstocking, drought, and erosion.[14] Bluff itself became a respectable town through tremendous effort, but since the settlers stripped the banks of the San Juan, the river undermined that town by becoming increasingly more difficult to tame and washing away many acres of its farms. They were part of the "farming, grazing, and, to a lesser extent, mineral extraction on the San Juan" that have "hastened more erosion than a Pleistocene flood."[15] As was true in other Mormon settlements, the ethic of intensive development of resources let the colonists survive but "made some deserts as well as gardens."[16]

---

12. Albert R. Lyman, "History of San Juan County," 101; Perkins, Nielson, and Jones, *Saga of San Juan*, 84.

13. Pincock, "Time Line"; Perkins, Nielson, and Jones, *Saga of San Juan*, 87; McPherson, *History of San Juan County*, 254–62.

14. For the specific effects, see Aton and McPherson, *River Flowing from the Sunrise*, 68–70.

15. Aton and McPherson, *River Flowing from the Sunrise*, 10.

16. Geary, "For the Strength of the Hills," 81.

Bluff's mission to the Indians was also successful in part. The town's strategic position on the San Juan buffered not just Indian-Mormon relations but also the rivalry [412] between Native Americans that might have resumed if the Navajos had tried their northern expansion directly at the Utes' expense. San Juan County was certainly more peaceful because of Bluff. The settlers were rightfully proud of their pacific record compared with the annual eruptions and murders that happened between Indians and gentile settlers. To the settlers, this was "as marvelous … as any of the miracles of old."[17] Bluff's citizens had responded peacefully to provocations, and they had tried not to provoke the Indians themselves. Over time the Mormons and Indians had developed acquaintances, understandings, and even, in some cases, trust, respect, and friendship. Kumen Jones in his later years declared, "I have become very much prejudiced in favor of the Navajo as a nation."[18] But the Bluff missionaries were never able to significantly convert the Indians to their way of living or to their way of believing. Bluff's residents always wished their neighbors well, but their direct efforts decreased over time.[19] Brother Jones was left to reflect wistfully, "When I … have seen an Indian school completed and in use at Bluff, I will be ready to pass on."[20]

The Native Americans in San Juan County had their own objectives, and Bluff fit into those plans in varying ways. The town presented no obstacle to the expansion of the Navajos' reservation to the south bank of the San Juan River in 1884. It provided a [413] convenient place where Navajos could trade products, hire out their labor, and attend occasional celebrations. If the settlers' desire for dividends raised prices at the co-op store too high, the Navajos could take their trade upriver.[21] Since Bluff

---

17. Kumen Jones, "Writings," 43.

18. Kumen Jones, "Writings," 172.

19. The policy and pattern of Indian interaction as well as the disappointment in the results are similar to those of Brigham Young. See Arrington, *Brigham Young*, chap. 13.

20. Kumen Jones, "Writings," 24.

21. See Aton and McPherson, *River Flowing from the Sunrise*, 71–78, for details of important trading posts on the San Juan. The San Juan Co-op store was apparently fair in its pricing in 1908, when an army officer reported that 950 adult Navajos traded at the co-op, even though only half of them lived within sixty miles of the store. Aton and McPherson, *River Flowing from the Sunrise*, 74.

never boomed as its founders had hoped, the town never tried to expand
south of the San Juan. But when Navajo herders increasingly crossed
north of the river during the droughts of the 1890s and early 1900s,
they came into conflict with those in Bluff. Navajo herders may have
felt they were re-occupying land they had used before in times of want,
but Bluff's stockmen felt the Indians were violating their reservation
and common-law boundary of the San Juan River, and the stockmen
responded with what they felt was justified aggressiveness. But Bluff's
frustration never turned into physical aggression. The Navajos turned
to other allies, the Methodist missionary Howard Antes and the federal
government, and won reservation lands north of the San Juan around
Antes's Aneth mission. On the whole, the northern Navajos were better off because of Bluff's presence, providing a rare example of Indian
expansion during that time.

It was a different story for the Utes and Paiutes. Beneath Bluff's
benevolent demeanor was its inexorable expansion onto the ranges and
into the new settlements farther north. The Utes and Paiutes were slowly
squeezed out of their traditional lives and land. They also turned to the
federal government and the state of Colorado in their competition with
Mormon settlers, but in this case the crusade to convert the county into
[414] a reservation failed. Especially when drought added to their misery,
these tribes increased their demands on Mormon hospitality, and both
sides built up resentments that weren't fully resolved until the collision
called Posey's War in 1923. The Utes and Paiutes became strangers in their
own land, an experience typical of American Indians across the continent.

As the limitations and frustrations of their mission became more
apparent, Bluff's settlers began to look inward more than outward for
the vindication of their efforts. If nothing else, their mission was successful for what it had done to them. The colonists were pleased with
their record in the Church: they had practiced "the full program," paid
full tithing, and sent out a large number of missionaries for such a small
town. Bluff's isolation became a sanctuary for the settlers and their children, with fewer outside influences than most Mormon places.[22] As the
town itself faltered, the townspeople preserved its ideals inside themselves. "Bluff is but a sorry remnant of what might be expected to show

22. Francis A. Hammond, letter to editor, *Deseret News*, December 29, 1886, 798.

for the lives that were worn out with toil to carry it on to its destiny,"
Albert Lyman reflected. But Bluff was "an extraordinary school" to which
people were called for training, and its graduates salted many communities.[23] The unique identity that started with the Hole-in-the-Rock expedition and increased through Bluff's relative isolation became embedded
in the town's legacy and has trickled down through its descendants. [415]

Bluff is an unusually stubborn study in persistence. It reinforces the
idea that even into the twentieth century, some Mormon pioneers were
committed enough to religious ideals to deny themselves the American
dream. But it was always a struggle. The town was settled at that spot
almost by accident but became doggedly defended. The colonists who
feuded with each other during the first land lottery in April 1880 had no
idea that would be the last time people would clamor for land at Bluff.
That awful ditch became the symbol and annual test of their determination to stay where they were and make the desert bloom. But the
pioneers were pragmatic enough to sense not only the faith but the folly
of what they were doing. As Parley Butt put it, only half-jokingly, "I am
pretty familiar with the San Juan River, which I wish I hadn't been."[24]
What was said of the Sanpete settlements would easily be echoed farther
south: "Every man ought to marry a wife from San Juan because, no matter what happens, she's seen worse."[25]

Many reasons accounted for Bluff's improbable ability to overcome
its challenging situation. The group that stayed was a peculiar bunch.
Many of them suffered together through the Hole in the Rock and multiplied that suffering on the ditch. The bonds forged in adversity were
strengthened through celebration and mourning and inscribed in their
institutions. The more they suffered together the more they invested
of themselves in their town. Bishop Nielson was an anchor for their
determination to make all their sacrifice worth something. He also
became a leading [416] example of the delicate balance of steadfastness
and pragmatism that they needed to practice if they were to stay. Kumen
Jones felt that these unusual characters, with "their 'hanging and rattling

---

23. Albert R. Lyman, "Bishop Jens Nielson: The Old Wagon," 76–77.
24. Aton, "River, the Ditch," 18.
25. Geary, "For the Strength of the Hills," 75. Geary also quotes J. Golden Kimball on another marginal settlement. Elder Kimball said that if he had a lot in
St. George and another lot in hell he would sell the lot in St. George.

stickitatutiveness' attracted other 'birds of a feather' so that it looks now
that the better element will prevail over all obstacles."[26] But only a small
minority of those who came through Bluff had the requisite mix to stick
it out.

Other factors were crucial to the town's survival. Bluff's isolation and
adversity kept outsiders away, which helped forge that vital communal
identity. Ironically, the town could survive where it was only with the
help of the Gentiles it tried to keep out of the county. The jobs, products, markets, and credit supplied by the communities in Colorado were
indispensable to Bluff's viability as it weaned itself from the ideal of
the agricultural village and based its life on livestock. Finally, Bluff's
core of settlers found ways to live with each other. They argued at some
point over everything, but underneath the disputes ran a stronger commitment to the greater good. Sometimes it was excruciatingly difficult,
but their leaders provided the incentive and the example to keep their
differences from becoming contentions. In all, as Leonard Arrington
concluded, "The settlement of Bluff is a superb example of the faith that
moves mountains."[27]

But the mountains also modified faith. The town and its residents
changed significantly by 1906. It had started as an idealistic throng of
young families packed [417] together in a fort hoping to live as farmers,
independent of any outside influence but religious direction. By the time
Jens Nielson died, the town had built up into private, usually comfortable
homes, whose residents made their living by various individual enterprises. Some were Republicans and some were Democrats; they got their
grain from Monticello and Colorado, their frills by way of Montgomery
Ward, Colorado merchants, or Salt Lake City, and the money to finance
it all from whatever the national markets would bear for their cattle
and sheep. The transformation in Bluff was its own particular chapter
in something that was happening throughout the Mormon settlements.
As opportunities increased and persecution withdrew, the siege men-
tality of Mormonism departed. Without outside pressure, cooperation
and economic independence no longer seemed so crucial. As with many
old ideals, they continued to be preached often and saluted regularly

---

26. Kumen Jones, "Writings," 217.

27. Arrington, *Utah's Audacious Stockman*, 19.

but practiced less. Mormons' social patterns became more recognizable to the rest of the country, shifting from "staunch communitarianism to modified individualism," and their peculiarity took refuge in their religious beliefs.[28]

Viewed in human terms, the "affair on the San Juan" was a tragic waste.[29] The Church's cooperation and organization as well as its leaders' charisma and moral pressure held people to a life of privation and labor far longer than they would have withstood it on their own. In this sense, it was a fitting continuation of the Hole-in-the-Rock trek, the heroic quest that led ultimately to more of the same prolonged, slow-motion struggling in [418] Bluff.[30] But the same argument could be made against the entire Mormon exodus of the nineteenth century. These people were not, in general, trying to move up to a nicer neighborhood. Prosperity was welcomed and often seen as a sign of God's favor. But it was supposed to be a consequence, not a goal, and could create its own mischief. Instead, the majority of those who moved to Bluff believed, as Jens Nielson did, that it was "the voice of the Lord" for them to go.[31] But even within this spiritual context, spiritual men such as Bishop Nielson, Platte Lyman, Francis Hammond, and the General Authorities of the Church never entirely agreed on whether Bluff was worth the sacrifices required to keep it. Those who stayed with Bishop Nielson were out-voted by many more who left Bluff but not Mormonism. Although the question cannot be ultimately answered on this side of the grave, those who stayed felt they had their reward. While their faith impelled them to reside in such a harsh environment, struggling against that environment strengthened their faith.[32] Even though most of the stalwarts groused while they were there and left Bluff as soon as they felt it was spiritually safe to do so, when they balanced accounts in their minds, they found, as did their bishop, great satisfaction rather than great bitterness at the bottom of their experiences.

Even in human terms, those who lived in Bluff found compensation for their extreme and prolonged labors. From the distance of over a

28. Ridge, "Mormon 'Deliverance,'" 148.
29. The epithet is from Platte D. Lyman, "Diary," November 2, 1884.
30. Peterson, *Look to the Mountains*, 37.
31. Cedar Ward General Minutes, October 19, 1879.
32. O'Dea, "Effects of Geographical Position," 358.

century, Bluff reminds us of a [419] time when people with few conveniences labored for something besides abundance. A stone home, a shingled roof, a cushioned buggy passed for luxuries in the town's early years,
but water in the ditch, "a good time had by all," and a day when the sand
stayed still were at least as valuable. Community meant more than living
near each other; it was a common commitment to resolve differences
and pursue cooperative goals. The Bluff Saints lived in an unusual environment, even for their times, and accomplished unusual things. The fact
that changing circumstances eroded their communal values and pitched
the town into the stream of modernity does not eliminate this toilsome
attempt to construct an alternative to the American dream. Modern
society would not trade its luxuries or its privacy with Bluff, but sometimes it longs for what it left behind: the strong community and sense
of shared purpose. To insist on these values at the expense of comfort is
difficult. Even back in those days, there were few like the stubborn old
Dane who would not leave. [420]

Bluff Population Statistics

Profile of Bluff and Montezuma Population, June 1880

Total population: 193

107 at Bluff and 86 at Montezuma (according to 1880 Manuscript Census, though more probably lived in Bluff and less in Montezuma according to what Platte Lyman wrote in his diary about who lived where)

Age and Gender

Men (% of males/total pop.)	Women (% of females/total pop.)	Total (% of total pop.)
		60–69: 2 (1.0)
60–69: 2 (2.1/1.0)	60–69: 0 (0.0/0.0)	50–59: 1 (0.5)
50–59: 1 (1.1/0.5)	50–59: 0 (0.0/0.0)	40–49: 9 (4.7)
40–49: 4 (4.3/2.1)	40–49: 5 (5.1/2.6)	30–39: 16 (8.3)
30–39: 11 (11.7/5.7)	30–39: 5 (5.1/2.6)	20–29: 53 (27.5)
20–29: 29 (30.9/15.0)	20–29: 24 (24.2/12.4)	10–19: 31 (16.1)
10–19: 13 (13.9/6.7)	10–19: 18 (18.2/9.3)	15–19: 17
15–19: 6	15–19: 11	10–14: 14
10–14: 7	10–14: 7	0–9: 81 (42.0)
0–9: 34 (36.2/17.6)	0–9: 47 (47.5/24.4)	5–9: 32
5–9: 10	5–9: 22	2–4: 24
2–4: 10	2–4: 14	0–1: 25
0–1: 14	0–1: 11	30+: 28 (14.5)
30+: 18 (19.1/9.3)	30+: 10 (10.1/5.2)	20+: 81 (42.0)
20+: 47 (50.0/24.4)	20+: 34 (36.4/18.7)	under 20: 112 (58.0)
under 20: 47 (50.0/24.4)	under 20: 65 (65.7/33.7)	Total: 193
Total: 94 (48.7)	Total: 99 (51.3)	

average age: 17.5, median: 15.5

% under 15: 49.2

Place of Birth

Foreign Born (% of age group)	Born Elsewhere in U.S. (% of age group)	Born in Utah (% of age group)
60–69: 1 of 2 (50)	60–69: 1 of 2 (50)	60–69: 0 of 2 (0)
50–59: 0 of 1 (0)	50–59: 1 of 1 (100)	50–59: 0 of 1 (0)
40–49: 6 of 9 (67)	40–49: 3 of 9 (33)	40–49: 0 of 9 (0)
30–39: 9 of 16 (56)	30–39: 5 of 16 (31)	30–39: 2 of 16 (13)
20–29: 11 of 53 (21)	20–29: 4 of 53 (8)	20–29: 38 of 53 (72)
10–19: 3 of 31 (10)	10–19: 0 of 31 (0)	10–19: 28 of 31 (90)
0–9: 1 of 81 (1)	0–9: 0 of 81	0–10: 80 of 81 (99)
30+: 16 of 28 (57)	*30+: 10 of 28 (36)*	*30+: 2 of 28 (7)*
20+: 28 of 81 (35)	*20+: 16 of 81 (20)*	*20+39 of 81 (46)*
below 20: 4 of 112 (4)	*below 20: 0 of 112 (0)*	*below 20: 109 of 112 (97)*
Total: 32 (17)	Total: 14 (7)	Total: 147 (76)

Places of Birth of Foreign Born

England: 19 (59% of foreign born/10% of total population)
Wales: 5 (16/3)
Scotland: 1 (3/1)
British Isles: 25 (78/13)
Australia: 1 (3/1)
Denmark: 5 (16/3)
Switzerland: 1 (3/1)

Families

Marriages

36 married couples (including two marriages of James Harvey Dunton)
average age of husband: 31.4, average age of wife: 28.3
average length of marriage 7.94 years
average age at marriage, men: 23.4, women: 19.8
children (under 15) per marriage: 2.6
polygamous families, both families in Bluff or Montezuma: 2 (5.6%)
polygamous families, one family in Bluff or Montezuma: 2 (5.6%)
residents in polygamous family: 23 of 193 (12%)

Households

44 households, 35 with married couples (77%)
average size of household: 4.4

5 households with a single man; 4 with a married man whose family was somewhere else
7 singles living with relatives, no single above 24 yrs. old.

Those who were in the Hole-in-the-Rock expedition but not in 1880 census
who later returned: Hanson Bayles, Willard Butt, Amasa Barton, Sarah Harriman,
and possibly the Gurrs and Barneys (church records list ordinances performed later
than 1880 in Bluff).

Profiles of Bluff and Montezuma Population, 1884

Total Population:
January 1, 1884: 245 population; 117 men 128 women (47.8%/52.2%)
    average age: 17.91 years old
December 31, 1884: 79 population; 36 men 43 women (45.6%/54.4%);
    average age: 21.63 years old
173 left Bluff and Montezuma during the year; 85 men 88 women (49.1%/50.9%)
    average age: 16.92 years old (measuring from Dec. 31 1884)
3 deaths (2 male/1 female), 10 births (7/3) during the year

January 1, 1884

Age and Gender

Men (% of males/total pop.)	Women (% of females/total pop.)	Total (% of total pop.)
		60–69: 4 (1.6)
60–69: 3 (2.6/1.2)	60–69: 1 (0.8/0.4)	50–59: 5 (2.0)
50–59: 2 (1.7/0.8)	50–59: 3 (2.3/1.2)	40–49: 12 (4.9)
40–49: 5 (4.2/2.0)	40–49: 7 (5.5/2.9)	30–39: 26 (8.2)
30–39: 15 (12.8/6.1)	30–39: 11 (8.6/4.5)	20–29: 49 (20.0)
20–29: 22 (18.8/9.0)	20–29: 27 (21.1/11.0)	10–19: 44 (18.0)
10–19: 21 (18.0/8.6)	10–19: 23 (18.0/ 9.4)	15–19: 17
15–19: 11	15–19: 6	10–14: 27
10–14: 10	10–14: 17	0–9: 105 (42.9)
0–9: 49 (41.9/20.0)	0–9: 56 (43.8/22.9)	5–9: 38
5–9: 14	5–9: 24	2–4: 36
2–4: 18	2–4: 18	0–1: 30
0–1: 16	0–1: 14	*30+: 46 (18.8)*
30+: 25 (21.4/10.2)	*30+: 22 (17.2/9.0)*	*20+: 93 (40.0)*
20+: 47 (40.2/19.2)	*20+: 49 (38.3/20.0)*	*under 20: 149 (60.8)*
under 20: 70 (59.8/28.6)	*under 20: 79 (61.2/32.2)*	Total: 245
Total: 117 (47.8)	Total: 128 (52.2)	

average age: 17.91, median 12
% below 15: 52.8%

Place of Birth

Foreign Born (% of age group)	Born Elsewhere in U.S. (% of age group)	Born in Utah (% of age group)
60–69: 4 of 4 (100)	60–69: 0 of 4 (0)	60–69: 0 of 4 (0)
50–59: 3 of 5 (60)	50–59: 2 of 5 (40)	50–59: 0 of 5 (0)
40–49: 8 of 12 (67)	40–49: 4 of 12 (33)	40–49: 0 of 11 (0)
30–39: 16 of 26 (62)	30–39: 5 of 26 (19)	30–39: 5 of 26 (19)
20–29: 8 of 49 (16)	20–29: 0 of 49 (0)	20–29: 41 of 49 (84)
10–19: 1 of 44 (2)	10–19: 1 of 44 (2)	10–19: 42 of 44 (96)
0–9: 0 of 105 (0)	0–9: 1 of 105 (1)	0–9: 104 of 105 (99)
30+: 31 of 46 (67)	*30+: 10 of 46 (22)*	*30+: 5 of 46 (11)*
20+: 39 of 95 (41)	*20+: 10 of 95 (11)*	*20+: 46 of 95 (48)*
under 20: 1 of 149 (1)	*under 20: 2 of 149 (1)*	*under 20: 146 of 149 (98)*
Total: 40 (16)	Total: 13 (5)	Total: 192 (78)

Places of Birth of Foreign Born

England: 16 (40.0% of foreign born/6.5% of total population)
Wales: 6 (15.4/2.5)
Scotland: 4 (10.3/1.7)
Ireland: 1 (2.6/0.4)
British Isles: 26 (66.7/10.9)
Australia: 1 (2.6/0.4)
Denmark: 10 (25.6/4.2)
Germany: 1 (2.6/0.4)
Sweden: 1 (2.6/0.4)

Families

Marriages

married couples: 48
average age of husband: 36.3; average age of wife: 31.9
average length of marriage: 12.2 years
average age at marriage, men: 24.1, women: 19.7
children (under 15) per marriage: 2.8
polygamous families, both families in Bluff or Montezuma: 14 of 48 (29.2%)
polygamous families, one family in Bluff or Montezuma: 2 of 48 (4.2%)
residents in polygamous family: 65 (26.5%)

Households

c. 48 households, c. 46 with married couples (95.8%)
average size of household: 5.1
three single men without parents in town, all twenty-six years old, two have broth-
    ers in town

Those Who Left in 1884 (figures as of 12/31/84)

Age and Gender

Men (% of males/total pop.)	Women (% of females/total pop.)	Total (% of total pop.)
		60–69: 0 (0.0)
60–69: 0 (0.0/0.0)	60–69: 0 (0.0/0.0)	50–59: 4 (2.3)
50–59: 2 (2.4/1.1)	50–59: 2 (2.3/1.1)	40–49: 10 (5.8)
40–49: 7 (8.2/4.0)	40–49: 3 (3.4/1.7)	30–39: 20 (11.6)
30–39: 10 (11.8/5.8)	30–39: 10 (1.1/5.8)	20–29: 28 (16.2)
20–29: 11 (12.9/6.4)	20–29: 17 (19.3/9.8)	10–19: 28 (16.2)
10–19: 11 (12.9/6.4)	10–19: 17 (19.3/9.8)	15–19: 7
15–19: 4	15–19: 3	10–14: 21
10–14: 7	10–14: 14	0–9: 83 (48.0)
0–9: 43 (50.6/24.9)	0–9: 40 (45.5/23.1)	5–9: 38
5–9: 19	5–9: 19	2–4: 36
2–4: 18	2–4: 11	0–1: 30
0–1: 6	0–1: 10	30+: 34 (19.7)
30+: 19 (22.4/11.0)	30+: 15 (17.0/8.7)	20+: 62 (35.8)
20+: 30 (35.3/17.3)	20+: 32 (36.4/18.5)	under 20: 111 (64.2)
under 20: 55 (64.7/31.8)	under 20: 56 (63.6/32.4)	Total: 173
Total: 85 (49.1)	Total: 88 (50.9)	

average age: 16.92 years
% below 15: 63.6%

Place of Birth

Foreign Born (% of age group)	Born Elsewhere in U.S. (% of age group)	Born in Utah (% of age group)
60–69: 0 of 0 (0)	60–69: 0 of 0 (0)	60–69: 0 of 0 (0)
50–59: 2 of 4 (50)	50–59: 2 of 4 (50)	50–59: 0 of 4 (0)
40–49: 7 of 10 (70)	40–49: 3 of 10 (30)	40–49: 0 of 10 (0)
30–39: 12 of 20 (60)	30–39: 3 of 20 (15)	30–39: 5 of 20 (25)
20–29: 7 of 28 (25)	20–29: 0 of 28 (0)	20–29: 21 of 28 (75)
10–19: 1 of 28 (4)	10–19: 1 of 28 (4)	10–19: 26 of 28 (93)
0–9: 0 of 83 (0)	0–9: 1 of 83 (1)	0–9: 82 of 83 (99)
30+: 21 of 34 (62)	*30+: 8 of 34 (24)*	*30+: 5 of 34 (15)*
20+: 28 of 62 (45)	*20+: 8 of 62 (13)*	*20+: 26 of 62 (42)*
under 20: 1 of 111 (1)	*under 20: 2 of 111 (2)*	*under 20: 108 of 111 (97)*
Total: 29 (17)	Total: 10 (6)	Total: 134 (77)

Places of Birth of Foreign Born

England: 16 (55% of foreign born/9% of total population)
Wales: 4 (14/2)
British Isles: 20 (69/12)
Denmark: 7 (24/4)
Australia: 1 (3/1)
Sweden: 1 (3/1)

Families

Marriages

married couples: 30
average age of husband: 34.3; average age of wife: 29.6
average length of marriage: 11.8
average age at marriage, men: 22.5; women: 18.8
children (under 15) per marriage: 3.5
polygamous families, both families in Bluff or Montezuma: 5 of 30 (16.7%)
polygamous families, one family in Bluff or Montezuma: 1 of 30 (3.3%)
residents in polygamous family: 17 (9.8%)

Households

c. 30 households with 30 married couples
average size of household: 5.8
1 single man, no immediate family

Departures

percent of population that left in 1884: 173 of 245 (70.6%).

1884 co-op total stock declined from $1,700 to $700 (59.8% drop)

amount in co-op per emigrant 20 and over: $11.29

    per male 20 and over: $23.33

amount in co-op per settler over 20 who remained in Bluff: $18.42

    per male 20 and over: $38.89

Numbers lost (% of age group—ages as of 1/1/84)

60–69: 0 of 4 (0%)

50–59: 4 of 5 (80%)

40–49: 10 of 12 (83.3%)

30–39: 20 of 26 (76.9%)

20–29: 28 of 49 (57.1%)

10–19: 28 of 44 (63.6%)

0–9: 83 of 105 (79.0%)

Total: 173 of 245 (70.6%)

Those Who Stayed in 1884 (figures as of 12/31/84)

Age and Gender

Men (% of males/total pop.)	Women (% of females/total pop.)	Total (% of total pop.)
		60–69: 4 (5.1)
60–69: 3 (8.3/3.8)	60–69: 1 (2.4/1.3)	50–59: 4 (5.1)
50–59: 1 (2.8/1.3)	50–59: 3 (7.0/3.8)	40–49: 2 (2.5)
40–49: 0 (0/0)	40–49: 2 (4.9/2.5)	30–39: 5 (6.3)
30–39: 3 (8.3/3.8)	30–39: 2 (4.9/2.5)	20–29: 23 (29.1)
20–29: 11 (30.6/13.9)	20–29: 12 (29.3/15.2)	10–19: 18 (22.8)
10–19: 10 (27.8/12.7)	10–19: 8 (19.5/10.1)	15–19: 8
15–19: 6	15–19: 2	10–14: 10
10–14: 4	10–14: 6	0–9: 23 (29.1)
0–9: 8 (22.2/10.1)	0–9: 15 (36.6/19.0)	5–9: 9
5–9: 1	5–9: 8	2–4: 7
2–4: 3	2–4: 4	0–1: 7
0–1: 4	0–1: 3	30+: 15 (19.0)
30+: 7 (19.4/8.9)	30+: 8 (19.5/10.1)	20+: 38 (48.1)
20+: 18 (50.0, 22.8)	20+: 20 (48.8/25.3)	*under 20:* 41 (51.9)
under 20: 18 (50.0/22.8)	*under 20:* 23 (51.2/29.1)	Total: 79
Total: 36 (45.6)	Total: 43 (54.4)	

average age 21.63 yrs. old
percentage of population under 15: 42.8%

Place of Birth

Foreign Born (% of age group)	Born Elsewhere in U.S. (% of age group)	Born in Utah (% of age group)
60–69: 4 of 4 (100)	60–69: 0 of 4 (0)	60–69: 0 of 4 (0)
50–59: 2 of 4 (50)	50–59: 2 of 4 (50)	50–59: 0 of 4 (0)
40–49: 2 of 2 (100)	40–49: 0 of 2 (0)	40–49: 0 of 2 (0)
30–39: 2 of 5 (40)	30–39: 1 of 5 (20)	30–39: 2 of 5 (40)
20–29: 1 of 23 (4)	20–29: 0 of 23 (0)	20–29: 22 of 23 (96)
10–19: 0 of 18 (0)	10–19: 0 of 18 (0)	10–19: 18 of 18 (100)
0–9: 0 of 23 (0)	0–9: 0 of 23 (0)	0–9: 23 of 23 (100)
30+: 10 of 15 (67)	*30+: 3 of 15 (20)*	*30+: 2 of 15 (13)*
20+: 11 of 38 (29)	*20+: 3 of 28 (8)*	*20+: 24 of 38 (63)*
under 20: 0 of 41 (0)	*under 20: 0 of 41 (0)*	*under 20: 41 of 41 (100)*
Total: 11 (14)	Total: 3 (4)	Total: 65 (82)

Place of Birth of Foreign Born

England: 1 (9% of foreign born/1% of total population)
Wales: 2 (18/3)
Scotland: 4 (36/5)
Ireland: 1 (9/1)
British Isles 8 (73/10)
Denmark: 2 (18/3)
Germany: 1 (9/1)

Families

Marriages

married couples: 18
average age of husband: 37.6; average age of wife: 33.5
average length of marriage: 13.6 years
children (under 15) per marriage: 1.83
polygamous families, both families in Bluff: 6 (33%)
polygamous families, one family in Bluff: 3 (17%)
residents in polygamous families: 36 (45.6%)

Households

c. 18 households with 18 married couples
average size of household: 4.4
1 single man, brother also in town

Profile of Bluff's Population, 1900 Census

Total Population: 193

Age and Gender

Men (% of males/total pop.)	Women (% of females/total pop.)	Total (% of total pop.)
70–79: 3 (3.2/1.6)	70–79: 1 (1.0/0.5)	70–79: 4 (2.1)
60–69: 0 (0.0/0.0)	60–69: 3 (3.0/1.6)	60–69: 3 (1.6)
50–59: 5 (5.4/2.6)	50–59: 3 (3.0/1.6)	50–59: 8 (4.1)
40–49: 12 (13.0/6.2)	40–49: 8 (7.9/4.1)	40–49: 20 (10.4)
30–39: 12 (13.0/6.2)	30–39: 6 (5.9/3.1)	30–39: 18 (9.3)
20–29: 10 (10.9/5.2)	20–29: 17 (16.8/8.8)	20–29: 27 (14.0)
10–19: 24 (26.1/12/4)	10–19: 28 (27.7/14.5)	10–19: 52 (27.0)
15–19: 10	15–19: 11	15–19: 21
10–14: 14	10–14: 17	10–14: 31
0–9: 26 (28.3/13.5)	0–9: 35 (34.7/18.1)	0–9: 61 (31.6)
5–9: 17	5–9: 13	5–9: 30
2–4: 6	2–4: 15	2–4: 21
0–1: 3	0–1: 7	0–1: 10
30+: 32 (34.8/16.6)	*30+: 21 (21.0/10.9)*	*30+: 53 (27.5)*
20+: 42 (45.7/21.8)	*20+: 38 (37.6/19.7)*	*20+: 80 (41.5)*
under 20: 50 (54.3/25.9)	*under 20: 63 (62.4/32.6)*	*under 20: 113 (58.5)*
Total: 92 (100/47.7)	Total: 101 (100/52.3)	Total: 193

average age: 21.5, median age: 16

% under 15: 47.7

Place of Birth

Foreign Born (% of age group)	Born Elsewhere in U.S. (% of age group)	Born in Utah (% of age group)
70–79: 4 of 4 (100)	70–79: 0 of 4 (0)	70–79: 0 of 4 (0)
60–69: 3 of 3 (100)	60–69: 0 of 3 (0)	60–69: 0 of 3 (0)
50–59: 2 of 8 (25)	50–59: 6 of 8 (75)	50–59: 0 of 8 (0)
40–49: 2 of 20 (10)	40–49: 6 of 20 (30)	40–49: 12 of 20 (60)
30–39: 3 of 18 (17)	30–39: 4 of 18 (22)	30–39: 11 of 18 (61)
20–29: 0 of 27 (0)	20–29: 5 of 27 (19)	20–29: 22 of 27 (81)
10–19: 0 of 52 (0)	10–19: 3 of 52 (6)	10–19: 49 of 52 (94)
0–9: 0 of 61 (0)	0–9: 7 of 61 (11)	0–10: 54 of 61 (89)
30+: 13 of 53 (25)	*30+: 16 of 53 (30)*	*30+: 24 of 53 (45)*
20+: 14 of 80 (18)	*20+: 21 of 80 (26)*	*20+: 45 of 80 (56)*
below 20: 0 of 113 (0)	*below 20: 10 of 113 (9)*	*below 20: 103 of 113 (91)*
Total: 14 (7)	Total: 31 (16)	Total: 148 (77)

Places of Birth of Foreign Born

Denmark and Scotland: 4 each (29% of foreign born/ 2% of total population)
Wales: 2 (14/1)
England, Germany, Switzerland, Ireland: 1 (7/0.5)

Families

Marriages

31 families
average age of husband: 47.4, average age of wife: 41.4
average length of marriage 18.7
average age at marriage, men: 28.7, women: 22.7
children (under 15) per marriage: 3.0
polygamous families, both families in Bluff: 5 (16%)
polygamous families, one family in Bluff or Montezuma: 2 (7%)
residents in polygamous families: 62 of 193 (32%)

Households

38 total households, average size: 5.2 people
23 households with married couples (2 of these households had 2 plural-marriage
    wives living in the same residence)
8 households with single men or migrant workers
5 households with plural-marriage wives living separately from their husbands
2 households with absent fathers
5 people (4 men, 1 woman) boarding with Bluff families
17 people non-Mormon (mostly cowboys and stock herders)

Note: figures in charts sometimes total more than 100% due to rounding

Sources:

U.S. Manuscript Census, 1880 and 1900
Bluff Ward Records
Ancestral File on FamilySearch.com
people mentioned in documentary sources

After Hole in the Rock: What Happened to the Members of the Expedition

* = returned to live in Bluff later

1. Those who never intended to settle in the San Juan Mission (and where they went):

Milton and Wilson Dailey and their families (Colorado)
Thomas Box (Colorado)
Mons Larson and his family (Snowflake, Arizona)
probably David Alma Stevens, James Edwards Stevens, as well as Walter Joshua and Elizabeth Kenney Stevens (Snowflake, Arizona, Holden, Colorado, or New Mexico)

2. Those who assisted family members on the trek then returned to their homes soon after (relation in parentheses):

Amasa Miles Barton* (brother of Joseph F. Barton)
George William Decker (son of Zachariah Decker Sr., brother of Zachariah Decker Jr., James Bean Decker, and Nathaniel Alvin Decker)
Amasa Lyman (half brother of Platte Lyman and Joseph Lyman)
Edward Lyman (brother of Platte Lyman and Joseph Lyman)
Rasmus Mickelsen (father of Peter Mickelsen and Anna Mickelsen Decker)
Peter Nelson (brother-in-law of George Urie)
James Monroe Redd* (brother of Lemuel Hardison Redd, Jr.)
Lemuel Hardison Redd, Sr.* (father of Lemuel Hardison Redd, Jr.)
Reuben Sevy (son of George Sevy from his first marriage)
George Henry Westover (brother of Eliza Ann Westover Redd)
Thomas Williams (brother of Mary Ann Williams Perkins and Sarah Williams)

3. Those who left before June 1880 (or who were not there for the census and did not return for long afterward) for unknown reasons (and where they went):

Noah Barnes (unknown)
Danielson Buren Barney and family* (unknown, possibly Arizona)
Samuel Bryson (unknown)
Marius Ensign Dunton and family (unknown)
William Eyre (returned to Parowan)
Isaac Haight and Caleb Haight (Cedar City)
David and Sarah Jane Hunter* (returned to Cedar City)
James Lewis (Taylor, Arizona)
George Morrell (unknown)
Peter and Hannah Mariah Mortensen (possibly Colorado)
Adam Franklin Robb and family (Animas, Colorado)
George Drummond Robb and family (returned to Paragonah, Utah)
John Robb and family (Mancos, Colorado)
William Robb and family* (returned to Paragonah)
George Sevy and family (returned to Panguitch)
Samuel Smith (unknown)
Edward Taylor and Warren Taylor (unknown)
George and Alice Jane Urie (returned to Cedar City)
Joseph Walker (unknown)
Francis Webster (probably returned to Cedar City)
Joseph Smith Woolsey* (returned to Panguitch)
Henry Wilson (unknown)

4. Those who left by the end of 1881 (and where they went):

Zachariah B. Decker, Sr. (possibly Parowan)
Zachariah B. Decker, Jr. and family (Snowflake, Arizona)
William Hutchings and family (returned to Beaver)
John Peter Jensen and family (Taylor, Arizona)
William Goddard and family (Colorado)
Sidney Goddard (unknown)
William Heber Gurr and family (Parowan)
James Wilkerson Pace and family (returned to Panguitch)
John Robinson (returned to Paragonah)
Silas S. Smith, Sr. and family (Manassa, Colorado)
Silas S. Smith, Jr. and family (Manassa, Colorado)
John Aikens Smith and family (Manassa, Colorado)
William Warren Taylor, Jr. (unknown)

5. Those who may have left by the end of 1881 and were definitely gone by the end of 1883 (and where they went):

James Harvey Dunton and families (Mancos, Colorado)
Hyrum Fielding and family (Mancos, Colorado)
John and Harriet Gower (Cedar City)
George Hobbs (eventually Nephi)
Henry Holyoak and family (returned to Paragonah, then Moab)
George Lewis (unknown)
Joseph W. Lillywhite and family (Woodruff, Arizona)
Wilford Woodruff Pace (unknown)
James Riley and family (returned to Beaver)
Jacob Roner (Bryner? Roper?) (unknown)
Joseph Stanford Smith and family (Mancos, Colorado)
George Henry Westover (possibly returned to New Harmony)
George Westwood (probably returned to Beaver)

6. These are the families that left sometime in 1884 for at least a year (with the total number in their family and their destination):

Danielson and Laura Barney (10, Thatcher, Arizona)
Hanson and Mary Ann Bayles* (4, probably Cedar City or Parowan)
Samuel and Sarah Cox (3, Emery County, Utah)
James and Elisabeth Davis (came with 1879 expedition, 9, Bear Lake, Utah)
Cornelius and Elizabeth Decker (6, Snowflake, Arizona)
James Cyrus and Eliza Dunton (4, possibly Paragonah, Utah)
Henry and Elizabeth Harriman (came with 1879 expedition, 5, Huntington, Utah)
David and Sarah Jane Hunter* (returned to Cedar City)
Joseph and Nellie Lyman* (3, Oak City, Utah)
Platte and Adelia Lyman* (6, Oak City then Scipio, Utah)
Samuel and Adelia Mackelprang (10, Huntington, Utah)
John and Paulina Pace (6, Huntington, Utah)
Benjamin and Mary Ann and Sarah Perkins* (11, Cedar City, later to Monticello)
William and Ellen Robb (3, maybe Paragonah)
Samuel and Ann Rowley (9, Huntington, Utah)
Joseph and Mary Woolsey (8, Arizona).

Others who left in 1884 for at least a year who were not members of the Hole-in-the-Rock expedition:

John, Jr. and Jennie Allan* (6, Burnham, New Mexico)
Nephi and Annie Bailey* (6, probably returned to Cedar City, Utah)
Lars and Anna Christensen (7, returned to Richfield, Utah)
David and Eliza Edwards (3, returned to Paragonah)

Brigham and Johanna Harrison (3, Manassa, Colorado)
William and Mary Ann Hyde (3, Riverview, Utah or Colorado)
Frederic and Mary Jones* (5, probably Cedar City, Utah)
George Ipson (1, possibly Emery County, Utah)
Lars and Mattie Jensen (9, Richfield, Utah)
Orren and Emeretta Kelsey (9, New Harmony, Utah)
Peter and Harriet and Ida Mickelsen (8, possibly Manassa, Colorado)
Elsie and Julia Nielson* (2, Cedar City, Utah)
Job and Martha Jane Openshaw (4, Moab)
Thomas and Margaret Rowley (4, Huntington, Utah)
Samuel and Josephine Wood* (6, probably Cedar City)

One of the reasons so many of the families that left in 1884 went to Huntington was that the Denver & Rio Grande ran through there starting in 1883, making it one of the more accessible new communities by way of Durango.

7. Those who left by 1900 (and where they went):

Parley Rogerson Butt (about 1888, Verdure)
Nathaniel Alvin Decker and family (about 1889, Mancos, Colorado)
Lemuel Hardison Redd, Sr. (about 1890, Colonia Juarez, Mexico)
Charles E. Walton and family (1888, Monticello)

8. Those who left later than 1900 (married name, when and where they went)

Joseph Franklin Barton (1908, Monticello)
Harriett Eliza Barton (1905, Moab)
Mary Viola Barton (1906, Moab)
Ole Hanson Bayles (1908, Blanding)
Anna Lillian Decker (Wood, 1904, Monticello)
Anna Marie Mickelsen Decker (after 1910, Monticello)
Lena Deseret Decker (Hammond, 1901, probably Moab)
Nancy Genevieve Decker (Wood, 1905, Monticello)
Kumen and Mary Nielson Jones (after 1920, Blanding)
Ida Evalyn Lyman (Nielson, 1913, Blanding)
Caroline Nielson (Redd, 1909, Blanding)
Francis Nielson (c. 1915, Blanding)
Jens Peter Nielson (1908, Blanding)
Julia Nielson (Butt, after 1920, possibly Blanding)
Lucinda Nielson (Hyde, after 1917, Salt Lake City)
Margaret Nielson (Adams, between 1910 and 1920, Blanding)
George William Perkins (about 1912, Blanding)
Rachel Corry Perkins (after 1920, probably Blanding)
James Monroe Redd and family (1905, Monticello)

Lemuel Hardison Redd, Jr. and family (1914, Blanding)
Sarah Williams (Perkins, 1907, Monticello)

9. Those who died in Bluff (and year of death):

Amasa Miles Barton (1887)
Harriett A. Richards Barton (1896)
Willard George Butt (1919)
James Bean Decker (1901)
Lydia May Lyman (1906)
Jens Nielson (1906)
Joe Nielson (1903)
Kirsten Nielson (1908)
Hyrum Perkins (1917)
Roswell Stevens (1880)

My estimates of who went where come from the lists of Hole-in-the-Rock pioneers from Miller, *Hole in the Rock*, 142–147; Perkins, Nielson, and Jones, *Saga of San Juan*, 346–347; and Crabtree, *Incredible Mission*, 146–154; also the 1880 Manuscript Census for San Juan County, Bluff Ward records, Personal Ancestral Files on FamilySearch.org, and mentions of these people in the documentary sources.

Photographs

All pictures from "Jens Nielson History" CD-ROM and San Juan county Historical Commission.

Figure 1. Jens and Kirsten Nielson Family, Cedar City, c. 1878. *Left to right with ages at the end of 1878:* Cindy, 6; Jens, 58; Jens Peter, 16; Caroline, 4; Joe, 18; Margaret, 14; Kirsten, 44; France, 10.

Figure 2. Jens Nielson

Figure 3. Bluff Ward Bishopric. *Left to right:* Kumen Jones, 1st Counselor; Bishop Jens Nielson; Lemuel Hardison Redd, Jr., 2nd Counselor

Map D

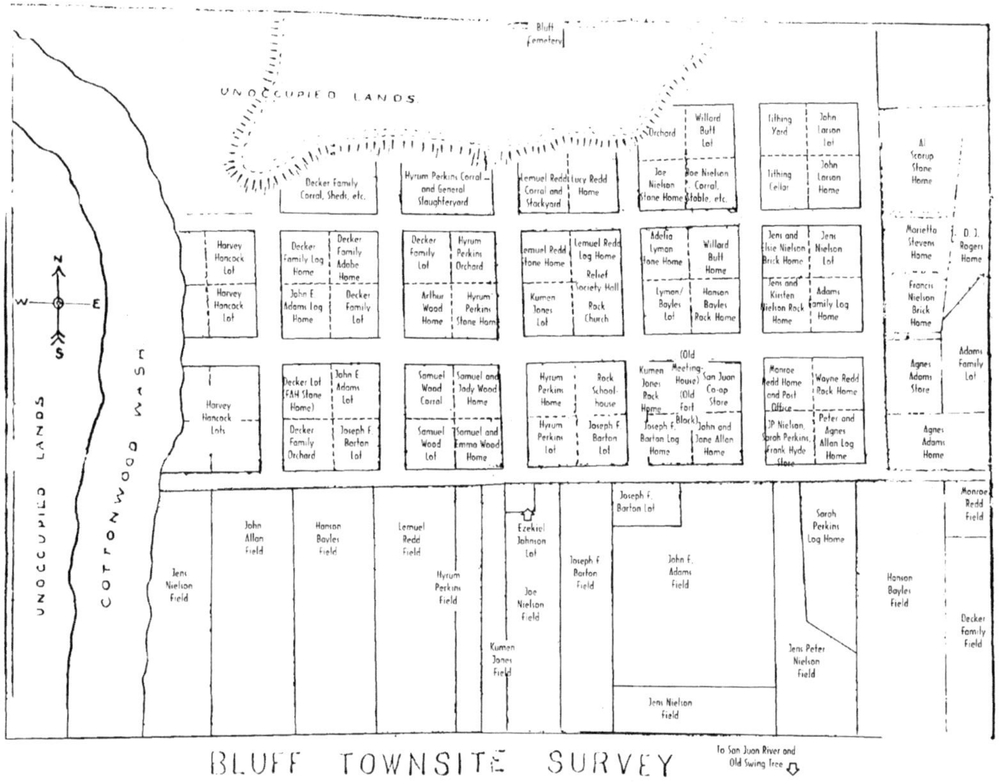

BLUFF TOWNSITE SURVEY

Map 1. Bluff, Utah, 1903, Modified Survey (page 469). I have taken the 1903 survey plat from Bryant L. Jensen, "An Historical Study of Bluff City, Utah, 1880–1906" (M.A. thesis, Brigham Young University, 1966), 37, and placed the names of the landholders in their properties. The sources for who owned what are Utah District Court, San Juan County, April 21, 1903, BYU, and Albert R. Lyman, "Accounts of the Homes of Bluff, 1890–1900," 1970, USHS.

Sources Consulted

Unpublished Works

Spelling and punctuation have been modernized in quoted material, unless the original version added meaning to the message of the document.

Abbreviations

BYU: L. Tom Perry Special Collections, Harold B. Lee Library, Brigham Young University, Provo, Utah.

FHL: Family History Library, Harold B. Lee Library, Brigham Young University, Provo, Utah.

JNCD: "Jens Nielson History" CD-ROM. Eds. Mike Halliday and Donna Jensen.

CHL: Archives of the Church of Jesus Christ of Latter-day Saints, Salt Lake City.

USHS: Research Library of the Utah State Historical Society, Salt Lake City.

Adams, Mary Kisten. "Life of Margaret Adams." JNCD, 187.

Adams, William. "Autobiography." January 1894. BYU.

Adams, William. "History of William Adams." 1894. Typescript. JNCD, 314–333.

Allred, Mary Ann Mackelprang. "Life Sketch of Samuel William Mackelprang and Adelia Terry." April 1, 1933. Typescript. CHL.

"Ann Taylor Rowley." Rowley Family Collection, CHL.

"'Aunt Mary' Nielson Jones." N.d. JNCD, 85–86.

Barney, Alma. "Diary of Alma Barney." 1922. CHL.

Bluff Ward, General Minutes. CHL.

Bluff Ward. Letter to President John Taylor, May 19, 1884. John Taylor Presidential Papers, 1877–87, CHL, as provided by archives staff.

"Bluff Ward Manuscript History." CHL.

"Bluff Ward Relief Society Minutes." CHL.

Butt, Julia Nielson. "Ane Katrine Jorgensen Nielson." In "Bishop Jens Nielson: History and Genealogy," comp. Jay P. Nielson. N.d. JNCD, 227–28.

Cannon, George Q. Letters to Francis A. Hammond, January 1, 1887; February 2, 1898. Francis A. Hammond Papers, BYU.

Cedar Ward, General Minutes. CHL.

"Cedar Ward Manuscript History." CHL.

Christensen, C. L. Diary. BYU.

Church of Jesus Christ of Latter-day Saint. "Bluff Ward Record of Members, 1880–1921." FHL.

Davis, James L. Journal. CHL.

———. "San Juan Mission Reminiscence." 1917. CHL.

Day, Franklin D. "The Cattle Industry of San Juan County, Utah, 1875–1900." Master's thesis, Brigham Young University, 1958.

Decker, Cornelius Isaac. "Pioneering in Utah, Arizona, and Colorado." N.d. Typescript. CHL.

Egler, Daniel. "A Blessing by Daniel Egler, Patriarch, upon the Head of Jens Nielson, Son of Niels and Doratha Nielson." November 23, 1875. CHL.

Ellertson, Norman W., and Carol A. Ellertson. "Julia Ann Nielson and Willard (Dick) Butt." N.d. JNCD, 133–137.

Elliott, Vilate. Diary, 1899–1900. BYU.

First Presidency Bulletin, February 9, 1898. Francis A. Hammond Papers, BYU.

First Presidency, "General Bulletin," June 6, 1888. Francis A. Hammond Papers, BYU.

Frost, Melvin J. "Factors That Influenced Homesteading and Land Abandonment in San Juan County, Utah." Master's thesis, Brigham Young University, 1960.

Gabbart, Helena N., and Caroline Nielson Redd. "A Brief History of Kirsten Jensen Nielson." In "Bishop Jens Nielson: History and Genealogy," comp. Jay P. Nielson. N.d. JNCD, 134–39.

Hammond, Francis A. Journals. December 13, 1884 to September 9, 1885; April 6, 1886 to January 23, 1887; September 15, 1888 to May 5, 1889; January 22, 1890 to February 2, 1891; September 25, 1891 to March 17, 1893; July 23, 1893 to November 25, 1900, Francis A. Hammond Papers, BYU.

———. Journals. September 10, 1885 to April 5, 1886; January 24, 1887 to September 17, 1888; May 6, 1889 to January 21, 1890; February 3, 1891 to September 24, 1891; March 18, 1893 to July 22, 1893, Francis A. Hammond Collection, CHL.

———. Letters to Capt. D. M. Edwards, June 14, 1889; January 1899; October 22, 1900. Francis A. Hammond Papers, BYU.

———. Letter to Bishop Jens Nielson, January 27, 1885. In "Bishop Jens Nielson, History and Genealogy," comp. Jay P. Nielson. 1965. BYU.

———. Letter to D. H. Edwards, January 1899. Francis A. Hammond Papers, BYU.

Hammond, Martha. Letters to Francis A. Hammond, December 11, 1889; January 21, February 26, 1890; March 29, 1895. Francis A. Hammond Papers, BYU.

Hammond, Silas S. Letters to Francis A. Hammond, February 12, 1891; July 25, 1892. Francis A. Hammond Papers, BYU.

Hyde, Herbert. "As I Recall Grandfather Jens Nielson." N.d. JNCD, 25–28.

Jensen, Bryant L. "An Historical Study of Bluff City, Utah, from 1878 to 1906." Master's thesis, Brigham Young University, 1966.

Johnson, Ezekiel. "Autobiography." USHS.

Jones, Gwen H. "History of Kumen Jones." N.d. JNCD, 98–109.

Jones, Kumen. "Aunt Mary Jones, My Wife." JNCD, 90.

———. "Bishop Jens Nielson Sketch." JNCD, 21.

———. "Writings of Kumen Jones." Ed. Albert R. Lyman. N.d. Typescript. BYU.

Jones, Lenora. "Pioneer Story: Dorthea Jensen Bayles, Handcart Veteran of 1857." In "Bishop Jens Nielson: History and Genealogy," comp. Jay P. Nielson.

Journal History of the Church (chronology of typed entries and newspaper clippings, 1830–present). CHL, microfilm copy in Harold B. Lee Library, Brigham Young University, Provo, Utah.

Kimmerle, Myrna. "A Little Visit with Aunt Caroline Nielson Redd." August 1957. JNCD, 233–36.

Lewis, James. "Life History of James Lewis, Son of James, Son of George." In "Utah Pioneer Biographies," 18:154–59. FHL.

"Life History of Mary Elizabeth Openshaw Ipson." N.d. CHL.

"Life of Thomas Rowley." Rowley Family Papers, CHL.

Lunt, Henry. "A Blessing by Henry Lunt, Patriarch, upon the Head of Kirsten Nielson." October 23, 1879. CHL.

Lyman, Albert R. "Accounts of the Homes of Bluff, 1890–1900." 1970. USHS.

———. "Bishop Jens Nielson." 1936. In "Bishop Jens Nielson, History and Genealogy," comp. Jay P. Nielson. 1965. BYU.

———. "Bishop Jens Nielson: The Old Wagon." N.d. JNCD, 68–77.

———. "Experiences and Impressions." N.d. Typescript. # vols. Albert R. Lyman Collection, BYU.

———. "Hans Joseph Nielson." 1958. JNCD, 146–51.

———. "History of San Juan County, 1879–1917." 1965. Typescript. BYU.

———, ed. "History of San Juan Stake." 1946. Typescript. BYU.

———. Interviews by Charles S. Peterson, February 3, 1970; [?], 1970. Transcript. USHS.

———. Journals, 1893–1973. Albert R. Lyman Collection, BYU.

———. "Letter to the Family of My Dear Bishop Jens Nielson of Bluff, Utah," September 21, 1965. JNCD, 46–48.

———. "Notes on the Life of Sarah Williams Perkins." April 27, 1930. Typescript. CHL and BYU.

———. "Platte DeAlton Lyman." N.d. USHS.

———. Summaries of Each Year. 1935. Typescript. Albert R. Lyman Collection, BYU.

Lyman, Francis Marion. Letters to Platte D. Lyman, February 27, 1880; July 3, 1899. In Platte D. Lyman Collection, CHL.

Lyman, Platte D. "Diary of Platte D. Lyman." Typescript. BYU.

Meo, Ruth, ed. "Uriah and Annie Butt Talk about Elsie Rasmussen." N.d. JNCD, 81–82.

Morgan, John. Letter to Francis A. Hammond, February 13, 1886. Francis A. Hammond Papers, BYU.

Nielson, Floyd. "Francis and Leona Nielson." N.d. JNCD, 191–92.

———. "Jens Nielson, A Personal Experience." N.d. JNCD, 58.

Nielson, Hans Joseph. "Letter to Ida Nielson, July 1, 1902." JNCD, 165.

———. Letter to Ida Nielson, September 14, 1902. JNCD, 173–74.

Nielson, Jay P. "Jens Peter Nielson, As I View Him." 1994. JNCD, 173–75.

———, comp. "Bishop Jens Nielson, History and Genealogy." 1965. Typescript. BYU.

Nielson, Jennie R. "Memory Gems of Jens Peter Nielson." 1958. JNCD, 170–72.

Nielson, Jens. Letter to Francis A. Hammond, June 15, 1887. John Taylor Presidential Papers, 1877–87, CHL.

———. Letter to Uriah Nielson, March 20, 1901. JNCD, 29–31.

———. "Short History of Jens Nielson." N.d. CHL.

Nielson, Jens P. "Settlement of Bluff." N.d. JNCD, 178–79.

Nielson, Katrine. Letters to Jens Nielson, April 15, 1883; June 9, 1884; n.d. JNCD, 229–231, 233, 240.

Nielson, Kirsten. Letter to Mr. and Mrs. John Lollin and Family, January 10, 1904. JNCD, 142–43.

Nielson, Marion G. "Apostle on Horseback." N.d. JNCD, 248–51.

Nielson, Maxine. "Grandpa Uriah Nielson History." N.d. JNCD, 239–42.

Nielson, Uriah. "Elsie Nielson." 1935. JNCD, 80.

Nuttall, John H. Diary. BYU.

Parowan Stake, General Minutes. CHL.

"Parowan State Manuscript History." CHL.

Perkins, Kisten. "Address Made in Evening Services, Blanding Ward Chapel." July 24, 1956. JNCD, 41.

———. "Life of Kirsten Jensen Nielson." N.d. JNCD, 132–33.

———. "Life of Margaret Adams." 1944. JNCD, 180–85.

Preston, William B. Letter to Francis A. Hammond, July 1, 1893. Francis A. Hammond Papers, BYU.

Redd, Alice. "Sketch of the Life of Caroline Nielson Redd." N.d. JNCD, 208–12.

Redd, L. Wayne. "Jens Nielson Family." 1997. JNCD, 59–67.

Redd, Leland W. "Bishop Jens Nielson." 1965. JNCD, 34–37.

Redd, Lemuel Hardison, Sr. Autobiographical Sketches. 1902 and 1907. CHL.

———. Letter to Family, January 22, 1889. CHL.

Redd, Lucinda Alvira Pace. Journal, 1898–1902. CHL.

Redd, Wayne H. Journals, 1895–1928. CHL.

———. Letter to L. H. Redd Sr., October 13, 1895. CHL.

Reeve, Mary Lyman. "Lucinda Diantha Nielson Hyde." May 21, 1955. JNCD, 197–207.

Roring, Corinee. "Leona Jane Walton—As I Remember My Little Grandmother." N.d. JNCD, 195.

Rose, Bobbette Reading. "Annetta Nielson, 1875–1930." N.d., JNCD, 234.

Rowley, Samuel. Autobiography. N.d. Typescript. Rowley Family Collection, CHL.

"Samuel Rowley." Typescript. Rowley Family Papers. CHL.

"A Short History of Elsie Rasmussen Nielson." N.d. JNCD, 81–83.

San Juan Cooperative Association. Ledger, 1887–1916. CHL.

San Juan County Minute Book. Photocopy. USHS.

San Juan County, Utah, County Clerk. "Marriage License Records, 1888–1966. FHL.

San Juan County, Utah, County Clerk. "Register of Births and Deaths, 1897–1917." FHL.

San Juan Stake General Minutes, 1880–1914. CHL.

"San Juan Stake Manuscript History." CHL.

San Juan Stake Relief Society Records. CHL.

Smith, Joseph F. Letter to Francis A. Hammond, March 4, 1886. Francis A. Hammond Papers, BYU.

Smith, Silas S. Letter to Platte D. Lyman, August 5, 1880. Platte D. Lyman Collection, CHL.

Snow, Erastus. Letter to Platte D. Lyman and Jens Nielson and to the Saints on the San Juan, October 26, 1883. CHL.

———. Letter to John Taylor, September 19, 1884. CHL.

Snow, Lorenzo, George Q. Cannon, and Joseph F. Smith. Circular Letter, December 1, 1898. Francis A. Hammond Papers, BYU.

Taylor, John. Letters to Erastus Snow, January 9, 1879; February 15, 1879. John Taylor Presidential Papers, 1877–87, CHL.

Taylor, John, and George Q. Cannon. Letters to Francis A. Hammond, September 7 and December 8, 1885; January 14, 1886; March 25, 1887. Francis A. Hammond Papers, BYU.

United States Manuscript Census. Iron County, Utah. 1860 and 1870. FHL.

United States Manuscript Census. San Juan County, Utah. 1880, 1900, and 1910. FHL.

Utah District Court, San Juan County. "District Court Minutes, 1896–1921; and County Court Minutes, 1892–1899." Microfilm. FHL.

Utah District Court, San Juan County. Probate Division. "Probate Records and Register of Estates, 1888–1966." Microfilm. FHL.

Walton, Charles Eugene. Diary, 1872–94. Photocopy. USHS.

Wilson, Helen. "Recollections of Her Father, Francis Nielson, and Her Mother, Leona Jane Walton Nielson." 1997. JNCD, 186–88.

Wilson, Mary Ann Perkins. Personal History. In "Utah Pioneer Biographies," 30:75–88. FHL.

Wood, Josephine Catherine Chatterley. Journal. JNCD.
Woodruff, Wilford. Letters to Francis A. Hammond, October 3, 1887; December 11, 1888. Francis A. Hammond Papers, BYU.

Published Works

Abbreviations

BMS: *Blue Mountain Shadows*
UHQ: *Utah Historical Quarterly*
NEI: *Nearly Everything Imaginable: The Everyday Life of Utah's Mormon Pioneers.* Ed. Ronald Walker and Doris R. Dant. Provo, Utah: BYU Studies and Joseph Fielding Smith Institute for Latter-day Saint History, 1999.

Abruzzi, William S. "Ecology, Resource Redictribution, and Mormon Settlement in Northeastern Arizona." *American Anthropologist* 91, no. 3 (1989): 642–55.
Adams, Julie. "Tales of a Cowboy." *BMS* 15 (Summer 1995): 49–50.
Adamson, Nathan W. *Francis Asbury Hammond, Pioneer and Missionary.* Salt Lake City: David H. Allred and West Hammond, 1993.
Alder, Douglas D. "Writing Southern Utah History: An Appraisal and a Bibliography." *Journal of Mormon History* 20 (Fall 1994): 156–78.
Alexander, Thomas G. *Mormonism in Transition: A History of the Latter-day Saints, 1890–1930.* Urbana: University of Illinois Press, 1986.
———. *Utah, the Right Place: The Official Centennial History.* Salt Lake City: Gibbs Smith, 1996.
Allen, Stephen. "The Killing of Jane McKechnie Walton." *BMS* 10 (1992): 13–15.
Arrington, Leonard J. *Brigham Young: American Moses.* Urbana: University of Illinois Press, 1986.
———. *From Quaker to Latter-day Saint: Bishop Edwin D. Woolley.* Salt Lake City: Deseret Book, 1976.
———. *Great Basin Kingdom: An Economic History of the Latter-day Saints, 1830–1900.* Cambridge: Harvard University Press, 1958. Reprint. Salt Lake City: University of Utah Press, 1993.
———. "The Mormon Tithing House: A Frontier Business Institution." *Business History Review* 28 (March 1954): 24–58.
———. *Utah's Audacious Stockman: Charlie Redd.* Logan: Utah State University Press; Provo, Utah: The Charles Redd Center for Western Studies, 1995.
Arrington, Leonard J., and Davis Bitton. *The Mormon Experience: A History of the Latter-day Saints.* New York: Alfred A. Knopf, 1979. Reprint. Urbana: University of Illinois Press, 1992.
Arrington, Leonard J., Feramorz Fox, and Dean L. May. *Building the City of God: Community and Cooperation among the Mormons.* Salt Lake City: Deseret Book, 1976.

Aton, James M., and Robert S. McPherson. *River Flowing from the Sunrise: An Environmental History of the Lower San Juan.* Logan: Utah State University Press, 2000.

Aton, Jim. "The River, the Ditch and the Volcano: Bluff, 1879–1884." *BMS* 12 (Summer 1993): 15–23.

Austin, Thomas E., and Robert S. McPherson. "Murder, Mayhem, and Mormons: The Evolution of Law Enforcement on the San Juan Frontier, 1880–1900." *UHQ* 55 (Winter 1987): 36–49.

Bachman, Daniel, and Ronald K. Esplin. "Plural Marriage." In *Encyclopedia of Mormonism,* ed. Daniel H. Ludlow, 3:1091–95. 4 vols. New York: Macmillan, 1992.

Bannon, John Francis. *The Spanish Borderland Frontier, 1513–1821.* New York: Holt, Rinehart, and Winston, 1970.

Bean, Lee L., Geraldine P. Mineau, and Ken R. Smith. "The Effect of Pioneer Life on the Longevity of Married Couples." In *NEI,* 387–403.

Bennion, Lowell "Ben." "The Incidence of Mormon Polygamy in 1880: 'Dixie' versus Davis Stake." *Journal of Mormon History* 11 (1984): 27–42.

"Bert Loper and the Gold Rush of 1893: Adventures of a Placer Miner on the San Juan River." *BMS* 17 (Summer 1996): 25–26.

Black, Marcia, and Robert S. McPherson. "Soldiers, Savers, Slackers, and Spies." *UHQ* 63 (Winter 1995): 4–23.

Blackburn, Fred, and Winston Hurst. "Charley Lang: Pioneer Photographer, Musician, and Archaeologist." *BMS* 14 (Winter 1994): 5–13.

Bolton, Herbert E. *The Spanish Borderlands: A Chronicle of Old Florida and the Southwest.* New Haven: Yale University Press, 1921.

Booher, Gary. "The Mormon Village and Bluff, Utah." In *Migrations, Settlement Patterns, and Ethnic Groups in the United States,* ed. Richard H. Jackson, 227–49. Occasional Papers in Historical Geography, vol. 1. Provo, Utah: Brigham Young University, 1972.

Brooks, Juanita. "Indian Relations on the Mormon Frontier." *UHQ* 12 (January to April 1944): 1–48.

Bushman, Claudia L. "Reports from the Field: The World of the *Women's Exponent.*" In *NEI,* 297–313.

Carter, Kate B., comp. *Heart Throbs of the West.* 12 vols. Salt Lake City: Daughters of Utah Pioneers, 1939–51.

———. *Our Pioneer Heritage.* 20 vols. Salt Lake City: Daughters of Utah Pioneers, 1958–77.

———. *Treasures of Pioneer History.* 6 vols. Salt Lake City: Daughters of Utah Pioneers, 1952–57.

Christy, Howard A. "Handcart Companies." In *Encyclopedia of Mormonism,* ed. Daniel H. Ludlow, 2:571–73. 4 vols. New York: Macmillan, 1992.

———. "Weather, Disaster, and Responsibility: An Essay on the Willie and Martin Handcart Story." *BYU Studies* 37, no. 1 (1997–98): 6–74.

Correll, J. Lee. "Navajo Frontiers in Utah and Troublous Times in Monument Valley." *UHQ* 39 (1971): 145–61.

Crabtree, Lamont J. *The Incredible Mission: The Hole-in-the-Rock Expedition/San Juan Mission Story and Trail Guide.* Salt Lake City: Lamont J. Crabtree, 1980.

Cronon, William, George Miles, and Jay Gitlin, eds. *Under an Open Sky: Rethinking America's Western Past.* New York: W.W. Norton, 1992.

Dalton, Luella Adams, ed. *History of Iron County Mission, Parowan, Utah.* [Parowan, Utah]: n.p., [1973?].

Embry, Jessie L. *Mormon Polygamous Families: Life in the Principle.* Salt Lake City: University of Utah Press, 1987.

Foster, Lawrence. *Religion and Sexuality: The Shakers, The Mormons, and the Oneida Community.* Oxford: Oxford University Press, 1981. Reprint, Urbana: University of Illinois Press, 1984.

Geary, Edward A. "For the Strength of the Hills: Imagining Mormon Country." In *After 150 Years: The Latter-day Saints in Sesquicentennial Perspective*, ed. Thomas G. Alexander and Jessie L. Embry, 73–94. Provo, Utah: Charles Redd Center for Western Studies, 1983.

Gonzalez, William H., and Genaro M. Padilla. "Monticello, the Hispanic Cultural Gateway to Utah." *UHQ* 52 (Winter 1984): 9–28.

Hartley, William G. "Common People: Church Activity during the Brigham Young Era." In *NEI*, 249–95.

———. "The Priesthood Reorganization of 1877: Brigham Young's Last Achievement." *BYU Studies* 20, no. 4 (1979): 3–36.

Hedges, Andrew H. "Battle of the Homefront: The Early Pioneer Art of Homemaking." In *NEI*, 118–36.

Holzapfel, Richard Neitzel, and David A. Allred. "A Peculiar People: Community and Commitment in Utah Valley." In *NEI*, 89–115.

Hoopes, Francis Hansen. "The Birth Records of 'Aunt Jody': Josephine Catherine Chatterley Wood," *BMS* 17 (Summer 1996): 55–65.

———. "Josephine Catherine (Jody) Chatterley Wood: Midwife of San Juan." *BMS* 2 (Fall 1988): 32–41.

Hurst, Winston. "Colonizing the Dead: Early Archaeology in San Juan County." *BMS* 17 (Summer 1996): 2–13.

Ivins, Stanley. "Notes on Mormon Polygamy." *Western Humanities Review* 10 (Summer 1956): 229–39. Reprinted in *UHQ* 35 (Fall 1967): 309–21.

Jackson, Richard H. "The Mormon Village: Genesis and Antecedents of the City of Zion Plan." *BYU Studies* 17, no. 1 (1977): 223–40.

———. "Myth and Reality: Environmental Perception of the Mormon Pioneers." *Rocky Mountain Social Sciences Journal* 9 (January 1972): 33–38.

Jackson, Richard H., and Robert L. Layton. "The Mormon Village: Analysis of a Settlement Type." *Professional Geographer* 28 (May 1976): 136–41.

Jenson, Andrew. *Autobiography of Andrew Jenson*. Salt Lake City: Deseret News Press, 1938.

———. *History of the Scandinavian Mission*. Salt Lake City: Deseret News Press, 1927. Reprint, New York: Arno Press, 1979.

———. *Latter-day Saint Biographical Encyclopedia: A Compilation of Biographical Sketches of Prominent Men and Women in The Church of Jesus Christ of Latter-day Saints*. Salt Lake City: Andrew Jenson History Company, 1914. Reprint, Salt Lake City: Western Epics, 1971.

Johnson, Donald Bruce, comp. *National Party Platforms: Volume I, 1840–1956*. Urbana: University of Illinois Press, 1978.

Jones, Evelyn K. *Henry Lunt: Biography and History of the Development of Southern Utah and Settling of Colonia Pacheco, Mexico*. Cedar City, Utah: E. K. Jones, 1996.

Kane, Elizabeth Wood. *Twelve Mormon Homes Visited in Succession on a Journey through Utah to Arizona*. Philadelphia: n.p., 1874. Reprint, Dallas: R. K. Taylor Publishing, 1973.

Lambert, Neal. "Al Scorup: Cattleman of the Canyons." *UHQ* 32 (Summer 1964): 301–20.

Larson, Andrew Karl. *Erastus Snow: The Life of a Missionary and Pioneer for the Early Mormon Church*. Salt Lake City: University of Utah Press, 1971.

Larson, Gustive O. *The "Americanization" of Utah for Statehood*. San Marino, Calif.: Huntington Library, 1971.

Leone, Mark P. "The Evolution of Mormon Culture in Eastern Arizona." *UHQ* 40, no. 2 (1972): 122–41.

Lesson Committee, comp. *Chronicles of Courage*. 7 vols. Salt Lake City: Daughters of Utah Pioneers, 1990–96.

———. *An Enduring Legacy*. 12 vols. Salt Lake City: Daughters of Utah Pioneers, 1978–89.

Limerick, Patricia Nelson. *Legacy of Conquest: The Unbroken Past of the American West*. New York: Norton, 1987.

Logue, Larry M. *A Sermon in the Desert: Belief and Behavior in Early St. George, Utah*. Urbana: University of Illinois Press, 1988.

Lyman, Albert R. "Fort on the Firing Line." *Improvement Era* 51 (October 1948) to 53 (March 1950).

———. *Indians and Outlaws: Settling of the San Juan Frontier*. Salt Lake City: Bookcraft, 1962.

Lyman, Edward Leo. *Political Deliverance: The Mormon Quest for Statehood*. Urbana: University of Illinois Press, 1986.

Madsen, Carol Cornwall. *Journey to Zion: Voices from the Mormon Trail*. Salt Lake City: Deseret Book, 1997.

Madsen, Susan Arrington. "Growing Up in Pioneer Utah: Agonies and Ecstasies." In *NEI*, 317–28.

May, Dean L. "A Demographic Portrait of the Mormons, 1830–1980." In *After 150 Years: The Latter-day Saints in Sesquicentennial Perspective*, ed. Thomas G. Alexander and Jessie L. Embry, 73–94. Provo, Utah: Charles Redd Center for Western Studies, 1983.

———. "The Making of Saints: The Mormon Town as a Setting for the Study of Cultural Change." *UHQ* 45 (1977): 75–92.

———. "Rites of Passage: The Crossing as Cultural Credo." *Journal of Mormon History* 29 (Spring 2003): 2–41.

———. *Three Frontiers: Family, Land, and Society in the American West, 1850–1900.* New York: Cambridge University Press, 1994.

McPherson, Robert S. *A History of San Juan County: In the Palm of Time.* Salt Lake City: Utah Historical Society, 1995.

———. "Howard Antes and the Navajo Faith Mission: Evangelist of Southeastern Utah." *BMS* 17 (Summer 1996): 14–24.

———. "Navajos, Mormons, and Henry L. Mitchell: Cauldron of Conflict on the San Juan." *UHQ* 55 (Winter 1987): 50–65.

———. *The Northern Navajo Frontier, 1869–1900: Expansion through Adversity.* Albuquerque: University of New Mexico Press, 1988.

———. "The Ute Invasion of San Juan County, 1894: A Study in Differing Perception." *BMS* 17 (Summer 1996): 46–50.

McPherson, Robert S., and Mary Lou Mueller. "Divine Duty: Hannah Sorenson and Midwifery in Southeastern Utah." *UHQ* 65 (Fall 1997): 335–54.

McPherson, Robert S., and Winston B. Hurst. "The Fight at Soldier Crossing, 1884: Military Considerations in Canyon Country." *UHQ* 70 (Summer 2002): 258–81.

Meinig, D. W. "The Mormon Culture Region: Strategies and Patterns in the Geography of the American West, 1847–1964." *Annals of the Association of American Geographers* 55, no. 2 (1965): 191–219.

Miller, David E. *Hole-in-the-Rock: An Epic in the Colonization of the Great American West.* Salt Lake City: University of Utah Press, 1959.

Mulder, William. "Five Years on the San Juan." *Improvement Era* 44 (January 1941): 20–21, 53–55.

———. *Homeward to Zion: The Mormon Migration from Scandinavia.* Minneapolis: University of Minnesota Press, 1957.

Nelson, Lowry. *The Mormon Village: A Pattern and Technique of Land Settlement.* Salt Lake City: University of Utah Press, 1952.

Newell, Linda King. *A History of Piute County.* Salt Lake City: Utah State Historical Commission, 1999.

Newell, Linda King, and Vivian Linford Talbot. *A History of Garfield County.* Salt Lake City: Utah State Historical Commission, 1998.

Noall, Clair. "Mormon Midwives." *UHQ* 10 (1942): 84–144.

O'Dea, Thomas F. "The Effects of Geographical Position on Belief and Behavior in a Rural Mormon Village." *Rural Sociology* 19, no. 4 (1954): 358–64.

Palmer, Jay W., and Merilyn Palmer Lisenby. "First Woman Elected to Public Office in San Juan County." *BMS* 19 (Fall 1997): 41–42.

———. "Law, Order, Print and Political Developments in Southeastern Utah." *BMS* 17 (Summer 1996): 65–68.

Perkins, Cornelia Adams, Marian Gardner Nielson, and Lenora Butt Jones. *Saga of San Juan*. 2d ed. Monticello, Utah: San Juan County Daughters of Utah Pioneers, 1968.

Perkins, Hilda, and Deanna Cook. "Another Bluff Pioneer: Samuel Rowley." *BMS* 6 (Spring 1990): 53–56.

Peterson, Charles S. "Imprint of Agricultural Systems on the Utah Landscape." In *The Mormon Role in the Settlement of the West*, ed. Richard H. Jackson, 91–106. Provo, Utah: Brigham Young University Press, 1978.

———. "Life in a Village Society." *UHQ* 49 (Winter 1981): 78–96.

———. *Look to the Mountains: Southeastern Utah and the La Sal National Forest*. Provo, Utah: Brigham Young University Press, 1975.

———. "San Juan in Controversy: American Livestock Frontier vs. Mormon Cattle Pool." In *Charles Redd Monographs in Western History: Essays on the American West, 1972–1973*, ed. Thomas G. Alexander. Provo, Utah: Brigham Young University Press, 1974.

———. *Take Up Your Mission: Mormon Colonizing along the Little Colorado River, 1870–1900*. Tucson: University of Arizona Press, 1973.

Peterson, Levi S. "The Development of Utah Livestock Law, 1848–1896." *UHQ* 32 (Summer 1964): 198–216.

Pincock, Renee. "Time Line." *BMS* 19 (Fall 1997): 33–40, 75.

Poll, Richard D., Thomas G. Alexander, Eugene Campbell, and David E. Miller, eds. *Utah's History*. Provo, Utah: Brigham Young University Press, 1978.

Powell, Allan Kent, ed. *San Juan County, Utah: People Resources, and History*. Salt Lake City: Utah State Historical Society, 1983.

———. *Utah History Encyclopedia*. Salt Lake City: University of Utah Press, 1994.

Redd, Amasa Jay, ed. *Lemuel Hardison Redd, Jr., 1856–1923*. Salt Lake City: Amasa Jay Redd, 1967.

Ricks, Joel E. *Forms and Methods of Early Mormon Settlement in Utah and Surrounding Regions, 1847–1877*. Logan: Utah State University Press, 1964.

Ridge, Martin. "Mormon 'Deliverance' and the Closing of the Frontier." *Journal of Mormon History* 18 (Spring 1992): 137–152.

Riis, John. *Ranger Trails*. Richmond, Va.: Dietz Press, 1937.

Riverton Wyoming Stake. *Remember: The Willie and Martin Handcart Companies and Their Rescuers, Past and Present*. Salt Lake City: Publishers Press, 1997.

Roring, Corinne. *Beautiful Bluff*. Bluff, Utah: By the author, 1991.

Rosenvall, Lynn A. "Defunct Mormon Settlements: 1830–1930." In *The Mormon Role in the Settlement of the West*, ed. Richard H. Jackson, 51–74. Provo, Utah: Brigham Young University Press, 1978.

Ross, Drew. "I Have Struck It Rich at Last." *BMS* 17 (Summer 1996): 30–36.

Salmon, Rusty, and Robert S. McPherson. "Cowboys, Indians, and Conflict: The Pinhook Draw Fight, 1881." *UHQ* 69 (Winter 2001): 4–28.

Samuel Wood Family Book. N.p.: Samuel Wood Family Organization, 1982.

Seegmiller, Janet Burton. *A History of Iron County.* Salt Lake City: Utah State Historical Society, 1998.

Sherlock, Richard. "Mormon Migration and Settlement after 1875." *Journal of Mormon History* 2 (1975): 53–68.

Shumway, Gary L. "Blanding: The Making of a Community." *UHQ* 48 (Fall 1980): 390–405.

Shumway, Larry V. "Dancing the Buckles Off Their Shoes in Pioneer Utah." In *NEI*, 195–221.

Smith, Albert E., ed. *Thales Hastings Haskell, Pioneer—Scout—Explorer—Indian Missionary, 1847–1909.* Salt Lake City, A. E. Smith, 1964.

Smith, James E., and Phillip R. Kunz. "Polygny and Fertility in Nineteenth-Century America." *Population Studies* 30 (1976): 465–80.

Smith, Joseph, Jr. *History of The Church of Jesus Christ of Latter-day Saints.* Ed. B. H. Roberts. 2d ed., rev. 7 vols. Salt Lake City: Deseret Book, 1971.

Lorenzo Snow, George Q. Cannon, and Joseph F. Smith. Circular Letter, December 1, 1898. Francis A. Hammond Papers, BYU.

Stegner, Wallace. *The Gathering of Zion.* New York: McGraw-Hill, 1964. Reprint, Lincoln: University of Nebraska Press, 1981.

———. *Mormon Country.* New York: Hawthorn Books, 1942.

Tate, Laverne Powell. "Elk Mountain." *BMS* 6 (Spring 1990): 6–19.

———. "The Real Gold Mine of San Juan." *BMS* 17 (Summer 1996): 27–29.

Tennity, Margaret Perkins. "The Elk Mountain Cattle Company." *BMS* 10 (Summer 1992): 16–17.

Thompson, Gregory C. "The Unwanted Indians: The Southern Utes in Southeastern Utah." *UHQ* 49 (Spring 1981): 189–203.

Turk, Toni Richard. *Rooted in San Juan: A Genealogical Study of Burials in San Juan County, 1879–1995.* [Blanding, Utah]: T. R. Turk, 1995.

Turner, Frederick Jackson. "The Significance of the Frontier in American History." 1893. In *The Frontier in American History.* New York: Henry Holt, 1921.

Utah since Statehood: Historical and Biographical. 4 vols. Salt Lake City: S. J. Clarke Publishing, 1920.

Walker, Don D. "The Carlisles: Cattle Barons of the Upper Basin." *UHQ* 32 (Summer 1964): 268–84.

———. "The Cattle Industry of Utah, 1850–1900: An Historical Profile." *UHQ* 32 (Summer 1964): 182–97.

———. "Cowboys, Indians, and Cavalry: A Cattleman's Account." *UHQ* 34 (Summer 1966): 255–62.

Walker, Ronald W. "Golden Memories: Remembering Life in a Mormon Village." In *NEI*, 47–74.

Wahlquist, Wayne. "Population Growth in the Mormon Core Area: 1847–1890." In *The Mormon Role in the Settlement of the West*, ed. Richard H. Jackson, 107–34. Provo, Utah: Brigham Young University Press, 1978.

White, Jean Bickmore, ed. *Church, State, and Politics: The Diaries of John Henry Smith*. Salt Lake City: Signature Books, 1990.

White, Richard. *"It's Your Misfortune and None of My Own": A New History of the American West*. Norman: University of Oklahoma Press, 1991.

Winkler, Albert. "The Circleville Massacre: A Brutal Incident in Utah's Black Hawk War." *UHQ* 55 (Winter 1987): 4–22.

Index

Page numbers in **bold** indicate pictures.

spoke at dedication of new meetinghouse, 242
spoke to newlyweds, 238
statehood celebration and, 257
on success of San Juan Mission, 289
supported woman suffrage, 193
sustained Silas Smith, 35
threw dinner party for newlyweds,
210, 229
urged forgiving Navajos, 154
urged frugality and cooperation, 232,
278
urged unity on co-op question,
198–200
visited in Cedar City, 67–70, 93
warned about dangers of herding, 167
willing to go to Four Corners area,
28–30, 32
worried about antipolygamy laws,
90, 141
youth of, 9–10
Nielson, Jens (baby), 20
Nielson, Jens Lyman, 140, 282
Nielson, Jens "Niels," 12, 15
Nielson, Jens Peter
asked mother about handcart journey, 38
birth of, 20
brought rest of family to Bluff, 120
called to help establish North Montezuma settlement, 157
contracted to cut and haul wood, 249
description of, 170, 196
drinking and, 210, 229, 253
endorsed as missionary, 280
helped with dairy, 158
herded cattle, 158
interested in Native American artifacts, 202, 230
jury duty of, 248
married, 296
moved to White Mesa (Blanding),
299, 325
picture of, 327
reception for, 297
returned from Colorado, 59, 77

returned from mission, 291
worked in Colorado, 57, 73
youth of, 34
Nielson, Joe. See Nielson, Hans Joseph "Joe"
Nielson, John, 22, 23
Nielson, Julia. See Butt, Julia Nielson
Nielson, Kirsten Jensen
accompanied Jens Nielson to San
Juan Mission, 30, 33
attended general conference, 177, 217
attended Utah jubilee, 264
became member of suffrage association, 193
Christmas and, 68
as counselor in Relief Society, 114
died, 326
domestic duties of, 172–73, 270
illnesses of, 58, 290, 298
life of, after Manifesto, 270
married, 18–19
moved into log home, 65
as oldest in Bluff, 44
picture of, 327
as president of Relief Society, 173, 271
Nielson, Leona "Lone" Jane Walton, 208,
211, 293
Nielson, Lisle, 280, 300
Nielson, Lucinda "Cindy". See Hyde,
Lucinda "Cindy" Nielson
Nielson, Maggie Perkins, 296
Nielson, Margaret. See Adams, Margaret
Nielson
Nielson, Martha Jane "Jennie" Roberts,
296, 297
Nielson, Mary. See Jones, Mary Nielson
Nielson, Nettie. See Johnson, Annetta
"Nettie" Nielson
Nielson, Uriah
attended Brigham Young Academy,
260
called on mission, 280
married, 296
ordained as deacon, 175
as pallbearer, 213
returned from mission, 291
youth of, 24, 93, 120, 205